Dispatches from the Front

Nathaniel Lande

A HENRY HOLT REFERENCE BOOK

Henry Holt and Company
New York

DISPATCHES FROM THE FRONT

News Accounts of American Wars, 1776–1991

A Henry Holt Reference Book
Henry Holt and Company, Inc.
Publishers since 1866
115 West 18th Street
New York, New York 10011

Henry Holt ® is a registered
trademark of Henry Holt and Company, Inc.

Published in Canada by Fitzhenry & Whiteside Ltd.,
195 Allstate Parkway, Markham, Ontario L3R 4T8.

Library of Congress Cataloging-in-Publication Data
Lande, Nathaniel.
Dispatches from the front
Nathaniel Lande — 1st ed.
p.   cm. — (A Henry Holt reference book)
Includes bibliographical references and index.
1. War in the press—United States.   2. War correspondents—
United States.   I. Title.   II. Series.
PN4784.W37L36   1995   95–13277
070.4'333'0973—dc20   CIP

ISBN 0-8050-3664-4

Henry Holt books are available for special promotions and
premiums. For details contact: Director, Special Markets.

First Edition—1995

DESIGNED BY KATE NICHOLS

Printed in the United States of America
All first editions are printed on acid-free paper. ♾
1   3   5   7   9   10   8   6   4   2

CONTENTS

INTRODUCTION

Since the founding of the United States, war has been a recurring phenomena in American history. We have fought for many reasons: independence, national unity, manifest destiny, international democracy. Americans have fought in almost every corner of the world, from deserts to mountains to jungles. And in every war on every front, we have paid intense attention. Typewriter patriots, equipped with telegraphs, radio microphones, or satellite links, have been the conduit for a public eager to imagine and feel every musket fire and missile blast from Lexington to Baghdad.

Here we have unique and special dispatches from ten American wars. In the correspondents' words ring the passion and drama of war: the first shots at Lexington and Concord; the interrogation of the determined John Brown at Harpers Ferry; the women rushing to the Charleston battery to witness the bashing of Fort Sumter; the massacres at the German front in the Great War; the orchestrated accomplishment at Normandy in 1944, the immediacy of the war in the Gulf.

These reports speak to much more than the bravery, destruction, and heroism found in war. With extraordinary writing, they document the evolution of warfare and the development of the war correspondent. From the American Revolution to the Gulf War, these dispatches note the gradual changes in combat technique. The almost intimate approach of the minutemen, who were ordered to hold their fire until they could distinguish the whites of the enemies' eyes, gave way over time to the distant blur of V2 missile mass destruction in World War II. The development of machine guns, aircraft, and submarines placed new demands on the valor of soldiers and exponentially increased the cost of battle.

To be sure, the reports bear witness to all the horror, bitterness, courage, and gallantry that drives war. Imagine Thomas Jefferson, the conscience behind the Declaration of Independence, asking for shoes for freezing soldiers at a Virginia encampment or a Rhode Island soldier offering water to a dying Confederate partisan. Even the professional assembly line landing on D day inspired typewriter soldiers to consider fate and fatality.

These dispatches also chronicle the changes in the way war is reported. In the eighteenth and nineteenth centuries, pamphleteers and newspapermen perfected their craft from war to war. By the mid-twentieth century, war no longer belonged to ink, with radio and television shifting the discussion from taverns and coffeehouses to living rooms. By the time cruise missiles bore down on Iraq, satellite links made war not only prime time, but real time. Through the centuries, however, one constant remains: war fascinates America.

The earlier chapters of this collection trace the historical development of the war correspondent. The writing evolves from correspondence and letters to factual accounts, combining drama with action in the developing style of each succeeding war.

ALWAYS, THE BIGGEST NEWS STORIES in American history have been the nation's many wars. Whether the nation turned to armed conflict to gain independence, to fight off an invasion, to protect national unity, or to further democracy, the hostilities characterized Americans in a way no other events have done. It could hardly be otherwise, for no other events were so critical in shaping the destiny of the nation. Nothing touched directly or indirectly the lives of so many people. In no other circumstances were the lines between good and evil, friend and foe, so clearly drawn.

Dispatches are the intelligence and information that helped us see into our national future.

In researching and planning this anthology, I have found it fascinating to explore how fundamental changes in our society gave rise to the issues that led Americans into war. Even more compelling are the varied and often contradictory words, phrases, and images of battle journalists have used to make sense of it all. Through ten American wars, with powerful prose, they speak to us now as they did in their times, linking book to battleground, peace to conflict.

For the two centuries spanning the American Revolution and Operation Desert Storm, the United States has engaged in successive, almost constant cycles of conflict. While the nature and objectives of conflict change over time and place, military encounter seems to be a persistent and central element in the national experience. This book presents press dispatches that invite exploration of the grand theme of our society on many levels. Warfare, disrupting the daily routines of life, has been a profound personal experience for most of us, both soldier and civilian, with reports connecting front lines to the home front. More broadly, each conflict, as the key nationalist venture of its day, delineated American society politically, geographically, and culturally. Public values that bound the country together were established, often contested, but always memorialized in the crucible of war.

Throughout the Republic's amazing history, the battles have ranged widely in size and circumstance. In 1776 a relative handful of ragged and disparate colonists fought doggedly to gain collective independence from England, the world's foremost military power. By contrast, in 1991 the United States demonstrated its preeminent position as the arbiter of global power by dispatching to the Persian Gulf more than 400,000 troops and thousands of tanks, planes, and supporting vehicles to enforce a United Nations Security Council resolution. Along this trajectory, the country underwent a gradual economic, social, and political transformation. Beginning in the eighteenth century as a collection of primarily agricultural states, the federal union strengthened, but not enough to erase significant regional differences. As American settlers expanded across the continent in the nineteenth century, they struggled mightily to reach a common vision of their nation's destiny. In the twentieth century, having consolidated the western territorites, they continued to debate their relationship to the rest of the world.

During times of crisis, Americans often debated the cause and circumstance and meaning of the fighting. After the troops returned home, remembrances gradually erased past disagreements. Now and then we honored our heroes with parades and oratory, celebrated them with songs and boulevards. We remember the past in fragments: the face of a daughter reading her father's name on the Vietnam War Memorial; "The Ballad of the Green Beret" playing on the radio; a ticker-tape gala for General MacArthur; a sailor kissing his sweetheart in Times Square on V-E Day; the marble monuments to the Confederate army that stand before every courthouse in every southern town. In a thousand different ways, some great, some small, these images reflect the community that is our nation.

Over the years, the words of press observers have been central in fostering wartime nationalism. Reporters functioned as frontline poets, scratching the first impressions into the culture's consciousness. Here is their writing in chronological order. Brief essays introduce each war by discussing the important changes taking place in American society and providing a series of "national snapshots" of the economic, political, and technological character of the world and the country at the time. The impact of these factors on each episode of warfare is considered, followed by a focus on the experiences of the war itself. The tone and character of the press coverage shaped the nation's understanding of itself. From commentary on ten American wars, we gain insight into the culture of the United States at each crisis point, from its beginnings through to the present time.

Regardless of time and place, war correspondents have always faced obstacles that hindered them in practicing their craft. Censorship often prevented them from telling the full story. Sometimes a factual account contained an unpleasant truth that political or military officials preferred to hide from the general public. At other times the details of a report might compromise the safety or reveal the plans of the army. Those in power sometimes viewed the war correspondent as little better than a spy. Even when censorship did not trouble reporters, miliary commanders frequently barred them from the battlefield or from areas where the best news stories might have been found. In those instances where commanders were antagonistic to newspeople in general or to one correspondent in particular, the very life of the reporter might be in danger.

BETWEEN 1775 AND 1991, technology changed the nature of both reporting and warfare.

As it transformed the face of the battlefield, it made warfare progressively more deadly and horrible. Throughout the nineteenth century, the accuracy, range, and speed of fire for all types of weapons increased, culminating with the machine gun. The ability of armies and navies to inflict casualties on each other grew greater and greater. At sea, battleships grew larger. World War I brought in the submarine, the airplane, the tank, and poison gas. The infantry remained the backbone of the land-based armed forces, but artillery became the biggest killer on the battlefield. The increased firepower of the infantry and artillery rendered the gallant cavalry charge a thing of the past. World War II witnessed the arrival of the aircraft carrier, the rocket, the atomic bomb, and a fuller realization of broadcast journalism. Improved weaponry led to losses that would have astonished any observer of earlier wars. War correspondents and commentators introduced the public to artillery through eyewitness accounts and described its deadly impact on the front lines and the home front.

In the first wars, Americans could not expect to read the news of a battle until weeks later. The reporter's handwritten story had to be delivered by hand. Not until after the Civil War did the typewriter allow the reporter to leave behind the handwritten dispatch. While the typewriter did not speed the delivery of the message to the public, other technological innovations did. Improved modes of transportation made it possible for dispatches to reach newspaper offices sooner. The stale news that filled the newspapers of the early republic—often news copied from other newspapers—was gradually replaced by fresher news. Better printing presses accelerated the printing of newspapers, while technological innovations made paper much cheaper to manufacture. These changes spurred the growth of hundreds of new newspapers throughout the nineteenth century. Americans became a newspaper-reading public.

Far and away the most significant technological advances were those that enabled reporters to send in their stories by means other than hand delivery. Time has always been a consideration in war reporting. As early as the Mexican-American War, George Kendall of the New Orleans *Picayune* demonstrated his understanding of this fact by purchasing a fast steamer, outfitting her with typewriters and printing presses, and speeding stories of the war from Veracruz to New Orleans. The advent of telegraphy in the years immediately before the Civil War greatly sped the transmission of news stories. The introduction of the telephone after that conflict further simplified the delivery of stories over long distances. Despite these advances, Americans were still entirely dependent on the print media for their news until radio emerged after World War I and television after World War II. The broadcasting media quickly recognized that they could release news to the public more quickly than newspapers and magazines. They could even offer eyewitness reports as events were unfolding. During Desert Storm, war news went live, reported by hotel warriors via satellite. All of these technological advances made the work of the war correspondent much easier.

Throughout American history, the reporter's dispatch adapted to meet the changing demands of the public. We wanted news and more news. We wanted to know even when generals and admirals thought it unwise to be open and frank. We wanted news quickly. We wanted to see and hear newsworthy events as they took place. The American media applied technological innovations to respond, documenting history in the making. In this context, war reporting can certainly be called instant history. With words and war in perspective, the correspondent writes about victories and defeat, heroism and blunders, bullets and bombs in copy fired around the world in a minute.

So many journalists have gone to war, never thinking of themselves as heroes but giving their lives and words courageously. For several hundred years, war correspondence has evinced an authenticity borne of the editor's directive to get the story right. For a reporter it is a most essential obligation, yielding dispatches that leave an impression. The stories in this anthology evoke mood and reveal character. They are examples of exceptional writing with emotional intensity. The narrative account, like a well-written piece of fiction, entertains the reader, who is drawn in by a lively lead that demands attention.

The investigative article based on character and the descriptive story that focuses on scenes and events are made possible by keen observation. The historical report adds background and with time, provides evaluation to give the reader a better perspective and analysis of selected news events. Good writing leaves an impression. The words and pictures of these correspondents reflect humanity in motion, filling the day's small history.

The reader will note that some chapters are longer than others. This balance is based on the author's interest and intent. Some wars, in my considered opinion and from our historical research, while not of greater importance in the scheme of things, are really more dramatic than others. No omission is intended. But these collected dispatches, I believe, represent good writing, clear thought, accurate interpretation, dramatic incident, varied style, and reflective passage.

Sincere appreciation is made to Carol Mann and my editor, Mary Kay Linge, whose insightful dispatches helped craft this book; and to Tony Fins, Melanie deForrest, Andrew Zack, Jenny Lawrence, Gerry Lawrence, and Danny deCellis, whose research and organization counted immeasurably.

And special thanks to the following contributors who made this book possible: Colonel David Hackworth, Eve Karlin, *Newsweek;* Lupe Salazar, *Los Angeles Times;* Norm Golden, *Associated Press;* Arthur Ochs Sulzburger, John Brewer, A. M. Rosenthal, Max Frankel, *New York Times;* Jason McManus, Lance Morrow, Bobbie Baker Burrows, Edward Barnes, George Church, John Arbour, Carl Mydens, Strobe Talbott, Abigale Silzer, Elaine Felsher, Richard Zoglin, Time, Incorporated; Teressa Buswell, Houghton Mifflin; John Smyntek, Detroit *Free Press,* Susan LeClair, *U.S. News and World Report;* Diana Daniels, Washington Post Company; Mary Lou Marusin, Scrips Howard Foundation; Henry Stokes, *The Commercial Appeal;* Faith Barbato, HarperCollins; Russell Burrows, William F. Buckley, Jr., and my former students at the School of Journalism, University of North Carolina at Chapel Hill.

THE REVOLUTIONARY WAR

THE AMERICAN REVOLUTION

1775–1783

FOR ALL THE SPEECHES and mythmaking, the American Revolution started as a desperate dispute over finance. The long war of the American Revolution was the culmination of a period of acute political and economic crises within the British Empire. At stake were the political and commercial autonomy of the prospering North American provinces. In essence, their populations and economies had grown robustly, straining the transatlantic ties of governance by the remote English Crown and Parliament. As King George's ministers pursued policies aimed at consolidating their control of the trade and revenue from the colonies, they increasingly cut across the grain of citizens who, though royal subjects, had grown accustomed to ruling themselves via provincial legislatures and lively participatory civic procedures such as petitions and town or county meetings. "The quarrel," as a reader of the *Publick Ledger* so aptly stated, "is about a paltry threepenny Duty on Tea."

British taxes, along with production and trade laws enacted by Parliament, fettered the merchants and farmers of English America. Efforts to reach a compromise on imperial policy were fruitless, and tensions mounted. A growing number of colonists regarded Parliament's acts as intolerable encroachments on their rights as citizens, and the imperial officials grew frustrated by the difficult enforcement of the tariffs, duties, and decrees. In the early 1770s, civil unrest polarized the empire. In ironic efforts to maintain order, royal governors alienated many of their countrymen by using force against them during the Boston Massacre and the suppression of a backcountry uprising in North Carolina. By the middle of the decade, loyalty and patriotism became hotly

The Boston Massacre.
(Library of Congress)

contested values as dissatisfaction with imperial policies coalesced into a rudimentary nationalism. As it unfolded, the war became a test of citizenship; some maintained allegiance to the old order and others embraced a new, ill-defined liberty. When warfare erupted in 1775, friends and family became divided in their loyalties and often faced one another on opposite sides of bayonet charges. But by the time Cornwallis's forces capitulated at Yorktown in 1781, the conflict had acquired a much higher purpose. John Warren gushed that the United Colonies were "the glorious constellation of the western hemisphere." In part, the meaning of the conflict was altered not by battle itself but by the words of war.

Far from being unbiased reporters, the revolutionary-era press was a committed advocate for or against independence. Tory and patriot pamphleteers alike printed virulent defenses for their causes from which readers selected their views and judged each dispatch by the politics of the source. The following selections give insight into how orators and thinkers of the late eighteenth century fueled the ideological transformation that changed a war to end mercantile allegiance to the British Crown into a revolution for national independence, personal liberty, and representative government. These selections serve to show how the written word anchored this transformation. What the eighteenth-century newspapers and pamphlets lacked in accuracy, they made up in passion. The rhetoric of pamphleteers and the debate over the rights and duties of American citizens established an argumentative tone for journalism that would last for over one hundred years.

In the eyes of rebel leaders, the conflict had to represent more than a revolt against taxes. Tories could fight for money, but American patriots could die for no less than the right of an untainted people to break from the corruption and politically constraining norms of the Old World. Indeed, Europe, with its monarchies and material excess, was seen and depicted as a corrupt land where the common man was enslaved by tyrannical kings. The freshness of the American continent, where farmers, common laborers, and artisans breathed freely, could be secured only by independence and democratic government.

In forming their ideology, patriot leaders tapped the visions of such intellectuals as Immanuel Kant. His *The Critique of Pure Reason* argued that every person ought to pursue his own path, in essence, freedom of speech, and thought. "Let each thinker," Kant wrote, "pursue his own path." The passion of Kant influenced writers like Thomas Paine. With conviction, Paine charged that "America can never be happy until she gets clear of foreign domination."

Yet at times the intense rhetoric on both sides created only confusion. Historians estimate that almost a third of the 2.75 million Americans who fought sided with the Crown. American-on-American conflict registered some of the most gruesome accounts of war.

For all the glory and fruits that victory in war brings, the problem with armed conflict is that it follows its own trajectory, regardless of the course intellectuals and thinkers may wish upon it. Thomas Jefferson, the symbol of American virtue, quickly realized that fighting a war took more than signatures on the Declaration of Independence. His letter to General Friedrich von Steuben pleaded for a shipment of shoes to soldiers at Williamsburg given "the murmurings of mutiny." At Valley Forge, many poorly clothed Continental army soldiers froze. The war, as Paine warned, was not for the summer soldier.

The British command was no more successful in its efforts to keep its armies and leaders in synchronization, not to mention at holding the rebel army regulars and militiamen at bay. Isaiah Thomas closed his dispatch by quoting the desperate commands of a British unit leader at Lexington: "Disperse you damn'd rebels! Damn you, disperse!"

Yet, the most significant irony in the war is that the greatness of the American Revolution was lost on the rest of the world at that time. Indeed, as the world approached 1776, three Londoners, calling themselves the Society of Gentlemen were busy with the first edition of the *Encyclopaedia Britannica*. Dutch scientists were ardently developing the study of photosynthesis, and Spain was more interested in learning the steps to the bolero. On the North American continent, some Americans shrugged off commitments at Saratoga, Morristown, and Charleston in order to seek adventure elsewhere. Daniel Boone set out to explore lands beyond the Appalachian Mountains and named the region Kentucky. Even as the American colonies were on the verge of being lost, the British Crown still attended to additional expansion with Captain Cook, then returning from his second voyage to the Pacific.

The first blows in the war for freedom were struck with the great toppling of royal emblems and a rush of citizens to arms around Boston. Opposed to the rebels were British general Gage's four thousand men, the main British force in the colonies. As the fighting went on, Britain brought over as many as fifty-five thousand soldiers, including about thirty thousand German-speaking mercenaries; to these were added many American Tories and Indians. The redcoats generally were well equipped; although the heavy muskets were dismally inaccurate, they were supplemented by that very useful weapon, the glittering twenty-one-inch bayonet.

After the battles of Lexington and Bunker Hill, the guns of Ticonderoga, and the liberation of Boston, after the blood-stained-turned-peaceful village greens and the bold assaults inside the walls of Quebec, all that remained for Congress was to justify its stand before the world.

The Declaration of Independence was an eloquent and persuasive statement for the causes that forced the colonies to dissolve their "political bands" and "to assume among the powers of the earth, the separate and equal station to which the laws of nature and of nature's God entitle them."

Within fifty years, the egalitarian spirit unleashed by the American Revolution extended from the streets of Paris to Latin America. The pens, like the muskets, of the American Revolution were driven by passion and pamphlet. In the difficult early decades of independence, the "Spirit of '76" served as a unifying call for the setting aside of partisan or regional difference and promoted a tightened union of the sovereign states under the Constitution of 1789. To have been a part of the revolution was the greatest of public honors well into the nineteenth century. The experience of the war created a small pantheon of national heroes and a host of militiamen of renown. John Adams, Thomas Jefferson, Alexander Hamilton, and George Washington were influential architects of the Republic.

The revolutionary war did not have correspondents as such. News from the battlefield probably first arrived in the form of unconfirmed rumors. Newspapers relied principally on letters received from regular correspondents who might be best considered stringers. Such a person in Cambridge or Philadelphia reported, usually briefly, on latest events in the community. Sometimes this news was war related. A newspaper also included letters from those who were not regular contributors. If a battle was not reported by a stringer or another observer who had written a letter, the newspaper often printed an official report of the engagement as submitted by the commanding officer. Regardless of the source of a battle report, it was usually not fresh news when it appeared in print. In the case of reports of the victory at Kings Mountain in the interior of the Carolinas, for example, weeks passed before newspapers printed accounts of it.

Newspapers in the period of the American Revolution were filled more with passion than news. They included only reports and commentaries that reflected favorably on their publisher's own political position. They rarely corrected the numerous errors that filled their pages. An American who was anxious to learn the latest events of the war would not have found these newspapers reliable sources of information. Reporting the news accurately, comprehensively, and honestly fell victim to the passions of the moment.

ISAIAH THOMAS

MASSACHUSETTS *SPY,* MAY 3, 1775

"Do thou great liberty inspire our souls and make our lives in thy possession happy or, our deaths glorious in thy just defence." These bold words appeared in each issue of the Massachusetts Spy *in the early months of 1775. An even more provocative part of the masthead was an illustration of a snake representing the colonies facing up to a threatening dragon representing Great Britain. "Join or die" was the clear warning to the colonies. The four-page Boston newspaper was a regular affront to British authorities.*

Isaiah Thomas, the publisher and editor of the Massachusetts Spy, *was just twenty-six years old in 1775. A member of the Sons of Liberty, Thomas realized that his newspaper could not last long in Boston given the rising tensions and the likelihood that British authorities would shut down his press. On 16 April 1775, he quietly removed his press to Worcester under cover of darkness. Between that day and the third of May, when he published the first issue of his newspaper in Worcester, the revolutionary war began. Three days after moving his press, a large British force confronted a few dozen patriot minutemen. Someone fired his musket—"the shot heard round the world"—and the American Revolution began.*

Isaiah Thomas's account appeared in the first issue of the Massachusetts Spy *printed in Worcester.*

ON THE NINETEENTH DAY OF April, one thousand, seven hundred and seventy-five, a day to be remembered by all Americans of the present generation, and which ought and doubtless will be handed down to ages yet unborn, in which the troops of Britain, unprovoked, shed the blood of sundry of the loyal American subjects of the British King in the field of Lexington.

Early in the morning of said day, a detachment of the forces under the command of General Gage, stationed at Boston, attacked a small party of inhabitants of Lexington and some other towns adjacent, the detachment consisting of about nine hundred men, commanded by Lieutenant Colonel Smith. The inhabitants of Lexington and the other towns were about one hundred, some with and some without

The Massachusetts *Spy,* originally based in Boston, was published and edited by Sons of Liberty member Isaiah Thomas—and openly in favor of independence from Great Britain. *(Smithsonian Institute)*

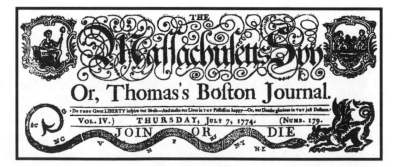

fire arms, who had collected upon information that the detachment had secretly marched from Boston the preceding night, and landed at Phip's Farm in Cambridge, and were proceeding on their way with a brisk pace towards Concord (as the inhabitants supposed) to take or destroy a quantity of stores deposited there for the use of the colony; sundry peaceable inhabitants having the same night been taken, held by force, and otherwise abused on the road, by some officers of General Gage's army, which caused a just alarm to the people, and a suspicion that some fatal design was immediately to be put in execution against them.

This small party of the inhabitants so far from being disposed to commit hostilities against the troops of their sovereign that, unless attacked, were determined to be peaceable spectators of this extraordinary movement; immediately on the approach of Colonel Smith with the detachment under his command they dispersed. But the detachment, seeming to thirst for BLOOD, wantonly rushed on, and first began the hostile scene by firing on the small party in which they killed eight men on the spot and wounded several others before any guns were fired upon the troops by our men.

"PHILADELPHIA, MAY 15"

NEW YORK *GAZETTE*, MAY 22, 1775

Isaiah Thomas had been present to witness at least some of the events of 19 April 1775 and could offer a report based on his own experience. Numerous other accounts of the action were offered by other men who had been present. The following are two of nineteen "Affidavits and Depositions, relative to the commencement of the late hostilities in the province of Massachusetts" appearing in a New York newspaper edited by Hugh Gaine. Captain John Parker, one of those who described what had happened, was a veteran of the French and Indian War. A farmer and mechanic in Lexington, Parker had led a force guarding a house in which Samuel Adams and John Hancock were staying.

AFFIDAVITIS AND DEPOSITIONS relative to the commencement of the late hostilities in the province of Massachusetts Bay; continued from our loft:

LEXINGTON, April 25, 1775
JOHN PARKER, OF LAWFUL AGE, and commander of the colonial militia in Lexington, do testify and declare, that on the 19th instant, in the morning, about one of the clock, being informed that there was a number of regular officers riding up and down the road, stopping and insulting people as they passed the road; and also was informed that a number of regular troops were on their march from Boston, in order to take Concord; ordered our militia to meet on the common in said Lexington, to consult what to do, and conclude not to be discovered, nor meddle or make with said regular troops (if they should approach)

unless they should insult or molest us, and upon their sudden approach I immediately ordered our militia to disperse and not to fire; immediately said troops made their appearance and rushed furiously, fired upon and killed eight of our party, without receiving any provocation therefor from us. John Parker.

We, Nathaniel Parkhurst, Jonas Parker, John Munroe, junior, John Winship, Solomon Pierce, John Murray, Abnes Meeds, John Bridge, junior, Ebenezer Bowman, William Munroe, the 3d, Micah Hager, Samuel Sanderson, Samuel Hastings, and John Brown, of Lexington, in the county of Middlesex, and colony of Massachusetts Bay, in New England; and all of lawful age, do testify and say, that on the morning of the nineteenth of April inst.

about one or two o'clock, being informed that a number of regular officers had been riding up and down the road the evening and night preceding, and that forms of the inhabitants as they were passing had been insulted by the officers, and stopped by them; and being also informed that the regular troops were on their march from Boston, in order (as it was said) to take the colony stores there deposited at Concord! We met on the parade of our company in this town; after the company had collected, we were ordered by Captain John Parker (who commanded us) to disperse for the present, and be ready to attend the beat of the drum; and accordingly the company went into houses near the place of parade. We further testify and say, that about five

The Battle of Lexington. *(National Archives)*

o'clock in the morning we attended the beat of our drum and were formed on the parade—we were faced towards the regulars then marching up to us, and some of our company were coming to the parade with their backs towards the troops; and others on the parade began to disperse when the regulars fired on the company, before a gun was fired by any of our company on them; they killed eight of our company, and wounded several, and continued the fire until we had all made our escape.

"NEW YORK, AUGUST 19"

CONNECTICUT *COURANT*, SEPTEMBER 2, 1776

In the weeks after the signing of the Declaration of Independence, the new nation faced a serious crisis. British general William Howe was on Staten Island with a force of more than thirty thousand men poised to launch an attack on New York City. The American army, led by General Israel Putnam, General John Sullivan, and General William Alexander (more commonly known as Lord Stirling), positioned itself on southern Long Island to halt the expected British advance. Howe's forces finally crossed from Staten Island to Long Island toward the end of August. Historians call the clash that took place between August 27 and 29 the Battle of Long Island.

The correspondent who sent the following report to the Connecticut Courant *wrote before this engagement had reached its final conclusion. The Hartford newspaper was clearly in the camp of the patriots and welcomed an upbeat appraisal of the happenings on Long Island.*

THE GREAT, THE IMPORTANT DAY, big with the fate of America and Liberty seems to draw near! The British troops began to land on Long Island last Thursday, nearly their whole force, supposed to be more than 20,000 British and foreign troops. They marched through the small town of New Utrecht, on their way to Flat Bush, another town about five miles from this city, near which they encamped; but were much harassed by our riflemen. Scouting parties were sent from our army to the adjoining woods, but were rather scanty in their numbers considering the extent of ground they had to guard. The British forces, in three divisions, taking three different roads, and the advantage of the night almost surrounded the whole of our out-parties, who though encircled with more than treble their number, bravely fought their way through the enemy, killing great numbers of them, and brought off some prisoners. The New York first battalion behaved with great bravery. Lord Stirling's brigade sustained the hottest of the enemy's fire, it consisted of Col. Miles' two battalions, Col. Attlee's, Col Smallwood's and Col. Hatch's regiments; they were all surrounded by the enemy, and had to fight their way through the blaze of their fire—they fought and fell like Romans!

Lieut. Col. Barry, of the Pennsylvania musquetry, was shot through the head, as he was giving orders to, and animating his men. The major part of Col. Atlee's and Col. Piper's regiments are missing. Doctor Davis and his Mate were both taken prisoners as they were dressing a wounded person in the woods. Col. Miles is missing (a truly amiable character) and supposed to be slain. Generals Stirling and Sulivan are thought to be killed. Gen. Parsons, with seven men, came in yesterday morning, much fatigued, being for ten hours in the utmost danger of falling into the enemy's hands. Our killed, wounded and missing are imagined to be about 1,000; but for our encouragement the missing are hourly coming in. Gen. Grant, of the British troops, from good intelligence, is among the killed: his hat with his name on it, was found lying near the dead body: the bullet had gone thro' and thro' the hat, and carried some of his grey hairs with it. Thus fell the hero, who boasted in the British House of Commons, he would march thro' America with 5,000 men, having only marched five miles on Long Island with an army of four times the number. Our out guards have retreated to the main body of the army within the lines. The British army have two encampments about a mile from our lines, and by their maneuvers, 'tis plain, they mean to attack us by surprize, and storm our intrenchments. Our men shew the greatest bravery, and wish to come to action. The firing continued yesterday all the day.

The alarm was so great last Tuesday (occasioned by the attack of the British troop) the day appointed for fasting, humiliation and prayer in this state, for imploring Divine assistance in forming the new government, that the churches were not opened nor public worship performed.

THOMAS PAINE

"THE AMERICAN CRISIS, NO. 1"

PENNSYLVANIA *GAZETTE*, DECEMBER 19, 1776

The Battle of Long Island began a campaign in which the British forced George Washington's Continental army to retreat again and again. By the middle of December 1776, the patriot forces had withdrawn across the Delaware into Pennsylvania not far from Philadelphia. In the meantime, the Continental Congress, fearing that the enemy might take Philadelphia, had removed to Baltimore. As the year drew to a close, it was obvious that the rebellion against the mother country might soon fizzle out.

The course of the war had blurred the line of distinction between the battlefield and the home front. Both the Loyalists and the patriots struggled for dominance on and off the battlefield. In December 1776 the war had become one for the hearts and minds of Americans. Would the battered patriots become so demoralized that they would give up their quest for independence?

A patriot with pen in hand sought to reverse flagging morale. Thomas Paine was already well known for his pamphlet Common Sense, *but what he wrote in December 1776 may have been more important.* Common Sense *appealed to the head, "The American Crisis" appealed to the heart. It sought to encourage the soldiers and citizens to persevere. Paine had witnessed the retreat of the Continental army, but he admired the fortitude of the beleaguered force.*

THESE ARE THE TIMES THAT TRY men's souls. The summer soldier and the sunshine patriot will, in this crisis, shrink from the service of his country; but he that stands it NOW deserves the love and thanks of man and woman. Tyranny, like hell, is not easily conquered; yet we have this consolation with us, that the harder the conflict, the more glorious the triumph. What we obtain too cheap, we esteem too lightly:—'Tis dearness only that gives every thing its value. Heaven knows how to put a proper price upon its goods; and it would be strange indeed, if so celestial an article as FREEDOM should not be highly rated. Britain, with an army to enforce her tyranny, has declared that she has a right (*not only to* TAX but) "*to* BIND *us in* ALL CASES WHATSOEVER," and if being *bound in that manner,* is not slavery, then is there not such a thing as slavery upon earth. Even the expression is impious, for so unlimited a power can belong only to God. . . .

I have as little superstition in me as any man living, but my secret opinion has ever been, and still is, that God Almighty will not give up a people to military destruction, or leave them unsupportedly to perish, who have so earnestly and so repeatedly sought to avoid the calamities of war, by every decent method which wisdom could invent. Neither have I so much of the infidel in me, as to suppose that He has relinquished the government of the world, and given us up to the care of the devils; and as I do not, I cannot see on what grounds the king of Britain can look up to heaven for help against us: a common murderer, highwayman, or a housebreaker, has as good a pretence as he. . . .

As I was with the troops at Fort Lee, and marched with them to the edge of Pennsylvania, I am well acquainted with many circumstances, which those who live at a distance know but little or nothing of. Our situation there was exceedingly cramped, the place being a narrow

This symbol was used on newspapers in defiance of the 1765 Stamp Act. The Pennsylvania *Journal* printed this on its famed "Tombstone Edition" to protest the revenue tax Great Britain imposed on newspapers. *(Library of Congress)*

neck of land between the North River and the Hackensack. Our force was inconsiderable, being not one fourth so great as [General William] Howe could bring against us. We had no army at hand to have relieved the garrison, had we shut ourselves up and stood on our defence. Our ammunition, light artillery, and the best part of our stores, had been removed, on the apprehension that Howe would endeavor to penetrate the Jerseys, in which case Fort Lee could be of no use to us; for it must occur to every thinking man, whether in the army or not, that these kind of field forts are only for temporary purposes, and last in use no longer than the enemy directs his force against the particular object, which such forts are raised to defend. Such was our situation and condition at Fort Lee on the morning of the 20th of November, when an officer arrived with information that the enemy with 200 boats had landed about seven miles above: Major General [Nathaniel] Greene, who commanded the garrison, immediately ordered them under arms, and sent express to General [George] Washington at the town of Hackensack, distant by way of the ferry six miles. Our first object was to secure the bridge over the Hackensack, which laid up the river between the enemy and us, about six miles from us, and three from them. General Washington arrived in about three quarters of an hour, and marched at the head of the troops towards the bridge, which place I expected we should have a brush for; however they did not choose to dispute it with us, the greatest part of our troops went over the bridge, the rest over the ferry, except some which passed at a mill on a small creek, between the bridge and the ferry, and made their way

through some marshy grounds up to the town of Hackensack, and there passed the river. We brought off as much baggage as the wagons could contain, the rest was lost. The simple object was to bring off the garrison, and march them on till they could be strengthened by the Jersey or Pennsylvania militia, so as to be enabled to make a stand. We staid four days at Newark, collected our outposts with some of the Jersey militia, and marched out twice to meet the enemy, on being informed that they were advancing, though our numbers were greatly inferior to theirs. Howe, in my little opinion, committed a great error in generalship in not throwing a body of forces off from Staten Island through Amboy, by which means he might have seized all our stores at Brunswick, and intercepted our march into Pennsylvania: but if we believe the power of hell to be limited, we must likewise believe that their agents are under some providential control.

I shall not now attempt to give all the particulars of our retreat to the Delaware; suffice it for the present to say, that both officers and men, though greatly harassed and fatigued, frequently without rest, covering, or provision, the inevitable consequences of a long retreat, bore it with a manly and martial spirit. All their wishes centered in one, which was, that the country would turn out and help them to drive the enemy back. Voltaire has remarked that King William never appeared to full advantage but in difficulties and in action; the same remark may be made on General Washington, for the character fits him. There is a natural firmness in some minds which cannot be unlocked by trifles, but which, when unlocked, discovers a cabinet of fortitude; and I reckon it among those kind of public blessings, which we do not immediately see, that God hath blest him with uninterrupted health, and given him a mind that can even flourish upon care.

I shall conclude this paper with some miscellaneous remarks on the state of our affairs; and shall begin with asking the following question, Why is it that the enemy have left the New-England provinces, and made these middle ones the seat of war? The answer is easy: New-England is not infested with tories, and we are. I have been tender in raising the cry against these men and used numberless arguments to show them their danger, but it will not do to sacrifice a world either to their filly or their baseness. The period is now arrived, in which either they or we must change our sentiments, or one or both must fall. And what is a Tory? Good God! what is he? I should not be afraid to go with an hundred Whigs against a thousand tories, were they to attempt to get into arms. Every Tory is a coward; for servile, slavish, self-interested fear is the foundation of toryism; and a man under such influence, though he may be cruel, never can be brave.

But, before the line of irrecoverable separation be drawn between us, let us reason the matter together: your conduct is an invitation to the enemy, yet not one in a thousand of you has heart enough to join him. Howe is as much deceived by you as the American cause is injured by you. He expects you will all take up arms, and flock to his standard with muskets on your shoulders. Your opinions are of no use to him, unless you support him personally, for 'tis soldiers, and not tories, that he wants.

I once felt all that kind of anger, which a man ought to feel, against the mean principles that are held by the tories: a noted one, who kept a tavern at Amboy, was standing at his door, with as pretty a child in his hand, about eight or nine years old, as I ever saw, and after speaking his mind as freely as he thought was prudent, finished with this fatherly expression, *"Well! give me peace in my day."* Not a man lives on the continent but fully believes that a separation must some time or other finally take place, and a generous parent should have said, *"If there must be trouble, let it be in my day, that my child may have peace"*; and this single reflection, well applied, is sufficient to awaken every man to duty. Not a place upon earth might be so happy as America. Her situation is remote from all the wrangling world, and she has nothing to do but to trade with them. A man can distinguish in himself between temper and principle, and I am as confident, as I am that God governs the world, that America will never be happy till she gets clear of foreign dominion. Wars, without ceasing, will break out till that period arrives, and the Continent must in the end be conqueror; for though the flame of liberty may sometimes cease to shine, the coal can never expire.

"BOSTON, FEBRUARY 4"

NEW HAMPSHIRE *GAZETTE*, FEBRUARY 9, 1779

No international agreements governed the treatment of prisoners of war during the American Revolution. Both sides were particularly anxious to induce deserting or captured enemy soldiers and sailors to switch sides. The British, who had taken more than a thousand prisoners in the Battle of Long Island and nearly three thousand in taking Fort Washington three months later, were particularly known for their attempts to force prisoners of war to put on their uniform.

Those captives unwilling to serve the Crown were often held aboard prison ships in conditions not unlike those endured by slaves being brought from Africa to the Americas. Perhaps the most notorious collection of these prison ships was in Wallabout Bay on the East River, securely in the hands of the British after Washington's Continental army had retreated from Long Island and Manhattan.

IT IS PAINFUL TO REPEAT THE indubitable accounts we are constantly receiving, of the cruel and inhuman treatment of the subjects of these States from the Britons in New York and other places. They who hear our countrymen who have been so unfortunate as to fall into the hands of those unrelenting Tyrants, relate the sad story of their captivity, the insults they have received, and the slow, cool, systematical manner in which great numbers of those who could not be prevail'd on to enter their service have been murdered, must have hearts of stone not to melt with pity for the sufferers, and burn with indignation at their tormentors. As we have daily fresh instances to prove the truth of such a representation, public justice requires that repeated public mention should be made of them. A cartel vessel lately arrived at New London in Connecticut, carrying about 136 American prisoners from the prison ships in New York to New London. Such was the condition in which these poor creatures were put on board the cartel,

that in the short run, 16 died on board; upwards of 60 when they were landed were scarcely able to move; and the remainder greatly emaciated and enfeebled; and many who continue alive, are never likely to recover their former health. The greatest inhumanity, we are told, was experienced by the prisoners in a ship, of which one Nelson, a Scotchman, had the superintendence. Upwards of 300 American prisoners were confined at a time on board this ship. There was but one small fire place allowed to cook the food of such a number. The allowance of the prisoners was, moreover, frequently delayed, insomuch that in the short days of November and December, it was not begun to be delivered out 'till eleven o'clock in the forenoon, so that the whole could not be served 'till three o'clock. At sunset the fire was ordered to be quenched; no plea for the many sick, from their absolute necessity, the shortness of the time, and the smallness of the hearth was allowed to avail. The known consequence was, some had not their food dressed at all; many were obliged to eat it half raw. On board the ship, no flour, oatmeal, and things of like nature, suited to the condition of infirm people, were allowed to the many sick: Nothing but ship-bread, beef and pork. This is the account given by a number of prisoners, who are credible persons; and this is but a part of their sufferings. So that the excuse made by the enemy, that the prisoners were emaciated, and died by a contagious sickness, which no one could prevent, is futile; it requires no great sagacity to know, that crowding people together without fresh air, and feeding, or rather starving them in such a manner as our prisoners, produce contagion. Nor is it a want of candour to suppose, that many of our enemies saw with pleasure this contagion, which might have been so easily prevented, among the prisoners who could not be persuaded to enter their service. Some of them, no doubt, tho't they acted in all this, with the true spirit of the British parliament; who began hostilities against America, by shutting up the port of Boston, interdicting the fishery those branches of trade that were deemed necessary to our subsistence; and when some members objected to the cruelty of such acts, some well known friends to the minority, had the face to ring in the ears of others, Starvation, Starvation to the Rebels—Starvation is the only thing that will bring them to their senses. In short, the inhumanity of the Britons, from the beginning of the war, through every stage of it, is without a parallel in the annals of any civilized nation. These things ought never to be forgotten, tho' some would fain wink them out of sight. We are not indeed to resolve never to make peace with our enemies; but never to make a peace that will leave it in their power to act over again their intolerable oppressions and cruelties. We can never secure ourselves against this, but by maintaining at all adventures, the Sovereignty and Independence of these States. Nothing but this can effectually prevent the present generation from enduring the severest punishment for their noble resistance to the tyranny of Britain; nor our posterity from groaning throughout all generations under the most abject and cruel bondage.

GENERAL HORATIO GATES

LETTER TO THOMAS JEFFERSON

NEW JERSEY *GAZETTE*, NOVEMBER 15, 1780

Major Patrick Ferguson and his force of more than one thousand Loyalists were making their way toward Charlotte, North Carolina, to join up with Lord Cornwallis when they set up camp on a hill known as Kings Mountain. Ferguson was confident that his men could easily defeat the rebels in the interior of the Carolinas and looked forward to hanging their leaders. The patriot militia force surprised the Loyalists at Kings Mountain early on the morning of October 7, 1780.

The following account of the battle is from General Horatio Gates, who transmitted the report to Thomas Jefferson on November 1, 1780.

LAST NIGHT, COL. CAMPBELL, who commanded our victorious troops in the action of the 7th ultimo at Kings Mountain, arrived here. He has delivered to me the enclosed authentic and particular account of that affair. I beg your Excellency will immediately, after perusal, forward it to Congress.

A state of the proceedings of the western army, from the 25th day of Sept. 1780, to the reduction of Major Furguson and the army under his command. On receiving intelligence that Major Furguson had advanced up as high as Gilbert-Town, in Rutherford county, and threatened to cross the mountains to the western waters, Col. William Campbell, with 400 men from Washington county of Virginia, Col. Isaac Shelby, with 240 men from Sullivan county of North-Carolina, and Lieut. Col. John Sevier, with 240 men from Washington county, North-Carolina, assembled at Wattaugo (Watauga), on the 25th day of September, where they were joined by Col. Charles McDowell, with 160 men from the counties of Burk and Rutherford who had fled before the Enemy to the western waters. We began our march on the 16th, and on the 30th we were joined by Col. Cleveland, on the Catawba River, with 350 men from the counties of Wilkes and Surrey: no one officer having property a right to the command-in-chief, on the 1st of October we dispatched an express to Major General Gates, informing him of our situation, and requested him to send a general officer to take command of the whole. In the mean-time Col. Campbell was chosen to act as commandant, till such general officer should arrive. We marched to the Cowpens on Broad River, in South Carolina, where we were joined by Col. James Williams, with 400 men, on the evening of the 6th of October, who informed us that the enemy lay encamped somewhere near the Cherokee Fjord of Broad River, about 30 miles distant from us. By a council of the principal officers it was thought advisable to pursue the enemy that night with 900 of the best horsemen, and leave the weak horse and footmen to follow as fast as possible. We began our march with 900 of the best men about 8 o'clock the same evening, and marching all night, came up with the enemy about 3 o'clock, P.M. of the 7th, who lay encamped on the top of Kings Mountain, 12 miles north of the Cherokee fjord, in the confidence that they could not be forced from so advantagious a post; previous to the attack, on our march, the following dispositions were made: Col. Shelby's regiment formed a column in the centre on the left; Col. Campbell's, another on the right; part of Col. Cleveland's regiment, headed in front by Maj. Winston's, and Col. Sevier's formed a large column on the right wing: the other part of Cleveland's regiment, headed by Col. Cleveland himself, and Col. Williams' regiment, composed the left wing. In this order we advanced, and got within a quarter of a mile of the enemy before we were discovered. Col. Shelby's and Col. Campbell's regiments began the attack, and kept up a fire on the enemy, while the right and left wings were advancing forward to surround them, which was done in about five minutes, and the fire became general all round. The engagement lasted an hour and five minutes, the greatest part of which time a heavy and incessant fire was kept up on both sides. Our men in some parts where the regulars fought, were obliged to give way a small distance two or three times, but rallied and returned with additional ardour to the attack. The troops upon the right having gained the summit of the eminence, obliged the enemy to retreat along the top of the ridge to where Col. Cleveland commanded, and were there stopped by his brave men: a flag was immediately hoisted by Captain Depeister, the commanding officer (Major Furguson having been killed a little before), for a surrender. Our fire immediately ceased, and the enemy laid down their arms, the greatest part of them loaded: and surrendered themselves prisoners to us at discretion. It appears from their own provision returns for that day, found in their camp, that their whole force consisted of 1,125 men. . . . Total loss of the enemy, 1,105 men, at Kings Mountain.

> Given into our hand at Camp,
> William Campbell
> Isaac Shelby
> Benjamin Cleveland

The loss on our side was—
Killed, 1 colonel, 1 major, 1 captain, 2 lieutenants, 4 ensigns, 19 privates; total—28
Wounded, 1 major, 3 captains, 3 lieutenants, 53 privates; total—69

ALEXANDER HAMILTON

LETTER TO ISAAC SEARS

ROYAL GAZETTE, DECEMBER 1780

Probably no newspaper more ably presented the Loyalist position than James Rivington's New York Gazette, *later known as the* Royal Gazette. *At the outbreak of the revolutionary war, Rivington attempted to present both sides in the conflict, but he soon offended the Sons of Liberty and they destroyed his press in November 1775. Chief among Rivington's tormentors in the patriot group was Isaac Sears, a ship owner and merchant who had first gained a reputation as a commander of privateers in the French and Indian War. The newspaper publisher left New York and spent some time in London, but then returned to New York, then occupied by British forces, as the king's partner.*

James Rivington's new newspaper, the Royal Gazette, *took a firm stance against the "rebels" in the American colonies. One of his means of discrediting the enemies of the Crown was to publish their letters when Loyalists could intercept them in the mail. The following letter from Alexander Hamilton, General Washington's aide-de-camp, to Isaac Sears was published together with a number of other letters in a single-page extra of the* Royal Gazette. *In preferatory remarks, Rivington noted that the letters offered "the most decisive proof of a concerted scheme to establish a military, upon the ruins of civil government."*

FREEDOM OF THE PRESS

Thomas Jefferson was a staunch defender:

> I am persuaded that the good sense of the people will always be found to be the best army. They may be led astray for a moment, but will soon correct themselves. The people are the only censors of their governors; and even their errors will tend to keep these to the true principles of their institution. To punish these errors too severely would be to suppress the only safeguard of the public liberty. The way to prevent these irregular interpositions of the people, is to give them full information of their affairs through the channel of the public papers, and to contrive that those papers should penetrate to the whole mass of the people. The basis of our government being the opinion of the people, the very first object should be to keep that right; and were it left to me to decide whether we should have a government without newspapers, or newspapers without a government, I should not hesitate a moment to prefer the latter.

A most important development in the 1780s was the government reporting provided by the *National Intelligencer*. Endorsed by Jefferson, it was nonpartisan and a success financially and editorially. The Niles' *Weekly Register* began publishing soon after with a weekly roundup of speeches, documents, and honest evaluations of current events. Now both sides of controversy found space in the *Register,* and its material was indexed so comprehensively that the entire publication has been reprinted issue by issue to give librarians and historians an authoritative index of the politics of the first half of the nineteenth century.

I WAS MUCH OBLIGED TO YOU, MY dear Sir, for the letter which you did me the favour to write me since your return to Boston. I am sorry to find that the same species of indifference to public affairs prevails. It is necessary we should rouse and begin to do our business in earnest, or we shall play a losing game. It is impossible the contest can be much longer supported on the present footing. We must have a government with more power. We must have a tax in kind. We must have a foreign loan. We must have a bank on the true principles of a bank. We must have an administration different from Congress, and in the hands of single men under their orders. We must, above all things, have an army for the war, and on an establishment that will interest the officers in the service.

Congress are deliberating on our military affairs; but I apprehend their resolutions will be tinctured with the old spirit: We seem to be proof against experience.

The surrender of Cornwallis at Yorktown, Virginia. Over seven thousand British and Hessian soldiers were taken prisoner. *(National Archives)*

They will, however, recommend an army for the war, at least as a primary object: All those who love their country ought to exert their influence in the states where they reside to determine them to take up this object with energy. The states must sink under the burden of temporary enlistments, and the enemy will conquer us by degrees during the intervals of our weakness.

Clinton is now said to be making a considerable detachment to the southward. My fears are high; my hopes low.

We are told here, there is to be a Congress of the neutral powers at the Hague for mediating a peace: Good send it may be true. We want it. But if the idea gets abroad, 'tis ten to one if we do not fancy the thing done, and fall into a profound sleep till the cannon of the enemy awaken our next campaign. This is our national character.

IN RETROSPECT

JOHN WARREN

AN ORATION . . . IN CELEBRATION OF THE ANNIVERSARY OF AMERICAN INDEPENDENCE, JULY 4, 1783

John Warren (1753–1815) rushed from Salem to Boston in June 1775 to aid those Americans wounded during the battle of Bunker Hill, but he arrived too late to help his brother, General Joseph Warren, who had been killed in that bloody encounter. Appointed a hospital surgeon by General Washington, John Warren served with the Continental army until 1778, when he became superintendent of military hospitals in Boston. In 1783 that city asked him to give an address to commemorate the Fourth of July, the first of Boston's annual celebrations of American independence. Warrens' theme was the fragility of a republic. Of course, the analogy of the human life cycle—of birth, maturation, and decay—sprang readily to Dr. Warren's mind. But it was a commonplace way for Americans to express their belief in the precarious life of their republican experiment. Likewise, the doctor's prescription was understandable to all of his listeners: stimulate and preserve public virtue. Only if the citizens of the American republic were virtuous would they be able to postpone the political diseases to which a republic was most susceptible—chaos and absolutism. Warren was more optimistic about the outcome than were many of his contemporaries who were loudly lamenting the loss of American political virtue.

FATHERS, BRETHREN, AND FELLOW-Citizens! To mark with accuracy and precision, the principles from which the great and important transactions on the theatre of the political world originate, is indispensable duty, not only of legislators, but of every subject of a free State; fraught with the most instructive lessons on the passions that actuate the human breast, the inquiry is amply adapted to the purpose of regulating the social concerns of life. . . .

That we may learn wisdom by the misfortunes of others, that by tracing the operation of those causes which have proved ruinous to so many states and kingdoms, we may escape the rocks and

quicksands on which they have been shipwreck'd, it may be useful to take a cursory retrospect of the motives and opinions, which have effected the dismemberment of a very large and valuable part of the British dominions, and thereby deprived them of a principal source of strength and greatness; under a constitution which has ever been the boast of Englishmen, we have seen a most shameful prostitution of wealth to the purposes of individuals, which when exorbitant, must always be injurious to the common interest.

We have seen the members of a House of Commons, which was once the bulwark of the nation, and the palladium of Liberty, availing themselves of the meanest artifices for securing a seat, because it enabled them to gratify their favorite passions; and shame to human nature! We have seen a people, once famed for honesty and temperance, intoxicated at the gambols of an election, and stupidly selling their suffrages for representatives in Parliament!

The whole business of government had become an affair of trade and calculation, the representative who expended his property for the purchase of a vote, was sure to make his profits, by the sale of his influence for the support of ministerial prodigality, or absolute domination; and to extend the security with which the members might plunder the people and trample on their rights, the prolongation of their parliaments to a term of time sufficient to inveterate their power, was at length adopted, for the purpose of riveting those chains which an undue influence in elections had previously forged.

Religious tyranny had forced from the unnatural bosom of a parent, a race of hardy sons, who chose rather to dwell in the deserts of America with the savage natives, than in the splendid habitations of *more* savage men.

Scarcely had these persecuted fugitives breathed from the fatigues of a dangerous voyage, when behold the cruel hand of power stretched over the Atlantic to distress them in their new possessions! Having found a rude uncultivated soil, inadequate to the supply of the conveniences of life, they attempted those arts of which they stood immediately in need; a prohibition of the manufactures necessary to clothe them in these then inhospitable wilds was early threatened, and though they were afterwards permitted, yet it was under the most humiliating restrictions.

From a principle of avarice and the most unjustifiable partiality in prejudice of these infant settlements, all commercial communication between them was forbidden, the importation of mercantile articles was laid under the heaviest restraints, none were to be freighted, not even the produce of foreign countries, from any other than British ports, and all exportations were finally to terminate in Britain.

The manifest object of these measures, was to enrich some crouching favorites at home, 'till at night, plunged into debt, even in the midst of success and conquest, by the rapaciousness of an insatiable ministry, and a general corruption of manners, every sinew was strained amongst their domestic subjects for the acquisition of a large revenue, but this resource having been found insufficient for the purpose, the expenses of the war, out of which they had just emerged, were made the pretext for levying taxes on the unrepresented subjects of America; the first requisition for the supply of an army was too readily submitted to, and the subsequent acts, which have led to that war, in which these states have been called upon to contend for every thing dear in life, are too recent to be yet forgotten by you my fellow citizens, on whom the vengeance they were designed to execute has so largely fallen.

The mild voice of supplication and petition had in vain assailed the royal ear, the blood of your fellow-countrymen was wantonly shed on the memorable plains of *Lexington*, you flew to arms and made *your last appeal to Heaven.*

Never did an enthusiastic ardor in the cause of an injured country blaze forth with such resistless fury, never did patriotic virtue shine out with such transcendent lustre, as on that solemn day! Scarcely was there to be seen a peasant through the land "whose bosom beat not in his country's cause." Angels must have delighted in the fight! A wide extended country, roused into action at the first flash of arms, and pouring forth her thousands of virtuous yeomen to avenge the blood of their slaughtered brethren on the unprincipled aggressors! Quickly they fled from merited destruction, and fleeing, shed their blood, an immolation to the beloved names of those who fell the early martyrs to this glorious cause, you then convinced *deluded* Britons, that bravery was not the growth of any one *peculiar* spot or soil.

The enterprize 'tis true was bold and daring! The nations of the world stood still, astonished at the desperate blow! The brave alone are capable of noble actions. Defenseless, and unfurnished with the means of war, you placed your confidence in that God of armies who approves the struggles of the oppressed, and relying on the honest feelings of the heart for your success, you ventured to contend with veteran armies, and to defy the formidable power of a nation accustomed to success and conquest. . . .

By means of their union, the states, alone and unassisted, have vanquished a numerous army of brave and veteran troops, and led their chief a captive to your capital.—As long as time shall last the noble example you have set the world shall be produced, to shew what wonders may be done by men united, and determined to be free.

Your virtue has supplied the place of wealth in the prosecution of the war; the taxes that have been levied, have generally been submitted to with cheerfulness, and in a free state, where the people themselves are the assessors, so far were they from being considered as a grievance, that you wisely *esteemed them* as the symptoms of virtue, because they evince that the safety of the public is the supreme object of attention.

Nor shall the powerful aids of a magnanimous Ally be suffered here to pass unnoticed; the generous terms on which assistance and support were granted, shall leave impressions of esteem and friendship which time and age shall not be able to efface. Under the conduct of *One* illustrious General, the brave allied armies have together contended for the rights of human nature, have mingled blood, conquered a formidable host of *chosen* troops, *and laid the British Standard at your feet.* . . .

What miseries and tortures have we not escaped! Go search the records of tyranny and usurpation, and learn the insolence forever consequent on the suppression of insurrections in the behalf of violated rights! . . .

Had conquest crowned the efforts of our enemies, numbers of our *worthy patriots*, had *now* been bleeding under the vindictive hand of a successful foe, and *we* perhaps in mines or dungeons, been dragging out a life of wretchedness, and weeping in silence, over the memory of *those*, to whom were justly due, the applause and gratitude of every friend to liberty and virtue.

What a contrast to this frightful picture does the joyfulness of the occasion which has this day assembled us together, exhibit to our view! Many of these illustrious freemen now meet us here, and mingle tears of joy and gratitude with ours!

Thousands of brave, deserving members of society, have fallen an untimely prey to the poisonous exhalations of a *prison*, and *filthy guardships*, have been the charnel houses of our brethren; confined within those dreadful regions of horror and despair, where no refreshing breezes ever entered, the tainted element itself was charged with pestilence and death! . . .

But smiling peace returns, and death and carnage shall prevail no more to swell the number of the slain; we wish not Britons, too severely to upbraid you, we only mean to hold you up as an example to the world, from which the best of lessons may be learnt.

—Let us however contemplate those unfictitious scenes of misery and distress, which an arduous struggle for our liberties have cost us; let us remember the principles that produced the opposition, as well as those that gave occasion for it, and then if we can tamely bear to see our liberties destroyed, let us flee, *quickly* flee, from these yet hallowed shores, nor dare pollute the land which holds *our fathers' tombs*.

A time of *tranquility* and *peace* is often a season of the greatest danger, because it is too apt to involve a general opinion of perfect security. The Roman state, whilst Carthage stood her rival, retained her virtue, Carthage was destroyed, and Rome became corrupt; unless *we* are properly apprized of, and duly armed against this

evil, the *United States* will *one day* experience a similar fate. . . .

When you forget the value of your freedom, read over the history that counts the wounds from which your country bled; peruse the picture which brings back to your imaginations, in the lively colours of undisguised truth, the wild, distracted feelings your hearts!—but if your happy lot has been not to have felt the pangs of a convulsive separation from *friend* or *kindred*, learn them of *those that have*. . . .

I might proceed—but permit me *here* to draw the sable veil, and leave to your imaginations to suggest the rest—but stay—forbear, nor longer mourn for those who have no cause for tears.—

"Glory with all her lamps shall burn
"To watch the warrior's sleeping clay,
"Till the last trump shall raise his urn,
"To share the triumphs of the day."

———

If to latest ages we retain the *spirit* which gave our INDEPENDENCE birth; if taught by the fatal evils that have subverted so many *mighty states*, we learn to sacrifice our dearest interests in our country's cause, enjoin upon our children a *solemn veneration* for her laws, as next to adoration of their God, the *great* concern of man, and seal the precept with our last expiring breath, these STARS, that even now enlighten half the world, shall shine a glorious constellation in this *western hemisphere*, 'till *stars* and suns shall shine no more, and all the kingdoms of *this* glove shall vanish like a scroll.

THE WAR OF 1812

"MR. MADISON'S WAR"

1812–1814

N THE THREE DECADES after the American Revolution, the population of the United States more than doubled, spilling settlements over the Appalachian Mountains into the vast, forested, and fertile tablelands beyond. In 1803 the purchase of the Louisiana Territory from France secured the whole of the Mississippi Valley, quickly transforming the meadows and forests of the Ohio watershed into a boom region marked by cash crop cultivation and riverboat traffic. Meanwhile, New England's shipping industry prospered from a stepped-up European trade due to the Napoleonic wars.

George Washington's final words as president to the young nation he had helped to create had warned Americans to steer clear of international conflict. "Observe good faith and justice toward all nations," he implored his fellow citizens. "Cultivate peace and harmony with all."

But the territorial and oceanic expansion of U.S. commerce brought the fledgling Republic into conflict with the British Empire in Canada and on the high seas. Threatened in Europe by its perennial rival, France, the English navy aggressively patrolled the Atlantic Ocean and Caribbean Sea, intercepting any American merchant ships it suspected of trading with its enemy. This practice, coupled with on-the-spot impressment of any English-speaking men deemed to be deserters from the Royal Navy, outraged many people in the United States. Even greater enmity arose from the widespread conviction that the British government deliberately encouraged fierce Native American resistance to American settlement of the Great Lakes region.

But the American citizenry was divided over the proper policy for its government to follow. By the spring of 1812, regions that exported farm products, particularly the West and the South, clamored loudly for war, while New England merchants feared that hostile British warships would destroy, rather than merely impede, their commercial fleets. Split on this crucial issue, Congress declared war on June 18 with more than one-third of the House and two-fifths of the Senate opposed to fighting such a powerful foe.

Great Britain immediately fielded a veteran army of seven thousand regulars supported by the Canadian militia and Native American allies; additional scores of war-hardened regiments could be transported to North America from the battlefields of Europe if peace were restored there. Even more dangerous were the two hundred British frigates and ships of the line, which boasted twice the firepower of their American counterparts. Patriotism, if not military prudence, won the day as the American government committed its scattered regular army of sixty-seven hundred and its sixteen naval vessels to avenging the humiliation the United States had suffered at English hands for a whole generation. Succeeding Thomas Jefferson, President James Madison used his authority to induct 100,000 state militiamen into federal service, but this body of volunteers was undercut in numbers and quality by the virtual neutrality of the New England states, which maintained the best-trained and best-equipped troops. This split strengthened state and regional allegiances within the national system.

Due in part to this disunity, the U.S. forces fared poorly during the first campaigns of the war. Attempts to seize forts in lower Canada ended in surrender, rout, and retreat as the British and their allies occupied large portions of the old Northwest Territories. Only the celebrated victories at sea by the USS *Constitution* and USS *United States* buoyed the war effort as state electors narrowly endorsed Madison the new president in November 1812. The proadministration newspaper The *Spirit of '76* exhorted patriots to support Thomas Jefferson's successor in this hour of republican need.

In the next year the Americans captured Lake Erie and secured an uneasy stalemate in the North. Combat shifted to the southwestern territories of the United States, where Creek warriors in Alabama battled American militiamen commanded by young Andrew Jackson, who was aided by his Cherokee allies. The fighting was especially brutal, with both sides constantly ambushing each other and making few distinctions between combatants and noncombatants. On both fronts, American troops were subjected to extended marches into unfamiliar territory, supported by unreliable supply lines and wholly dependent on Native American scouts. But gradually the U.S. forces learned to hold their ground.

By 1814 the Americans had become proficient enough in land warfare to defend themselves from a three-pronged British attack spearheaded by fourteen thousand veterans fresh from their triumph over Napoleon. First they checked the English advance southward through New York at Lake Champlain. Then in Baltimore they held firm against an invasion in which Washington, D.C., was burned. And finally, they soundly defeated the British army attempting to seize New Orleans, although this battle, General Jackson's most famous, occurred fifteen days after diplomats had signed a peace accord.

This historical disjuncture was able to occur because news traveled slowly. The

Francis Scott Key observes the Battle of Fort McHenry. This experience was the inspiration for Key's poem "The Star-spangled Banner." *(Smithsonian Institute)*

printers and newspapers transformed firsthand narratives and reports into often reflective stories. The news of New Orleans spread across the land and in early February came the word from Ghent, where the treaty had been signed. Torchlights flared. Crowds surged shouting through the streets. "A peace! A peace!" was the cry—and the fact that the peace had been signed before New Orleans was fought seemed to matter not at all.

Americans bestowed greater confidence and glory upon their fighting men after the war than they did during the conflict. Eventually William Henry Harrison and Andrew Jackson would ride their reputations as frontier warriors to the White House, and Francis Scott Key's "The Star-spangled Banner" would become the nation's anthem. Since the popular imagination makes symbols of complicated events, in retrospect the War of 1812 confirmed the nationalistic view that the rough-hewn volunteer forces of a New World republic could easily thwart invasion by the polished professionals of a European monarchy. This frontier myth held that pioneers invariably made superior warriors. It was this romantic view of the United States as a fighting nation that would be tested and modified in the next war.

"DECLARATION OF WAR"

KENTUCKY *PALLADIUM*, JULY 1, 1812

The news of war met with a mixed response in Congress, the public, and the press. The vote in Congress, seventy-nine to forty-nine in the House and nineteen to thirteen in the Senate, was the narrowest margin on any declaration of war in American history. Around the nation, Republican supporters of the war huzzahed the inauguration of hostilities, while Federalists reluctantly agreed to support the war, though muttering their fears of destruction, destitution, and humiliation.

The highly partisan press echoed these divisive sentiments. News from Washington of congressional debates reached editors in bits and pieces, mail often moved at a snail's pace, and Madison's supporters did their best to keep the debates quiet. In the weeks after the news finally broke, Republican papers ran stories of jubilant celebrations. Federalists countered with doleful warnings and laments of their countrymen's foolhardy decision.

Two such papers were the Kentucky Palladium *of Frankfort and the Connecticut* Courant *of Hartford. The* Palladium, *a thoroughly Republican weekly, captured the feelings of its western audience, while the* Courant, *staunchly Federalist, like most in New England, tolled a note of despair.*

ON THE ARRIVAL OF THE EASTern mail on Monday, bringing the official intelligence of a Declaration of War against Great Britain, it was announced by a federal salute; and after the public meeting had adjourned (the proceedings of which are published in this paper) a second salute was fired, accompanied by the loud huzzas of the numerous assemblage present.

GOVERNOR HARRISON.

ON FRIDAY EVENING LAST HIS EXcellency WILLIAM H. HARRISON arrived in this place, on his way to Cincinnati. His arrival was announced by a federal salute, and the Frankfort Infantry Company, and a large number of citizens, met him at the ferry and escorted him into town. On Saturday a public dinner was given him at Capt. Weisiger's tavern, where his excellency Gov. Scott acted as President, and Col. John M. Scott as Vice-President. The greatest good humor and hilarity pervaded the whole company, and the pleasure that sparkled in every eye evinced the gratification it afforded them to entertain their distinguished guest. After the cloth was removed, a number of appropriate toasts were drank [sic], among which were the following:

By Gov. Harrison. The Militia of Kentucky—Prompted by patriotism and organized by experienced valor, they will disseminate the fame of American backwoods men to the ends of the earth.

By the same the Governor of Kentucky—May the mighty spirit which animates the feeble frame of the veteran hero, diffuse itself amongst the military sons of our country, and enable them to tear from the ramparts of Quebec the last emblem of British power in America.

By Gov. Scott. Governor Harrison and the brave officers and soldiers who were engaged in the action of Tippecanoe—3 cheers.

In reply to the above toast by Governor Scott, Gov. Harrison observed, "That he highly appreciated the honor which was done him by the toast. He was happy also to find that the gallantry of the army which he had the honor to command at Tippecanoe, had received its just tribute of applause—None in fact can deserve more. With troops who were determined to conquer or perish, the task of the commander is not difficult. It was his good fortune to be placed in that situation, and he should be contented with a small share of the laurels which the company were pleased to say were won on that occasion."

We are informed that as Gov. Harrison passed through Shelbyville, on his way to Frankfort, the troop of cavalry of that place solicited the pleasure of escorting him; and on his departure from this place, on Monday last, the company of mounted volunteer riflemen commanded by Capt. John Arnold, who lately returned from Vincennes, offered to escort him to Lexington: both of which polite offers Governor Harrison modestly declined.

"WAR! WAR! WAR!"

HARTFORD, CONNECTICUT *COURANT*, JUNE 23, 1812

The partisan press did not soon quiet down; the events of war—mostly bad in its first months—only gave Federalists more to moan about. Republicans called the opposition traitorous. The divided response to the war's opening salvos only portended far deeper divisions to come.

THE DREADFUL TIDINGS HAVE just reached us, that on Thursday last Congress declared War against Great-Britain. We cannot express the sensations which are excited in the minds of all classes of our citizens, on the receipt of this Intelligence. Dissatisfaction, disgust, and apprehensions of the most alarming nature, have seized on every mind. If war were necessary, we could encounter it as a necessary evil, with fortitude, with heroism, and submit to all its evils with resignation. If war were necessary, poor as we are, in the spirit and valor of our fellow-citizens we should find means, or make them. Exposed, as we are, to destruction on every side, if the war was just we could brave the enemy undaunted; we could see our cities smoking, our ships swept from the ocean; we could, unmoved, hear the war-whoop echoing around our frontiers: willingly would we resign our sons to the sword, and cheerfully see them go to death, in defence of their country's rights. But, alas! it is too late to reason. "The die is cast, the scabbard thrown away." The evil is here, it is upon us.—We would ask one question—with every thing to lose, what have we to gain? Let this be answered at the conclusion of the war.

Let it be remembered, war never leaves where it finds a nation. We cannot, will not predict the consequences. We can only say, the crisis is big with events. What will result from the heavy taxes, a cumbersome national debt, the divided sentiment of our citizens, must be left to time to unfold. The greatest evil we have to deplore is that we may not experience the fate of Switzerland; that God would not visit us with the plagues of Holland.

"BRILLIANT NAVAL VICTORY"

BOSTON *GAZETTE*, AUGUST 19, 1812

The Hull family provided America with both its highest and lowest moments in the first year of the war. William Hull, a grizzled veteran of the revolution and governor of Michigan Territory, assumed command of the U.S. Army's western division in the summer of 1812, despite his failing health, and—yet unaware that Congress had declared war—prepared an invasion of Canada. But indecision, which his subordinates decried as cowardice, led Hull to surrender Fort Detroit and his entire army. Hull, unable to defend his surrender with mountains of powder still at his disposal, was court-martialed and handed a suspended death sentence.

His nephew Isaac fared far better. As captain of the commanding American frigate USS Constitution, *he captured the British frigate HMS* Guerriere, *which had plagued American merchant ships before the war. One of the* Constitution's *crew, witnessing a shot bounce off his ship, cried, "Huzza, her sides are made of iron"—and the* Constitution *entered the annals of history as "Old Ironsides." An officer on board sent the following dispatch to the Boston* Gazette *on returning to port. Highly factual and detailed, it shows readers' thirst for every scrap of information about the war.*

THE UNITED STATES FRIGATE Constitution, Captain HULL, anchored yesterday in the outer harbour, from a short cruise, during which she fell in with the English frigate Guerriere, which she captured, after a short, but severe action.—The damage, sustained by the fire of the Constitution, was so great, that it was found impossible to tow her into port, and accordingly the crew were taken out, and the ship sunk. The brilliancy of this action, however we may regret the occasion that has produced it, will still excite the liveliest emotions in every American bosom.

PARTICULARS OF THE LATE ACTION BETWEEN THE U.S. FRIGATE *CONSTITUTION*, AND THE BRITISH FRIGATE *GUERRIERE*

(COMMUNICATED TO THE EDITORS of the Boston *Gaz.* by an officer on board the *Constitution*) Lat. 41, 42, N. long. 55, 33, W.

Thursday, Aug 19, fresh breeze from N.W. and cloudy; at 2 P.M. discovered a vessel to the southward, made all sail in chase; at 3, perceived the chase to be a ship on the starboard tack, close hauled to the wind; hauled S.S.W. at half past 3,

Frigates fight at sea during the War of 1812 *(Library of Congress)*

made out the chase to be a frigate; at 4 coming up with the chase very fast; at quarter before 5, the chase laid her main topsail to the mast; took in our top gallant sails, stay-sails, and flying gib; took a second reef in the topsails, hauled the courses up; sent the royal yards down; and got all clear for action; beat to quarters, on which the crew gave three cheers; at 5 the chase hoisted three English Ensigns, at five minutes past 5, the enemy commenced firing; at 20 minutes past 5, set our colours, one at each mast head, and one at the mizen peak, and began firing at the enemy and continued to fire occasionally, he wearing very often, and we maneuvering to close with him, and avoid being raked; at 6, set the main top gallant sail, the enemy having bore up; at five minutes past 6, set the main top gallant sail, the enemy having bore up; at 5 minutes past 6, brought the enemy to close action, standing before the wind; at 15 minutes past 6, the enemy's mizen-mast fell over on the starboard side; at 20 minutes past 6, finding we were drawing ahead of the enemy, luffed short round his bows, to rake him; at 25 minutes past 6, the enemy fell on board of us, his bowsprit foul of our mizen rigging. We prepared to board, but immediately after, his fore and main mast went by the board, and it was deemed unnecessary. Our cabin had taken fire from his guns; but soon extinguished, without material injury; at 30 minutes past 6, shot ahead of the enemy, when the firing ceased on both sides; he making the signal of submission, by firing a gun to leeward; set fore sail and main sail, and hauled to the eastward to repair damage; all our braces and much of our standing and running rigging and some of our spars being shot away. At 7, wore ship, and stood under the lee of the prize—sent our boat on board, which returned at 8, with Capt. Dacres late of his Majesty's ship Guerriere, mounting 49 carriage guns, and manned with 302 men, got our boats out, and kept them employed in removing the prisoners and baggage from the prize to our own ship. Sent a surgeon's mate to assist in attending the wounded, wearing ship occasionally to keep in the best position to receive the boats. At 20 minutes before 2 A.M. discovered a sail off the larboard beam, standing to the south; saw all clear for another action; at 3 the sail stood off again; at daylight was hailed by the lieut.

on board the prize, who informed, he had 4 feet of water in the hold, and that she was in a sinking condition; all hands employed in removing the prisoners, and repairing our own damage through the remainder of the day. Friday the 20th commenced with light breezes from the northward, and pleasant; our boats and crew still employed as before. At 3 P.M. made the signal of recall for our boats, (having received all the prisoners) that immediately left her on fire, and quarter past 3, she blew up. Our loss in the action was 7 killed, and 7 wounded; among the former, Lieut. Bush of Marines, and among the latter, Lieut. Morris severely. Mr. Aylwin, the master, slightly. On the part of the enemy, 15 men killed, and 64 wounded. Among the former, Lt. Ready, 2d of the ship; among the latter, Capt. Dacres, Lieut. Kent, 1st; Mr. Scott, master, and master's mate.

"THE INVASION OF WASHINGTON"

BOSTON *COLUMBIAN CENTINEL*, AUGUST 31, 1814

Most often, news from the various fronts reached editors piecemeal, dispatched by army officers when hostilities paused or by seamen returning to port. Reports were often unreliable and editors sometimes printed disclaimers admitting that they harbored doubts as to the accuracy of the stories they ran. When reports contradicted one another, as they often did, or when the trickle of letters from participants in the war dried up, one newspaper might reprint the words of another with only a brief reference to the original source.

Such was the case after the British invasion of Washington in the late summer of 1814. Redcoats burned much of the town, including the White House, the Treasury, and the Capitol, which included the Library of Congress. President Madison fled the city along with most of its inhabitants, his wife Dolley saving vital documents and national treasures. Although some American witnesses generously praised the invaders for their restraint in not putting the torch to private property, much of the capital lay in ruins, and even members of Parliament joined in denouncing their troops' behavior. The city's major newspaper,

The *National Intelligencer and Washington Advertiser* began to be published by Samuel Harrison Smith in October 1800, becoming a daily in 1813. It was the first paper dedicated to objective national news and one of the few that hired Washington correspondents before 1850. *(Library of Congress)*

the National Intelligencer, *was not spared, and amid the confusion of rampaging soldiers and fleeing inhabitants, only sparse and contradictory reports escaped the district. This story from the Boston* Columbian Centinel *is an attempt by one editor in a distant city to piece together what news he could find and present it to his readers in reasonably clear form.*

After sacking Washington, the British turned their sights to Baltimore, where they bombarded the port's main defense, Fort McHenry. The best-known dispatch from this battle was penned by an obscure attorney named Francis Scott Key, whose poem "The Star-spangled Banner"—set to an eighteenth-century British drinking song—would become the American national anthem in 1931.

THE WAR—THIRD YEAR

In the Vicinity of Washington

REMARK

The accounts which are daily received of War Events—particularly of the Invasion of the CAPITAL OF THE UNITED STATES BY THE British army, are found to be most contradictory, exaggerated or extenuated.— So much so, that the most experienced Editors find it a hard task to develope [sic] the TRUTH, or any consistent features of it, from the mass of crudities continually received. TO publish it en masse were to waste paper and time, and would serve more to distract than to inform the People—The best thing then that can be attempted appears to be, to examine the mass carefully and give such SKETCHES as are found to be corroborated and confirmed, and which may least stand in need of correction. We have, therefore, noted the following minutes of one of the most important events of the war.

SKETCHES OF THE INVASION OF WASHINGTON

BETWEEN THE 16TH AND THE 18th of Aug, a British Naval Force, comprised of upwards of 50 sail, including transports, entered the Potowmac [sic] and Patuxent. [*On the former river the city of Washington is located. The latter runs to within fifteen miles of the Capital.*]

These vessels had on board a large body of troops estimated at from 5 to 10,000—probably rising 7000; with considerable artillery [from 20 to 40 pieces]. The troops are commanded by Gen. Ross; and are part of the Duke of WELLING-TON's army. The fleet is commanded by Ad. COCHRANE. Of the vessels upwards of 40 entered the Patuxent, and from 6 to 10 remained in the Potowmac.

AUG. 19, 1814. The British troops commenced landing near Benedict [40 miles E. of Washington], on the western side of the Patuxent. We have not accounts of the number (if any) which landed on the Potowmac.

AUG. 20. The Mayor of Washington issued this notification, stating, that the whole body of the militia had marched to meet the enemy.

AUG. 20–21. The British began their march towards Washington—their barges and craft following up the Patuxent.

AUG 22. The British were in Nottingham, 17 miles S.E. of Washington.

AUG. 22. Com. BARNEY's expensive gun-boat flotilla, which lay in one of the branches of the Patuxent, was deserted and blown up. Some accounts say by his orders, others by the British.

AUG 22. The American troops, including all the militia of Columbia District, ordered for the defense of Washington, are commanded by General WINDER. Their force variously stated from 3000 to 18,000.—The General advanced his army to the Wood Yards, 12 miles from the city; and the President of the U.S. slept in camp the 21st.

The public papers began to be removed from Washington; and all the horses, carriages, and drivers, are pressed. The roads are covered with women and children; and the greatest distress prevails. The President and secretaries returned on horseback.—The papers are printed on half sheets. The enemy are expected to be in Bladensburg by 11 o'clock, this day.

They are stated to have but little artillery, and less land transportation. (*Intelligencer.*)

AUG. 23. The advance of the enemy are stated to be at Oden's farms. Their main body, 5500, in Upper Marlborough—at the head of the waters of the Patuxent. BARNEY joined the army with his seamen. Fortifications are erected in Bladensburg, six miles from the city.

AUG. 24, A.M. Gen. WINDER is in the vicinity of the British. An officer of the Navy writes from Washington, that the British will probably be in that city the 24th at night.

Same Day, P.M. The enemy continue to advance, and our army under Gen. W. falling back on the city. The out-posts close to each other. The British force *now* estimated at from 7 to 12,000—Ours about 5000. The Commissary informs that he had only issued 7000 rations this day. Gen. SMITH writes, that the 5300 are exclusive of the Baltimore troops, and that our army have 20 pieces of artillery,

each drawn by four horses. Deserters say, the British have 9000 infantry under Gen. ROSS and PICTON, and 4000 artillery under gen. LORD HILL. [*Incorrect—The artillery do not exceed 500, and Lord HILL is not an artillery officer.*] The greatest distress prevails in Washington, among the women and children; their husbands, fathers, and brothers all under arms. Many have resolved to stay and share the fate of their houses.

Our main body was at the Battalion fields (8 miles) last night at sunset, in high spirits and full of confidence, and the enemy are advancing on them. We feel assured that the number and bravery of our men will afford complete protection to the city—2300 Baltimore, and 700 Virginia troops have reached the city. These and reinforcements every moment expected, added to our other forces, will secure the safety of the metropolis. A prisoner informs that Gen. ROSS commands, and that Lord HILL is expected with reinforcement. (*National Intelligencer.*)

"EVENTS OF THE WAR ON LAKE CHAMPLAIN FRONTIER"

BOSTON *COLUMBIAN CENTINEL*, SEPTEMBER 17, 1814

The dubious accuracy of most reports from the front prompted some editors to append some editorial comment to an article. The following excerpt from the Boston Columbian Centinel *late in the war shows the manner by which news reached the public, as well as the conflation of fact and opinion that comprised much of the news writing of the early nineteenth century.*

Whatever their feelings about the war, few Federalists stooped to the treason with which hawks charged them. It is to his credit that the editor of the Centinel *could cheer the heroism of American soldiers and militia on one hand while condemning their commander in chief and crying for secession on the other, as he would do but three months later.*

Colonel Miller at the Battle of Chippewa. *(National Archives)*

BURLINGTON, Sept. 9

BY GENTLEMEN FROM PLATTS-burg we learn, that the main body of the British army is about two miles from the village:—that the advance guard is near that river, and that the village is mostly destroyed. The American army is advantageously posted on the Eastern side of the river, 4000 strong. Several skirmishes have taken place since the affairs before noticed in General Orders; and several attempts of the British reconnoitering parties to cross the Saranac, have been repulsed. The riflemen and militia, it is said, conducted nobly.

We rejoice to find our militia are turning out with a spirit that does honor to themselves and their country. There can be but one voice on this subject. Whatever we think of the War, our country is dear to us, and we hope not to see an enemy within our borders. The militia of Vermont have heard the voice of their friends in distress. They will protect their firesides and their altars. Great numbers are constantly passing through town.

"DESCRIPTION OF THE HORRORS OF WAR"

HARTFORD, CONNECTICUT *COURANT,* NOVEMBER 15, 1814

As in all other American wars before the twentieth century, far more men died in the War of 1812 from disease than from wounds received in battle. Epidemics raged through the army camps, aided by poor sanitation. Battle, however, could still be horrific, producing death and destruction on a scale to turn the hardiest of stomachs. A participant in the battles between American and British regulars at Fort Erie in 1814 conveyed to his countrymen the events of that struggle, and the editor of the Courant, *eager for reliable news and for gore as well as glory that might capture his readers' attention, published the story in November of that year. The engagements at Fort Erie, bloody though they were, produced little strategic effect. Nevertheless, they provided a needed boost in morale, for Americans had proved the equal of the mighty redcoats in battle. Militia whose performance had until then disappointed their leaders fought gallantly, and the* Courant's *readers, though opposed to the war, could not but swell with pride at word of their countrymen's bravery. However, pride alone might not sell newspapers, and the* Courant's *editor was not above titillating his readers as well as educating them.*

THE FOLLOWING REMARKS ON the explosion of one of the bastions of Fort Erie is communicated in a letter from a gentleman, who was present on the occasion:—"The scene witnessed after the magazine had exploded on the morning of the late attack on this fort, was horrible beyond description; even Indian warfare, dreadful as the annals of history represent it to be, cannot be compared with what was now presented to our sight—the mangled limbs and mutilated bodies of the poor fellows who were thus exploded into eternity, laying [sic] scattered around, was an awful spectacle; in one instance, the body of a soldier was found at one hundred yards distance from where he had been thrown, deprived of its head and legs, and the cloaths entirely burnt off. But those who were alive were objects of the most wretched commiseration, they passed me in bodies of twenty and thirty, led by our soldiers to the water's edge, their eyes burnt out, their faces perfectly raw and black as negroes, and their arms rendered useless from the effects of the powder—they were, indeed, living monuments of human misery."

The Battle of New Orleans.
(Library of Congress)

"PEACE—SAFETY, AND THE PROSPECT OF RETURNING COMMERCE, AND PROSPERITY"

BOSTON *COLUMBIAN CENTINEL*, JANUARY 15, 1815

If the first news of the war trickled slowly onto the pages of America's papers, leaked by correspondence from Washington, the word of peace exploded in front-page headlines, despite fears that it might prove wishful thinking. Federalist and Republican editors alike rejoiced, although the former could not resist one final jab at their domestic enemies—as the following announcement in the Boston Columbian Centinel *shows.*

"To THEE, Great Sovereign of the Skies;
This day our grateful Hymns resound;
From ever heart the paeans rise,
And Praise on every tongue is found."

———

ON MONDAY MORNING LAST, A few minutes before Eight o'clock, we received by an Express in Thirty-Two hours from New-York, the following Letter, which was immediately issued from this office in a Handbill:

FOR THE PUBLIC

TO BENJAMIN RUSSELL, *Esq.*
Centinel-Office, Boston, & c.
New York, Feb. 11, 1815
　　　　—Saturday Evening, 10 *o'clock.*

SIR,

I HASTEN to acquaint you, for the information of the Public, of the arrival here, this afternoon of His Brittanic Majesty's sloop of War Favorite, in which has come passenger Mr. CARROLL, American Messenger, having in his possession

A TREATY OF PEACE

Between this country and Great-Britain, signed on the 24th December last.

Mr. BAKER also is on board, as Agent for the British Government, the same who was formerly *Charge des Affaires* here.

Mr. CARROLL reached town at eight o'clock this evening. He shewed to a friend of mine, who is acquainted with him, the pacquet containing the *Treaty,* and a London newspaper of the last date in December, announcing the signing of the Treaty.

It depends, however, as my friend observes, upon the act of the *President* to suspend hostilities on this side.

The gentleman left London the 2d. Jan. The *Transit* had sailed previously from a port on the Continent.

This city is in a perfect uproar of joy, shouts, illuminations, &c., &c.

I have undertaken to send you this by Express—the rider engaging to deliver it by Eight o'clock on Monday morning. The expense will be 225 dollars;—if you can collect so much as to indemnify me I will thank you to do so. I am with respect, Sir, your obedient servant,

　　　　JONATHAN GOODRUE

We most heartily felicitate our Country on this suspicious news, which may be relied upon as wholly authentic.

　　　　CENTINEL.

The money (225 dollars) paid the express for bringing the news of Peace to this town, was advanced by Mr. GOODRUE in New York.—It was immediately collected here—and would have been, had it been ten times the amount—and refunded to the partner of that gentleman (Mr. WARD) in this town. In acknowledging the distinguished disinterestedness of the attention of Mr. G. we do but express the universal sentiment.

Many hundreds of the above Handbills were circulated in all directions.

It is impossible to do justice to the expressions of joy and gratulation which sat on every countenance, animated every tongue, and flowed from the heart of every man, woman, and child, on learning the above news. The respectable source from whence it came prevented the least shadow of doubt of its authenticity.

In a few minutes after its promulgation, all the bells announced the receipt of happy tidings, and expresses posted off to all parts to diffuse them. Business of every kind was immediately suspended; and the whole population of the town devoted itself to expressions of joy. A holiday was directed in all the schools; the stores and shops were closed; and the thronged streets—where nothing was heard but the cheering sounds of gratulation and loud huzzas—were decorated with the ensigns of all the Commercial Nations, and the

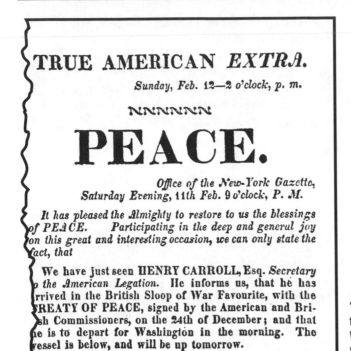

TRUE AMERICAN *EXTRA*.

Sunday, Feb. 12—2 o'clock, p. m.

NNNNNN

PEACE.

Office of the New-York Gazette,
Saturday Evening, 11th Feb. 9 o'clock, P. M.

It has pleased the Almighty to restore to us the blessings of PEACE.   Participating in the deep and general joy on this great and interesting occasion, we can only state the fact, that

We have just seen HENRY CARROLL, Esq. *Secretary* o the *American Legation.* He informs us, that he has rrived in the British Sloop of War Favourite, with the TREATY OF PEACE, signed by the American and Bri- sh Commissioners, on the 24th of December; and that he is to depart for Washington in the morning. The vessel is below, and will be up tomorrow.

"Extra" edition issued by the *New-York Gazette,* one of the oldest American newspapers. It was founded by William Bradford on November 8, 1725 and was the first to publish "extra" editions for fast-breaking news. *(Library of Congress)*

American and British flags were seen waving together, united by wreaths of *olive* and *laurel.*

The forlorn ships at the wharves and docks, once more displayed their colors; and yesterday the busy hum of the implements of the Mechanic was heard on board many of them in fitting them out for sea.

Orders were given for the immediate parade of all the elite of the industry; and in a very short time, the Ancient and Honorable Artillery, Independent Cadets, Boston Light Infantry, Winslow Blues, Fusiliers, Washing Light Infantry, and Rangers, were under arms, and made a brilliant *feu de joie* in State Street.

IN RETROSPECT

THE WAR OF 1812 WAS A SMALL WAR, a series of actions fought on distant fronts. Rarely were a few thousand men engaged in one place at one time. Yet the small conflict was played out on a world stage. At sea, it produced duels on the China Sea and along the Pacific coast of South America, in American harbors, and the home waters of Great Britain. On land, it was fought toward the North from Spanish Florida to Maine and reached west to New Orleans, and along the thousand-mile border between the United States and Canada. The sheer distance promoted constant frustration.

The same poor communications that plagued diplomacy and military strategy throughout the war also hampered attempts to report the war to the American people. Editors relied heavily on letters from participants in or witnesses to battles—letters that might reach them days or weeks after the events had taken place. As often as not, the news that reached distant cities was muddled, inaccurate, or contradictory, and editors faced a major challenge in piecing together the information they received. Much of what was printed about the war was editorial commentary in the political style of the day—rife with sarcasm and mudslinging that made even politicians themselves blush. The war had deepened the enmity between Federalists and Republicans so much that New England Federalists convened in late 1814 to consider seceding from the Union. "The nation," moaned publisher Mathew Carey, "is divided into two hostile parties, whose animosity towards each other is daily increased by inflammatory publications." Newspapers were overwhelmingly of one party or the other, and their editors' political views—often more than the news they conveyed—was the story of the coverage of the War of 1812. And the partisan sniping did not end with the war.

With England depleted by the Napoleonic Wars and America weakened by sectional dissension, neither side had the strength to sustain an effective outcome. Though both sides tried again and again, the war had comprised a pattern of scattered skirmishes that richly guaranteed that the outcome would be inconclusive. As if to illustrate the point, the war's bloodiest battle was fought near New Orleans on January 8, 1815—more than two weeks after peace was concluded in Ghent. With a wasteful courage that provided a fitting climax to years of futile conflict, Sir Edward Pakenham paraded his scarlet legions into impregnable American positions to die in a "leaden torrent no man on earth could face."

The Treat of Ghent granted the United States none of its goals, although the final defeat of Napoleon removed the cause of Britain's interference with American trade, making those goals moot. Federalists cried that it had been a useless war, that they had been right all along, and they condemned Madison all the more once the exigencies of war no longer provided an impetus to unity. God, warned the Baltimore *Federal Republican*, would "call him to a dreadful account hereafter." Republicans, meanwhile, cheered that the war had been a second war for independence, proving that Britain could not control its former colonies. They charged Federalist detractors with treason. Today historians continue to debate the significance of the war. For most Americans, however, the echoes of the battles—those in the field and those in the newspapers—have long since died away. Only a few highlights—Jackson's victory at New Orleans, Key's "The Star-spangled Banner"—remain.

A useless war? Perhaps. But to the Americans of the time, fighting this war was a matter of the young Republic's very existence. And in recording the nation's fight, journalists advanced its very being. Americans emerged from the War of 1812 certain, as we had always suspected, that we were a courageous nation. And, armed with that thought, Britain and the United States have since been able to exist as close friends.

The War of 1812 does not receive much attention from today's historians, but except for the Civil War, it was perhaps the most hotly debated conflict in which the country has ever been involved—including the one in Vietnam. Americans were bitterly divided by political party loyalties, economic considerations, religious views or patriotic and national sentiment. Usually these forces worked in combination. Thus, journalism from the period contained a great deal of propaganda and polemics. The strategic analysis, simple narration, poetical inspiration, patriotism, and treason of pamphleteers and politicians all contributed to the political, social, and economic dimensions of the war. With the pen replacing the sword, the war continued to be waged for many years after it was over.

THE MEXICAN WAR

THE MEXICAN WAR

1846–1848

THE MEXICAN WAR BEGAN AS the biggest land grab in American history and ended as a dress rehearsal for the Civil War. But the two-year conflict with America's neighbor to the south, the second war for continental expansion within a span of forty years, was a struggle much different from the War of 1812. It was fought with greater precision and ended with extensive tangible gains. Fanning the flames of this expansionist impulse were the trials of Texas. Rich in cotton, wide in space, and certain of manifest destiny, Texas had declared its independence in 1836; the blood shed at the Alamo guaranteed it. Americans, particularly southerners, demanded that the republic join the cavalcade of states in the burgeoning Union. By 1846, Americans were ready for another fight. President Polk sent a war message to Congress on May 11 declaring that Mexico had invaded our territory and American blood had been spilled on American soil. Congress declared that war existed by an act of Mexico's, and it voted an appropriation of $10 million and approved the enlistment of fifty thousand soldiers.

To a great extent, the war was defined by the enemy. The American Revolution was, as pamphleteers argued, a conflict for independence and the removal of corrupting influence. The war against its southern neighbor brought Washington into conflict not only with Mexico but with that country's Spanish colonial legacy—and with British designs on it. The issues alternately bolstered and frightened Americans, who often viewed their enemy as inferior. Decades later, Dudley Harmon of the New York *Sun* perpetuated this view, describing the scene as Veracruz was captured by the *Stars and*

Residents of a small town read news of the first battles in Mexico in this painting, "News of the War." *(Library of Congress)*

Stripes: "Armed with rifles from the Mexican armories and inflamed with liberal droughts of mescal [the convicts fighting in the Mexican ranks] were dangerous and treacherous adversaries. With them intense excitement prevailed. Half crazed peons ran hither and thither, shouting out aimlessly and apparently not knowing where to seek refuge." Mexico, wrote the *Examiner* in San Francisco, was a "Catholic Ireland . . . with a priesthood whose chief is in a foreign clime, who are too rich not to be despoiled, and who have a flock of ignorant paupers who can be excited to any folly."

The zeal of the correspondents, plus the wider use of the telegraph, allowed hometown America to follow the campaigns south of the Rio Grande closely. Reporters followed the troops and wrote dispatches from the field. Army officers often doubled as correspondents and, as a regular matter of practice, filed their accounts with the newspapers before they completed reports to their superiors. Eager to place their successes in the best light and to posit them as the most significant, they sent great news to New Orleans, Boston, Atlanta, and Washington.

The news was good, too, because the Mexican War generated few military defeats for the Americans. The combination of an increasingly professional cadre of West Point officers and high-spirited volunteers scored amazing victories in the two-year campaign. The cost of the war was a mere thirteen thousand dead and $115 million. Of that sum, $15 million went to Mexico for 530,000 square miles of territory ceded to the United States. It also created a political divide among the *norteamericanos* over the expansion of slavery and the admittance of the conquered ground to the Union. Those issues would be solved only by the next conflict, the Civil War.

President Polk signed the declaration of war on May 13, 1846. General Zachary Taylor took New Mexico without a major battle. Rebellion and chaos wrested California from Mexican control almost before war was declared. Taylor pushed south into Mexico in the fall of 1846, taking Monterrey after a five-day siege. When he took over Taylor's command, General Winfield Scott launched the first major amphibious operation in American history, landing his army on the beach near Veracruz in March 1847. Following the route that Cortes had chosen for his own conquest of Mexico three centuries before, Scott marched toward Mexico City. Halted only briefly on the way—and not by the Mexican army but by his own troops, who went home when their enlistments ran out, forcing him to have to wait for reinforcements—Scott led his army into the capital on September 13, 1847. Three days later, Mexican resistance quashed, the war was over.

Short though the Mexican War was, it saw some notable firsts in American journalism. News traveled from the front to the front pages in record time. Competing papers formed a cooperative network that conveyed information by steamboat to New Orleans, where it was telegraphed to offices throughout the United States. Correspondents even printed single-page news sheets—the *American Star*, *American Eagle*, and *Tampico Sentinel* were three—right on the battlefield. Americans at home were able to follow the war more closely and more quickly than ever before.

The events of the war were reported by the New Orleans *Picayune* and other major newspapers in a competitive atmosphere that was unprecedented in the history of journalism. From New Orleans, overland express or steamships carried dispatches to a point where newly erected telegraph lines could convey them to their final destinations. Many newspapers arranged at their own expense to speed the eyewitness accounts along, going to great lengths to beat out their rivals even by a few hours. The New York *Herald* kept a small vessel at sea to intercept any steamship bearing news, which was then rushed to dockside and the waiting typesetters. The New Orleans *Picayune* went this one better, installing a typesetter aboard its ship so that the report could immediately be sent to the press. To be first with the latest news became something of an obsession. If the news was deemed at all important, the newspapers printed a special edition, an "extra," for newsboys to take to the waiting public. Publishing as many as four editions in a single day, newspapers on more than one occasion sold out entire editions within a few hours. Accuracy was also essential, and editors relied on eyewitness reports by trusted correspondents. Reports from the field were valued above all others and were copied verbatim as soon as they arrived at their papers.

A giant and major contributor was George Wilkins Kendall. After founding the *Picayune* in 1837, Kendall quickly realized the advantage of covering events in the republic of Texas; under his lead, the *Picayune* became an instrument for American expansion at the expense of Mexico. Hearing of hostilities on the Rio Grande, Kendall quickly rode south to cover the action. He joined Taylor's army in Matamoros, set up a field office, and began his duties as a war correspondent. His desire to be at the forefront of the action also caused him to link up with a company of Texas Rangers. When Scott took center stage, Kendall signed on as a voluntary aide and participated in all of the fighting on the way to Mexico City. He used couriers and boats to rush the news back to New Orleans; his greatest coup came at the war's end, when he raced a copy of the Treaty of Guadalupe Hidalgo to American shores by chartered steamboat—ahead of his competitors and even the government's official dispatch. "Mr. Kendall's express" made him the most widely known reporter of his day.

The Mexican War allowed the penny press to flourish. The combined efforts of American reporters in Mexico and their editors at home made the Mexican War, in the words of historian Robert Henry, "The first War in history to be adequately and comprehensively reported in the daily press."

The Treaty of Guadalupe Hidalgo, which officially ended the war, gave the United States the disputed region of Texas as well as all of New Mexico and California—some one million square miles. But the long-term costs were great. What Ralph Waldo Emerson called the "discreditable means" by which that land was gained put a black mark on the Mexican War that outlived the names of Polk, Taylor, and Scott in the collective memories of Americans.

Still worse, though, was the ensuing debate over what to do with the new territory. Southerners wanted the land open to slavery so that the cotton kingdom could expand with the "empire of liberty." Northerners wanted the land for small farmers to live free of slavery's economic and moral influence. The two halves of manifest destiny—the republican and the racist—could no longer be held together. The argument over slavery and the fate of the western lands set off a chain reaction of events and rhetoric that culminated in the election of Abraham Lincoln as president in 1860. His promise to halt slavery's expansion resulted in the secession of the South and the start of the bloodiest conflict in American history. And even as the Mexican War helped drive a wedge between North and South, the sections' future Civil War heroes—Jefferson Davis, Robert E. Lee, Ulysses S. Grant, and countless others—cut their martial teeth as brothers fighting on the same side. What seemed in the short run a glorious triumph proved in the end only the first chapter of a far greater tragedy.

CHRISTOPHER HAILE

"CORRESPONDENCE OF THE *PICAYUNE*"

NEW ORLEANS *PICAYUNE*, JUNE 14, 1846

George W. Kendall spent most of the Mexican War in the field, organizing the New Orleans Picayune's *network of correspondents and express writers and sending back and sometimes hand-delivering detailed reports on the war's major battles. Among the reporters he relied on was Christopher Haile, a West Point graduate who served as the paper's "special army correspondent."*

Christopher Haile was the first of the Picayune's *correspondents to rendezvous with George W. Kendall in Mexico. Realizing the war offered his paper great opportunities, Kendall had assembled a small corps of reporters before his competitors were organized. Once Haile arrived, he and Kendall organized a system to gather news and send dispatches. By following different units of the expeditionary force, they were able to complement each other's reports to produce truly comprehensive coverage of the war.*

Point Isabel, Fort Polk, June 2, 1846
Editors of the Picayune:

GENTLEMEN—I LEFT MATAMO-ros yesterday morning in company with Capts. Ramsay and Hardee and four dragoons, and on route to this place had another view of the two battlefields. The *Resaca de la Palma* battle-ground is covered with the graves of our fallen countrymen, who fell, many of them, fighting hand to hand with the enemy. Terribly, were they avenged, however, on the spot, for the antagonists are buried around them by hundreds. I was shown one grave, near the spot where some brave Cochrane is interred, in which some eight Mexicans are said to have been placed, and there are many more which contain a score or two of each of the slaughtered foe. The grave of poor Inge was pointed out to me. It is near where one of the enemy's batteries was posted. It was with feelings of deep sadness that I recalled to mind the many virtues of this gallant and noble-hearted officer. He had left a young wife in Baltimore, and had arrived at Point Isabel, with a body of recruits, just in time to march with Gen. Taylor; had distinguished himself in both battles by his heroic bearing, and fell at the moment when the brilliant victory, to which he contributed so largely, was about to declare itself in favor of our arms. Mexican caps and remnants of their clothing are scattered here and there over the battleground, and the whole field is dotted with marks of the enemy's camp fires. It is a wild looking place, and so advantageous was the position of the enemy, that it will ever remain a wonder to me that our little army was not cut to pieces by their greatly superior force. Over a great portion of the ground on which our army prepared to attack them, the thickets are so dense that a dog would find it difficult to penetrate them. Men actually *pushed* each other through there thickets, and

The *Daily Picayune*, founded by editor and publisher George Kendall, later became the New Orleans *Picayune*.

were divided into small squads of from three to six.

The Palo Alto battlefield, on this side, near the edge of the chaparrals, is an open prairie, quite level, and a most magnificent place for the meeting of two armies. The positions of the Mexican lines was pointed out to me, and we rode over a part of the field where the battle raged the hottest. They are represented as having presented a very warlike and picturesque appearance as our troops approached them; their compact lines extending from an elevated point of the chaparrals on their right, about a mile; their left extending across the road near its entrance to the *pass.* I visited the place where some of their heavy artillery opened upon our army, and against which

our two 18 pounders were for a time directed. Convincing evidence of the skill with which our artillery was used against them are still perceptible upon that part of the field; for although they were permitted to bury their dead, and afterwards returned in numbers and spent considerable time in that employment, counted some thirty dead bodies, stretched out as they fell, in that immediate vicinity.

Some had been nearly severed in two by cannon balls; others had lost a part of the head, both legs, a shoulder, or the whole stomach. Of many of them nothing but the bones, encased in uniform, was left; whilst others had been transformed into mummies, and retained the expression of countenance which their death agonies had stamped upon them. One man who had been shot between the hips with a large ball lay doubled up as he fell, with his hands extended and his face downward between his knees. Another, whose shoulders and back were shot away, seemed to have died in the act of uttering a cry of horror. Dead horses were scattered about in every direction, and the buzzards and wild dogs were fattening upon the carrion.

During my stay with the army near Matamoros, nothing of any consequence occurred. Rumor is always busy enough, spreading ridiculous tales from one encampment to another, and the wages and "green'uns," and literary aspirants, have no doubt kept the newspapers abundantly supplied with this species of "important news." There is no probability of the army moving from its present position for a month at least. This you will have heard before this reaches you, from intelligent officers, one of whom has been sent to procure boats, &c. for the transportation of supplies up the Rio Grande. In the meantime the volunteers will be drilled, and those who are not at Matamoros with those who may arrive here, will be sent to Burita, to remain until their services may be needed. Colonel Dakin's regiment, which I left at this place, is now encamped at the point, at the bar, three miles from here, preparatory to marching to Burita. Col. Peyton's regiment is at the same place. You have been informed, I suppose, that the Alabama, with Col. Peyton's regiment, came near being lost off this place in the recent gale. Nothing but the remarkable vigilance, skill and coolness of Capt. Windle, saved the vessel and the brave men on board from complete destruction. Col. Peyton and his officers and men speak in the highest possible

terms of Capt. Windle, and have already made arrangements for presenting him with a fit testimonial of their high regard and the gratitude with which his noble conduct in that trying occasion is viewed by them. This reminds me of an omission for which I feel ashamed and which I hope will be pardoned by the parties concerned. The steamer Florida, on her way out here with 250 volunteers, encountered many difficulties from the wretched quality of her fuel, head winds and the crowded state of her decks, which latter caused much inconvenience in the management of her sails during a severe storm that she encountered. Capt. Butler's skill as a seaman, his gentlemanly deportment towards the volunteers, and the vigilant care which he manifested for their safety and comfort during the performance of his difficult duties drew from Captains Riusseau, Blanchard, and McNubar, and Lieutenants Seguine, Higgins, Hays, Herald, Laune and Miller, a highly complimentary letter, a copy which I was requested to send to you for publication, but which is not at present within my reach.

There are now about four thousand volunteers out here. So far as I have been able to learn, their health is good, and they are doing very well in the way of drills and discipline.

We had another heavy wind last night which like the recent gale, overthrew many of the tents. The tent in which I slept, in the dragoon camp, was stripped from over . . . it had been a sheet of tissue paper, and the way the lighter articles of our wardrobe danced about the prairie was quite uncomfortable to behold, especially to me, who gave chase to a portion of them. A certain dilapidated straw hat, of which I was the proprietor, gave me especial concern. I saw it moving off at a distance, at a rapid rate, and without stopping to dress, set off in pursuit. The night was black as pitch, except when the lightning reveals the objects around. Several times was I on the point of seizing my venerable castor, when the lightning would cease, and leave nothing but a muskeet shrub or a thistle in my grasp; and the next instant the truant could be discovered rolling off towards the bay at a fearful rate. I returned, however, after a hard race, with the old war-hat (it was in the battles of the 8th and 9th, though not on my head) firmly tied to my head.

It was stated at Matamoros, and generally believed before I left, that a proclamation had been received from some high Mexican functionary, declaring that any Mexican citizen who should hold communications with Gen. Taylor's army, would be punished as traitors, and any Mexican citizens who should hold communications with those who held communications with our troops would likewise be punished as traitors! I shall send you, with this, an account of the bombardment of Fort Brown, which I have been permitted to prepare from a journal kept by a very intelligent officer who was actively engaged in the works during the whole affair. It can be fully relied on. I also send a detailed account of the battles of the 8th and 9th, which I take from the journal of an officer who took an active part and distinguished himself in each. Although I do not mention his name here, it may be proper to state that the allusions to his name and deeds have been taken by me from one of his superior officers—he having modestly refrained from mentioning any act of his own. I also send you Col. Twigg's report, and an authentic account of the capture of Capt. Thorton and his squadron by the Mexicans. I do not believe that serious inaccuracies exist in any of these narratives. The officers who have undergone so many dangers and privations during this war are becoming disgusted and discouraged with the thousand ridiculous and injurious reports that have emanated from irresponsible sources. These scribblers frequently praise, censure, or omit to mention the deeds of members of the army without the slightest regard to truth. Glory, or at least a spotless name, is a soldier's greatest incentive to action. Our officers and men have acted nobly in this war—their country is justly proud of their achievements, and the press should be ready on all occasions to defend them against any imputations that could arise from the idle tattle of busy-bodies.

H.

"NEWS FROM THE ARMY"

NEW ORLEANS *PICAYUNE*, OCTOBER 4, 1846

The battle of Monterrey clearly established the Picayune's *leadership in reporting the events of the Mexican War. Relying on Kendall's organizational skills and Haile's ability to understand and write about military affairs, the paper reinforced its reputation as the first and best informed on the Mexican situation. Kendall's forethought in establishing the relay system to carry the news back to the paper proved a critical factor at Monterrey. It was the first battle to be reported by regular correspondents and, in fact, probably the first instance of foreign war correspondence by American writers. They rose to the challenge by providing a day-to-day account of the action on sheets delivered by express riders and steamships to a dispatch center in New Orleans.*

ARRIVAL OF THE STEAMSHIP JAS. L. DAY.

Capitulation of Monterrey!

Three Days' Hard Fighting!

THE STEAMSHIP JAMES L. DAY, Capt. Wood, arrived from Brazos' Santiago about 1 o'clock this morning. By her we have received the glorious news that MONTERREY HAS CAPITULATED, AFTER THREE DAYS OF DESPERATE FIGHTING. Capt. Eaton, one of the aids of Gen. Taylor, arrived on the Day, bearing despatches for Washington. He left Monterrey on the 25th ult. Colonel Kinney and one other gentleman accompanied him from Monterrey. Col. Kinney kindly took charge of packages of letters for us and brought them to Camargo, and there delivered them to his companion, by whom they were faithfully delivered. We shall not forget the service.

We cannot delay the press to attempt to write out a narration of the battles. The following "memoranda" are from the pen of an officer who was in the battles.

Gen. Worth, who lead the attack upon the city on the west side, has immortalized himself. The fighting was desperate on our side, the Mexicans outnumbering us by two to one, and being protected by strong entrenchments.

All our readers will delight to hear that the Louisiana boys did honor to the State. We knew they would.

Almost all our different accounts set down our loss at 500 or over, of whom 300 were killed. This best tells the character of the fight.

HASTY MEMORANDA OF THE OPERATIONS OF THE AMERICAN ARMY BEFORE MONTERREY, MEXICO, FROM THE 19TH TO THE 24th SEPT.

ON THE 19TH GEN. TAYLOR ARRIVED before Monterey, with a force of about 6000 men, and after reconnoitering the city at about 1500 or 1600 yards from the Cathedral fort, during which he was fired upon from its batteries, his force was encamped at the Walnut Springs, 3 miles short of the city. This was the nearest position at which the army could obtain a supply of water, and be beyond the reach of the enemy's batteries. The remainder of the 19th was occupied by the engineers in making reconnaissances of the city, battery, and commanding heights. On the 20th Gen. Worth was ordered with his division to move by a circuitous route to the right, to gain the Saltillo road beyond the west of the town and to storm the heights above the Bishop's Palace, which vital point the enemy appear to have strangely neglected. Circumstances caused his halt on the night of the 20th, short of the intended position. On the morning of the 21st he continued his route, and after an encounter with a large body of the enemy's cavalry and infantry, supported by artillery from the heights, he repulsed them with loss, and finally encamped, covering the passage of the Saltillo road. It was here discovered, that besides the fort at the Bishop's Palace and the occupation of the heights above it, two forts, on commanding eminences, on the opposite side of the San Juan, had been fortified and occupied. These two latter heights were then stormed and carried— the guns of the last fort carried being immediately turned with a plunging fire upon the Bishop's Palace. On this same morning [the 21st] the 1st Division of regular troops, under Gen. Twiggs, and the Volunteer Division under Gen. Butler, were ordered under arms to make a diversion to the left of the town, in favor of the important operations of Gen. Worth. The 10 inch mortar and two 24 pounder howitzers, had been put in battery the night of the 20th, in a ravine 1400 yards distant from the Cathedral fort or Citadel, and were supported by the 4th Regiment of Infantry. At 8 A.M. on the 21st the order was given for this battery to open upon the citadel and town, and immediately after the 1st Division, with the 3rd and 4th Infantry in advance, under Col. Garland, were ordered to reconnoitre and skirmish with the enemy on the extreme left of the city, and should prospect of success offer, to carry the most advanced battery. This attack was directed by Maj. Mansfield, Engineer, Capt. Williams, Topographical Engineer, and Maj. Kinney, Q. M. to the Texas Division. A heavy fire from the first battery was immediately opened upon the advance, but the troops soon turned it, entering and engaging with the enemy on the streets of the city, having passed through an incessant cross fire from the Citadel and the first and second batteries, and from the infantry who lined the parapets, streets and house tops of the city. The rear of the 1st battery was soon turned, and the reverse fire of the troops through the gorge of the works killed or dislodged the artillerists and infantry from it, and the building occupied by infantry immediately in its rear. The 1st Division was followed and supported by the Mississippi and Tennessee and 1st Ohio Regiments, the two former regiments being the first to scale and occupy the fort. The success of the day here stopped. The Mississippi, Tennessee and Ohio Regiments, though warmly engaged in the streets of the city for some time after the capture of the 1st battery and its adjoining defences, were unable, from exhaustion and the loss they had suffered, to gain more advantage. A heavy shower of rain also came up to cause a suspension of hostilities before the close of the day. The 3rd, 4th and 1st Infantry and the Baltimore Battalion, remained as the garrison of the captured position, under Col. Garland, assisted by Capt. Ridgely's battery. Two 12 pounders, one 4 pounder, and 1 howitzer, were captured in this fort, three officers and some 20 or 30 men taken prisoners. One of the 12 pounders was served against the 2nd fort and defences, with captured ammunition, during the remainder of the day, by Capt. Ridgely. The storming parties of Gen. Worth's Division also captured two nine pounders, which were also immediately turned against their former owners.

On the morning of the 22nd Gen. Worth continued his operations, and portions of his divisions stormed and carried successfully the heights above the Bishop's Palace. Both were carried by a command under Capt. Vinton, 3rd Artillery. In these operations the company of Louisi-

ana troops under Capt. Blanchard performed efficient and gallant service as part of Capt. Vinton's command. Four pieces of artillery, with a good supply of ammunition, were captured in the Bishop's Palace this day, some of which were immediately turned upon the enemy's defences in the city. On the evening of the 22nd, Col. Garland and his command were relieved as the garrison of the captured forts by Gen. Quitman with the Mississippi and Tennessee Regiments, and five companies of the Kentucky Regiment.

Early on the morning of the 23rd, Gen. Quitman, from his position, discovered that the second and third forts and defences east of the city had been entirely abandoned by the enemy, who, apprehending another assault on the night of

The Battle of Monterrey. *(Amon Carter Museum)*

the 22nd, had retired from all his defences to the main plaza and its immediate vicinity. A command of two companies of Mississippi and two of Tennessee troops were then thrown into the streets to reconnoitre, and soon became hotly engaged with the enemy, these were soon supported by Col. Wood's regiment of Texas Rangers, dismounted, by Bragg's Light Battery and the 3rd Infantry; the enemy's fire was constant and uninterrupted from the streets, house tops, barricades, &c. &c. in the vicinity of the plaza. The pieces of Bragg's artillery were also used with much effect far into the heart of the city—this engagement lasted the best part of the day, our troops having driven the scattered parties of the enemy, and penetrated quite to the defences of the main plaza. The advantage thus gained, it was not considered necessary to hold, as the enemy had permanently abandoned the city and its defences, except the main plaza, its immediate vicinity and the Cathedral fort or Citadel. Early in the afternoon (same day) Gen. Worth assaulted from the Bishop's Palace the west side of the city, and succeeded in driving the enemy and maintaining his position within short distance of the main plaza on that side of the city; towards evening the mortar had also been planted in the Cemetery enclosure, and during the night did great execution in the circumscribed camp of the enemy in the plaza—thus ended the operations of the 23rd.

Early on the morning of the 24th, a communication was sent to Gen. Taylor, from Gen. Ampudia, under a flag, making an offer of capitulation, to which the former refused to accede, as it asked more than the American commander would under any circumstances grant;—at the

same time a demand to surrender was in reply made to Gen. Ampudia—12 M. was the hour at which the acceptance or non-acceptance was to be communicated to the American General. At 11 A.M., the Mexican General sent, requesting a personal conference with Gen. Taylor, which was granted; the principal officers of rank on either side accompanying their Generals. After several offers in relation to the capitulation of the city made on either side and refused, at half-past 4 P.M., Gen. Taylor arose and saying he would give Gen. Ampudia one hour to consider and accept or refuse, left the conference with his officers—at the expiration of the hour, the discharge of the mortar was to be the signal for the recommencement of hostilities. Before the expiration of the hour, however, an officer was sent on the part of Gen. Ampudia, to inform the American General that to avoid the further effusion of blood, and the national honor being satisfied by the exertions of the Mexican troops, he had, under consultation with his General Officers, decided to capitulate, accepting the offer of the American General.

The terms of capitulation were in effect as follows:—

That the officers should be allowed to march out with their side arms.

That the Cavalry and Infantry should be allowed to march out with their arms and accoutrements.

That the Artillery should be allowed to march out with one battery of six pieces and twenty-one rounds of ammunition.

That all other munitions of war and supplies should be turned over to a board of American officers appointed to receive them.

That the Mexican Army, should be allowed seven days to evacuate the city and that the American troops should not occupy it until evacuated.

That the Cathedral, Fort or Citadel, should be evacuated at 10 A.M., next day, (25th) the Mexicans then marching out and the American garrison marching in. The Mexicans allowed to salute their flag when hauled down.

That there should be an armistice of eight weeks, during which time neither army should pass a line running from the Rinconada through Linares and San Fernando.

This lenient offer of the American General was dictated with the concurrence of his Generals and by motives of good policy and consideration for the good defence of their city by the Mexican Army.

CHRISTOPHER HAILE

"SPECIAL CORRESPONDENCE"

NEW ORLEANS *PICAYUNE*, OCTOBER 4, 1846

The following dispatch demonstrates the abilities that made Christopher Haile one of the most precise correspondents of the war. The reporter kept meticulous notes, complete with explicit data: enemy troop strength, the position of U.S. forces, hours and miles marched. He lucidly described formations of soldiers on the march, as easily as he narrated the chase and capture of a Mexican spy.

His attention to detail was no accident. Before striking out as a newspaperman, Haile attended the United States Military Academy at West Point. At the siege of Veracruz, Haile was commissioned as a first lieutenant in the infantry, leaving Kendall without his ace reporter at a critical point. But the Picayune *by now had a steady reserve of writers, and the paper missed not a beat.*

IN INTRODUCING THE FOLLOWING series of letters from Mr. Haile, it can hardly be necessary to remind the reader that they were written amid the bustle of the camp and din of arms. He asks us to say so much for him, but we feel it is unnecessary. In the last letter dated from him—a private one dated the 25th ult.— he says: "I omitted to state in my letters that the Mexicans had seven thousand regulars and between three and four thousand rancheros in the city. Their killed and wounded was small compared with ours—their legs and walls protecting them."

Again he says: "Capt. Bragg's battery was terribly cut up—he lost twenty horses. I am told he behaved nobly. His orderly sergeant, Waitman, was killed. Ridgely had three fine horses killed—no men. The dragoons had no chance to fight, but were very active as scouts, etc."

Mr. Haile's private letter assures us of his fine health and spirits. Our troops he represents to be almost worn out with the fatigue of their several days' labors, but otherwise in high spirits.

SAN FRANCISCO, MEXICO, Sept. 13, 1846

GENTLEMEN: WE ARE, AT LENGTH, within five hour's march of Monterrey, say twelve miles distant. The army left the camp near Marin, this morning, the 1st Division starting at six o'clock, and 2d Division at seven o'clock. The advance consisted of McCulloch's and Gillispie's companies of Rangers, and a squadron of Dragoons, under Col. May. The pioneer corps was broken up and returned to their respective regiments. The baggage of the 1st Division, and one-half the ordnance train followed that command, and the 2d Division was followed in like manner by its baggage and the other part of the ordnance train. The Volunteer Division marched at eight o'clock, followed by its baggage and the supply train. The rear guard was composed of two companies of Regulars, one from each Division, and closed the march, following the supply train. In case Gen. Henderson should arrive with his Texan Rangers, they were to form the advance, with the exception of four companies, which were to take the place of the two companies of Infantry, which formed the rear guard. Gen. Henderson overtook the army about four miles from here, and his command was disposed of according to the above named arrangement. The habitual order of battle was directed to be as follows: "1st Division on the right, the 2d on the left, and the Volunteer Division in the centre," the chiefs of Divisions to organize such reserves as they might judge proper. This order of battle not to be considered invaluable, but to be controlled by the nature of the ground. Four men from Gillespie's

company were attached to each of the two (2d and volunteer) divisions.

Everything connected with this day's march has been intensely interesting to all, and novel to many. The troops marched in closed columns, and were always held in readiness to act promptly. The column embracing the trains, reached nearly or quite three miles. It was a grand sight, and so much did the men feel interested in coming events, that every one went at it in a business manner, and, although it has been hot and dusty, not half a dozen out of nearly six thousand five hundred have given in to-day on the march. We have forded a number of streams to-day, commencing near Marin, with the San Juan, which was nearly waist deep. Of course, we are now in the midst of the mountains, but so imperceptibly have we ascended what appeared like mountains, this morning, that we now seem to be on a great plain, with mountains rising into peaks, in every direction around us. Our road has been through a richer region since leaving Marin than any I have seen since leaving the Rio Grande. We passed two or three large haciendas, where sugar-cane is cultivated to a considerable extent, and the second corn crops are in a flourishing state. All these plantations are irrigated from the mountain streams.

Soon after we arrived here this evening, a Mexican who has been following the Army from Seralvo, was seen writing in one of the houses at the hacienda near the camp. On being pointed out by one of the drummer boys of the 7th Infantry, he bolted out the door, and was pursued and caught. A little while later he broke from the guard and ran for the chaparral, but, unfortunately for the poor devil, he was running directly into the camp of the 2d

Division, which lies hid in the bushes. A hue and cry was raised, the guard not wishing to shoot him, and, after a smart foot-race through the thorn bushes and various extraordinary feats of dodging, he was captured by some of the soldiers of the 7th after receiving a bayonet wound. He is a spy.

Well, to-morrow evening or next day morning we shall have seen the question decided, with regard to the strength of Monterrey. Information came into camp from Monterrey last evening, which Mr. Kendall forwarded to you. This evening the report is that there are 8,000 (one report says 15,000) troops there, and that the city is surrounded by a ditch and breast-works, and the streets all fortified.

How do the troops act on the eve of an expected battle? Only that they are a little more precise in the performance of their duties—a little more careful in arranging their arms and knapsacks to be in readiness for an instant's notice—and little more careful to procure rest while they may—I see no change in their demeanor. The only conversation is, how they will probably go to work to take the city, should resistance be offered. It is the settled belief that the Mexicans will fight, and it is also believed that many lives will be sacrificed on both sides. I predict that on their retreat, the Army will be awfully cut up. About twelve hundred Texan horsemen are now with us, and they are desirous of paying off old scores. In taking the town they cannot engage very actively, but in overtaking the retreating troops they will be active and destructive.

Nine o'clock, P.M.—The impression of those who ought best to know is still that the troops at Monterrey will resist. Our troops will be greatly disappointed if no re-sistance is offered them. They have come a long distance to seek a fight. I was amused at a remark made by Col. Persifor F. Smith some days ago, when asked what he thought of the probabilities of a battle. "I never knew a man to seek perseveringly for a thing a long time, but what he found it," replied he, "and Gen. Taylor will not, I think, seek in vain for another set-to with the Mexicans." One thing is certain, the enemy has been at a heavy expense to fortify Monterrey, and if we do not find out, before to-morrow night at this time, that they do not intend to expend their money and labor for nothing, I shall then be satisfied that there is no spirit left among them. Two hundred Mexican troops left this place this morning, after ill-treating and pillaging the inhabitants as usual. But these people are singular beings, and very ungrateful. In Marin, where Torrejon's troops had, a day or two before, robbed, whipped, and insulted the citizens shamefully, I saw a family selling *muscal* to Americans for two dollars per bottle, and at the same time selling it to Mexicans for four bits per bottle. We march to-morrow at 6 o'clock, to encamp three miles from Monterrey.

Camp before Monterrey, Sept. 18, at 12 o'clock, M.—Well, "the ball has opened!" When within about four miles of the city, we heard a brisk cannonading in that direction. On arriving here we learn that Gen. Taylor, with a detachment of Dragoons and the Texan Rangers, advanced within a few hundred yards of the city, when the enemy opened upon them with twelve pounders. The first ball came within about ten yards of the General. Some twenty-five or thirty shot were fired at the Dragoons and Rangers, passing through their lines, but hurting neither man nor horse. A picket of 200 Mexican

Cavalry appeared on the plain when our advance first approached, and after firing a volley or two with their escopettes, retired into the city. Bishop's Hill is strongly fortified, and they are hard at work on a height commanding that place. So to-night or early in the morning we will probably have hot work. They will fight, now, without a doubt.

H.

CAMP BEFORE MONTERREY, Sept. 19, 1846

GENTLEMEN—THIS HAS BEEN A day of excitement and interest to our isolated little army. The General left the Camp at San Francisco this morning at sunrise, and by 8 o'clock the whole column was in motion, the Texan Rangers, and Col. May with a squadron of Dragoons, in advance. The men started off briskly, and the road was fine. After two hours' march a bridge was found broken up by the Mexicans. A corn field near at hand afforded materials for filling up the place, and the Army proceeded over the first corn stalk bridge I ever heard of. When within about four or five miles of the city we heard a brisk cannonading. Some of the men had just previous to this begun to lag, some suffering from blistered feet, and others from the intensity of the heat, but no sooner did the sound of cannon reach their ears, than they straightened themselves up and pressed forward with an eagerness that showed that their sufferings were all forgotten. Cap. Scott (the veritable), or rather now Major Scott, who commands the 5th Infantry, marched immediately before us, and the moment the brave old soldier heard the enemy's cannon, he drove his spurs into his horse and pranced about his regiment as if he would give a liberal

portion of his life to be at Monterrey. Captain Miles, commander of the 7th Infantry, by whose side I was riding at the moment, likewise rose in his stirrups, with his keen black eyes sparkling, and his nostrils slightly dilated, and gave orders to his regiment to close up, but his orders were useless, for the noble fellows were already pressing upon the staff, to the very rumps of the horses. Again, again and again, noise of the twelve pounders reverberated through the lofty mountains which rose before us and upon each side [I will describe this grand scenery at another time], and a buzz, a suppressed hurrah ran through the line. The officers ran their eyes over their commands with looks of pride and confidence, and the men returned the glance, as if to say, "we are ready," and pressed on still more eagerly. I rode out of the column and fell back to look at the Louisiana boys. Every eye among them was bright with eager excitement. Capt. Blanchard, and Lieutenants Tenbrink and the two brothers Nicholls, wore a peculiar smile upon their countenances, an expression that I never shall forget. I translated its meaning thus: "Now we are about to be rewarded for all our sacrifices and toils, and we'll show old Louisiana that we can represent her worthily, though our numbers are small." They regretted the absence of their fellow citizens who had returned to their quiet homes, for they well knew how many a brave heart would burn with bitter disappointment and laudable envy, could their returned friends but see them and know their feelings at that moment.

On reaching the place of encampment we came up with Gen. Worth, sitting his horse in beautiful style. A handsomer officer than he appeared then, I never saw.

Every one remarked the change that had suddenly come over him. From the somewhat dejected air, and saddened countenance that he is said to have worn of late, Richard was now himself again—and the gallant soldier, forgetting of all his cares, now appeared before us, the personification of an accomplished military chieftain. His handsome face was lighted up with a proud, but affable smile, as he motioned gracefully to his officers, pointing out to them the direction they were to take with their respective commands, and not a man who saw him, but what would at that moment have followed him to the cannon's mouth.

Such is the feeling manifested by the whole army—which renders this body of men invincible.

This evening the enemy's batteries have been opened again upon a reconnoitering party of ours. Generals Taylor, Twiggs, Worth, and others, have been out looking at their works.

9 o'clock, P.M.—An attack is expected, and every man in the Army will rest to-night on his arms. A night attack is what a soldier dislikes very much, because it is then difficult to distinguish friend from foe.

September 20th.—Everything remained quiet last night. To-morrow an attempt will be made to take Monterrey. A stout resistance is expected, for the town is strongly fortified, as well as the heights that command it, and the enemy has troops and ammunition enough there to defend it. A movement will no doubt be made to-night. No one expects an easy victory, on the other hand, all have made up their minds to see much bloodshed. It is believed that a large number of the enemy is in our rear—in fact there is little doubt on the subject.

An express rider is off this morning for Camargo. I finish hastily—having already taken notes that will enable me to re-write what I have already penned in my two last communications.

H.

GEORGE W. KENDALL

"CAPTURE OF MONTERREY"

NEW ORLEANS *PICAYUNE*, NOVEMBER 19, 1846

Kendall covered the battle of Monterrey while accompanying the Texas Rangers, who rode without supplies—no blankets, no food. Stopping in hamlets or small ranches, they chased chickens and pigs. They were vulnerable to Mexican sharpshooters and to the cold rains that often fell.

When the rangers charged toward Monterrey, the surrounding fields of corn and chaparral were raked with bullets from Mexican batteries. The fierceness of these skirmishes, Kendall writes in the following passage, promptly changed the minds of those who had believed that the enemy would not fight for the city. After fighting his way into Monterrey's perimeter, General Zachary Taylor negotiated a truce with General Pedro de Ampudia that allowed the Mexican army to withdraw and regroup while U.S. forces occupied the city.

President Polk was indignant at this, believing that Taylor had missed an opportunity to crush the enemy and end the war. Until the Picayune's *dispatches arrived, it was unclear just how costly such a fight would have been.*

THE FOLLOWING ACCOUNT OF General Worth's operations has been written by one of the editors of this paper, from hasty notes taken at the time and recollections of the varied scenes: yet he is confident it will be found in the main correct. The names of many of the subaltern officers, both among the Regulators and Rangers, who took part in the active operations of the three days, he has been unable to gather; else they would have appeared in this report. Many incidents of personal gallantry, performed by officers and privates and which came under his personal observation, he has also been compelled to exclude, as to make mention of all would swell out this account to an unreasonable length and as many of the incidents have already appeared in print. That the report has errors and important omissions is conceded; but they are such as must inevitably occur in describing a succession of brilliant events following so close upon each as did those at Monterrey—by day and night, amid sunshine and storm—and it is not taxing the indulgence of those who participated too far, the writer thinks, to ask them to overlook what could hardly be avoided. The accompanying map was drawn by Lt. Benjamin on the spot, and has been lithographed by Messrs. Manouvrier & Snell of this city. The drawing is faithful in every particular—the execution shows for itself. With this short preface and apology the writer commences the report.

Before commencing in detailed account of the part taken by the 2d division of Gen. Taylor's army, under Gen. Worth, in the capture of Monterrey, it may be necessary to carry the reader back to the events of the four or five days preceding the combined attack upon the city.

The two slight skirmishes between McCulloch's Rangers and Torrejon's Lancers, which occurred on the 11th September, opened the eyes of many of those who had all along held firmly the belief that the Mexicans would not make a stand at Monterrey. One of the skirmishes above mentioned, which occurred midway between the miserable rancho of Papa Gallos and Ramos, resulted without loss to McCulloch's men, although two or three of the Mexicans were badly wounded and one of their horses was killed. The Texan commander had but 35 men in all, while the Mexicans numbered at least 300; yet the latter, fearful as they afterwards said of being drawn into an ambuscade, retreated precipitately to Ramos, dropping several lances and escopetas in their flight.

G.W.K.

GEORGE W. KENDALL

"ANOTHER GLORIOUS VICTORY!"

NEW ORLEANS *PICAYUNE*, MAY 1, 1847

On April 17, the opening day of the battle of Veracruz, Kendall reported: "I write this in great haste, with noise, confusion and everything else around me." After dispatching his first reports from Veracruz, Kendall left the battle area and rode forward to Jalapa, where the main American units had stopped for rest. He remained there for a month following the battle, sending a steady stream of correspondence to the Picayune. *Following the fall of Mexico City, Kendall monitored the peace negotiations and interpreted scores of reports from both sides, which he distilled and sent to his editors at the* Picayune.

BATTLE OF CERRO GORDO.

Santa Anna again Defeated in a Pitched Battle by Gen. Scott—Six Thousand Mexicans taken Prisoners—Five Hundred Americans Killed and Wounded—Gen. La Vega Again a Prisoner.

BY THE STEAMSHIP McKIM, CAPT. Pillsbury, which left Vera Cruz on the 20th inst., we have glorious news from the army under Gen. Scott. Mr. Bugbee, who was sent from the scene of the action by Mr. Kendall, with despatches for this office, left the McKim twenty miles below the city, and came up to the city, express, with his glorious tidings.

On the afternoon of the 17th, the advance under Gen. Twiggs encountered the enemy, when a severe but indecisive conflict ensued. As the general orders, which we give below, show that it was Gen. Scott's intention to give battle only on the 18th, it may be that this engagement was brought on by the Mexicans. The main battle occurred on the 18th, and resulted in the complete triumph of the American arms.

Santa Anna made his escape after his army was routed. Gen. La Vega is again among the prisoners. Besides him there were four generals taken, and along list of colonels and subordinate officers. We give below a list of such of the officers as are coming to this place. They were to leave Vera Cruz about the 25th April.

The first letter which we give to-day from Mr. Kendall did not appear in our extra of yesterday—we had not time to print it. It will show the dispositions made for the attack by our troops, for every thing done by Gen. Scott evinced his skill and science as well as gallantry.

Various typographical errors unavoidably crept into our extra. These are in a measure corrected to-day; the names of the Mexican officers, particularly, which suffered unduly from our types, are given more accurately.

Many inquiries are made of us by friends and acquaintances as to the wounded. Mr. Kendall's letters give all the

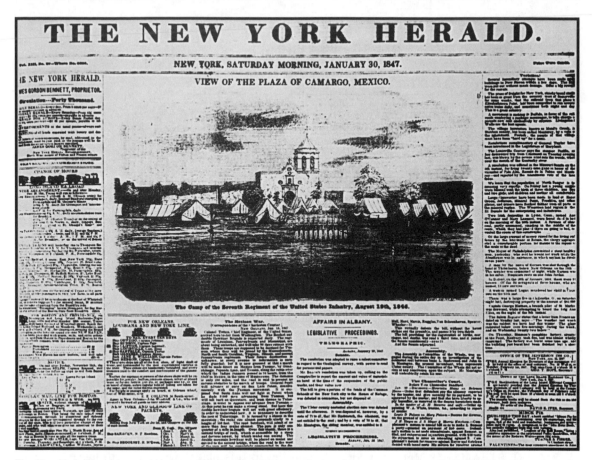

The *New York Herald*, founded by James Gordon Bennett, was a leader of war correspondence in the Mexican and Civil Wars. It was one of the first papers to use "lightning presses" with cylinders capable of printing twelve thousand impressions an hour. It eventually merged with the *New York Tribune*.

information which we possess, and it must be recollected that they were written under circumstances of excitement and in great haste. It is a delicate matter for gentlemen who have reached the city from the field of the conflict to speak of the state of the wounded with any positiveness. In individual cases their hopes may be blasted by the result, and again their fears amounting almost to certainty may in other cases be happily disappointed. We must wait for further arrivals to dispel the uncertainty which hangs over the fate of many brave men.

In this connection all will learn with pleasure that Capt. Johnston is doing so well. This gentleman, captain of the Topographical Engineers and appointed lieutenant colonel of the Voltigeurs, was so desperately wounded that little hope was felt for him. He has a strong constitution and is in fine spirits, and Capt. Hughes thinks he will recover.

The health of the troops at Vera Cruz

is absolutely improving. Great ameliorations are making in the city, but above all things it has been undergoing a thorough purification. There is no yellow fever there nor other malignant epidemic. This is good news.

Ampudia was in the battle of Cerro Gordo, but neither he nor Santa Anna ventured within the lines which their countrymen strenuously defended. *They were prepared to run the moment the day should seem to go against them*, and run they did. Ampudia came near being taken close to Jalapa, and to save himself had to take to the fields. But we will not longer detain the reader from our correspondence.

PLAN DEL RIO, MEXICO, April 16, 1847—EVENING

MEETING LIEUT. MCLANE OF the navy this afternoon, at Puente Nacional and on his way here, I joined his party and rode over. Major Beall, with a small squad of dragoons, was also along with us. On the road, some six miles back, we came up with a forage party of the 2d Dragoons under Lieut. Anderson, and also Capt. Caswell's company of Tennessee volunteers which had been out after beef. The latter had had a brief skirmish with a party of rancheros, in which Capt. C. had two men wounded, one of them, a young man of great promise, named J. L. Roberson, sadly. His thigh bone was completely shattered, and the poor fellow's sufferings were most acute as they bore him along in a wagon over the rough road. The Mexicans stood their ground in the chaparral with some little bravery at first, but were finally routed in every direction.

I find all excitement and bustle here.

The Mexicans, under Santa Anna, are occupying a chain of works along the road, the nearest of which is about a mile and a quarter from Gen. Scott's headquarters in a direct line. The road this side is cut up and barricaded, and every possible means of defence and annoyance has been resorted to. Beyond the first work there are three or four others, completely commanding the gorge through which the road to Jalapa runs—these fortifications on hills, and rising so as to defend one another. It is thought that Santa Anna has 20,000 men with him—the lowest estimate gives him 15,000—and with these he had 24 pieces of field artillery, besides some 14 heavy cannon in position. Some of the prisoners and deserters from the enemy's camp place even higher estimates as to the number of men and guns.

To turn these different works a road has been partially cut through the rough ground and chaparral to the right; and although the reconnaissance is as yet imperfect, it is still thought that a point near the enemy's farthest work can be reached. Gen. Twiggs, with his division, is to march at 8 o'clock to-morrow morning by the new road, and on the following morning it is thought the attack will commence on the works on this side. If Gen. Twiggs succeeds in reaching the rear of Santa Anna, and he will use every exertion, I do not see what is to save him. He is generally fox enough to have plenty of holes out of which to escape, however, and from the great difficulty of reconnoitering his position fully he may have some means of escape here. The general impression now in camp is, that this is to be the great battle of the war; and the immense natural strength of Santa Anna's works would justify the belief.

The Mexicans are more on the alert than they have ever been before, and more bold in throwing out their pickets. Not a party can go near their works without being fired upon, and yesterday a soldier of the 7th Infantry fell with no less than seven bullets in his body. It is said that Almonte is with Santa Anna, as also all the principal generals of the country.

Gen. Worth left Puente Nacional this afternoon with his division, and he will be up during the night. He started a little after 1 o'clock this morning, with near 2000 picked men, determined to make a force march through; but learning on the road that the attack upon the Mexican works was not to commence as soon as anticipated, he returned to Puente Nacional after marching a mile and a half. Capt. Pemberton, one of his aids, rode over here last evening after dark, and returned with the information that the attack had been postponed.

The wounds of Capt. Johnston are doing well. I regret to state that Gen. P. F. Smith is confined to his bed—utterly unable either to ride or walk. He has a violent inflammation of the right ankle and knee, resembling erysipelas, which from neglecting several days when he should have remained in his cot, has finally compelled him to lay up. I will write again tomorrow.

Yours, G.W.K.

PLAN DEL RIO, MEXICO, April 17, 1847—8 o'clock, A.M.

GEN. WORTH'S DIVISION CAME up during last night and this morning, ready for anything that turns up. A section of the siege train, comprising two 24-pounders and an 8-inch howitzer will be along this afternoon. A subsistence train is also close by, and is very much needed as the army is nearly out of provisions.

Gen. Twiggs's division will march by 9 o'clock. The 1st Brigade, composed of the 1st Artillery, 2d Dragoons and Capt. K.'s company of the 1st and the 7th Infantry is under command of Col. Harney during the illness of Gen. Smith; the 2d Brigade consists of the 4th Artillery and 2d and 3d Infantry, under Col. Riley; and to these must be added Taylor's battery and Talcott's mountain howitzer and rocket men, acting under the immediate orders of Gen. Twiggs. The latter company will probably have plenty of work on their hands, as this is just the country for their operations.

I have written this off so as to be able to send you an account of the operations thus far in case any one is going to Vera Cruz.

G.W.K.

PLAN DEL RIO, April 17—11 A.M.

THE DIVISION OF GENERAL Twiggs started two hours since, and a heavy cannonade has already commenced upon his line from the furthest of the Mexican works. At intervals, too, the rattling of small arms can be heard distinctly from the dragoon camp where I am writing this. I am going out, with Cols. Duncan and Bohlan and Capt. Pemberton, to the seat of action, and will return here at night to report the progress of the fight. It was not intended, I believe, that Gen. Twiggs should open the fight to-day, at least to bring on a general action, and it is therefore presumable the Mexicans have commenced upon him. I write in great haste. G.W.K.

5 P.M.—I have just returned from the

scene of conflict, and a bloody one it has been, considering the number engaged. A hill this side of the furthest Mexican work, and on which there was no one seen last evening, was found occupied by the enemy's light troops this morning, and to force it was at once deemed indispensable. For this purpose the Rifles under Major Sumner, besides detachments of artillery and infantry, were ordered to charge up the rugged ascent. This they did in gallant style, driving the Mexicans, after a resistance which may be put down as most obstinate. Great numbers of the enemy were killed, while on our side the loss was also severe. Major Sumner was shot in the head with a musket ball— severely but not mortally: Lieuts. Maury and Gibbs, of the Rifles, were also wounded, but not as severely, as was also Lieut. Jarvis of the 2nd Infantry. I could not learn that any of our officers were killed. The entire loss on our side, in killed and wounded, is estimated at about one hundred; but from the nature of the ground—broken, covered with brush, and extremely uneven—it is impossible to tell with accuracy. Nor can I, at this time, give even the names of the officers who were immediately engaged.

About 3 o'clock the enemy made a demonstration from the fort on the neighboring height to the one our men had captured, as if with the intention of retaking it; but it all ended in marching down the hill, blowing a most terrific charge on their trumpets, firing a few shots, and then retiring. Their appearance, as they came down the slope, was certainly most imposing. The cannon on the height meanwhile kept up a continuous fire upon Gen. Twiggs's lines, yet doing little execution other than cutting down the trees and brush. As we returned to camps, the fire still continued— the enemy had evidently ascertained the position of the road, which had just been cut, with accuracy, but their balls principally went over.

Gen. Shields, at 3 o'clock, was ordered out to support Gen. Twiggs, with three regiments of volunteers—two from Illinois under Cols. Baker and Barnett. They will have warm work to-morrow, if the Mexicans stand up as they did to-day.

There has been not a little skirmishing to-day between the forage and beef parties, sent out in the rear, and the rancheros. One Illinois man was killed, and one of the same regiment and a Tennessean wounded. I could not learn their names.

To-morrow the grand attack, both upon the front and rear of the enemy, is to be made. Gen. Worth is to move at sunrise, and little peace will the Mexicans have for one twenty-four hours at least.

If possible I shall report and send off the progress of the conflict, although one has little time or convenience in the chaparral for writing.

G.W.K.

CAMP NEAR DEL RIO, APRIL 18—1 o'clock, P.M.

THE AMERICAN ARMS HAVE achieved another glorious and most brilliant victory. Outnumbering Gen. Scott's force materially, and occupying positions which looked impregnable as Gibraltar, one after another of their works have been taken to-day, five generals, colonels enough to command ten such armies as ours, and other officers innumerable, have been taken prisoners, together with 6000 men, and the rest of their army driven and routed with the loss of every thing, ammunition, cannon, baggage train, *all*. Nothing but the impossibility of finding a road for the dragoons to the rear of the enemy's works saved any part of Santa Anna's grand army, including his own illustrious person.

Among the prisoners is our old friend La Vega, who fought with his accustomed gallantry. The other generals are Jose Maria Jarero, Luis Pinzon, Manuel Noriega, and Jose Obando. The names of the colonels I have not been able to gather. Nothing saved Santa Anna but the want of dragoons on the other side of their lines. As it is, his travelling coach, together with all his papers, valuables, and even his *wooden leg*, have fallen into our hands, together with all the money of his army. No one anticipated, when they arose from their hard bivouack this morning, such a complete victory.

The loss on both sides has been heavy.
G.W.K.

"DEEDS OF PERSONAL VALOR"

AMERICAN STAR, MAY 2, 1847

One of the most valuable functions of the American journalist during the war was to keep Americans at home and in Mexico informed on the issues. American printers who followed the army into Mexico established the American Star *and the* North American *there. Their rebellious impulse to establish papers in Mexican cities arose from a mixture of patriotism, politics, and personal gain. The resistance helped Americans in the 1840s to better understand the war.*

John Peoples, formerly a printer at the New Orleans Delta, *was active for almost the entire two-year period, establishing a number of papers in the occupied territory and continuing a steady stream of correspondence via the* American Star. *The New Orleans* Crescent *called him "the reporter, who without any other motive than a desire of spreading truth before the public, has been so indefatigable in furnishing his contemporaries in the United States everything of interest and importance." In Mexico City, the* American Star *became the most important of all war papers, serving as the semiofficial publication of the American army and giving news to the troops during their eight-month occupation of the Mexican capital.*

The Veracruz Eagle *and the* American Star, *both published by Charles Callahan and Peoples, two former* Picayune *staff members, printed a three-column, one-page tabloid containing official orders, sentences, court-martials, and a few news items from the United States. With his letters, George W. Kendall now sent current issues of the* Star, *published twice a week in Pueblo.*

WE HAVE BEEN FAVORED BY A friend with the following names of officers, who were engaged in a hand-to-hand conflict, with the enemy while storming the height of Cerro Gordo. Our informant is a man of high metal and valor, and one who would much rather speak of the deeds of his friends, than to rehearse what he himself achieved:

Capt. E. B. ALEXANDER, who commanded the gallant 3d Infantry, did much to inspire his men. One of his sergeants fell wounded in the charge. The captain, not wishing to see an idle musket in the command, sheathed his sword, and picking up the shooting iron of the sergeant, went to work with good will, and continued to fire as fast as he could load, and with great effect, until one of his men came up and begged for the gun, saying that his own was out of order. He handed it to him, and then drawing his revolver, fired, and shot down two of the enemy, and wounded one with each of the other barrels. The pistol being useless then was belted, and the sabre drawn, which in his unerring hand, severely wounded an enemy upon the head.

Lt. D. C. BUELL, adjutant of the third—the man who, Gen. Twiggs says, knows not what fear is—cut down two men with his sabre. His conduct at Monterrey, would prepare us for any feat of daring performed by him.

Lt. E. VAN DORN, 7th Infantry aide-de-camp to Col. Harney, on the 18th, cut two men down with his sabre.

Lt. B. E. BEE, was wounded in the thumb, by a bayonet, but succeeded in cutting the man down with his sword.

As we said before, we will consider it a great favor if those who are cognizant of "deeds of personal valor," in either officers or privates, will furnish us with their names. It will afford us the greatest pleasure to refer to them in such length as our space will admit. If the commanders of companies would but furnish the names of non-commissioned officers and privates who distinguished themselves, it would be an incentive to exertions in other frays.

SECOND DRAGOONS

Gallant Conduct of Sergeant Tucker and His Part of Dragoons.

ON THE 19TH INSTANT SERGEANT Tucker, with four men, was sent by Capt. Merrill, from Plan del Rio, as bearer of important dispatches of Gen. Scott detailing the battle, to Vera Cruz. On reaching the bridge six miles beyond Puente Nacional, the party was fired upon by some thirty men, Mexicans, and the Sergeant and one man wounded. The enemy had concealed themselves in the chaparral, for the purpose of cutting off any small party that might attempt to pass. Before receiving this fire from the enemy the sergeant had the precaution to send one of his men ahead to reconnoiter who soon returned and reported that from several indications he believed that the enemy were near. Upon the receipt of this information, sergeant extended his rear, placed the mail in the centre, and giving the word forward charged over the bridge at full speed—through a shower of musket balls, and was soon out of the way of the enemy. He arrived at Vera Cruz in good season, notwithstanding his wound, and delivered the mail to the proper person. Such conduct as this even in the epauletted officer, is worthy of the highest encomium and should be doubly so to the enlisted soldier. The sergeant carried out the instructions he received to the very letter—that of endeavoring to carry the mail through at all hazzard.

The Battle of Churnbusco and the capture of the Tête de Pont. *(National Archives)*

ATTACK ON THE TRAINS

ON MONDAY, APRIL 26TH, A SMALL train of wagons left Vera Cruz, escorted by Capt. Nixon, with detachments of sick from the hospitals in that place. When they arrived at a ranch, a few miles this side of Santa Fe, they were attacked by a body of Rancheros, about 125 in number. Lieut. Gibbs, with a small party of men, were sent to attack, and if possible, to dislodge them. But finding most of his men in a disabled condition, and discovering the strong position of the Rancheros, he deemed it prudent to withdraw. A man by

the name of Joiner, belonging to company G., of the Alabama regiment, was killed by an escopeta ball, discharged from the chaparral. A short time after, the large train under Capt. Bell, escorted by Capt. Kerr with about sixty men, belonging to the 2nd dragoons, came up to them. Captain K. ordered the whole body to advance. When he arrived at the place of attack, he found the Rancheros posted on the right and left of the road, just at the foot of a mountain, over which the train would be obliged to pass. The dragoons formed in line, and with Captain Kerr at their head, charged them, and drove them

THE MEXICAN WAR 75

in confusion over the hills. A short distance from this place the train was again fired upon by about twenty-five Rancheros, but without doing any injury.

Sergeant Henry and Captain Bell (the wagon master) we are told behaved with great prudence and courage in this affair. The former was entrusted with an advance or reconnoitering party, which he managed with great credit to himself, and the latter, as is always the case with him in time of trouble was up and doing.

GEORGE W. KENDALL

"MR. KENDALL'S LETTERS FROM THE ARMY"

NEW ORLEANS *PICAYUNE*, OCTOBER 14, 1847

In the following series, George W. Kendall relates the assault on the Mexican capital. Although victory was at hand, he focuses on the unusually high number of casualties. Such emphasis was uncommon in a war that trumpeted U.S. military superiority—and in which dispatches were often written by officers themselves. The reports from Tacubaya, thus, are the first to openly question commanders' decisions that seemed to have resulted in unnecessary losses.

After the fighting ended, Kendall remained in Mexico City and wrote about the war's aftermath, including the ambushing of U.S. troops by vengeful "armed ruffians." Kendall soon became bitter about the way the conflict had ended, accusing General Winfield Scott of manipulating the armistice to improve his chances of capturing the White House.

TACUBAYA, Sept. 8, 1847

FORENOON, 10 O'CLOCK.— I HAVE just returned from another battle field—one on which the victory of the American arms was complete, and on which our troops contended against an enemy immensely superior in number and strongly posted. Gen. Worth commenced the attack at early daylight, and in less than two hours every point was carried, all the cannon of the enemy were in our possession, an immense quantity of ammunition captured, and nearly 1000 men, among them fifty-three officers, taken prisoners.

For more than an hour the battle raged with a violence not surpassed since the Mexican war commenced, and so great the odds opposed that for some time the result was doubtful. The force of the enemy has been estimated at from 12,000 to 15,000, strongly posted behind breastworks, and to attack them our small force of scarcely 3000 was obliged to approach on an open plain and without the least cover; but their dauntless courage carried them over every obstacle, and notwithstanding the Mexicans fought with a valor rare for them, they were finally routed from one point or another until all were driven and dispersed. The defeat was total.

But to gain this victory our own loss has been uncommonly severe—it has been purchased with the loot of some of the most gallant spirits of the army. The

SPOT NEWS

American newspapers published by American printers on foreign soil is a phenomenon seldom reported in American journalism history. Before the Mexican War came to an end, enterprising Americans had established no fewer than twenty-six papers in thirteen locations.

The Corpus Christi *Gazette,* organized and published by Samuel Bangs, made its appearance on January 1, 1846. The four-page *Gazette* bore the motto "Be Sure You Are Right, Then Go Ahead." When General Taylor decided to move his army toward the Rio Grande, the *Gazette* expressed its disapproval.

> What are they going to do there, and the object of their going, are to us a profound mystery. One thing is certain. If the United States are to occupy the east bank of the Rio Grande . . . they must send a much stronger force than the one now here. . . . Instead of black-eyed senoras . . . we predict that our Army of Occupation will find some less agreeable subjects to digest.

To support its claim, the *Gazette* added:

> Our sources of information are in no way inferior to those of the United States Government itself. The policy which has dictated the removal (of the army). . . . We have reason to believe is founded in error. (Corpus Christi *Gazette,* February 12, 1846)

Another American paper, the *Reveille* (named for the Saint Louis *Daily* with the same title), first appeared in Matamoros on June 24, 1846. It was printed in English and Spanish. Again, it was operated by Samuel Bangs. The *Reveille*'s motto was one of the longest of the war: "We must ever maintain the principles that the peoples of this continent alone have the right to decide their own destiny." An item in the first issue of the paper, headed HOW TO WRITE FOR A NEWSPAPER, explained:

1. Have something to write about.
2. Write plain: dot your i's, cross your t's, point your sentences.
3. Begin with capitals.
4. Write short: to the point; stop when you have done.
5. Write only on one side of a leaf.
6. Read it over, abridge and correct it, until you get it into the shortest space possible.
7. Pay the postage.

The *American Star* and the *Flag* were two other newspapers that appeared before the end of the war. As quoted in the New Orleans *Delta,* October 13, 1847, Secretary of the Navy John Mason remarked on the American press in Mexico when speaking at the University of North Carolina:

(continued)

Nothing is more remarkable, or more indicative of the intelligence and education of our people than the fact newspapers have been established in every town of importance which had been captured from the enemy. (In them) American journals have been busy in imparting information, in combating crime, in inculcating virtue, in fostering all the attributes of humanity in the bosoms of American soldiery, and in striving to extend over the benighted territory conquered by our arms, the ameliorating influence of our civilization.

The final issue of the Mexico City *American Star,* on May 30, 1848, marked the end of the movement:

With this number ends the *American Star.* Peace is made and ratified, and with its coming ends our mission here. The deed is done. The *Star,* which has risen in every city occupied by our arms on this line, has set for the last time in the capital of those, who, but a few days since, ranked on our list of enemies. May there never be a cause for another rupture between us. The *Star* has advocated an honorable peace—it has been brought about. We are satisfied—our country is satisfied—Mexico is satisfied—may peace rest continually with all.

5th Infantry has suffered the most. This regiment along with the 6th and 8th, was engaged in the attack upon a strong work on the enemy's right, and was opposed to such superior numbers that it was compelled to retire along with the others. The celebrated Col. Martin Scott was killed in this attack, along with Lieuts. Burwell and Strong, while Col. McIntosh and many other officers were badly wounded. The worse than savage miscreants in the fort, after our men retired, set up a yell and came out and massacred such of our wounded as were unable to get off. In this way poor Burwell lost his life. Full were they avenged, however; for within half an hour Duncan's battery, aided by the fall of another of their works, drove the dastardly wretches in full flight across the fields. No one knew or even surmised the strength of the place; it was an old fort, constructed long since, and was one of the main defences of the line of works.

On the enemy's left, and nearer Chapultepec, our loss was also great, although not as severe. It was here that Col. Wm. M. Graham, as brave a spirit as ever lived, was killed; Capts. Merrill and Ayres also fell in this part of the field. The wonder now is how any one could come out safe under such a terrible fire as the enemy poured from his entire line of works. Nothing but the daring and impetuosity of our men who rushed onward while their comrades were falling thick around them, gained the victory—had they once faltered all would have been lost.

The broken ground on the right of the enemy, cut up by deep ravines, saved many of Santa Anna's troops in their flight; yet as it was our dragoons killed and captured many of the fugitives. Large bodies of the Mexican cavalry approached the scene of strife several times, but they were driven like sheep by Duncan's battery.

The Mexican loss has been even more severe than our own. Gen. Balderas, Gen. Leon, and many other officers are numbered among the dead, while the interior of their works, the tops of the houses from which they fought, and the ground over which they fled are strewn with lifeless bodies. Such was the panic that many of our officers say that a few fresh troops might have taken Chapultepec itself almost without a struggle; but other than a few shots fired at that point from some of the captured cannon, no demonstration was made.

After the battle was over Gen. Scott came out, accompanied by his staff, and also by Mr. Trist. The Mexicans at the time were throwing shells at some of the wagons Gen. Worth had sent out to pick up the dead and wounded. They had placed a howitzer in position on Chapultepec at the close of the action, and now, seeing no enemy within reach, the cowardly wretches opened upon the ambulances and those who were gathering the bodies of their wounded and lifeless comrades. On seeing this worse than savage outrage, one of our officers, with a sarcastic expression of countenance, asked whether Mr. Trist had any new peace propositions in his pockets. Mackintosh did not come out after the battle to gain more time for his friend Santa Anna, nor worm out fresh intelligence of the strength and movements of our army, in order that he might be of service to the Mexicans by communicating it.

The Mexican prisoners say that Santa Anna himself was on the ground in the rear of their works, but left at the commencement of the rout. They admit that their entire force was 15,000; it is certain that including killed, wounded, prisoners and dispersed their loss has been near 5,000. Many of them were regulars, the 11th and 12th Infantry Regiments suffering most. The commander of the latter, Col. Tenorio, is a prisoner in our hands; some fourteen officers belonging to the former are also prisoners, but the commander, Gen. Perez, escaped.

The foundry, in which several moulds for casting cannon and other apparatus were found, was entirely demolished, and after ascertaining this, Gen. Scott, not wishing to hold the position, ordered all the forces to retire. The whole affair, as a military movement, is severely criticized by many of our officers. They contend that no result has been gained commensurate with the immense loss we have sustained in the battle. This is a matter I do not feel myself qualified to discuss, but it must be certain that the *morale* upon the Mexicans, of a defeat so disgraceful and so disastrous, must be important. They have now (it is 5 o'clock in the afternoon) returned to their positions; and if Santa Anna was on the ground as is stated, and can find no one to lay the blame upon, he may twist the whole affair into a victory— *on paper.* It will not be the first time he has done this thing.

Since I commenced this letter I have been out endeavoring to obtain a full list of the killed and wounded officers, but so far have been unable. Knowing the deep anxiety felt in the United States by the families of all, this shall be my first care. The entire loss in Gen. Worth's division, out of some 1,800 or 2,000 that went into action, will not fall much short of 600.

The Dragoons and Gen. Cadwalader's brigade did not suffer so severely in comparison. What the next movement is to be no one knows, but it is thought the city will be attacked immediately.

Yours, &c. G.W.K.

TACUBAYA, Sept. 9, 1847

I HAVE BEEN ENABLED TO GATHER a full list of all the killed and wounded officers in Gen. Worth's division in the great battle of the Molino del Rey, as also of those in Maj. Sumner's command of Dragoons. Gen. Cadwalader's loss I will obtain before I close this letter. The list which follows may be relied upon.

Major Sumner's Command.

CAPT. CROGHAN KER, 2D DRAGOONS, severely; Lieut. Tree, 2d Dragoons, severely; Lieut. Walker, Mounted Rifles, slightly; Lieut. Williams, 3d Dragoons slightly.

The above list is complete and perfect. There had been much difficulty in obtaining it, as nearly all the orderly sergeants and executive officers have been killed or wounded. The conduct of all the non-commissioned officers had been gallant and most conspicuous, while several of them behaved so nobly that they have been recommended for immediate promotion to Gen. Scott. Their names are Sergeants Benson, Wilson and Robinson of the 2d Artillery; Sergeant Heck of the 3d Artillery; Sergeants Updegraff, Farmer, Archer and Daily of the 5th Infantry; Sergeant Major Thompson of the 6th Infantry; Sergeant Major Fink of the 8th Infantry. I trust and hope that Gen. Scott will at once promote these brave fellows. More than half the officers in Gen. Worth's division have been struck down,

either killed or wounded, in the actions of Churubuaco and El Molino del Rey, and many of the companies have absolutely no one to command them.

Of our wounded officers, I cannot learn that one of them has received mortal injury, although three or four are in a dangerous situation. The wound of Major Waite, although severe, will not keep him long from duty. The same may be said of Capt. Mason and Lieut. Foster of the engineers. Major Wright was struck in the stomach by a partially spent ball, while gallantly leading the storming party of 500 picked men, but is now recovering from the effect. I shall make further enquiries in relation to the wounded officers before I close this letter.

No less than *nineteen* of the deserters, captured by Gens. Twiggs and Shields at Churubuaco, have been found fully guilty, and are to be hung to-morrow morning. The miscreant Riley, who commanded them, escapes the punishment of death, as he proved that he deserted before the war. He has been sentenced, however, to be severely whipped, to be branded as well, and to wear a ball and chain in front of the army during the war! A deserter taken among the prisoners at the Molino, on the 8th, was summarily dealt with. It seems that he deserted from Monterey last fall, and a comrade who recognized him, to save the trouble of a court martial, at once pitched him into the mill flume and he was crushed to pieces by the wheel! Another batch of deserters, who have been undergoing a trial here in Tacubaya, will be hung in a day or two it is said. Most richly do they deserve their fate.

The following list of the officers killed and wounded in Gen. Cadwalader's brigade I believe to be nearly correct. If there is any inaccurate in it I will correct it. It so happened in the order of battle that the 11th Regiment was immediately engaged. The brigade of Gen. Pierce was called into action towards the close of the battle. He lost a few men, but I learn that no officers were killed. Both Gens. Cadwalader and Pierce behaved with the greatest alacrity and gallantry on the occasion. Here is the list of the killed and wounded in the brigade of the former:

Gen. Cadwalader's Brigade.
(list of dead and wounded)

THE LOSS OF NON-COMMISSIONED officers and privates in this brigade I have not yet ascertained; it will not exceed 100. The loss in Major Sumner's command, which consisted of 280 men, was 6 killed and 33 wounded. Of horses he had 27 killed and 78 wounded. Nearly every officer had a horse shot under him.

I may possibly send this letter off to-night by a Mexican, but it will depend upon whether there is a prospect of another battle to-morrow or next day. Matters are approaching a crisis, while the great mistake in not entering the capital on the night of the 20th, when the Mexicans were perfectly panic stricken and in full flight, is hourly developing itself. The great sacrifice of life yesterday—the loss of so many gallant spirits—has all been owing to the cessation of hostilities and the armistice which followed, and an awful responsibility rests either with the Government or with Gen. Scott and Mr. Trist. The instructions will show, but I am of the opinion that the former is mostly to blame. The latter are censurable for placing faith in Mackintosh, in giving Santa Anna so much time, or even in having any reliance upon his power and ability to make peace under all the circumstances, however much he might have desired it personally. I will say nothing of the bribery—that dark side of the picture is undoubtedly the work of the exceedingly wise men at Washington. Bad advisers have been busy, both here and at home, in recommending measures to bring about a peace, and their counsels have prevailed to the exclusion of the opinions of men who might have been listened to with profit. I trust the experience of the past may prove a lesson for the future, and that by this time our rulers must see and feel that in order to bring about a peace with the Mexicans they must use hard blows instead of soft words.

Yours, &c. G.W.K.

TACUBAYA, Sept. 10, 1847

WE HAVE ACCOUNTS FROM MEX-ico, brought in by Frenchmen and other foreigners, to the effect that Santa Anna's loss at El Molino was much more severe than any one here had anticipated. They say that during the afternoon of the 8th no less than 1500 wounded men came into the city, while the number of killed was over 600. The slaughter from the batteries of Col. Duncan and Capt. Drum must have been terrific. Santa Anna, it is said, would have laid all the blame of the defeat upon Gen. Leon, but that officer, unfortunately for him, died. He has since torn the epaulettes from the shoulders of Col. Miguel Andrade, commander of the celebrated regiment of Hussars, accuses him of everything, has thrown him into prison, and denied him all communication. He must have some one to break out upon.

Everything looks quiet to-day, but the

Mexicans are busily employed in fortifying at every point. At Chapultepec they can be seen at work, while they are also repairing the damage done at El Molino and other points on that line. On the Pledad road they have strong works, while at the Nino Perdido and San Antonio Abad entrances to the city they are also fortifying with the greatest vigor. Gen. Pillow's division, as also Col. Riley's brigade, attached to that of Gen. Twiggs, occupy the village of La Pledad and neighborhood, in plain sight and in fact under the guns of the enemy. Gen. Worth remains here in Tacubaya, but he is sending all his sick and wounded to Mixcoac, out of the range of the guns of Chapultepec. No one knows what point will be first attacked, but this question will soon be determined. The next blow struck will be hard, and all hope decisive. It must read strange, the story that some 7 or 8000 men have set themselves down before a strongly fortified city of over 200,000 inhabitants, with an army of at least 25,000 men to defend it; but the tale is a true one and the proud captain of Mexico must fall.

Yours, &c. G.W.K.

TACUBAYA, Sept. 11, 1847

A SMALL PARTY OF US HAVE JUST returned from a ride over to La Pledad, the headquarters of Gen. Pillow. Gen. Scott was there, as also were some of his principal officers, holding a council as to the best mode and point of attack. The result of their deliberations is not known, but it is thought that the infantry will have some respite after their hard labors, and that all the heavier cannon recently captured from the Mexicans will be employed in sending their own balls back at them. With their own guns, and those brought up by Gen. Scott, at least fifty pieces of heavy calibre can be opened at any one point—enough to demolish any work the Mexicans have constructed in time incredibly short, and give them a lesson they will not soon forget.

From the Puente del Hermita, which has been destroyed by the Mexicans, they can plainly be seen at work on several fortifications between the roads of San Angel and San Antonio de Abad. These works are but little more than half a mile from the city, which is also in plain view. Shortly after we left, the enemy opened with two of their heavy guns upon our pickets or engineers, and continued the fire for near an hour. I cannot learn that they did any injury. On our return to Tacubaya we found that Maj. Sumner and Col. Duncan had had a little brush with the enemy's lancers near the battle ground of El Molino. Capt. Ruff, with his company of Mounted Riflemen, drew a large party of the Mexican cavalry immediately within the range of one of Duncan's guns, when one or two discharges sent them scampering off in every direction. Only one man was wounded on our side, but it is known that the enemy lost several in the skirmish. They opened with one heavy gun from Chapultepec on our men, but did no harm other than frightening the inhabitants of this place half out of their wits.

Lieut. Burbank, who was mortally wounded at El Molino, died yesterday, and Capt. E. Kirby Smith this afternoon of wounds received at the same time. Lieut. Col. Dickinson, shot badly in the ankle at Churubuaco, is also dead. All were gallant officers, and their loss is much regretted.

I have already mentioned the execution of nineteen of the deserters captured on the 20th August at Churubuaco. Gen. Scott has just signed the death warrant of thirty others, taken at the same time, and they will suffer the same fate in the course of a day or two.

From various movements, there is certainly strong reasons to believe that Gen. Scott will open a heavy fire upon Chapultepec to-morrow morning, from not only his own siege guns but from those captured from the enemy. Whether it is a feint to draw the Mexicans to that point and weaken other defences is not known.

Yours, &c. G.W.K.

TACUBAYA, Sept. 12, 1847

A T EARLY DAYLIGHT THIS MORNing a heavy cannonade was opened upon the stronghold of Chapultepec, which was increased during the day as additional siege guns were placed in position. The Mexicans returned the fire with great spirit at intervals during the day, but with little effect other than dismounting one of our guns—I cannot learn that a man has been killed at any of the batteries. Several of the Voltigeurs, while skirmishing with the enemy's sharpshooters at the foot of Capultepec, were wounded, but none of them severely. A 10 1/2 mortar was opened upon the place during the afternoon, and as several shells have been seen to fall and explode directly within the enemy's works it is certain that great damage has been caused. A firing of heavy guns has also been heard in the direction of La Pledad, showing that the Mexicans have been diverted in that quarter.

At dusk this evening several loads of scaling adders were sent down towards the foot of Chapultepec, and the move-

ments of our infantry and other light corps would indicate that the strong works upon the crest are to be stormed early to-morrow. A large portion of the entire army will be brought to the struggle, and it is thought the contest will be terrible. I have little time to write.

Yours, &c. G.W.K.

CITY OF MEXICO, Sept. 14, 1847

A NOTHER VICTORY, GLORIOUS IN its results and which has thrown additional lustre upon the American arms, has been achieved to-day by the army under Gen. Scott—the proud capital of Mexico, has fallen into the power of a mere handful of men compared with the immense odds arrayed against them, and Santa Anna, instead of shedding his blood as he had promised, is wandering with the remnant of his army no one knows whither.

The apparently impregnable works on Chapultepec, after a desperate struggle, were triumphantly carried—Gens. Bravo and Mouterde, besides a host of officers of different grades, taken prisoners; over 1000 non-commissioned officers and privates, all their cannon and ammunition, are in our hands; the fugitives were soon in full flight towards the different works which command the entrance to the city, and our men at once were in hot pursuit.

Gen. Quitman, supported by Gen. Smith's brigade, took the road by the Chapultepec aqueduct towards the Belen gate and the Cindadela; Gen. Worth, supported by Gen. Cadwalader's brigade, advanced by the San Cosme aqueduct towards the garita of that name. Both routs were cut up by ditches and defended by breastworks, barricades, and strong works of every description known to military science; yet the daring and impetuosity of our men overcame one defence after another, and by nightfall every work to the city's edge was carried. Gen. Quitman's command, after the rout at Chapultepec, was the first to encounter the enemy in force. Midway between the former and the Belen gate, Santa Anna had constructed a strong work; but this was at once vigorously assaulted by Gen. Quitman, and aided by a flank fire from two of Duncan's guns, which Gen. Worth had ordered to approach as near as possible from the San Cosme road, the enemy was again routed and in full flight. They again made a stand from their strong fortifications at and near the Belen garita, opening a tremendous fire not only of round shot, grape and shell, but of musketry; yet boldly Gen. Quitman advanced, stormed and carried the works, although at great loss, and then every point on this side of the city was in our possession. In this onslaught two of our bravest officers were killed—Capt. Drum and Lieut. Benjamin.

Meanwhile Gen. Worth was rapidly advancing upon San Cosme. At the English burying ground the enemy had constructed a strong work. It was defended by infantry for a short time, but could not resist the assault of our men—the affrighted Mexicans soon fled to another line of works nearer the city, and thus Gen. Worth was in possession of the entrance to San Cosme. As his men advanced towards the garita, the enemy opened a heavy fire of musketry from the house tops, as well as grape, canister and shell from their batteries, thus sweeping the street completely. At this juncture the old Monterrey game, of burrowing and digging through the houses, was adopted. On the right, as our men faced the enemy,

the aqueduct afforded a partial shelter; on the left, the houses gave some protection; but many were still killed or wounded by the grape which swept every part, as well as by the shells which were continually bursting in every direction. About 3 o'clock the work of the pick-axe and the crow-bar, under the direction of Lieut. G. W. Smith, of the Sappers and miners, had fairly commenced, and every minute brought our men nearer the enemy's last stronghold. In the meantime two mountain howitzers were fairly lifted to the top of one of the houses and into the cupola of the church, from which they opened a plunging and most effective fire, while one of Duncan's guns, in charge of Lieut. Hunt, was run up under a galling fire to a deserted breastwork, and at once opened upon the garita. In this latter daring feat, four men out of eight were either killed or wounded, but still the piece was most effectively served. The work of the Miners was still going on. In one hour after they had entered, by the pick-axe, a favorite aide of Santa Anna's was found. The great man had just fled, but had left his friend and supper! Both were well cared for—the latter was devoured by our hungry officers; the former, after doing the honors of the table, was made a close prisoner. Just as dark was setting in, our men had dug and mined their way almost up to the very guns of the enemy, and now, after a short struggle, they were completely routed and driven with the loss of everything. The command of the city by the San Cosme route was attained.

During the night, Gen. Quitman commenced the work of throwing up breastworks and erecting batteries, with the intention of opening a heavy cannonade upon the Cuidadela with the first light

General Scott triumphantly enters Mexico City. *(National Archives)*

this morning. At 10 o'clock at night Gen. Worth ordered Capt. Huger to bring up a 24-pounder and a 10-inch mortar to the garita or gate of San Cosme, and having ascertained the bearings and distance of the grand plaza and palace, at once opened upon those points. The heavy shells were heard to explode in the very heart of the city. At a little after midnight Major Palscios, accompanied by two or three members of the municipal council of the city, arrived at Gen. Worth's head-quarters, and in great trepidation informed him that Santa Anna and his grand army had fled, and that they wished at once to surrender the capital! They were referred to the commander-in-chief, and immediately started for Tacubaya; but in the mean time the firing upon the town ceased.

At 7 o'clock this morning Gen. Scott, with his staff rode in and took quarters in the national palace, on the top of which the regimental flag of the gallant Rifles and the stars and stripes were already flying. An immense crowd of blanketed leperos, the scum of the capital, were congregated in the plaza as the commander-in-chief entered it. They pressed upon our soldiers, and eyed them as though they were beings of another world. So much were they in the way, and with such eagerness did they press around, that Gen. Scott was compelled to order our Dragoons to clear the plaza. They were told, however, not to injure or harm a man in the mob—they were all our friends!

About five minutes after this, and while Gen. Worth was returning to his division near the Alameda, he was fired upon from a house near the Convent of San Francisco. Some of the cowardly Polkas, who had fled the day previous without discharging their guns, now commenced the assassin game of shooting at every one of our men they saw, from windows, as well as from behind the parapets on the azoteas of tops of the houses. In half an hour's time our good friends, the leperos, in the neighborhood of the hospital of San Andrea and the church of Santa Clara, also commenced discharging muskets and throwing bottles and rocks from the azoteas. I have neglected to mention that just previous to this Col. Garland had been severely wounded by a musket, fired by some miscreant from a window.

For several hours this cowardly war upon our men continued, and during this time many were killed or wounded. It was in this species of fighting that Lieut. Sidney Smith received his death wound. The division of Gen. Twiggs in one part of the city, and Gen. Worth in another, were soon actively engaged in putting down the insurrection. Orders were given to shoot every man in all the houses from which the firing came, while the guns of the different light batteries swept the streets in all directions. As the assassins were driven from one house they would take refuge in another; but by the middle of the afternoon they were all forced back to the barriers and suburbs. Many innocent persons have doubtless been killed during the day, but this could not be avoided. Had orders been given at the outset to blow up and demolish every house or church from which one man was fired upon, the disturbances would have been at once quieted. As it is, I trust that the lesson the rabble and their mischievous leaders have received today may deter them from future outrages.

On entering the palace Gen. Scott at once named Gen. Quitman governor of Mexico—a most excellent appointment. Some wag immediately proclaimed aloud in the plaza as follows: "Gen. John A. Quitman, of Mississippi, has been appointed governor of Mexico, vice Gen. Jose Maria Ternel, resigned—*very suddenly!*" It seems that the valiant Ternel ran off at an early hour, and his magnificent house has been converted into a hospital for our wounded officers.

Yours, &c. G.W.K.

CITY OF MEXICO, Sept. 17, 1847

THE CAPITAL IS NOW QUIET enough, and although the inhabitants say but little they are probably not altogether contented with their new masters. They say that the Lord and Santa Anna are to blame for all their misfortunes—their own lack of prowess or courage is not thought of. They say that Providence withheld the rains and gave the Yankees fair weather for their operations, while Santa Anna deserted them in their extremity, and gave up the city without even making terms for them. The latter has gone no one knows whither. Some contend that he is on his way to the coast, with the intention of leaving the country; others say that he has gone towards Queretaro; while many think that he is lurking about Guadalupe or San Christobal, within a few miles of this, yet with only a small force of cavalry at his command. His wife, who has been living all the while at the house of his particular friend Mackintosh, has gone out in the direction of San Christobal in search of him. Santa Anna just before he left the city grossly insulted Gen. Torres, who commanded at the Belen gate, for deserting his post. It is also said that he has quarreled with Lombardini. These are old tricks of the tyrant—throwing the blame upon others to cover his own shameless conduct.

Yours, &c. G.W.K.

CITY OF MEXICO, Sept. 24, 1847

NOT A LITTLE JOY HAS BEEN manifested by all at the arrival here of the American prisoners—Capts. Clay, Heady and Smith, Lieuts. Churchill, Davidson and Barbour, and sixteen privates—who have recently been confined at Toluca. It seems that they were released by the Governor, Olaguibel, on his own responsibility, they promising that the same number of Mexican prisoners, and of equal rank, should be delivered up to him. Those officers who refused to give their parole when all were ordered to Toluca, and who afterwards escaped, have performed active service here in different battles. Major Gaines has been serving on the staff of Gen. Scott, Midshipman Rogers on that of Gen. Pillow, Major Borland on that of Gen. Worth, and Capt. Danley on that of Gen. Quitman. The latter was severely wounded on the 13th, but will recover.

Yours, &c. G.W.K.

CITY OF MEXICO, Sept. 26, 1847

ASSASSINATIONS CONTINUE. NO less than ten murdered soldiers were found this morning in the vicinity of the quarter of San Pueblo, and eight on the previous day. The fault lies partially with our own men, who straggle from their quarters and get intoxicated at the first pulqueria or grog shop; yet the fact that even in this state they are set upon by gangs of armed ruffians shows that a feeling of revenge and deep hatred obtains against us; and the frequency of the murders would prove that a regular system of assassination has organized, the wire workers very likely some of the priests and leading men.

In my last letter I stated that Col. McIntosh was sinking under his wounds—that brave officer died last night, and is to be buried to-morrow with all military honors. He fell pierced by two balls while gallantly leading his men to attack the Casa Maia on the 8th September, and his system, suffering under wounds received in former battles, was not able to overcome the shock.

Yours, &c. G.W.K.

CITY OF MEXICO, Sept. 28, 1847

WE HAVE RUMORS WITHOUT number from Peubla today. One is that Santa Anna has been killed in an encounter with Col. Childs in the vicinity of that city, another story would make us believe that he has been taken prisoner, after defending himself for some time at the paper mill called La Constancia, in the neighborhood of Puebla. The accounts say that Col. Childs was reinforced by Maj. Lally, and that he immediately entered the city, drove out the guerrilleros and surrounded the mill above named. What credit to place in these rumors I know not; but if Santa Anna is really a prisoner, it has been intentional—he has given himself up. If he has been killed, it has been what the Mexicans would term one *casualidad*, a sheer accident, for no such intention ever entered his head.

As a prisoner, Santa Anna knows perfectly well that he can humbug Mr. Polk with ease, and all his friends besides. We shall know the whole truth of the matter in the course of a day or two.

It is said that the Mexican Congress is to assemble at Queretaro, on the 5th of October—next week—and that Pena y Pena has gone out to be installed as the acting President. I have heard Mexicans say that the body has many members who will deliberate manfully and seriously in favor of peace; but my opinion is, that a majority of them will talk of little save honor and ditches and glory, and last extremities and ruins, and of being buried under them, and kindred nonsense. Some of them may be bribed, or hired, to espouse the peace side. We shall see.

Rejon, in his letters to Santa Anna, told him that if he would continue the war, he would perish by his side; but they say, that when the armistice was broken, he remained at Queretaro and forgot all about fighting. Valiant man is Manuel Cresceneia Rejon! but he has a prudent way of manifesting it in the hour of peril.

Paredes was here in the city a few days since, without followers, and has gone North, perhaps towards Guadalajara, his old and favorite ground, to stir and influence the minds of the people against the Yankees, and try his hand against them. He is, no doubt, one of the bravest and best generals Mexico has ever produced.

Gomez Farias is at Queretaro, but we do not hear what he is doing. Gen. Herrera is also there, and if any leading man in Mexico is in favor of peace, he is the one. His influence, however, is confined almost entirely to the *moderandos*.

Mr. Wells, the partner of Hart in the Army theatre, died here a day or two since. He may be recollected in the United States, not only as a pantomimist but as a dancer and actor of some distinction. Capt. Pemberton Waddell, of one of the new regiments of infantry, is also dead. The wound of Gen. Shields, although painful, is improving. A musket ball struck him in the left arm at the storming of Chapultepec, but binding a handkerchief round it he continued with his men until every thing was calmed. Gen. Pillow has almost entirely recovered. Since commencing this I have heard another rumor to the effect that Alvarez and the Congress of Puebla have risen upon Santa Anna and put him to death. This can hardly be credited. Alvarez is doubtless in that direction. He took especial good care to keep himself and his pintos out of harm's way during the recent struggles in this vicinity.

The loss in the different divisions in the storming of Chapultepec and capture of the city on the 13th is as follows: in that of Gen. Quitman about 300, in that of Gen. Twiggs 268, in that of Gen. Pillow 142, in that of Gen. Worth 138. Owing to his previous heavy loss the latter only had about 1000 men engaged in the last battles. As I know it will be of great interest to their friends, before closing this letter I will state that the wounds of almost all the officers are doing well. I can speak positively of Col. Garland, Majors Wade, Waite, Loring and Gladden, of Capts. Mason, Walker, Danley, and of Lieuts. Foster, Shackelford, Selden and Lugeneel, and I mention them as being some of the most severely wounded.

I send you a few papers and documents of interest, which, I trust, will reach safely. Had I an opportunity, I could furnish you with a volume of letters, papers, &c., all found in the palace and other places, which would be a rare treat to our readers. You shall have them all in good time. I send you a species of diary from the 30th August up to this date in the shape of letters, written day to day. In the main, I believe I was correct in my surmises, although not always right. I write in great haste, as the courier is just starting.

Yours, &c. G.W.K.

D. SCULLY

"LETTERS FROM MEXICO"

NEW ORLEANS *PICAYUNE*, MARCH 23, 1848

When Christopher Haile defected to the infantry, George W. Kendall quickly turned to D. Scully as his point man at Veracruz. Scully had managed the Picayune's *Point Isabel headquarters, which followed General Zachary Taylor's march through northern Mexico. It was Scully's job to gather the other correspondents' letters and dispatches, combine them with his own, and forward them all to New Orleans. Scully's attention now shifted to General Winfield Scott and his trek from Veracruz to Mexico City.*

In the aftermath of the battles at Monterrey and Veracruz, Scully's letters made heroes of the officers whose exploits he described. This created envy among other army officers—which the Picayune's *competitors used to their advantage. Generally, such unbalanced stories were not deliberate but rather were the result of imperfections in the courier system. The Mexican War reporters might have been the first modern war correspondents, but their methods of operation were still limited.*

THE BIRTH OF GEORGE WASHINGton was yesterday celebrated in the city of Mexico by men composing what has been magnificently termed "the proudest army in the world!" Early in the morning Gen. F. P. Smith's brigade proceeded to the fields in the immediate vicinity of the city, on the Penon road, and after witnessing some fine target shooting by Capt. Taylor's battery (of the brigade) returned and marched through the streets in lively and patriotic airs. On arriving at the plaza a national salute was fired, and it was highly amusing to witness the effect of the rapid discharge of the artillery upon the Mexicans. They had heard that Gen. Scott was recalled, and that Gen.

Butler was appointed chief in command, and at once concluded that a revolution was raging. Knowing from sad experience that if the Yankees fired guns in anger the result would not be so harmless as their own social wars, they rushed in every direction to their homes for protection. In a few minutes scarcely a Mexican was to be seen in the streets, not a few of the shops were closed, and the market women abandoned their fruits and vegetables to the care of leperos and ladrones. Some, however, whose curiosity was greater than their fears, carefully approached the plaza, and discovering that no harm was being done to friend or foe, spread the news and alarm was banished. Almost every corps in the city and its vicinity had a dinner in honor of the occasion, and during the evening rockets blazed from the palace and the engineer quarters until the midnight bells announced the entrance of another day. It was not alone the birth of the greatest and purest of the men that was being celebrated; yesterday, a year ago, opened the battle of Buena Vista, and the gallant men who fought their way into this city, knee deep in blood, mingled with their manifestations of respect for "the father of his country," rejoicings in a victory that has given quality to American arms and has proved the prowess of the citizen soldier.

Commissioners have met here to negotiate armistice. The commissioners on our side are Gens. Worth and Smith, and in behalf of the Mexicans Gen. Mora y Villamil and Senor Quijano. As an armistice is not required by us, it is said our commissioners will neither make propositions nor suggest what will be acceptable; the Mexicans will therefore have to play the Yankee and try their hand, or rather their heads, at guessing—a faculty they have hitherto displayed a costly deficiency in.

Herewith you will find a copy of the order of Gen. Butler on assuming the command of the army. The sentiments expressed by him are such as were expected by his modesty and generosity, and becomes one who, whenever occasion offered, ... freely spilled his blood in his country's cause. It is no disparagement to Gen. Butler to say that the whole army regrets the withdrawal of Gen. Scott. The late commander-in-chief has shared with this army a year of privations, hardships, and fatigues, and, to use the words of Gen. Butler himself, he has brought to a glorious termination one of the bloodiest campaigns to be found in the annals of war.

Yesterday an incident occurred as Gen. Smith's brigade was returning to the plaza, the relation of which was hearkened to every American in Mexico with delight. The Rifles—a regiment that landed at Vera Cruz nearly 800 strong, and has been cut down to little over 200—on coming opposite the quarters of Gen. Scott, unable to restrain themselves, broke through the barriers of discipline with the same impetuosity they have many a time rushed over an enemy's battery, and halting, gave three as hearty cheers as were ever heard from stout fellows with big lungs.

Gen. Butler has made no changes in the staff officers. He still retains Major Thomas, a gentleman having the reputation of an able and efficient officer, as his adjutant general. Lieut. Lay, late military secretary of Gen. Scott, occupies the same position in the staff of the new commander-in-chief. Lieut. Butler, nephew of the general, Dr. Hunt, Mr. Wickliffe and Mr. Meriwether continue to be his aides—the three latter are volunteers.

An order has been drafted which will be gratifying to the officers and soldiers on this line, and to their friends at home, in affording a regular semi-monthly mail to and from Vera Cruz, to be dispatched with the greatest possible celerity.

D.S.

IN RETROSPECT

The biggest scoop of the Mexican War can be credited to the Baltimore *Sun*. In April 1847, a pony express rider brought the news that Veracruz had fallen. The capture of this fortress was a decisive victory for the invading forces; aware that his rider was at least a day ahead of the War Department courier, the Baltimore publisher sent a telegram to President Polk. It was the first news of the victory to reach the White House. The *Sun*, curiously enough, printed the news on page two, in the column where editorials ordinarily appeared. But the column was topped with running ponies and gave the news in fourteen different typefaces. The first six read:

By Special Overland Expresses of
Nearly One Thousand Miles
Exclusively for The Baltimore Sun
Independent of All Telegraphic Communication!

Unparalleled Effort of
Newspaper Enterprise

Highly Important
From the South

Unparalleled Achievement
of the
American Arms!

The Greatest Military Exploit
of the
Present Century

Fall, Surrender,
And Unconditional Capitulation of
The City of Vera Cruz
and
The Castle of San Juan D'Ulloa

It had taken twelve days for the news to reach Baltimore by runner, steamer, and pony express, illustrating the energy and aggressiveness that characterized news coverage during the Mexican War. Newspaper publishers and editors could now provide more facts and more accurate information than the public had ever seen before.

After the fighting ended, some American soldiers stayed on to try their luck in Mexico or California, but most went home—to new assignments if they were regulars or to be mustered out if they were volunteers. Many volunteers, when they signed up, had been promised both a certificate redeemable for up to 160 acres of land and travel money to get them home from the point of discharge. One newspaper estimated that with these benefits, plus a bonus of three months' wages, a private in the Massachusetts volunteers was due at least $170. "No army ever mustered out of service," the newspaper stated approvingly, "was better paid than that of the United States."

Reality, however, did not always match the promise. Some volunteers were released in their regiment's home state and consequently got no travel pay. As one officer wrote to the secretary of war, the denial of travel money meant that the men "will not be enabled to clothe themselves with decent clothing without disposing of their land scrip." Indeed, many cash-short veterans were fleeced out of their grants by unscrupulous speculators who paid half value or less to soldiers who were ignorant of the grants' true worth.

When the troops did reach home, they were feted as heroes. Parades were commonplace. Nashville threw a great barbecue. In Charleston, South Carolina, "a Grand Torch light Procession marched through the principal streets to the Gardens where a splendid display of Fire Works took place."

But such excitement did not last. Soon the men who had marched with Taylor and Scott, Fremont and Kearny went their separate ways—many to pioneer the recently enlarged West, and some to climb to new heights of glory and despair in the Civil War.

THE CIVIL WAR

THE WAR BETWEEN THE STATES

1861–1865

O F ALL THE CONFLICTS IN AMERICAN HISTORY, the Civil War intrigues writers and historians more than any other. In the North, Yankees resolved to quash the "Great Rebellion." In the South, rebels rallied for a cause they called the "War for Southern Independence." By any name, it was the costliest military confrontation ever to take place on the North American continent. More Americans died in the Civil War, it is often noted, than in all other wars fought by the United States since the fall of Yorktown. The emotions, sights, and sounds of the war are captured in the following dispatches.

The four-year-long clash between the states marked a transitional stage of warfare, away from the Napoleonic style toward modern machine battle. In 1861 war was still a personal conflict. Regiments were categorized by state; often a town's entire population of young men composed a company. The telegraph and railroads made transportation of men and machines much faster and gave the North a technological superiority that the South's better-qualified generals could never overcome. The advanced, deadlier weaponry, such as more accurate rifles and cannons, changed military strategy and gave the North's less indoctrinated field officers a further advantage over their Southern counterparts.

The stakes in this war, men and women on both sides felt, were just too great to ignore. In the North, fighting was a question of patriotism. In the South it was a question of honor. Love of one's homeland was a common underlying theme; as in most wars, the cause was just, for both sides. Said John Brown: "It is my sympathy with the oppressed and the wronged, that are as good as you and as precious in the sight of God." Yet the decisive factor was never the level of ideological fervor or fanaticism. "What we need," William T. Sherman said with firm determination, "is cool thoughtful soldiers—no more hurrahing."

The newspapers that covered the Civil War differed greatly from those that had informed the public on the developments of the American Revolution. Large staffs produced many of the Civil War newspapers, often printing daily editions. By the second half of the nineteenth century, newspapers overwhelmed their readers with column after column and page after page of timely, substantive news reporting. The residents of northern and southern cities turned first to the newspaper for the latest news. The development of an extensive network of telegraph lines allowed the reporter in the 1860s to transmit at least his shorter dispatches straight from the front lines to his newspaper by telegraph. Even when he hand-delivered his dispatches, he could do so speedily because the railroads made cross-country travel much quicker than ever before. Correspondents harbored a keen desire to get the scoop. The best reporters were not always those whose dispatches represented the best writing, they were those who got their reports to their newspapers before their competitors. The paper that was the first to get the latest information was the most successful.

Reporting by and large reflected the sectional sentiments of the correspondents, although editorials critical of both governments' war policies were abundant on both sides of the Mason-Dixon Line. No federal ban on sedition was enacted, partly because Lincoln was a strong advocate of a free press and mostly because enforcement of such a ban would have been politically and practically impossible. The Associated Press, centered in New York, disseminated telegraph and rail-post dispatches from the hundreds of "specials" who followed the fighting. Seceding from this network, the publishers in Dixie formed the Press Association of the Confederate States. Northern and southern papers trumpeted their armies' victories and preached their sections' perspective. At stake was the popular understanding of American democracy and government. Wartime governors on both sides occasionally censored papers that published compromising information or false proclamations, or that violated the proper bounds of a loyal opposition. More than once the public, not state officials, pilloried editors who took unpopular stands: the offices of Horace Greeley's New York *Tribune* were stoned by a mob during the 1863 draft riots for its support of the administration's measure.

Civil War newspapers printed news whether it was good or bad. Reporting in the 1860s was not entirely objective or accurate, but it was a marked improvement over that of years gone by. Correspondents from northern newspapers thought nothing of lambasting blue-coated generals or dwelling on the carnage of a particularly costly battle. They might passionately denounce the inhumanity of the rebels in one breath while blaming the president or a general for costly Union losses. Generally unhampered by censorship, reporters were usually allowed the freedom to be candid in their dispatches.

During the Mexican War, the individual war correspondent had begun to emerge as a distinct figure on the battlefield, and this trend continued in the Civil War. Some newspapers printed bylines, particularly for its more noted reporters. Sometimes the identity of the reporter was concealed behind a nom de plume. Still, a remarkable number of reports were ascribed simply to a "special correspondent." The greatest share of the hundreds of reporters who were eyewitnesses to campaigns and battles remained unknown to the general public. Presented to readers in black and white, the harsh realities of actual warfare changed their romantic notions of combat. Mourning fallen brothers and sons, northern and southern composers produced doleful ballads. Both sides claimed authorship of "The Picket Guard," a poem often put to music, which contemplated the relative insignificance of one private's death on an otherwise uneventful night. Indeed, the loss of life in the Civil War was staggering. By the time Lee surrendered to Grant at Appomattox, 650,000 soldiers had been killed. Twenty-six thousand fell in a single day at Antietam Creek. Millions of wounded men survived as amputees. Like living ghosts, they reminded the broken Republic of its bloody sacrifices near the white church at Shiloh and on the green fields of Gettysburg. For a generation, the country grieved for the trampled "flower of the nation's manhood." In the ensuing decades, citizens would erect thousands of granite and marble markers in memory of the blue and gray veterans who lay dead.

Slavery, the institution at the root of the conflict, also lay dead. In 1863 Lincoln's

Soldiers in the trenches before battle at Petersburg. *(National Archives)*

Emancipation Proclamation made abolition a central Union war aim. The flight of thousands upon thousands of African-Americans from plantations to federal armies profoundly weakened the "peculiar institution." In the waning days of the fight, even the Confederate government offered freedom to any slaves who would bear arms against the Union. Its economic and social landscape devastated, the defeated South endured a long and costly Reconstruction, in which African-Americans would only briefly enjoy their hard-won voting and political rights.

As the nation cleaned its littered battlefields and rebuilt its burned bridges, the shattered national community searched for lasting meaning in its apocalyptic experience. It would be many years before Americans would again take up arms with as much zeal.

Despite the flaws and abuses of the Reconstruction era, the war did ultimately bring cohesion to the nation. Like the mortally wounded Confederate and Federal soldiers, placed side by side to die together, the healing nation put down its weapons and put away the past. Previous animosity seemed to slowly dissipate, unlike shared memories of the fury of war itself.

"HARPERS FERRY OUTBREAK"

NEW YORK *HERALD*, OCTOBER 21, 1859

In the years leading up to the Civil War, newspapers in the North included Republican organs that opposed slavery and Democratic organs that argued for unity and tolerance of slavery. One of the leading Democratic newspapers was James Gordon Bennett's New York Herald.

John Brown's October 1859 attack on the federal arsenal with a force of twenty-one men was particularly odious to northern Democrats. The day after his capture, a group of political leaders and reporters secured permission from Colonel Robert E. Lee to interview Brown. The men found him with one of his men, Aaron D. Stephens, lying wounded on mattresses on the floor. One of Brown's questioners was an unknown reporter for the New York Herald. *The others included former congressman Charles J. Faulkner of Virginia, Senator James M. Mason of Virginia, and Congressman Clement L. Vallandigham of Ohio. No one present had any sympathy for John Brown.*

The interview with Brown was one of many stories on the abolitionist militant and his friends that appeared in the New York Herald. *Newspaper reporters were able to establish links between Brown and a number of well-known northern abolitionists who had provided him with financial support.*

John Brown was tried, convicted, and hung on December 2, 1859, while Aaron D. Stephens went to the gallows a few days later. In the eyes of many abolitionists, Brown was a martyr whose spirit would live on as an inspiration. For defenders of slavery he was emblematic of the northern fanaticism that boldly threatened the South.

VERBATIM REPORT OF THE QUESTIONING OF OLD BROWN BY SENATOR MASON, CONGRESSMAN VALLANDIGHAM, AND OTHERS

From Our Special Correspondent

HARPERS FERRY, October 19, 1859

"OLD BROWN," OR "OSAWATOmie Brown," as he is often called, the hero of a dozen fights or so with the "border ruffians" of Missouri, in the days of "bleeding Kansas," is the head and front of this offending [sic]—the commander of the abolition filibuster army. His wounds, which first were supposed to be mortal, turn out to be mere flesh wounds and scratches, not at all dangerous in their character. He has been removed, together with Stephens, the other wounded prisoner, from the engine room to the office of the armory, and they now lie on the floor, upon miserable shakedowns, covered with some old bedding.

Brown is fifty-five years of age, rather small-sized, with keen and restless gray eyes, and a grizzly beard and hair. He is a wiry, active man, and should the slightest chance for an escape be afforded, there is no doubt that he will yet give his captors much trouble. His hair is matted and tangled, and his face, hands, and clothes are smutched and smeared with blood.

Colonel Lee stated that he would exclude all visitors from the room if the wounded men were annoyed or pained by them, but Brown said he was by no means annoyed; on the contrary, he was glad to be able to make himself and his motives clearly understood. He converses freely, fluently, and cheerfully, without the slightest manifestation of fear or uneasiness, evidently weighing well his words, and possessing a good command of language. His manner is courteous and affable, while he appears to be making a favorable impression upon his auditory, which, during most of the day yesterday averaged about ten or a dozen men.

When I arrived in the armory, shortly after two o'clock in the afternoon, Brown was answering questions put to him by Senator Mason, who had just arrived from his residence at Winchester, thirty miles distant, Colonel Faulkner, member of Congress who lives but a few miles off, Mr. Vallandigham, member of Congress of Ohio, and several other distinguished gentlemen. The following is a verbatim report of the conversation:

Mr. Mason: Can you tell us, at least, who furnished the money for your expedition?

Mr. Brown: I furnished most of it myself. I cannot implicate others. It is by my own folly that I have been taken. I could easily have saved myself from it had I exercised my own better judgment rather than yield to my feelings. I should have gone away, but I had thirty-odd prisoners, whose wives and daughters were in tears for their safety, and I felt for them. Besides, I wanted to allay the fears of those who believed we came here to burn and kill. For this reason I allowed the train to cross the bridge and gave them full liberty to pass on. I did it only to spare the feelings of these passengers and their families and to allay the apprehensions that you had got here in your vicinity a band of men who had no regard for life and property, nor any feeling of humanity.

Mr. Mason: But you killed some people passing along the streets quietly.

Mr. Brown: Well, sir, if there was anything of that kind done, it was without my knowledge. Your own citizens, who were my prisoners, will tell you that every possible means were taken to prevent it. I did not allow my men to fire, nor even to return a fire, when there was danger of killing those we regarded as innocent persons, if I could help it. They will tell you that we allowed ourselves to be fired at repeatedly and did not return it.

A Bystander: That is not so. You killed an unarmed man at the corner of the house over there [at the water tank] and another besides.

Mr. Brown: See here, my friend, it is useless to dispute or contradict the report of your own neighbors who were my prisoners.

Mr. Mason: If you would tell us who sent you here—who provided the means—that would be information of some value.

Mr. Brown: I will answer freely and faithfully about what concerns myself—I will answer anything I can with honor, but not about others.

Mr. Vallandigham (member of Congress from Ohio, who had just entered): Mr. Brown, who sent you here?

Mr. Brown: No man sent me here; it was my own prompting and that of my Maker, or that of the devil, whichever you please to ascribe it to. I acknowledge no man [master] in human form.

Mr. Vallandigham: Did you get up the expedition yourself?

Mr. Brown: I did.

Mr. Mason: What was your object in coming?

Mr. Brown: We came to free the slaves, and only that.

A Young Man (in the uniform of a volunteer company): How many men in all had you?

Mr. Brown: I came to Virginia with eighteen men only, besides myself.

Volunteer: What in the world did you suppose you could do here in Virginia with that amount of men?

Mr. Brown: Young man, I don't wish to discuss that question here.

Volunteer: You could not do anything.

Mr. Brown: Well, perhaps your ideas and mine on military subjects would differ materially.

Mr. Mason: How do you justify your acts?

Mr. Brown: I think, my friend, you are guilty of a great wrong against God and humanity. I say it without wishing to be offensive—and it would be perfectly right for anyone to interfere with you so far as to free those you willfully and wickedly hold in bondage. I do not say this insultingly. I think I did right and that others will do right who interfere with you at any time and all times. I hold that the golden rule, "Do unto others as you would that others should do unto you," applies to all who would help others to gain their liberty.

Lieut. Stewart: But you don't believe in the Bible.

Mr. Brown: Certainly I do.

Mr. Vallandigham: Have you had any correspondence with parties at the North on the subject of this movement?

Mr. Brown: I have had correspondence.

Bystander: Do you consider yourself an instrument in the hands of Providence?

Mr. Brown: I do.

Bystander: Upon what principle do you justify your acts?

Mr. Brown: Upon the golden rule. I pity the poor in bondage that have none to help them; that is why I am here; not to gratify any personal animosity, revenge, or vindictive spirit. It is my sympathy with the oppressed and the wronged, that are as good as you and as precious in the sight of God. [Brown then proceeded to deny that he ever took any slaves against their will, to justify secrecy as necessary to success, and, when told of Gerrit Smith's published letter criticizing moral suasion as hopeless and advocating an insurrection in the South as the only effective way of Negro emancipation, declared:] I should concur with it. I agree with Mr. Smith that moral suasion is hopeless. I don't think the people of the slave states will ever consider the subject of slavery in its true light till some other argument is resorted to than moral suasion.

Mr. Vallandigham: Did you expect a general rising of the slaves in case of your success?

Mr. Brown: No, sir; nor did I wish it; I expected to gather them up from time to time and set them free.

Mr. Vallandigham: Did you expect to hold possession here till then?

Mr. Brown: Well, probably I had quite a different idea. I do not know that I ought to reveal my plans. I am here a prisoner and wounded, because I foolishly allowed myself to be so. You overrate your strength in supposing I could have been taken if I had not allowed it. [Brown ad-

John Brown on the courthouse
steps. *(Library of Congress)*

mitted that he had purchased the arms that enabled him to seize the armory, but refused to say just where he had obtained them.]

Reporter of the Herald: I do not wish to annoy you; but if you have anything further you would like to say I will report it.

Mr. Brown: I have nothing to say, only that I claim to be here in carrying out a measure I believe perfectly justifiable, and not to act that part of an incendiary or ruffian, but to aid those suffering great wrong. I wish to say, furthermore, that you had better—all you people at the South—prepare yourselves for a settlement of that question that must come up for settlement sooner than you are prepared for it. The sooner you are prepared, the better. You may dispose of me very easily. I am nearly disposed of now; but this question is still to be settled—this Negro question, I mean; the end of that is not yet.

Q.: Brown, suppose you had every nigger in the United States, what would you do with them?

A.: Set them free.

B. S. OSBON

"THE BALL IS OPENED. WAR IS INAUGURATED."

NEW YORK *WORLD*, APRIL 13, 1861

Wars often begin with an air of excitement. At the outset of the Civil War, young men were eager to put on the blue uniform of the Union army or the gray uniform of the Confederate army. The people of the two parts of the fractured nation shared the enthusiasm of their young men. Those who witnessed the bombardment of Fort Sumter felt the elation of seeing history in the making.

Bradley Sillick Osbon was one of those who watched the spectacle of Fort Sumter from the harbor of Charleston. The reporter's dispatch was one of the first to announce the beginning of the war.

THE BALL IS OPENED.
WAR IS INAUGURATED.

CHARLESTON, April 12

THE BATTERIES OF SULLIVAN'S Island, Morris Island, and other points were opened on Fort Sumter at four o'clock this morning. Fort Sumter has returned the fire, and a brisk cannonading has been kept up.

The military are under arms, and the whole of our population are on the streets. Every available space facing the harbor is filled with anxious spectators.

The firing has continued all day without intermission.

Two of Fort Sumter's guns have been silenced, and it is reported that a breach has been made in the southeast wall.

The answer to General Beauregard's demand by Major Anderson was that he would surrender when his supplies were exhausted; that is, if he was not reinforced.

CHARLESTON, April 12, 3 P.M.

CIVIL WAR HAS AT LAST BEGUN. A terrible fight is at this moment going on between Fort Sumter and the fortifications by which it is surrounded. The issue was submitted to Major Anderson of surrendering as soon as his supplies were exhausted, or of having fire opened on him within a certain time. He refused to surrender, and accordingly at twenty-seven minutes past four o'clock this morning Fort Moultrie began the bombardment by firing two guns.

Major Anderson has the greater part of the day been directing his fire principally against Fort Moultrie, the Stevens and floating battery, these and Fort Johnson being the only ones operating against him. The remainder of the batteries are held in reserve.

The Stevens battery is eminently successful and does terrible execution on Fort Sumter. Breaches, to all appearances, are being made in the several sides exposed to fire. Portions of the parapet have been destroyed, and several of the guns there mounted have been shot away.

The excitement in the community is indescribable. With the first boom of the gun, thousands rushed from their beds to the harbor front, and all day every available place has been thronged by ladies and gentlemen, viewing the solemn spectacle through their glasses. Most of these have relatives in the several fortifications, and many a tearful eye attested the anxious affection of the mother, wife, and sister, but not a murmur came from a single individual.

Business is entirely suspended. Only those stores are open necessary to supply articles required by the army.

Troops are pouring into the town by hundreds, but are held in reserve for the present, the force already on the islands being ample. The thunder of the artillery can be heard for fifty miles around, and the scene is magnificently terrible.

HENRY VILLARD

"THE NEW YORK *HERALD*'S HENRY VILLARD SCORES A STUNNING BEAT"

NEW YORK *HERALD*, JULY 20, 1861

On July 18, 1861, a twenty-six-year-old German-born reporter was among a number of newspapermen and congressmen attached to Colonel Israel Richardson's brigade. General Daniel Tyler's First Division of Union forces, which included Richardson's brigade, advanced from Centreville toward Confederate forces said to be on the far side of a creek called Bull Run, at Blackburn's Ford. Henry Villard had just climbed a cherry tree to pick some fruit when concealed rebels opened fire on the advancing Union skirmishers. Scrambling for cover behind a farm building, the young reporter rejoined two of his colleagues, Edmund Clarence Stedman and Edward Howard House, both of the New York Tribune. *The three reporters remained pinned down until Union forces withdrew late in the afternoon. Nevertheless, they came away with stories for a public anxious to hear of one of the first major actions of the war.*

This clash at Blackburn's Ford between Union and Confederate troops was a prelude to the first important battle of the Civil War fought three days later at the same place. Villard would be present to report on the defeat of Union forces in that First Battle of Bull Run. Other reporters, anxious to get the scoop, had prematurely reported a Union victory. But the German-born correspondent, who had waited to see the final outcome of the battle, witnessed the disorderly retreat of General Irvin McDowell's defeated northern army.

Perhaps Henry Villard's report on the action on the eighteenth of July is most interesting for what it does not say. He does not suggest that he was in danger during the attack. He did not seem to know that General Irvin McDowell had ordered Tyler only to proceed to

Centreville, and not to continue on and engage the enemy. Indeed, the commanding general was displeased to learn that Tyler's forces had suffered eighty-three casualties in this engagement. Villard, who never caught a glimpse of the Confederate opponents concealed in the woods, did not know that Brigadier General P. G. T. Beauregard was in command across Bull Run. His eyewitness account of the action was from the worm's-eye view.

CENTREVILLE, SIX AND A HALF MILES FROM MANASSAS JUNCTION, THURSDAY, July 18, 5 P.M.

I HAVE JUST RETURNED FROM THE thickest of an action of considerable moment, between a portion of the rebel forces and the Fourth Brigade of General Tyler's division, composed of the Second and Third Michigan, the First Massachusetts, and Twelfth New York Volunteer regiments, under command of Colonel Richardson; and as the aide of General McDowell, who will carry the official report of the affair to General Scott, and who offers the only means of communication with Washington this evening, is about starting, I have only time to send you the following brief particular of to-day's operation. . . .

At eleven o'clock General Tyler proceeded to make a reconnaissance in force, with Captain Ayres' (late Sherman's) battery, four companies of cavalry, and Colonel Richardson's brigade, composed as above stated. Advancing up the road to Bulls Run for about two miles, the column came to an opening, after passing through a long stretch of timber, when sight was caught of a strong body of the enemy. General Tyler immediately ordered Captain Ayres' battery to advance and open on them, which they did from a commanding elevation. Eight shells had been thrown, when suddenly a volley was fired upon us from a hidden battery, about a mile down the road.

Our howitzers then threw some grape-shot into the timber, when at once a terrific series of volleys of musketry was poured out from the woods upon the troops outside. At the same time a battery commenced playing upon us from an elevation in the rear. Shot of every description flew about us for some minutes like hail; but it being, fortunately, nearly all aimed too high, hardly anyone was struck outside the woods.

A retreat was now ordered, when infantry, cavalry, and artillery fell back behind our battery on the hill. The Twelfth New York and a portion of the First Massachusetts broke ranks and scattered in different directions, in their hasty retreat, for some distance through the woods, in the rear of the battery.

Our troops fought under great disadvantage. Not one rebel ventured out of the woods during the action. *The affair was not an attack, but merely a reconnaissance* to discover the position and strength of the enemy.

HEADQUARTERS OF THE GRAND ARMY, CENTREVILLE, July 19, 8 A.M.

M UCH OF THE HASTE AND *confusion of the retreat was due to the inefficiency and cowardice of some of the officers.*

I can personally testify to the more than ordinary coolness and gallantry shown by Colonel Richardson during the action. A shower of rifle balls was constantly aimed at him, but they did not for a moment deter him from his whole duty. General Tyler also showed great courage on the occasion. He was exposed to the enemy's fire for nearly four hours.

The representatives of the press stood their ground as well as any, in spite of the shot, shell, and rifle balls that kept whizzing past them for hours.

GEORGE W. SMALLEY

"THE CONTEST IN MARYLAND"

NEW YORK _TRIBUNE_, SEPTEMBER 20, 1862

The bloodiest single day of the Civil War was September 17, 1862. The armies of General George McClellan and General Robert E. Lee clashed near Sharpsburg, Maryland, in an engagement that goes down in history as the Battle of Antietam.

Covering this bloody battle for the New York Tribune *was George W. Smalley, who had graduated from Yale, studied law at Harvard, and practiced law in Boston before the war. The attorney-turned-journalist not only was present to witness the Battle of Antietam but also delivered several orders for General Joseph Hooker in the heat of the battle.*

Smalley's dispatch describing the battle was particularly distinguished for two reasons. It was the first full account of the action to reach Washington, D.C., and President Lincoln. Smalley's report was also one of the finest pieces of writing to come out of the war, both in terms of clarity and accuracy. The following represents just part of the story that took up over five columns in the Tribune. *Numerous other newspapers reprinted Smalley's remarkable story as well.*

FIERCE AND DESPERATE BATTLE between 200,000 men has raged since daylight, yet night closes on an uncertain field. It is the greatest fight since Waterloo—all over the field contested with an obstinacy equal even to Waterloo. If not wholly a victory tonight, I believe it is the prelude to a victory tomorrow. But what can be foretold of the future of a fight which from 5 in the morning till 7 at night the best troops of the continent have fought without decisive result? . . .

The battle began with the dawn. Morning found both armies just as they had slept, almost close enough to look into each other's eyes. The left of Meade's reserves and the right of Rickett's line became engaged at nearly the same moment, one with artillery, the other with infantry. A battery was almost immediately pushed forward beyond the central woods, over a plowed field, near the top of the slope where the cornfield began. On this open field, in the corn beyond, and in the woods which stretched forward into the broad fields, like a promontory into the ocean, were the hardest and deadliest struggles of the day.

For half an hour after the battle had grown to its full strength, the line of fire swayed neither way. Hooker's men were fully up to their work. They saw their General everywhere in front, never away from the fire, and all the troops believed in their commander, and fought with a will. Two-thirds of them were the same men who under McDowell had broken at Manassas.

The half hour passed, the Rebels began to give way a little, only a little, but at the first indication of a receding fire, Forward, was the word, and on went the line with a cheer and a rush. Back across the cornfield, leaving dead and wounded behind them, over the fence, and across the road, and then back again into the dark woods which closed around them, went the retreating Rebels.

Meade and his Pennsylvanians followed hard and fast—followed till they came within easy range of the woods, among which they saw their beaten enemy disappearing—followed still, with another cheer, and flung themselves against the cover.

But out of those glooms woods came suddenly and heavily terrible volleys—volleys which smote, and bent, and broke in a moment that eager front, and hurled them swiftly back for half the distance they had won. Not swiftly, nor in panic, any further. Closing up their shattered lines, they came slowly away—a regiment where a brigade had been, hardly a brigade where a whole division had been victorious. They had met from the woods the first volleys of musketry from fresh troops—had met them and returned them till their line had yielded and gone down before the weight of fire, and till their ammunition was exhausted.

In ten minutes the fortune of the day seemed to have changed—it was the Rebels now who were advancing; pouring out of the woods in endless lines, sweeping through the cornfield from which their comrades had just fled. Hooker sent in his nearest brigade to meet them, but it could not do the work. He called for another. There was nothing close enough, unless he took it from his right. His right might be in danger if it was weakened, but his center was already threatened with annihilation. Not hesitating one moment, he sent to Doubleday: "Give me your best brigade instantly."

The best brigade came down the hill to the right on the run, went through the timber in front through a storm of shot and bursting shell and crashing limbs, over the open field beyond, and straight into the cornfield, passing as they went the fragments of three brigades shattered by the Rebel fire, and streaming to the rear. They passed by Hooker, whose eyes lighted as he saw these veteran troops led by a soldier whom he knew he could trust. "I think they will hold it," he said.

Gen. Hartstuff took his troops very steadily, but now that they were under fire, not hurriedly, up the hill from which the cornfield begins to descend, and formed them on the crest. Not a man who was not in full view—not one who bent before the storm. Firing at first in volleys, they fired them at will with wonderful rapidity and effect. The whole line crowned the hill and stood out darkly against the sky, but lighted and shrouded ever in flame and smoke. There were 12th and 13th Massachusetts and another regiment which I cannot remember—old troops all of them.

There for half an hour they held the ridge unyielding in purpose, exhaustless in courage. There were gaps in the line, but it nowhere quailed. There this General was wounded badly early in the fight, but they fought on. Their supports did not come—they determined to win without

The Battle of Gettysburg.
(Library of Congress)

them. They began to go down the hill and into the corn, they did not stop to think that their ammunition was nearly gone, they were there to win that field and they won it. The Rebel line for the second time fled through the corn and into the woods. I cannot tell how few of Hart-stuff's brigade were left when the work was done, but it was done. There was no more gallant, determined, heroic fighting in all this desperate day. Gen. Hartstuff is very severely wounded, but I do not believe he counts his success too dearly purchased.

The crisis of the fight at this point had arrived; Ricketts division, vainly endeavoring to advance, and exhausted by the effort, had fallen back. Part of Mansfield's corps was ordered to their relief, but Mansfield's troops came back again, and their General was mortally wounded. The left nevertheless was too extended to be turned, and too strong to be broken. Ricketts sent word he could not advance, but could hold his ground. Doubleday kept his guns at work on the right, and had finally silenced a Rebel battery that for half an hour had poured in a galling enfilading fire along Hooker's central line.

There were woods in front of Doubleday's hill which the Rebels held, but so long as those guns pointed that way they did not care to attack. With his left then able to take care of itself, with his right impregnable with two brigades of Mansfield still fresh and coming rapidly up, and with this center a second time victorious, Gen. Hooker determined to advance. Orders were sent to Crawford and Gordon—the two Mansfield brigades—to move directly forward at once, the batteries in the center were ordered on, the whole line was called on, and the General himself went forward.

To the right of the cornfield and beyond it was a point of woods. Once carried and firmly held, it was the key of the position. Hooker determined to take it. He rode out in front of his furthest troops on a hill to examine the ground for a battery. At the top he dismounted and went forward on foot, completed his reconnaissance, and returned and remounted. The musketry fire from the point of woods was all the while extremely hot. As he put his foot in the stirrup a fresh volley of rifle bullets came whizzing by. The tall soldierly figure of the General, the white horse which he rode, the elevated place where he was—all made him a most dangerously conspicuous mark. So he had been all day, riding often without a staff officer or an orderly near him—all sent off on urgent duty—visible everywhere on the field. The Rebel bullets had followed him all day, but they had not hit him, and he would not regard them. Remounting on this hill he had not ridden five steps when he was struck in the foot by a ball.

Three men were shot down at the same moment by his side. The air was alive with bullets. He kept on his horse for a few moments, though the wound was severe and excessively painful, and would not dismount till he had given his last order to advance. He was himself in the very front. Swaying unsteadily on his horse, he turned in his seat to look about him. "There is a regiment to the right. Order it forward! Crawford and Gordon are coming up. Tell them to carry these woods and hold them—and it is our fight!"

I see no reason why I should disguise my admiration of Gen. Hooker's bravery and soldierly ability. Remaining nearly all the morning on the right, I could not help seeing the sagacity and promptness of his maneuvers, how completely his troops were kept in hand, how devotedly they trusted to him, how keen was his insight into the battle; how every opportunity was seized and every reverse was checked and turned into another success. I say this the more unreservedly, because I have no personal relation whatever with him, never saw him till the day before the fight, and don't like his politics or opinions in general. But what are politics in such a battle? . . .

A LASTING RECORD OF A TRAGIC TIME

In the conflict of the 1860s, for the first time in history, the face of war was recorded in all its tragedy and grandeur by the sharp eye of the camera. Although a few pictures had been taken during the earlier Mexican War, photography then was limited in scope and quality. Civil War photographers captured the brutality of battle with shattering clarity despite the fact that their equipment was unwieldy and the processing incredibly difficult. The most famous of these photographers was Mathew Brady from New York, who covered the eastern war from Bull Run to Richmond at his own expense, producing unforgettable images of the war, sometimes shocking but always stirring.

The Civil War was the first American conflict involving citizen soldiers on a large scale—one American in twelve saw service, either Union or Confederate, and virtually every family had someone at the front. To satisfy their appetite for news of victories and defeats and how the menfolk were doing, a new breed of journalist came into prominence—the "special artist." His assignment was to go wherever the winds of combat blew and to sketch what he saw, whether battle, boredom, or bravado. One such notable artist was Winslow Homer, one of America's greatest artists. In 1861 he was an unknown young illustrator covering the Army of the Potomac. As every soldier knows, war is partly fighting, partly waiting—and Homer's pictures preserved an unmatched record of the Civil War's citizen-soldier in his unguarded moments between battles, in camp, on the move, and in the trenches. His work had a unique vitality. While other artists were busy drawing synthetic battle panoramas, with handsome soldiers in neat uniforms, Homer created combat scenes that had the smell of gunpowder and the shriek of death under trampling horses.

THOMAS W. KNOX

"THE BATTLE OF CHICKASAW BAYOU"

NEW YORK *HERALD*, JANUARY 18, 1863

Thomas W. Knox of the New York Herald *was to discover that the war correspondent was not always welcome at the wartime front. Before General William T. Sherman's expedition left Memphis for Vicksburg (shortly before Christmas 1862), the general issued the following order: "Any person whatever, whether in the service of the United States or transports, found making reports for publication which might reach the enemy giving them information and comfort, will be arrested and treated as spies." Knox, who arrived in Memphis only hours before the steamers departed downriver, was only vaguely aware of the order and thought it did not apply to him.*

Sherman's campaign to capture Vicksburg and give the Union full control over the Mississippi was a failure. Securely entrenched Confederate forces were able to resist a deter-

Wounded Zouave soldier. These were early Civil War volunteers who arrived in Washington wearing fancy uniforms copied from those of the French colonial troops in North Africa known as the Zouaves. Most American "Zouave" units eventually adopted regular Union dress: dark blue tunics and sky blue trousers. *(National Archives)*

mined Union assault at *Chickasaw Bayou as Sherman's men attempted to advance on the backside of Vicksburg.*

Knox collected information for his dispatch to the Herald *more from the accounts of eyewitnesses than from his own firsthand viewing of the fighting. Although the battle took place on December 28 and 29, 1862, Knox's account did not appear in print until nearly three weeks later. The following excerpts from this dispatch focus not on his coverage of troop movements and the battle but rather on the aftermath of the engagement and the abilities of General Sherman. These gratuitous comments would get the twenty-seven-year-old reporter into serious trouble.*

Less than two weeks after the New York Herald *published Knox's dispatch, General Sherman called the young correspondent on the carpet, pointing out numerous inaccuracies in what he had reported. In a letter to the general dated February 1, 1863, Knox readily admitted his "repeated errors." He went on to offer what amounted to a personal apology to Sherman: "I am fully convinced of your prompt, efficient, and judicious management of the troops under your control."*

Despite Knox's remorse, Sherman insisted on a general court-martial trying the reporter for "giving intelligence to the enemy, directly or indirectly," "being a spy," and "disobedience of orders." Found guilty in early February of only the third charge, the court sentenced Knox "to be sent without the lines of the army, and not to return under penalty of imprisonment." In March 1863 President Lincoln intervened in the case and allowed Knox to return to the headquarters of General Ulysses S. Grant, providing that Grant approved of his presence. Grant forcefully refused to allow the war correspondent for the Herald *to remain: "You came here first in positive violation of an order from General Sherman. Because you were not pleased with the treatment of army followers, who had violated his order, you attempted to break down his influence with his command, and to blast his reputation with the public. You made insinuations against his sanity, and said many things which were untrue, and, as far as your letter had influence, calculated to affect the public service unfavorably."*

ON TUESDAY MORNING LAST I mailed to the *Herald* a full account of the operations of the right wing of the Thirteenth army corps from the time it left Memphis to date. That letter, enclosed under cover to private parties in Cairo, was placed in the mail on board the steamer Forest Queen, General Sherman's flag boat, and was supposed to be safe from harm. Colonel A. H. Markland, special agent of the Postal Department, was in charge of the mails. I have ascertained that his clerk, by Colonel Markland's order, took that letter from the mail and turned it over to General Sherman. It was opened at the headquarters of Major General commanding, and has since been perused by his staff and by various officers of the army. If General Sherman has obtained from it any facts that may aid him in making up his official report he is welcome to the letter. Upon his proceeding in the matter I make no comment. I simply give the facts of the case. Major J. H. Hammond, chief of General Sherman's staff, has been prominent in the war upon the journalists by direction of his commanding officer. Had they all acted as earnestly and persistently against the rebels as against the representatives of the press, there is little doubt that Vicksburg would, ere this, have been in Union hands. . . .

Throughout the battle the conduct of the general officers was excellent, with a few exceptions. General Sherman was so exceedingly erratic that the discussion of the past twelve months with respect to his sanity, was revived with much earnestness. . . .

All through the long December day the wounded lay upon the hill uncared for by either contending party. The ground was that for which there had been so fierce a contest, and, while we could not take possession of it, the rebels did not choose to occupy it. Daybreak, sunrise, noon, sunset and night, and still the wounded uncared for. What must have been their suffering!

On the morning of Wednesday, the 31st of December the firing had been entirely stopped, and the rebels consented to receive a flag of truce. Five hours were allowed for burying the dead and taking away the wounded, and at the end of the time the work was accomplished. A few of the rebels came out and talked freely with the bearers of the flag. They stated that after the 1st of January they should shoot every officer captured, and put the privates at work on fortifications, with ball and chain, in retaliation for the emancipation proclamation of the President. They expressed the utmost confidence in their ability to hold Vicksburg against the force now before it. From their statements it was inferred that Price was in command at Vicksburg, and that Tilghman's division was to arrive there on that day. There were evidently strong grounds for their hopes. They were well

General Grant's council of war near Massaponax Church, Virginia in 1864. Grant is bending over General Meade's shoulder, reading a map. *(National Archives)*

posted as to our strength, and informed us of the exact number of our transports and gunboats, and gave the number of men in the expedition with surprising accuracy.

All the slightly wounded had been taken to Vicksburg as prisoners of war, and we were allowed to bring away only those that we found on the ground. The rain and cold combined, with fifty hours' continued exposure, had left but few men alive. Had the flag been taken out and received on the afternoon subsequent to the battle, there is little doubt that many lives would have been saved. Doctors Burke and Franklin attended as best they could to the wants of the sufferers. By some criminal oversight there had been little preparation for battle on the part of Sherman's medical director, and the hospitals were but poorly supplied with many needed stores. Since the battle General Sherman has persistently refused to allow a hospital boat to go above, though their detention in this region is daily fatal to many lives. The only known reason for his refusal is his fear that a knowledge of his management will reach the people of the North. . . .

Thursday, the 1st inst., was passed in lying idle in front of the enemy's position and on the transports at the landing. About three P.M. General Sherman issued orders for all the troops to embark on the original transports and make ready for moving. One of the commissaries had recently taken fifty thousand rations to a depot in the rear of the battlefield, only a mile and a quarter from the landing. General Sherman ordered these supplies destroyed by rolling them into the bayou, as there was no time for their removal. A part of the supplies were tumbled into the

bayou in obedience to instructions. . . . General Sherman also ordered commissary stores destroyed by General A. J. Smith's division, and there was much waste in consequence. All these stores might have been saved, and would have been, had General Sherman's orders been less preemptory.

For some days the camp had been full of rumors that General McClernand would shortly arrive and assume command of the right wing of the Thirteenth Army corps. Almost at the moment of the appearance of the order for evacuation we learned that General McClernand was at the mouth of the Yazoo, and that General Sherman had gone down to report to him. The brief authority of the latter officer had passed away, and a sane mind was not to conduct our operations. How unfortunate that General McClernand could not have arrived a week earlier. Had such been the case Vicksburg would doubtless be now in our possession, and the way open to the Gulf. . . .

Just as I am closing this account of the battle I have the pleasure of receiving the manuscript of my first letter, with a cool and refreshing note from Major Hammond. The letter is all right; but I fail to find two elaborate maps, drawn with great care. It is possible that General Sherman may need them for his instruction. Had he possessed them earlier it is possible that he would have taken Vicksburg. . . .

The second siege of Vicksburg is over. The battle of Chickasaw Bayou has been a repetition on a smaller scale of the great battle of Fredericksburg, a month ago. Had it been a success, the result could have been hardly less important than the defeat of the rebels at the latter place. It would have opened up the Mississippi river, the highway of America, now closed for nearly twenty months. The products of the great West, long pent up in the granaries of the wheat and corn growing States, would have found their natural outlet to the commerce of the world. Cincinnati, St. Louis and New Orleans would again have become the centres of active trade and shaken off their lethargy of the period of war. Our failure has dashed the hopes of the nation, and delayed for weeks the progress of our arms. When we again attack the steep bluffs and frowning batteries of Vicksburg we will do so with a better promise of success. Insanity and inefficiency have brought their result; let us have them no more. With another brain than that of General Sherman's, we will drop the disappointment at our reverse, and feel certain of victory in the future.

WHITELAW REID

"GETTYSBURG, LANDMARK BATTLE OF THE WAR"

CINCINNATI *GAZETTE*, JULY 5, 1863

Whitelaw Reid was just twenty-five years old when he covered the Battle of Gettysburg for the Cincinnati Gazette. Earlier in the war he had established his reputation with a nineteen thousand–word dispatch on the Battle of Shiloh in April 1862. His report, written under the pen name "Agate," was the best on that battle and was reprinted in newspapers other than the Gazette. Having proven his ability to get a story, Agate went to Washington, the best base from which to cover the war.

Though Reid missed the first day of action at Gettysburg, arriving late on the afternoon of July 1, he witnessed the next two days from atop Cemetery Hill. In his company during the battle was a much older reporter, Samuel Wilkeson of the New York Times, *who wrote: "My pen is heavy. Oh, you dead, who at Gettysburgh have baptised with your blood the second birth of Freedom in America, how you are to be envied! I rise from a grave whose wet clay I have passionately kissed, and look up and see Christ spanning this battlefield with his feet and reaching fraternal and lovingly up to heaven. His right hand opens the gates of paradise—with his left he beckons to these mutilated, bloody, swollen forms to ascend."*

After the battle, Reid rode by horseback to Westminster in order to catch the train to Baltimore, where he sent out his dispatch on the great battle, a report that took up fourteen columns in his newspaper.

. . . ASCENDING THE HIGH HILL TO the rear of Slocum's headquarters, I saw such a sight as few men may ever hope to see twice in a lifetime. Around our center and left, the rebel line must have been from four to five miles long, and over that whole length there rolled up the smoke from their two hundred and fifty guns.

The roar, the bursting bombs, the impression of magnificent power, "all the glory visible, all the horror of the fearful field concealed," a nation's existence trembling as the clangor of those iron monsters swayed the balance—it was a sensation for a century!

About two the fire slackened a little, then broke out deadlier than ever, till, beaten out against our impenetrable sides, it ebbed and closed in broken, spasmodic dashes.

The great, desperate, final charge came at four. The rebels seemed to have gathered up all their strength and desperation for one fierce, convulsive effort, that should sweep over and wash out our obstinate resistance. They swept up as before, the flower of their army to the front, victory staked upon the issue. In some places they literally lifted up and pushed back our lines, but that terrible "position" of ours!—wherever they entered it, enfilading fires from half a score of crests swept away their columns like merest chaff. Broken and hurled back, they easily fell into our hands, and on the center and left the last half-hour brought more prisoners than all the rest.

So it was along the whole line; but it was on the Second Corps that the flower of the rebel army was concentrated; it was there that the heaviest shock beat upon and shook and even sometimes crumbled our line.

We had some shallow rifle pits, with barricades of rails from the fences. The rebel line, stretching away miles to the left, in magnificent array, but strongest here—Pickett's splendid division of Longstreet's corps in front, the best of A. P. Hill's veterans in support—came steadily and, as it seemed, resistlessly sweeping up. Our skirmishers retired slowly from the Emmetsburg road, holding their ground tenaciously to the last. The rebels reserved their fire till they reached this same Emmetsburg road, then opened with a terrific crash. From a hundred iron throats, meantime, their artillery had been thundering on our barricades.

Hancock was wounded; Gibbon succeeded to the command—approved soldiers, and ready for the crisis. As the tempest of fire approached its height, he walked along the line, and renewed his orders to the men to reserve their fire. The rebels—three lines deep—came steadily up. They were in point-blank range.

At last the order came! From thrice six thousand guns there came a sheet of smoky flame, a crash of leaden death. The line literally melted away; but there came the second, resistless still. It had been our supreme effort—on the instant were not equal to another.

Up to the rifle pits, across them, over the barricades—the momentum of their charge, the mere machine strength of their combined action swept them on. Our thin line could fight, but it had not weight enough to oppose to this momentum. It was pushed behind the guns. Right on came the rebels. They were upon the guns, were bayoneting the gunners, were waving their flags above our pieces.

But they had penetrated to the fatal point. A storm of grape and canister tore its way from man to man and marked its track with corpses straight down their line! They had exposed themselves to the enfilading fire of the guns on the western slope of Cemetery Hill; that exposure sealed their fate.

The line reeled back—disjointed already—in an instant in fragments. Our men were just behind the guns. They leaped forward upon the disordered mass; but there was little need for fighting now. A regiment threw down its arms, and, with colors at its head, rushed over and surrendered. Webb's brigade brought in eight hundred taken in as little time as it requires to write the simple sentence that tells it. Gibbon's old division took fifteen stands of colors.

Over the field the escaped fragments of the charging line fell back—the battle there was over. A single brigade, Harrow's (of which the Seventh Michigan is part), came out with fifty-four less officers, 793 less men than it took in! So the whole corps fought—so, too, they fought further down the line.

It was fruitless sacrifice. They gathered up their broken fragments, formed their lines, and slowly marched away. It was not a rout, it was a bitter, crushing defeat. For once the Army of the Potomac had won a clean, honest, acknowledged victory.

H. J. WINSER

"OUR PRISONERS"

NEW YORK TIMES, NOVEMBER 26, 1864

Established in February 1864, Andersonville was the most infamous of Confederate prisoner-of-war camps. The camp was designed to hold ten thousand enlisted men, but within a few months more than twice that number were crammed into the limited space. Overcrowding, poor sanitation, disease, insufficient food, and the torrid summer heat played havoc with the health of the inmates.

The first reliable accounts of the atrocious conditions at Andersonville came at the time of a prisoner exchange near Savannah in November 1864. Henry J. Winser, a well-traveled war correspondent for the New York Times, *witnessed the exchange. Winser's story, which took up the entire first page, did not include his byline. Nevertheless, the* New York Times *attributed its front-page story to Winser elsewhere in the newspaper, adding the editorial comment that the "barbarities to helpless captives . . . would make the blood of a cannibal run cold."*

The treatment of Union prisoners at Andersonville outraged the people of the North. After the war, Captain Henry Wirz, the commander of the camp, was tried, convicted, and hung. The present-day national cemetery at Andersonville includes the graves of 12,912 prisoners of war who died there.

In addition to the following excerpts, the dispatch included a number of appeals by Confederate medical officers for the relief of the suffering soldiers in the camp during the summer of 1864 and figures for the number who died each day between late July and early September.

THE PAST FEW DAYS HAVE BEEN fraught with a very painful interest to everybody who has been connected in any way whatever with the exchange of our sick and wounded prisoners now in progress on the Savannah River. Col. Mulford began to receive our poor fellows last Friday, and the delivery is to continue at the rate of from eight hundred to twelve hundred per day, until the aggregate number of the wretched suffering creatures, estimated at ten thousand, return to our welcome keeping. I shall attempt in this letter to give some idea of the outward appearance, physical condition, animating spirit and expression of opinion of these soldiers of the Republic who have escaped from unutterable misery, with the sole object of presenting facts to the county which must result in the release of their fifty thousand comrades who cannot survive the coming Winter, under the conditions in which they are kept through the unparalleled vindictiveness of the Southern authorities. This is a hard charge, but I make it deliberately. The irrefragable proof is lying before me not alone in the ex parte testimony and wasted hungry aspect of the sufferers, whose filth and squalor and skeleton frames appeal for justice to the God of justice, but in the official papers of the rebel surgeons at Andersonville and the records of the charnel-houses, miscalled hospitals, at that terrestrial hell—records never meant to pass the limits of the Confederacy, but which a merciful Providence has brought to light, that out of their own mouths these barbarians, with whom we are at war, should be convicted. . . .

It is a distressing fact, but one of which I have found abundant proof in many conversations with the men so far brought back, that the prisoners very generally believe that they have been abandoned by our Government. This idea is sedulously inculcated by the rebel authorities. I am convinced that many a brave heart has succumbed under the cruel aspersion that the sympathies of the people are dead to their woes. Hunger, squalor, filth, nakedness and disease may be borne, but that hope deferred which results in heartsickness—that longing for home which superinduces mental depression, cannot long be survived. Nostalgia is the parent of physical ailments, and, under the terrible monotony and privations of the prison pens, it is more fatal than bullets on the field of battle. A very large proportion of these prisoners have been held as such for periods of from nine to sixteen months, and the exchange question between the two Governments as yet gives promise of a speedy settlement. The rebels assure the captives that they are prepared to yield all the points at issue, and have long since announced the fact to the United States Government, whose only reason for nonacceptance is one of simple expediency, viz: that by resuming the exchanges thousands of rugged, strong men would be sent into the armies of the South from the prison camps of the North and no equivalent would be received in the broken-down, emaciated wrecks of humanity that would be sent home from the pens at Andersonville, Columbus, Milan and Richmond. Is it a matter of marvel that under the innocence of this monstrous belief, hundreds of the disheartened soldiers endeavor to escape the horrors of the prisons by enlisting in the rebel service? Such is the fact and it behooves our Government to weigh it well. The exchanges are in abeyance on well-taken grounds, from which there can be no retraction without a sacrifice of national honor. But there are two sides to the question, and the national faith and honor are just as deeply plighted to the fifty thousand soldiers languishing and dying in captivity as it can possibly be in other quarters. Justice to the heroic men whom the fortune of war has placed in the hands of the enemy, demands that no effort should be relaxed to release them from a condition which will bring to the majority of them certain death during the fast approaching Winter. The resources of the North in men have scarcely been drawn upon as yet, in comparison with the resources of the South, and the question of expediency in releasing a few thousand Southern soldiers should not be entertained an instant, even if a draft in the Northern States were not able to put their equivalent in the field. . . .

When the rebel boat moves off and the men are huddled together on the decks of our own vessels, all fully understand that the last link which bound them to rebeldom has been severed, then rises hearty shouting and cheering, which only can be given under these circumstances. There is the music of intense gratefulness in it. Three cheers and a tiger for the old flag; there more and a tiger for Col. Mulford; then comes a burst of song, most often the words being "Rally round the flag, boys, from near and from far, down with the traitor and up with the star," the rebels still within hearing, probably gnashing their teeth at the pointed personal allusion, but everybody else feeling that the bad taste of the happy fellow is excusable, even though exhibited under the sacred folds of a flag of truce. Then vermin-infested rags, till now highly prized as the only cover for nakedness, are rudely torn off and flung into the water or cast with glee into the flaming furnaces of the steamers. and new clothes are issued, and a general cleaning-time inaugurated. But the bathing has long been needed and scarcely comes soon enough. Many of the men, through illness or carelessness, are so begrimed with filth, that, were it not for the dead color of the blackened epidermis, they might be taken for the sons of Ham. . . . It is a touching sight to see them, each with his quart can, file by the steaming coffee barrels, and receive the refreshing draught whose taste has long been unfamiliar. It seems scarcely possible that men should feel such childish joy as they express in once more receiving this common stimulant. And then, the eager, hungry glare which their glassy eyes cast upon the chunks of ham as they clutch and devour their allowance with a wolf-like avidity. . . .

Such is the condition of the men whom we are now receiving out of chivalrous Dixie. These the sons, brothers, husbands and fathers of the North. Men reduced to living skeletons; men almost naked; shoeless men, shirtless men, hatless men; men with no other garment than an overcoat; men whose skins are blackened by dirt and hang on their protruding bones loosely as bark on a tree; men whose very presence is simply disgusting, exhaling an odor so fetid that it almost stops the breath of those unaccustomed to it, and causes an involuntary brushing of the garments if with them there is accidental contact. Imagine 25,000 of such wretched creatures penned together in a space scarcely large enough to hold them, and

Death and destruction near Richmond, Virginia. *(National Archives)*

compare their conditions with the most miserable condition that can be imagined. The suffering of the Revolutionary captives on the prison ships at Wallabout Bay will not stand the comparison, and the horrible sight in the Blackhole of Calcutta scarcely exceeds it in atrocity. Remember, too, that the men thus returned are the beset specimens of the suffering. Only those are forwarded to us whom the rebel medical authorities decide to be strong enough to bear the fatigue of transportation. If those whose wretchedness I have vainly endeavored to portray, are the best specimens of our sick and wounded, is it not awful to contemplate what must be the woe of the remainder? . . .

The stockade or pen in which the prisoners at Andersonville are confined, is an enclosure of fourteen acres, five of which were a morass. Here the men were with-out shelter, and in many instances almost naked, huddled together without room for exercise. During the hot Summer months there were scattered about in this pen an average of at least 500 prisoners who were suffering from disease in almost every form incident to man, in a climate to which he is unaccustomed. Five acres of the surface of the ground were covered with human excrement, exhaling a morbidic influence which would prove fatal even to the rice plantation laborer, accustomed from infancy to breathing the malarious atmosphere of his native savannahs. Constantly drenched by rains, receiving bad food, always poorly prepared and often raw, in many instances naked and laboring under a mental depression verging upon melancholy, feeling that their days were numbered, the prisoners were kept in their dreadful prison. Under these circumstances the mortality became frightful, and as a matter of defence from an epidemic, the rebel authorities were compelled to thin out the shambles early in September, by sending several thousand of the prisoners to a new stockade established at Savannah, where their sufferings were considerably alleviated. Subsequently these men on the breaking out of yellow fever at Savannah were removed to another prison pen at Milan. Before the change from Andersonville was made eleven thousand victims had been buried, uncoffined, in the shallow trenches near the prison.

IN RETROSPECT

ROBERT PENN WARREN

"A MARK DEEP ON OUR NATION'S SOUL"

LIFE, MARCH 17, 1961

A winner of the Pulitzer Prize in both fiction and poetry, Robert Penn Warren was one of the nation's leading literary figures. During the Civil War centennial observances, Life *magazine asked Warren to place the war in contemporary perspective. At the time the nation was in the midst of racial turmoil and Great Society soul-searching.*

Warren's version of the Civil War reflected a position that historians and intellectuals widely shared. While most of their fellow citizens saw the conflict as a struggle over slavery, most scholars saw it as the crossroad of two visions of American society: one a republic of people who lived on "milk-and-honey, at small expense," the other a modern industrial power. But Warren's reference to the question of absoluteness and to the decision not to repeat such a calamity was disquieting. Americans were already having serious doubts about the war in Southeast Asia.

'The Great Single Event of Our History' Lives on in Pain and Pageant—and Unity

THE CIVIL WAR IS, FOR THE AMERican imagination, the great single event of our history. Without too much wrenching it may, in fact, be said to *be* American history. Before the Civil War, in the deepest sense, we had no history. There was, of course, the noble vision of the Founding Fathers, articulated in the Declaration of Independence and the Constitution: the vision of freedom incarnated in a more perfect union. But the Revolution did not create a nation except on paper, and too often in the following years the vision of the Founding Fathers became merely a daydream of easy and automatic victories, a vulgar delusion of Manifest Destiny, a conviction of being a people divinely chosen to live on milk and honey, at small expense.

The vision became a reality, and we became a nation, only with the Civil War.

The Civil War is our only "felt" history—history lived in the national imagination. This is not to say that it is always and by all men felt in the same way. But this fact is an index to the very complexity, massiveness and fundamental significance of the event. It is an overwhelming and vital image of human and national experience. We instinctively feel that we can best understand ourselves and our country by reference to it. The first fact we understand is that we *are* a united nation—in a union that is at least technologically, economically and politically validated. A second fact is that the war abolished slavery. However, we may assess slavery in the tissue of causes of the Civil War—with all the economic overlay and cultural collision—it looms up mountainously, and it did provide the occasion for all the mutual vilification, self-righteousness, spite, guilt and general exacerbation of feeling that was the natural atmosphere in which the event came to flower. Once slavery was out of the way, a new feeling about union was possible.

A third fact is that the War catapulted America from what had been in considerable part an agrarian, handicraft society into a society of Big Technology, Big Business Organization, with a vast industrial plant, a unified banking system and currency, a national debt insuring national stability far beyond Alexander Hamilton's rosiest dreams, and a financial system centered in New York that has done more than bayonets or railroads to curb any remaining centrifugal tendencies of the South or West.

The War meant, too, that Americans saw America and each other. Together, the farm boy of Illinois and the gutter rat of the Mackerelville section of New York shot it out against some Scot of the Valley of Virginia or a Jew from Louisiana. In the end the War claimed Ohio and New York for the Union at the same time that it claimed the South.

But in claiming the Confederate states the War made them, paradoxically enough, more southern—with all the mystique of a prideful "difference." There had been great disintegrating tensions within the Confederacy, but once the War was over the Confederacy became a City of the Soul, beyond the haggling of politicians and the jealousy of the localisms. We can say that only at the moment when Lee signed the document of surrender was the Confederacy born. At the moment of its death it entered upon its immortality, with all that that has meant for America even to the present moment.

The War has colored our whole view of politics. When the smoke of battle had cleared away, the American was apt to see that there had been a bloody collision between two absolute and uncompromising views of how society should be operated. Looking about him at the carnage, he was likely to say that he had had enough of such absolutes, and to decide never to permit anything like them again.

THE SPANISH-AMERICAN WAR

"THE SPLENDID LITTLE WAR"

1898

DURING THE 1890s the United States experienced the social strains and anxieties of an accelerated transformation. The nation's population more than doubled in the period 1865 to 1898, and it grew increasingly urban. Foreign immigration and the general decline of the domestic agricultural sector crowded millions of country folk into American cities to work in sprawling factories. Though the country reached full industrialization (its gross national product was the highest in the world), commerce could not keep all of its people working. Businesses failed by the thousands after the panic of 1893, and during the four years of depression that followed, ethnic and racial tensions rose. In the cities, native-born laborers blamed the newcomers from southern and eastern Europe for low wages, while in the South, white mobs lynched nearly one thousand African-American citizens in the most violent decade of Jim Crow. In all, the dislocating social and psychological effects of modernity prompted the nation to search for order.

Politics reflected the concentration of national wealth and power. Big business and finance had a great influence over federal policies at home and abroad. Few restrictions were put on commerce and protective tariffs were kept high. While refusing to meddle in domestic matters, the government asserted its right to intervene in the affairs of Latin American states throughout the turbulent 1890s. Proponents of this new foreign policy cited the Monroe Doctrine, promising to protect New World republics from European corruption and to foster the proper cultivation of the region's resources and markets in

"Newspaper Square," New York City. *(Bettman Archive)*

the fashion of the United States. This nationalistic program resulted in the expansion and modernization of a navy that would establish the Republic's place among world powers.

By 1898 many outspoken Americans were spoiling for a fight. They regarded the prolonged insurrection in Cuba, a Spanish colony, as a fitting opportunity to demonstrate their country's virility. It seemed the Spanish could not adequately rule the island, so the United States should intervene to negotiate Cuba's independence. Failing that, American forces should assist the Cuban revolutionaries, who seemed to be fellow democrats. From the outset the press was avidly interested in the situation. William Randolph Hearst, head of the New York *Journal,* and Joseph Pulitzer, chief of the New York *World,* competed to deliver the most sensationalistic coverage. The competition between the *World,* the *Journal,* and other papers became a war within a war. Pulitzer was a crusader who demanded breezy copy, clear headlines, and stunning illustrations. His reporters ventured in and out of Cuba, writing commentary on the supposedly downtrodden Cubans who yearned to free themselves from Spanish oppression. With the assistance of the New York papers, a small rebellion became a full-scale revolt.

Objectivity, an indispensable tool of a good reporter, was too often tossed aside during the Spanish-American War. Some months before fighting broke out, Hearst sent Frederic Remington, the famous artist and pictorial historian of the American frontier, to Cuba to wander the back country and sketch the insurgents. There were no skirmishes or battles of consequence, and the artist grew bored drawing scenes of burning cane fields and dejected families around their small homes. He cabled his boss from Havana:

W. R. Hearst
Journal, New York
Everything quiet. No trouble here. There will be no war. I wish to return.
REMINGTON

And the reply from the publisher that will forever be remembered:

Remington
Havana
Please remain. You furnish the pictures and I will furnish the war.
HEARST

Hearst soon made good on his promise. THE WARSHIP *MAINE* WAS SPLIT IN TWO BY AN ENEMY'S SECRET INFERNAL MACHINE, screamed the *Journal* on February 17, 1898. Although the cause of the explosion was uncertain, the story made it clear that the enemy was Spain. The next day the headline proclaimed: THE WHOLE COUNTRY THRILLS WITH THE WAR FEVER. This was the most truthful report the *Journal* had run in some time. Under the slogan of "Remember the *Maine*! To hell with Spain!" the nation surged toward war. On Monday, April 11, President McKinley asked Congress to give him war powers, stating: "I await your action." Everyone knew what the action would be. On the nineteenth, Congress declared Cuba independent from Spain and authorized McKinley to use the army and navy to guarantee that independence. Spain declared war on the United States on April 24. Congress voted a state of war on April 25. The hour of the expansionists, the big-navy men, and the warmakers had finally come.

In spectacular circumstances, then, the Spanish-American War was bred, not born. American newspapers responded to the country's expanding role in world affairs, manifesting their own destiny by winning more readers, creating financial stability through advertising, and popularizing their product with bigger headlines and sensational stories. In the new "yellow journalism," events were transformed into both hard drama and melodramatic stories driven by violence and action.

The yellow journalists had an eager audience. Enthusiasm for the war was very high, despite the obvious manipulation of the issues by politicians and publishers. Response to President McKinley's call to arms overwhelmed the regular army's ability to train recruits. As a result, the mobilization was seriously flawed. The government could not provide enough uniforms, horses, food, or medicine for the 270,000 volunteers. Coordination of the effort broke down and chaos prevailed at the ports from which the American invasion of Cuba was launched.

The war was short, the actual fighting lasting less than a month. Tropical disease killed more of the poorly fed and ill-prepared soldiers than did Spanish bullets. But the Spanish-American conflict became very much a war for the one million readers of the *Journal*, which offered $50,000 for information leading to the arrest and conviction of the criminals who had sunk the USS *Maine* in Havana Harbor.

Hearst, the *Journal*'s publisher, had cut his professional teeth at Pulitzer's New York *World* before assuming the editorship of the San Francisco *Examiner*. Experimenting with layouts, typefaces, and headlines, he had tripled that paper's circulation in just two years, setting the stage for his New York invasion. He had captured the New York *Journal*, marching into yellow journalism with his best San Francisco troops, raiding Pulitzer's staff, and declaring war on the New York *World* with the injunction, "While others talk the *Journal* acts." Hearst also liked to say, "Men of action in all walks of life heartily endorse the *Journal*'s fight on behalf of the people."

Pulitzer, meanwhile, demonstrated striking success with the New York *World*, boosting circulation not only through sensationalism. There was some solid credibility to his editorial pages. But to compete with the *Journal*, the *World*'s news coverage injected sensational entertainment in rich yellow shades. It was Pulitzer who understood the potential profit of Sunday papers and who first installed color presses for the comics. The most successful of these, "Hogan's Alley," featured a grimy kid drawn in yellow—"The Yellow Kid." Yellow came to symbolize a journalistic style; the two papers staged a full and outright battle for readership and circulation with staff raids, price cutting, and exaggeration.

Mark Twain, a former journalist and editor himself, was fascinated by the machinations of the *World* and the *Journal*. On occasion, for a terrific fee, he contributed to both, and eventually cast a critical eye on the quality of their writing and political commentary. The journalistic jingoism that helped set off the Spanish-American War never upset Twain, who believed in the crusade to liberate Cuba, but he became disenchanted with the papers in his twilight years.

America fought the war with zest, clumsiness, gallantry, and incredible good luck. Within a week the country had a smashing victory at sea and a new naval hero. In a fittingly bizarre opening to a curious war, this first battle took place not in Cuban waters but halfway around the world in the Spanish-ruled Philippine Islands, which even McKinley had to locate by looking at a globe.

The cost of wiping out Spanish sea power in the Pacific was eight men slightly wounded. Admiral George Dewey cabled the news back home and waited for the arrival of more troops in order to occupy Manila. His message had to be taken to Hong Kong before it could be transmitted, so Washington did not receive it until May 7, whereupon the country went mad. Dewey was voted a promotion, an elaborate sword, and a congressional vote of thanks. The war was off to a running start.

The war in the Philippines was fought with guerrilla tactics, search and destroy maneuvers, ambushes, booby traps, and torture. The United States resorted to concentration camps, the very abuse that had caused such outrage in Cuba. While the war in Cuba lasted a little over three months, the war in the Philippines lasted more than four years. A brutal business from the very beginning, it became even worse. It settled nothing except to show that the United States was a strong nation, which the world already knew.

SYLVESTER SCOVEL

"ALL NOW DEPENDS ON GOMEZ"

NEW YORK *WORLD*, JANUARY 19, 1897

Sylvester Scovel of the New York World *went to Cuba in 1895 in a spirit of adventure—"to see the fighting," he told friends. Shortly after the Cuban revolt, Scovel made arrangements to furnish letters for several Western papers and went to Havana. Without difficulty, he made his way into the eastern provinces and joined the forces of rebel leader Maximo Gomez. On his return to Havana after about six months, he was ordered to leave the island but apparently did not do so.*

Maximo Gomez had gathered a few thousand men willing to die for freedom under the command of Jose Macao. They burned cane fields, wrecked the railroads, and moved westward toward Havana, picking up supporters along the way.

Scovel's first World *dispatch, published on February 4, 1896, was datelined January 24 from a Cuban camp near Batabano in southeastern Havana province. He was with Gomez and a force of fifteen hundred Cubans playing hide-and-seek with a force of about three thousand Spaniards. On February 7, Scovel was arrested and imprisoned.*

Scovel was a superior field correspondent because he was able to get dispatches to his newspaper with fair regularity. Others might be as daring in facing danger or as enduring in undergoing hardships, but they failed to make arrangements to get their dispatches sent from the island. Scovel succeeded by the risky method of going into well-patrolled towns along the railroad and mailing or sending his articles by Cuban messengers to agents in Havana, to be sent by ship to Key West and telegraphed to New York. The stories sometimes appeared in print within a week but more often were two or three weeks late, or sometimes months. For example, the World *on February 15 published three Scovel stories about Gomez's activity in Havana province, one dated February 7, one February 3, and one January 27. Three months elapsed, however, before another batch of stories was received and printed.*

By November Scovel was in New York, writing long, analytical articles on the situation in Cuba and preparing for publication full details of the atrocities he had investigated and documented. On November 9, predicting a winter of heavy fighting after the summer rains, Scovel said there were 200,000 Spanish troops on the island and 75,000 rebels. The World *gave major display on November 21 and 30 to Scovel's documented evidence of atrocities. He said that he had proof of 212 cases of Spanish brutality in seventy days in the form of 196 affidavits in the Spanish language, and he concluded: "That extermination of the Cuban people under the cloak of civilized warfare is Spain's settled purpose is shown by facts already made public through the* World.*"*

HE FIGHTS CUBA MAY BE FREE; IF HE ACCEPTS TERMS OF PEACE CUBA MAY HAVE HOME RULE.

In the District at Havana's Gates, Where Weyler's Sway Is Least Hampered, Patriots Steadily Grow Stronger and More Confident.

DEFY THE BEST REGULAR TROOPS ON THE ISLAND.

The *World's* War Correspondent Tells What He Saw Riding Throughout the Section Where the Cubans Overcome the Greatest Obstacles.

In the Field, Playa Santa Anna, near Punta Brava.

PROVINCE OF HAVANA, CUBA, Jan. 8, 1897

HERE, LITERALLY IN THE MIDST of more and better Spanish troops than guard any equal area of this island, the Cuban revolution has steadily strengthened.

Under less favorable circumstances than obtain elsewhere in Cuba, the insurgents of this Spanish-ridden section have not only increased in numbers and armament, but are sanguine of ultimate success.

They will not listen now to a suggestion of autonomy under Spanish sovereignty. But if such a proposition were indorsed and guaranteed by the United States it would have great effect, and if it were approved by Maximo Gomez it would be accepted.

SPAIN CANNOT HOPE FOR ABSOLUTE SWAY AGAIN.

IF THE CUBAN REVOLUTION HAS held its ground in this district, conservatism itself says that Spain can never hope to regain absolute control of the Pearl of the Antilles.

This district extends eastward from the Mariel trocha in Pinar del Rio province and runs along the north coast through Havana province to the very gates of Havana city.

It is eighteen miles long by six miles average breadth, and lies between the Marianao-Guanajay pike road and the coast. The total is 108 square miles, just about one-third the area covered by Greater New York.

This diminutive theatre of war is fenced in by Spanish bayonets.

The part of the trocha which bounds it on the west counts fully 5,000 regular soldiers, of whom at least 4,000 can be marched eastward on an hour's notice.

The eastern end of the district is the heavily fortified and garrisoned suburb of Marianao, which is eighteen minutes by rail from the Spanish reserves in Havana, trains running every hour.

WEYLER CAN FLOOD THE DISTRICT WITH TROOPS IN SIX HOURS.

GEN. WEYLER CAN PUT 10,000 TROOPS of the line into this section within four hours and can follow them up with 10,000 volunteers two hours later.

In other words, on six hours' notice, fully 20,000 splendidly equipped and drilled soldiers of Spain can be poured

THE CISNEROS AFFAIR

The events leading up to the Spanish-American War were blown far out of proportion in the media. The press produced outrageous stories, and interventionists in Congress used them to support flamboyant oratory, calling upon the administration to get tough with the Spanish government.

Richard Harding Davis, a reporter of the New York *Journal,* was luxuriating in the pleasures of a long sea voyage in February 1897 when he met a pretty Cuban woman who introduced herself as Senorita Clemencia Arango. The woman had been strip-searched and interrogated three times by Spanish detectives for secret messages intended for the Cuban rebels. One of the searches had taken place on an American-registered ship. Davis's story was soon splashed across the front page of the *Journal* on Lincoln's birthday, accompanied by Frederic Remington's illustration of the naked lady being questioned.

DOES OUR FLAG SHIELD WOMEN?

TAMPA, Fla., Feb. 10—On the boat which carried me from Cuba to Key West were three young girls who had been exiled for giving aid to the insurgents. The brother of one of them, Miss Clemencia Arango, is in command of the Cuban forces in the field near Havana. More than once the sister has joined him there and has seen fighting and carried back dispatches to the Junta in Havana. So for this she and two other young women, who were also suspected, were ordered to leave the island.

I happened to sit next to Miss Arango at table on the steamer. I found that she was not an Amazon, or a Joan of Arc, or a woman of the people, with a machete in one hand and a Cuban flag in the other. She was a well bred, well educated young person who spoke three languages and dressed as you see girls dress on Fifth avenue after church on Sunday.

This is what the Spaniards did to these girls.

After ordering them to leave the island on a certain day, they sent detectives to their houses in the morning of that day and had them undressed and searched to discover if they were carrying letters to the Junta at Key West and Tampa. They then, an hour later, searched them at the Custom House as they were leaving for the steamer. They searched them thoroughly, even to the length of taking off their shoes and stockings, and fifteen minutes later, when the young ladies stood at last on the deck of an American vessel, with the American flag hanging from the stern, the Spanish officers followed them there and demanded that a cabin should be furnished them to which the girls might be taken, and they were then again undressed and searched for the third time. . . .

Now, suppose that letters and dispatches had been found on the

Senorita Clemencia Arango, a young Cuban woman expelled from Cuba, is searched on the United Mail steamer *Olivette.* (*Frederick Remington/New York Journal*)

persons of these young ladies, and they had been put on shore and lodged in prison; or suppose the whole ship and every one on board had been searched, as the captain of that vessel, the *Olivette,* said the Spanish officers told him they might decide to do, and letters had been found on the Americans, and they had been ordered over the side and put into prison—would that have been an act in any way derogatory to the dignity of the United States, or are we to understand that an American citizen, or a citizen of any country, after he has asked and obtained permission to leave Cuba, and is on board an American vessel, is no more safe there and then than he would be in the insurgent camp?

The latter would seem to be so, and to depend on the captain of the vessel and on her owners, from whom he receives his instructions, and not to be a matter in which the United States Government is in any way concerned. I do not believe the captain of a British passenger steamer would have allowed one of his passengers to be stripped on the main deck of his vessel, nor the captain of a British tramp steamer, nor of a coal barge.

(continued)

American women were horrified, and the *Journal* editorialized: "There are things more dreadful than even war and one of them is dishonor." The press war was more dreadful still. Pulitzer's *World* retaliated with a story on Arango's experience that contradicted Davis's account in every respect, and the fight to defend the sanctity of maidenhood was on.

The story of Evangelina Cisneros was an immediate precursor to the advent of the Spanish-American War. The seventeen-year-old Cisneros was the niece of the president of the nascent Cuban Republic. Her plight was first reported by Marion Kendrick in the *Journal* on August 17, 1897.

THE CUBAN GIRL MARTYR

HAVANA, Aug. 16—The trial of Evangelina Betancourt Cisneros for rebellion is concluded, but the court-martial's verdict is withheld, in accordance with the usual custom, until it is approved by the Captain-General. The fiscal at the opening of the trial demanded that she be sentenced to twenty years' imprisonment at Ceuta, the African penal settlement. The withholding of the verdict is almost certain evidence of her conviction. Even the Spaniards in civil life here are horror stricken at the idea of a young girl being condemned to the awful prison, but there is very little chance of her escape from this fate. Public opinion has not the slightest weight with a military court, such as tried her.

Evangelina Betancourt Cisneros, young, beautiful, cultured, guilty of no crime save that of having in her veins the best blood in Cuba, is in imminent danger of being sent to Spain's African penal settlement for twenty years.

This true daughter of the Revolution is now undergoing trial by a military tribunal at Havana on the charge of rebellion, after a hideous imprisonment of nine months in a jail filled with the vilest women of Havana.

There is nothing against the black-eyed, sweet-faced young girl except that she was in the Isle of Pines when an outbreak of Cuban prisoners occurred, and that she is the niece of President Cisneros y Betancourt, who heads the civil government of the rebels in the jungles of Camaguay.

Her conviction is a foregone conclusion. Under the Spanish system of trial of military prisoners there is no chance for acquittal. The accused never hears the evidence, never confronts the witnesses who appear against her. Unrepresented by counsel, she makes her statement to a judge, who asks her what he pleases and leaves unasked what he pleases. The fiscal prosecutor has demanded a verdict of guilty from the court with a sentence of twenty years' imprisonment at Ceuta.

The *World,* hoping to expose another fraud, cabled General Valeriano Weyler, the governor-general of Cuba, for an official statement on the Cisneros trial. Weyler condescended to reply to Pulitzer's editors, but the *World*'s accompanying report of August 21, 1897, only fanned the flames of public outcry.

GEN. WEYLER TO THE *WORLD*

CABLE MESSAGE
THE WESTERN UNION
TELEGRAPH COMPANY.
TRANSLATION.

World, N.Y.:   Havana, August 20. For judicial reasons there is on trial in the preliminary stages a person named Evangelina Cisneros, who, deceitfully luring to her house the military commander of the Isle of Pines, had men posted secretly, who tied him and attempted to assassinate him. This case is in the preliminary stages and has not as yet been tried by a competent tribunal, and consequently no sentence has been passed nor approved by me.

I answer The World with the frankness and truth that characterize all my acts.

WEYLER.

THE CUBAN VERSION

The beautiful Cuban girl was arrested with her father and sister on the charge of rebellion and exiled a year ago to the Isle of Pines, where they lived in the Calle Principal of the little town of Nueva Gerona. The Governor of the Isle of Pines was the Spanish Colonel Jose Berris, a nephew of the Spanish Prime Minister. He saw the beautiful girl and fell in love with her. He wrote frequently to her, and finally imposed a condition worse than death on the young and delicately reared girl.

Answering one of his letters, she told him to be at her house on a certain day. Then she told her friends, and they secreted themselves in her parlor on the day the Governor was to visit her. He came; her friends rushed on him, and he was bound hand and foot.

Just then the patrol passed, and the Colonel's cries were heard. The soldiers rushed into the house, and she, her father and nearly all her friends were captured. They were thrown into prison, and then Col. Berris, who had been an aide-de-camp to Weyler, visited the General, reporting he had discovered a conspiracy in the Isle of Pines. Then the girl and her father were taken to Havana She was sent to the Casa de Recojidas (House for Abandoned Women) and her father to the Cabana.

It has been reported that the young girl had been court martialled and that the verdict—twenty years' imprisonment in Ceuta, where no woman has ever been confined, and where her fate would be worse than death—had been withheld until it was approved by Gen. Weyler.

According to Gen. Weyler's message to The World, her case has not yet reached the stage of trial. This means months of delay before her sentence.

(continued)

To make the most of this story, Hearst sent reporters out to get the women of America to sign a petition to Maria Christina, the queen regent of Spain, demanding Evangelina's release. Among the fifteen thousand women who signed this extraordinary paper were Mrs. Jefferson Davis, Frances Hodgson Burnett, President McKinley's mother, General Grant's widow, Julia Ward Howe, and Clara Barton. Davis went so far as to send an impassioned personal plea to the queen, while Howe wrote to the pope, all to no avail.

THE WHOLE COUNTRY RISING TO THE RESCUE

MORE THAN TEN THOUSAND WOMEN IN ALL PARTS OF THE UNITED STATES SIGN THE PETITION FOR THE RELEASE OF MISS CISNEROS

Evangelina Cisneros, the fair young Cuban girl who, after a hideous year-long imprisonment among the degraded women of Havana, is threatened with twenty years' imprisonment in Spain's foulest African penitentiary, has found champions among the women of the United States.

The whole United States is aroused. Ministers in their pulpits yesterday took their texts from the horrible atrocity contemplated by Weyler's secret military court, which would damn this girl for defending her honor against the modern Tarquin who came to her room at night when he thought there was nobody to protect her from his four attentions.

From all parts of the Union came expressions of horror.

Weyler over his own signature has admitted that his creature, Berris, military commander of the Isle of Pines, where her father was a prisoner, came to the girl's room and was made prisoner by those who were summoned by her shrieks.

Now, the charge is that she lured him there in order to have him assassinated and help an insurrection of the prisoners.

An insurrection of unarmed men in the midst of a Spanish army!

For this the Butcher of Cuba would sentence her to an imprisonment where the fate she escaped when she was rescued from Berris would be certain at even meaner hands.

Unless the appeals move the Queen there is no hope for Evangelina Cisneros. (New York *Journal,* August 23, 1897)

Hearst, who some think was genuinely moved by Cisneros's plight—as well as its news value—finally wired his Cuban bureau chief, George Bryson, "Rescue Evangelina Cisneros, no matter what the cost." Bryson was soon expelled from the country by Weyler, who was incensed at the *Journal*'s inaccurate and inflammatory reporting, but another enterprising Hearst reporter, Karl Decker, was sent to Cuba to effect a jail break. His plan could have been lifted from a dime novel, with secret tunnels, ladders, hacksaws, sleeping potions, and a briefcase full of money, but on October 7, 1897, Decker managed to pull it off.

When Cisneros arrived in New York to a heroine's welcome, Hearst laid on an extravaganza in Madison Square Garden featuring military bands and, of course, the bewildered teenager. Later she was taken to Washington, where she was greeted by President McKinley. The *Journal* had succeeded where diplomacy had failed and, modestly, dubbed the episode "The greatest journalistic coup of the age."

William Randolph Hearst. *(New York Public Library)*

into this small territory by rail and by road from the east and the west.

This does not take into account the forces along its southern boundary on the pike road between Marianao and Guanajay. That fine macadamized highway is a trocha in itself.

From east to west are the towns of Marianao, La Lisa, El Cano, Arroyo, Arena, Punta Brava, Hoyo Colorado, Caimito and Guanajay. Each place is well fortified, has an efficient cavalry force, or "guerilla," and a strong infantry garrison.

WHERE THE CRUEL SAN QUINTIN BATTALION "OPERATES."

ONE OF GEN. WEYLER'S FIRST moves was to fortify these towns and gar-

rison them with troops of the line. Consequently they now form a hedge of well-guarded bases for the operations throughout this little inclosure of no less than ten bodies of irregular Spanish cavalry and the infantry battalion of San Quintin. These forces are in constant movement. Sometimes two columns from the trocha combine with the regular forces, and I have seen one Cuban position near here attacked by three infantry columns and thirteen different guerilla squadrons.

The heliograph signal station on the hill north of Caimito is one of a chain between Pinar del Rio and Havana. All day long the heliograph is winking in the steady Cuban sunshine, and all night long the powerful reflecting lamp is twinkling cipher messages to Havana.

RICHARD HARDING DAVIS

"THE DEATH OF RODRIGUEZ"

A YEAR FROM A REPORTER'S NOTE BOOK
(HARPER AND BROTHERS, 1897)

Richard Harding Davis, reporter, war correspondent, novelist, writer of short stories, dramatist, editor, and fashion-plate model, was idolized in his day. He burst into national prominence with the publication of a short story, "Gallegher," in the August 1890 issue of Scribner's Monthly. *Delighted with this "American Kipling," the reading public during the 1890s and early years of the twentieth century consumed his novels, stories, and reports of wars and coronations. Perhaps they saw through Davis's eyes a colorful young world full of romance, adventure, success, and wealth.*

It was said that no war was a success without the presence of this war correspondent, who was handsome, debonair, and splendidly equipped to chronicle it. His dispatches from Cuba immortalized a colonel of the Rough Riders and helped to make a president of the United States.

"I am Richard Harding Davis," he would announce in a superbly assured way. And for everyone who listened unimpressed, there were a thousand to whom that name meant the breath of romance and the spirit of adventure, to whom it was a symbol of youth and success, a token of friendship or kindness, a gauge of chivalry. Print and personality were his passports throughout the world.

He was dashing and always impeccably dressed, even when he traveled to the front. He probably knew more actors, nobles, and headwaiters than any president. Yet he had a seriousness of purpose as a war correspondent and in this respect he was remarkable. The "Death of Rodriguez" is one of his most personal and poignant accounts.

ADOLFO RODRIGUEZ WAS THE only son of a Cuban farmer, who lived nine miles outside of Santa Clara, beyond the hills that surround that city to the north.

When the revolution in Cuba broke out young Rodriguez joined the insurgents, leaving his father and mother and two sisters at the farm. He was taken, in December of 1896, by a force of the Guardia Civile, the corp d'elite of the Spanish army, and defended himself when they tried to capture him, wounding three of them with his machete.

He was tried by the military court for bearing arms against the government, and sentenced to be shot by a fusillade some morning before sunrise.

Previous to execution he was confined in the military prison of Santa Clara with thirty other insurgents, all of whom were sentenced to be shot, one after the other, on mornings following the execution of Rodriguez.

His execution took place the morning of the 19th of January, 1897, at a place a half-mile distant from the city, on the great plain that stretches from the forts out to the hills, beyond which Rodriguez had lived for nineteen years. At the time of his death he was twenty years old.

I witnessed his execution, and what follows is an account of the way he went to his death. The young man's friends could not be present, for it was impossible for them to show themselves in that crowd and that place with wisdom or without distress, and I like to think that, although Rodriguez could not know it, there was one person present when he died who felt keenly for him, and who was a sympathetic though unwilling spectator.

There had been a full moon the night preceding the execution, and when the squad of soldiers marched from town it was still shining brightly through the mists. It lighted a plain two miles in extent, broken by ridges, and gullies and covered with thick, high grass, and with bunches of cactus and palmetto. In the hollow of the ridges the mist lay like broad lakes of water, and on one side of the plain stood the walls of the old town. On the other rose hills covered with royal palms that showed white in the moonlight, like hundreds of marble columns. A line of tiny camp-fires that the sentries had built during the night stretched between the forts at regular intervals and burned clearly.

But as the light grew stronger and the moonlight faded these were stamped out, and when the soldiers came in force the moon was a white ball in the sky, without radiance, the fires had sunk to ashes, and the sun had not yet risen.

So even when the men were formed into three sides of a hollow square, they were scarcely able to distinguish one another in the uncertain light of the morning.

There were about three hundred soldiers in the formation. They belonged to the volunteers, with their band playing a jaunty quickstep, while their officers galloped from one side to the other through the grass, seeking a suitable place for the execution. Outside the line the band still played merrily.

A few men and boys, who had been dragged out of their beds by the music, moved about the ridges behind the soldiers, half-clothed, unshaven, sleepy-eyed, yawning, stretching themselves nervously and shivering in the cool, damp air of the morning.

Either owing to discipline or on account of the nature of their errand, or because the men were still but half awake, there was no talking in the ranks, and soldiers stood motionless, leaning on their rifles, with their backs turned to the town, looking out across the plain to the hills.

The men in the crowd behind them were also grimly silent. They knew that whatever they might say would be twisted into a word of sympathy for the condemned man or a protest against the government. So no one spoke; even the officers gave their orders in gruff whispers, and the men in the crowd did not mix together, but looked suspiciously at one another and kept apart.

As the light increased a mass of people came hurrying from town with two black figures leading them, and the soldiers drew up at attention, and part of the double line fell back and left an opening in the square.

With us a condemned man walks only

the short distance from his cell to the scaffold or the electric chair, shielded from sight by the prison walls, and it often occurs even then that the short journey is too much for his strength and courage.

But the Spaniards on this morning made the prisoner walk for over a half-mile across the broken surface of the fields. I expected to find the man, no matter what his strength at other times might be, stumbling and faltering on this cruel journey; but as he came nearer I saw that he led all the others, that the priests on either side of him were taking two steps to his one and that they were tripping on their gowns and stumbling over the hollows in their efforts to keep pace with him as he walked, erect and soldierly, at a quick step in advance of them.

He had a handsome, gentle face of the peasant type, a light, pointed beard, great wistful eyes, and a mass of curly black hair. He was shockingly young for such a sacrifice, and looked more like a Neapolitan than a Cuban. You could imagine him sitting on the quay at Naples or Genoa lolling in the sun and showing his white teeth when he laughed. Around his neck, hanging outside the linen blouse, he wore a new scapular.

It seems a petty thing to have been pleased with at such a time, but I confess to have felt a thrill of satisfaction when I saw, as the Cuban passed me, that he held a cigarette between his lips, not arrogantly nor with bravado, but with the nonchalance of a man who meets his punishment fearlessly, and who will let his enemies see that they can kill but not frighten him.

It was very quickly finished, with rough and, but for one frightful blunder, with merciful swiftness. The crowd fell back when it came to the square, and the condemned man, the priests, and the firing squad of six volunteers passed in and the line closed behind them.

The officer who had held the cord that bound the Cuban's arms behind him and passed across his breast, let it fall on the grass and drew his sword, and Rodriguez dropped his cigarette from his lips and bent and kissed the cross which the priests held up before him.

The elder of the priests moved to one side and prayed rapidly in a loud whisper, while the other, a younger man, walked behind the firing squad and covered his face with his hands. They had both spent the last twelve hours with Rodriguez in the chapel of the prison.

The Cuban walked to where the officer directed him to stand, and turning his back on the square, faced the hills and the road across them, which led to his father's farm.

As the officer gave the first command he straightened himself as far as the cords would allow, and held up his head and fixed his eyes immovably on the morning light, which had just begun to show above the hills.

He made a picture of such pathetic helplessness, but of such courage and dignity, that he reminded me on the instant of that statue of Nathan Hale which stands in the City Hall Park, above the roar of Broadway. The Cuban's arms were bound, as are those of the statue, and he stood firmly, with his weight resting on his heels like a soldier on parade, and with his face held up fearlessly, as is that of the statue. But there was this difference, that Rodriguez, while probably as willing to give six lives for his country as was the American rebel, being only a peasant, did not think to say so, and he will not, in consequence, live in bronze during the lives of many men, but will be remembered only as one of thirty Cubans, one of whom was shot at Santa Clara on each succeeding sunrise.

The officer had given the order, the men had raised their pieces, and the condemned man had heard the clicks of the triggers as they were pulled back, and he had not moved. And then happened one of the most cruelly refined, though unintentional acts of torture that one can very well imagine. As the officer slowly raised his sword, preparatory to giving the signal, one of the mounted officers rode up to him and pointed out silently that, as I had already observed with some satisfaction, the firing squad was so placed that when they fired they would shoot several of the soldiers stationed on the extreme end of the square.

Their captain motioned his men to lower their pieces, and then walked across the grass and laid his hand on the shoulder of the waiting prisoner.

It is not pleasant to think what that shock must have been. The man had steeled himself to receive a volley of bullets. He believed that in the next instant he would be in another world; he had heard the command given, had heard the click of the Mausers as the locks caught—and then, at the supreme moment, a human hand had been laid upon his shoulder and a voice spoke in his ear.

You would expect that any man, snatched back to life in such a fashion, would start and tremble at the reprieve,

or would break down altogether, but this boy turned his head steadily, and followed with his eyes the direction of the officer's sword, then nodded gravely, and with his shoulders squared, took up the new position, straightened his back, and once more held himself erect.

As an exhibition of self-control this should surely rank above feats of heroism performed in battle, where there are thousands of comrades to give inspiration. This man was alone, in sight of the hills he knew, with only enemies about him, with no source to draw on for strength but that which lay in himself.

The officer of the firing squad, mortified by his blunder, hastily whipped up his sword, the men once more leveled their rifles, the sword rose, dropped, and the men fired. At the report the Cuban's head snapped back almost between his shoulders, but his body fell slowly, as though some one had pushed him gently forward from behind and he had stumbled.

He sank on his side in the wet grass without a struggle or a sound, and did not move again.

It was difficult to believe that he meant to lie there, that it could be ended without a word, that the man in the linen suit would not rise to his feet and continue to walk on over the hills, as he apparently had started to do, to his home; that there was not a mistake somewhere, or that at least some one would be sorry or say something or run and pick him up.

But, fortunately, he did not need help, and the priests returned—the younger one with tears running down his face—and donned their vestments and read a brief requiem for his soul, while the squad stood uncovered, and the men in the hollow square shook their accoutrements into place, and shifted their pieces and got ready for the order to march, and the band began again with the same quickstep which the fusillade had interrupted.

The figure still lay on the grass untouched, and no one seemed to remember that it had walked there of itself, or noticed that the cigarette still burned, a tiny ring of living fire, at the place where the figure had first stood.

The figure was a thing of the past, and the squad shook itself like a great snake, and then broke into little pieces and started off jauntily, stumbling in the high grass and striving to keep step to the music.

The officers led it past the figure in the linen suit, and so close to it that the file closers had to part with the column to avoid treading on it. Each soldier as he passed turned and looked down on it, some craning their necks curiously, others giving a careless glance, and some without any interest at all, as they would have looked at a house by the roadside, or a hole in the road.

One young soldier caught his foot in a trailing vine just opposite to it, and fell. He grew very red when his comrades giggled at him for his awkwardness. The crowd of sleepy spectators fell in on either side of the band. They, too, had forgotten it, and the priests put their vestments back in the bag and wrapped their heavy cloaks about them, and hurried off after the others.

Every man seemed to have forgotten it except two men, who came slowly towards it from the town, driving a bullock-cart that bore an unplaned coffin, each with a cigarette between his lips, and with his throat wrapped in a shawl to keep out the morning mists.

At that moment the sun, which shown some promise of its coming glow above the hills, shot up suddenly from behind them in all the splendor of the tropics, a fierce, red disk of heat, and filled the air with warmth and light.

The bayonets of the retreating column flashed in it, and at the sight a rooster in a farm-yard near by crowed vigorously, and a dozen bugles answered the challenge with the brisk, cheery notes of the reveille, and from all parts of the city the church bells jangled out the call for early mass, and the little world of Santa Clara seemed to stretch itself and to wake to welcome the day just begun.

But as I fell in at the rear of the procession and looked back, the figure of the young Cuban, who was no longer a part of the world of Santa Clara, was asleep in the wet grass, with his motionless arms still tightly bound behind him, with the scapular twisted awry across his face, and the blood from his breast sinking into the soil he had tried to free.

"CRISIS IS AT HAND"

NEW YORK *JOURNAL*, FEBRUARY 16, 1898

The most important single event in the start of the Spanish-American War was the sinking of the USS Maine. *The incident ignited controversy and led to congressional investigation. Why the* Maine *actually sank is still a subject of debate. Was it the work of war or was it a mechanical malfunction from the* Maine's *engine rooms?*

253 KNOWN TO BE LOST

Cabinet in Session

Growing Belief in Spanish Treachery

Maine Destroyed by an Outside Attack, Naval Officers Believe.

*Censored Dispatches from Havana Say
a Shot Was Heard
Before the Ship's Magazines Blew Up.*

WASHINGTON, Feb. 16

THE PRESIDENT HURRIEDLY called a special meeting of the Cabinet at 11:30 A.M.

While the Cabinet was in session the following cable dispatch from Captain [Charles D.] Sigsbee was handed to the President.

"Advise sending wrecking vessel at once. The Maine is submerged dneep debris. It is mostly work for divers now. Jenkins and Meritt still missing. There is little hope for their safety. Those known to be saved are: Officers, twenty-four; uninjured crew, eighteen. The wounded now aboard steamer, city hospital and at Mascotte Hotel number fifty-nine as far as known.

"All others down on board nor near the Maine. Total loss of missing 253. With several exceptions no officer nor man has more than part of a suit of clothing, and that wet with harbor water.

"Ward steamer leaves for Mexico at 2 o'clock this afternoon. Officers saved are uninjured.

"Damage was in compartment of crew. Am preparing to telegraph list of wounded and saved.

"Olivette leaves for Key West at 1 P.M. Will send by her to Key West officers saved except myself, Wainwright, Holman, Heneberger, Ray and Holden. Will turn over three uninjured boats to caption of the port with request for safekeeping. Will send all wounded men to hospital at Havana."

After the Cabinet had been in session an hour and a half Long [John D. Long, Secretary of the Navy] sent this reply.

"Sigsbee, U.S.S. Maine, Havana: The President directs me to express for him and for the people of the Maine, and desires that no expense be spared in providing for the survivors and in caring for the dead."

Secretary Long also announced that an unsigned dispatch from Havana reported the number of dead at 275.

Vice President [Garrett] Hobart was in the Senate chamber at noon when he re-

The U.S.S. *Maine.* (Smithsonian Institute)

ceived a message from the President calling him at once to the White House.

The President and members of the Cabinet were still in conference but the Vice President was at once admitted.

A dispatch was received from General Lee [Fitzhugh Lee, Consul General of Havana], this afternoon, saying "All Quiet. Great Sorrow expressed by authorities. Sigsbee has telegraphed details to Navy Department. Not yet prepared to report cause of explosion."

Public opinion in Washington is rapidly changing. It is now believed that the destruction of the Maine could not have been due to an accident. There is a strong belief in Spanish treachery.

General Blanco has cabled Senor Du Bose, the Cuban Charge D' Affairs, that a dynamo boiler on the Maine blew up, causing the explosion of the magazine.

Admiral Sicard, of the North Atlantic squadron, will be communicated with at once respecting the sending of another battle ship to Havana.

The lighthouse tenders Fern and Mangrove have arrived at Havana. The coast survey steamer Bache has been ordered there from Key West.

The torpedo boat Ericsson has been dispatched from Key West with orders to Rear Admiral Sicard at the Bay Tortugas.

"TORPEDO HOLE DISCOVERED BY GOVERNMENT DIVERS IN THE *MAINE*"

NEW YORK *JOURNAL*, FEBRUARY 17, 1898

On February 17, an early edition of the Journal *declared in a huge banner headline:* DESTRUCTION OF THE WARSHIP *MAINE* WAS THE WORK OF AN ENEMY. *Below was a page-wide drawing purporting to show how the battleship had been blown up. It pictured the* Maine *moored to a buoy with a submarine mine anchored under her bow.*

While the Journal *asserted in the biggest type available that the* Maine *had been purposely blown up, the* World *in its second-day headlines and stories merely hinted at this. Its front-page banner on February 17 ended with a question mark:* MAINE EXPLOSION CAUSED BY BOMB OR TORPEDO?

FORTUNE OFFERED FOR EVIDENCE $50,000 REWARD.

Startling Evidence of Spanish Treachery Revealed

The Battleship and Hundreds of American Lives Sacrificed in Havana Harbor.

HAVANA, Feb. 17

DIVERS WHO HAVE DESCENDED and inspected the hull of the sunken battleship Maine have discovered an 8-inch percussion hole in one of her plates.

This indicates that the Maine was destroyed by a torpedo. It makes clear that the destruction of the Maine was not brought about by an accidental explosion aboard the battleship.

It is very clear that either a Spanish fanatic or a secret emissary of the Spanish Government floated the torpedo under the waterline against the Maine's forward magazine, and set it with a detonating device, giving him time to escape.

The danger lies in the fact that the proofs of the torpedo wound may be removed by secrete agents of the Spanish Government before the arrival of the United States investigating officers.

RUMORS OF DYNAMITE.

VAGUE RUMORS REACHED NEW YORK at noon to-day, that the Maine had been blown up by the bumping of a small boat filled with dynamite or other high explosive against the battleship's bows.

The press censorship at Havana had suppressed all but the most meagre news.

Newspapers and private corporations having Cuban interests have made every effort to get dispatches through in plausible cipher.

From a complicated dispatch received by the president of a coast-wise steamship company at noon to-day, the news of a dynamite plot to destroy the Maine was deciphered.

Hearst's *Journal* of February 17; the *Maine* sank on the night of February 15.

GEORGE B. REA

"THE NIGHT OF THE EXPLOSION IN HAVANA"

HARPER'S WEEKLY, MARCH 5, 1898

To George Bronson Rea and Sylvester Scovel, seated in a café near Havana's Central Park in the early evening of February 15, the city appeared animated and joyful. The carnival season had opened the day before, and the streets were rapidly filling with celebrants, faces hidden by grotesque masks. In contrast with the lively scenes in the city was the stillness of the harbor.

THE CITY OF HAVANA PRESENTED an animated and joyful appearance during the first hours of the night of February 15. The carnival season had only opened the day before, and the streets were rapidly filling with the happy and grotesque masqueraders. Out in the bay lay the men-of-war and merchant vessels, whose forms were barely distinguishable in the darkness. The night was dark, and the few stars were frequently shadowed by the thick clouds wafted out to sea by the light land-breeze.

On board the war-ships the buglers had sounded "taps" and the boatswains' mates had shrilly "piped down" for the night. The only life visible was the forms of the officers and sentries on watch, mechanically pacing to and fro in their respective stations.

In company with Mr. and Mrs. Sylvester Scovel, the writer was seated in one of the numerous cafes located near the park. Suddenly the sound of a terrible explosion shook the city; windows were broken and doors were shaken from their bolts. The sky towards the bay was lit up with an intense light, and above it all could be seen innumerable colored lights resembling rockets.

Hastily providing for the safety of his wife, Scovel and I jumped into a coach, and ordered the reluctant driver to drive for his life in the direction of the noise. The populace were evidently frightened, probably believing that the explosion was the forerunner of another riot, and very few essayed to leave their doors and venture into the street. As we approached the docks the excitement increased, and at last, reaching the custom-house gate, we found an excited crowd trying to force its way through, despite the energetic remonstrance and resistance of the guards.

Elbowing and pushing through, we informed the guards that we were two officers from the *Maine;* for by this time we understood something terrible had occurred on board. The gates were quickly opened, and closed immediately. Rushing through the baggage-inspection room and out on the open wharf, our worst fears were realized—the *Maine* was a wreck and burning brightly. Jumping into a boat with the chief of police, Colonel Paglieri, we were soon out in the harbor. Our progress was often retarded by huge masses of floating wreckage, and as we approached closer, the rapid-fire and small-arm ammunition began to explode and whiz through the air over our heads. Our boatmen were paralyzed with fear, and wished to turn back. The Colonel beat one of them with his cane, I whacked the other with a rope's end, until they concluded to proceed.

The scene as it unfolded itself to our vision was terrible in its significance. Great masses of twisted and bent iron plates and beams were thrown up in confusion amidships; the bow had disappeared; the foremast and smoke-stacks had fallen; and to add to the horror and danger, the mass of wreckage amidships was on fire, and at frequent intervals a loud report, followed by the whistling sound of fragments flying through the air, marked the explosion of a 6-pound shell.

The greatest danger for a time seemed to lie in another magazine explosion; but, despite this circumstance, we could see the boats of the Spanish cruiser and of the *City of Washington* darting in and out of the wreckage, bravely rescuing some poor fellow crying for help. We pulled close to the wreck, in the hope of being of some assistance. We arrived there fifteen minutes after the crash, the first to reach her from the shore, but in that short time everybody who survived had already been saved. Too much praise cannot be bestowed on the crews and officers of the two steamers mentioned, who were on the spot immediately after the catastrophe, and their vessels did not draw away for more than three-quarters of an hour after, or when it was deemed absolutely necessary to protect themselves from the danger of being struck by fragments of the shells and fixed ammunition which were constantly exploding.

We finally comprehended the full extent of the calamity. My strong companion gulped down a sob as he exclaimed: "Great God, old man, they are all gone! This is the work of a torpedo, and marks the beginning of the end." The stern old Spanish Colonel muttered, *"Ave Maria! how horrible!"* and, with another oath, made a pass at the boatmen with his cane, to urge them forward to where we could now discern the forms of Captain Sigsbee and his officers—many of them half-dressed—standing in their boats sadly viewing the remnants of their once-proud cruiser. Here we were hastily informed of what had occurred. At this time it was impossible to estimate the loss of life, and many were supposed to have been saved by swimming to other vessels. We followed Captain Sigsbee to the gangway of the *Washington,* and there the chief of police offered his services and expressed his sympathy to the Captain. Once on board I hastened below, and found eight wounded men being tenderly cared for by Surgeon Heneberger, who was attired in his pajamas. His faithful assistant was Father Chidwick, who has performed a hero's work since that terrible night.

I soon found that there were about thirty-seven survivors on board the *Washington.* All the officers except four were there, and were cared for by the passengers and officers of the steamer.

Only four marines and their captain were accounted for at first. These were the remnants of the full guard of forty-one men.

I received about forty cablegrams from the officers and crew to be forwarded to their families, and as I was about to leave I stepped in to interview Captain Sigsbee, who, in answer to my question, politely handed me his despatches to the Secretary of the Navy and the Admiral at Key West, and at the same time requesting me to see that they were put on the wire immediately.

While conversing with him, a large deputation of prominent Spanish officials, headed by Secretary-General Congosto, arrived on board to express their sympathy, and to offer all the aid in their power. Their attentions were kindly received and answered by Captain Sigsbee, and when they left the ship I accompanied them ashore, and I must say that I only heard the most profound expressions of sympathy and sorrow. When Dr. Congosto learned that I was the bearer of the official and private telegrams of the Captain and officers, he sent orders to the cable-office that all telegrams I might present for transmission should be given the right of way, and that all expenses should be paid by the Spanish government. This was indeed a delicate compliment to the noble officers who had been left destitute as a result of the explosion, and deserves at least our appreciation.

After a protracted tour of all the hospitals during the early hours of Wednesday morning, making up a list of the saved and wounded, I once more returned to the *Washington*, and later on in the day had the satisfaction of seeing many of the poor fellows and their officers sent back to their native land on board the steamship *Olivette*.

FREDERIC REMINGTON

"SOLDIERS WHO CRY"

HARPER'S WEEKLY, MAY 21, 1898

On the Western frontier, Frederic Remington had been a cowboy and a scout returning to the East with a portfolio of drawings he hoped to sell to a magazine publisher. He was assigned to Harper's Weekly, *where his drawings and paintings became famous.*

YESTERDAY I CALLED AT THE Ninth Infantry camp, and Colonel Powell told the following in the course of conversation, and it struck me as a new note. This regiment came from Plattsburg Barracks, New York, and when the order came to go the colonel asked his captains to draw up small details out of the companies which should be left behind to guard and look after the property of the government of Plattsburg.

The colonel drew these details up in line to instruct them in their duties, which he did at some length. He said he noticed tears running down the faces of some of the men, but it did not strike him seriously at the time. He dismissed the squad and left the building; but in a string behind him came the men, crying like children. One old mustached and grizzled chap was bawling as though at his mother's funeral; he begged, he pleaded, he implored the colonel by all his gods not to leave him behind. Others did the same, standing there crying, blubbering, and beseeching Colonel Powell not to make them stay behind. The old colonel was quite taken aback. He did not know just what to do. He liked the spirit, but the discipline had never had just this sort of a shock before, and it upset him. He told the men they had been detailed by their captains to stay behind to guard property because they were steady men. It did nothing but cause more pleading and blubbering, and the colonel walked away. He did not tell me if he had a tear in his own eye when he turned his back, but the men had to be rounded sharply up and regularly made to stay. That is the kind of boys to follow the band, I say.

STEPHEN CRANE

"STEPHEN CRANE AT THE FRONT FOR THE *WORLD*"

NEW YORK *WORLD*, JULY 7, 1898

By the time of his arrival in Siboney, Cuba, Stephen Crane was already a renowned author. His first work, Maggie: A Girl of the Streets *(1893), was self-published but* The Red Badge of Courage *and* The Black Riders *brought him fame and reached bookstores in 1895, the same year in which the Cuban insurrection against Spain began. Crane's reporting from the Caribbean theater received almost immediate acclaim. Richard Harding Davis called him "the coolest man, whether army officer or civilian, that I saw under fire at any time during the war." The following collage of anecdotes is Crane at his best—disembarking at Daiquiri, following a thicketed path blazed by the Rough Riders, and encountering a mortally wounded fellow correspondent.*

THE AUTHOR OF "THE RED BADGE OF COURAGE," THE MOST NOTABLE WAR STORY OF RECENT YEARS, WRITTEN BEFORE HE EVER SAW AN ACTUAL ENGAGEMENT, WAS IN THE THICK OF BATTLE WITH THE ROUGH RIDERS.

Heedless of Danger That Surrounded Them, Noisily, Carelessly They Went to Death with Superb Courage—The Heroism of Marshall, the Correspondent, and Other Thrilling Episodes Brought Intimately Before the Reader.

SIBONEY, June 24

AND THIS IS THE END OF THE third day since the landing of the troops. Yesterday was a day of insurgent fighting. The Cubans were supposed to be fighting somewhere in the hills with the regiment of Santiago de Cuba, which had been quite cut off from its native city. No American soldiery were implicated in any way in the battle. But to-day is different. The mounted infantry—the First Volunteer Cavalry—Teddie's Terrors—Wood's Weary Walkers—have had their first engagement. It was a bitter hard first fight for new troops, but no man can ever question the bravery of this regiment.

As we landed from a despatch boat we saw the last troop of the mounted infantry wending slowly over the top of a huge hill. Three of us promptly posted after them upon hearing the statement that they had gone out with the avowed intention of finding the Spaniards and mixing it up with them.

THROUGH THE THICKETS

THEY WERE FAR AHEAD OF US BY THE time we reached the top of the mountain, but we swung rapidly on the path through the dense Cuban thickets and in time met and passed the hospital corps, a vacant, unloaded hospital corps, going ahead on mules. Then there was another long lonely march through the dry woods, which seemed almost upon the point or crackling into a blaze under the rays of the furious Cuban sun. We met nothing but blankets, shelter-tents, coats and other impediments, which the panting Rough Riders had flung behind them on their swift march.

In time we came in touch with a few stragglers, men down with the heat, prone and breathing heavily, and then we struck the rear of the column. We were now about four miles out, with no troops nearer than that by the road.

I know nothing about war, of course, and pretend nothing, but I have been enabled from time to time to see brush fighting, and I want to say here plainly that the behavior of these Rough Riders while marching through the woods shook me with terror as I have never before been shaken.

SUPERB COURAGE

IT MUST NOW BE PERFECTLY UNderstood throughout the length and breadth of the United States that the Spaniards have learned a great deal from the Cubans, and they are now going to use against us the tactics which the Cubans have used so successfully against them. The marines at Guantanamo have learned it. The Indian-fighting regulars know it anyhow, but this regiment of volunteers knew nothing but their own superb courage. They wound along this narrow winding path, babbling joyously, arguing, recounting, laughing; making more noise than a train going through a tunnel.

Any one could tell from the conformation of the country when we were liable to strike the enemy's outposts, but the clatter of tongues did not then cease. Also, those of us who knew heard going from hillock to hillock the beautiful coo of the Cuban wood-dove—ah, the wood-dove! the Spanish guerilla wood-dove which had presaged the death of gallant marines.

For my part, I declare that I was frightened almost into convulsions. Incidentally I mentioned the cooing of the doves to some of the men, but they said decisively that the Spaniards did not use this signal. I don't know how they knew.

SILENCE—ACTION

WELL, AFTER WE HAD ADVANCED well into the zone of the enemy's fire mark that—well into the zone of Spanish fire—a loud order came along the line: "There's a Spanish outpost just ahead and the men must stop talking."

"Stop talkin', can't ye,—it," bawled a sergeant.

"Ah, say, can't ye stop talkin'?" howled another.

I was frightened before a shot was fired; frightened because I thought this silly brave force was wandering placidly into a great deal of trouble. They did. The firing began. Four little volleys were fired by members of a troop deployed to the rights. Then the Mauser began to pop— the familiar Mauser pop. A captain announce that this distinct Mauser sound was our own Krag-Jorgensen. O misery!

Then the woods became aglow with fighting. Our people advanced, deployed, reinforced, fought, fell— in the bushes, in the tall grass, under the lone palms—before a foe not even half seen. Mauser bullets came from three sides. Mauser bul-

U.S. soldiers in Cuban trenches. *(Library of Congress)*

lets—not Krag-Jorgensen—although men began to cry that they were being fired into by their own people—whined in almost all directions. Three troops went forward in skirmish order and in five minutes they called for reinforcements. They were under a cruel fire; half of the men hardly knew whence it came; but their conduct, by any soldierly standard, was magnificent.

GREEN HEROES

MOST PERSONS WITH A FANCY FOR military things suspect the value of an announcedly picked regiment. Better ga-

ther a simple collection of clerks from anywhere. But in this case the usual view changes. This regiment is as fine a body of men as were ever accumulated for war.

There was nothing to be seen but men straggling through the underbrush and firing at some part of the landscape. This was the scenic effect. Of course men said that they saw five hundred, one thousand, three thousand, fifteen thousand Spaniards, but—poof—in bush country of this kind it is almost impossible for one to see more than fifty men at a time. According to my opinion there were never more than five hundred men in the

Spanish firing line. There might have been aplenty in touch with their center and flanks, but as to the firing there were never more than five hundred engaged. This is certain.

The Rough Riders advanced steadily and confidently under the Mauser bullets. They spread across some open ground— tall grass and palms—and there they began to fall, smothering and threshing down in the grass, marking man-shaped places among those luxurious blades. The action lasted about one-half hour. Then the Spaniards fled. They had never seen men fight them in this manner and they fled. The business was too serious.

Then the heroic rumor arose, soared, and screamed above the bush. Everybody was wounded. Everybody was dead. There was nobody. Gradually there was somebody. There was the wounded, the important wounded. And the dead.

MARSHALL'S COURAGE

MEANWHILE A SOLDIER PASSING near me said: "There's a correspondent all shot to hell."

He guided me to where Edward Marshall lay, shot through the body. The following conversation ensued:

"Hello, Crane!"

"Hello, Marshall! In hard luck, old man?"

"Yes, I'm done for."

"Nonsense! You're all right, old boy. What can I do for you?"

"Well, you might file my despatches. I don't mean file 'em ahead of your own, old man—but just file 'em if you find it handy."

I immediately decided that he was doomed. No man could be so sublime in detail concerning the trade of journalism and not die. There was the solemnity of a funeral song in these absurd and fine sentences about despatches. Six soldiers gathered him up on a tent and moved slowly off.

"Hello!" shouted a stern and menacing person, "who are you? And what are you doing here? Quick!"

"I am a correspondent, and we are merely carrying back another correspondent who we think is mortally wounded. Do you care?

The Rough Rider, somewhat abashed, announced that he did not care."

NEW YORK TO THE FORE

AND NOW THE WOUNDED SOLDIERS began to crawl, walk and be carried back to where, in the middle of the path, the surgeons had established a little field hospital.

"Say, doctor, this ain't much of a wound. I reckon I can go now back to my troop," said Arizona.

"Thanks, awfully, doctor. Awfully kind of you. I dare say I shall be all right in a moment," said New York.

This hospital was a spectacle of heroism. The doctors, gentle and calm, moved among the men without the commonsenseless bullying of the ordinary ward. It was a sort of fraternal game. They were all in it, and of it, helping each other.

In the mean time three troops of the Ninth Cavalry were swinging the woods, and a mile behind them the Seventy-first New York was moving forward eagerly to the rescue. But the day was done. The Rough Riders had bitten it off and chewed it up—chewed it up splendidly.

Celebrating the end of hostilities off the coast of Cuba.

JAMES CREELMAN

"BATTLE IMPRESSIONS"

COSMOPOLITAN, SEPTEMBER 1898

Some reporters in Cuba wrote the news. James Creelman made the news. His personal exploits at El Caney turned out to be one of the best news stories of the war. Riding along Santiago's outer picket lines, Creelman cabled the Journal *a preliminary story on the preparations for the great attack.*

THERE WERE TWO VIVID, IMPRESsive moments during the battle of El Caney. One was when I stood beside General Chaffee and saw a button cut from his breast by a Mauser bullet. A moment before, he had been raging up and down the line, the only man in his whole brigade who was not lying flat on the grass. His hat was on the back of his head, and his lean, thirteenth-century face was glorified with the passion and fury of the fight—the toughest, profanest, divinest soldier I ever saw in battle, his eyes shining, and the muscles standing out on his neck and forehead like knotted cords. Then, as I stood beside him in the shadow for a moment, a Mauser bullet clipped the shining ornament from his breast, and he looked into my face with a half-startled, half-amused air.

The next tremendous moment of the fight was when I went alone to the edge of the trench in front of the stone fort, and saw the Spaniards who remained alive crouching there and waiting for death. The thing that fascinated me was a drop of blood which hung on the end of a dead man's nose. His lips were drawn back from his teeth and he seemed to be laughing, and there on the end of his pinched nose was a great bright drop of blood.

In every battle that I go through, I somehow get a melody in my head and hum it to the end of the action. I suppose it is the result of nervous excitement. A man's nerves play him some very curious tricks. All through the battle and massacre of Port Arthur in the Japanese war, I hummed the air from Mendelssohn's "Springtime," and during the shell fire I found myself actually shrieking it. When I started in the charge on Fort Caney, I began to hum "Rock of Ages," and I couldn't get rid of the tune even when I was lying among the dying of Chaffee's brigade in the hospital camp. I remember that when General Chaffee leaned over me after I had been shot and asked me how I was, I couldn't answer him until I had finished, in my mind, one phrase of "Rock of Ages."

WINSTON CHURCHILL, CUB REPORTER

On December 5, 1898, Winston Churchill, just a twenty-one-year-old reporter, witnessed a battle between the column of General Suarez Valdez and Maceo forces in Puerto Principe province. The battlefield was a mile-wide clearing in a dense forest, across which the Spaniards marched to meet the Cubans hidden in the underbrush among the trees. The Spanish infantry was within thirty yards when the rebels, as was their usual practice, turned and fled, "The insurgents are bad shots," Churchill wrote. "It appeared to me that tons of lead passed over the heads of General Valdez's staff, with whom I was. Three orderlies were wounded. . . . My general conclusion is that European methods of warfare are almost out of the question in a wild country where an enemy operates cavalry, as infantry is useless except for marching" (New York *World*, December 2, 1898).

The *World* headlined the dispatch CHURCHILL IN BATTLE; the editors were delighted to have the son of a British lord as a contributor. They could not, however, refrain from taking an editorial potshot at him on December 7, 1898:

> Concerning the report of Lieut. Winston Churchill, of the British Army, on the battle at the Reforma plantation on Dec. 2 between the Cuban insurgents and the Spanish forces, it may be said that certain statements in it are presumably accurate; others are undoubtedly erroneous.
>
> For instance, there is no reason to disbelieve the assertion that "the Spanish loss would have been heavy had the enemy's shots told": The trouble seems to have been that the enemy's shots did not tell, for, as our correspondent says, "the Spanish loss was ridiculously small." It appears to have been so small as to be imperceptible.
>
> But it is not impossible to believe that the Spanish troops marched slowly, in close formation, across an open plain up to within thirty yards of an army of 4,000 Cubans without a single man being killed, especially when it appeared to Lieut. Churchill that "tons of lead" passed over the heads of the staff of the attacking army.
>
> At any rate, a battle in which nobody is killed is not the kind of battle by which Cuban independence can be secured. If the Cubans wish to convince the world that they have a real army they must fight a real battle. Their cause cannot be won by a sham battle, or by newspaper despatches, however interesting.

IN RETROSPECT

RICHARD HARDING DAVIS

"OUR WAR CORRESPONDENTS IN CUBA AND PUERTO RICO"

HARPER'S MONTHLY, MAY 1899

By the time of his death in 1916, Davis had covered wars all over the globe and had encountered the best—and worst—of his peers. The piece that follows ran in Harper's Monthly *in May 1899. The war with Spain was over, but America's role in global politics was only beginning. As the nation's role expanded, the need for sophisticated analysis and reporting from the battlefront would clearly increase. Davis recognized that, and called for it here.*

THE NEWSPAPER CORRESPONDENTS who are allowed to accompany the British army during an active campaign are selected on account of their former experience and reputation, or on account of the importance of the paper they serve. Their number is extremely limited. The two great press associations, *Reuter's* and the *Central News*, which furnish the same matter to different papers in all parts of the United Kingdom, are each allowed one or two representatives, and a dozen of the more important London dailies, like the *Times*, the *Daily Telegraph*, and the *Mail*, and one or two of the provincial papers, such as the Manchester *Guardian* and the Dublin *Times*, are each allowed to send one special correspondent to the front.

This plan of selection and limitation is very different from the one pursued during the late war by our own government. With us, nearly every paper in the country that could afford to send a representative was permitted to do so. Even weekly periodicals of a strictly literary or religious character were represented by men who were anxious to get to Cuba in any capacity, and the big dailies were each given credentials for as many as twenty correspondents, artists, and photographers. As our country, unlike England, is not constantly engaged in military operations, only a few of the men who acted as correspondents during the war with Spain went to the front with any previous experience of the kind of work before them. But they had been trained in a school of journalism which teaches self-reliance and, above all other things, readiness of resource. In consequence they met the new conditions without anxiety, and by using the same methods they had formerly employed in reporting a horse show or a fire, they succeeded in satisfactorily describing the operations of our army.

Before the Santiago campaign had opened, and while our troops were still at Tampa, many of the newspapers promised their readers that when the war really came the "pencil-pushers of Park Row," with no experience of battle or of things military, would develop into great war correspondents, while, on the other hand, the men who had been employed to serve as descriptive writers merely, and who possessed some further experience in campaigning and in roughing it, would show that they were better suited to write fiction in a library than to recognize news when they saw it, or to collect facts.

The war, so far as it concerned itself with the correspondents, proved nothing of the sort. It did not show that the descriptive writer or novelist was capable of gathering news, nor did it prove to the contrary; not did it prove that the man who had previously reported criminal news and real-estate deals was equally at home when he found himself in a Cuban jungle two thousand miles from the office telephone, and with no friendly policeman to direct his steps. The success of the different men was entirely a question of intelligence and of individual character. Their past experience seemed to count for very little. Some of those who had seen much service with the army and navy in times of peace, who could harness a team to a gun-carriage, or drill a cavalry regiment, or name every part of a battle-ship, were, when "the real thing" came, lost absolutely from the sight of their fellowmen. All their experience on the plains and in the wardrooms of the White Squadron either failed to get them to the front at all, or did not enable them to take care of themselves once they got there. On the other hand, mere boys, who had been jerked out of the city room of a metropolitan daily and rushed to the front without even a rubber blanket, followed the soldiers from the first to the last, and never left them, except to tramp back to Siboney to file their despatches on the pressboats. Two of the very best correspon-

dents had served their respective papers, previous to the war, as dramatic critics, and their only knowledge of war had been gathered from performances of *Secret Service* and *Shenandoah*. These were H. James Whigham, of the Chicago *Tribune*, and Acton Davies, of the New York *Evening Sun*. Each of these gentlemen proved most conclusively that serious experience is not necessary to enable either an Englishman or an American to report a war correctly. I have seen the war correspondent whom Kipling describes as the "War Eagle" in his *Light that Failed*. I saw him in Greece, with three horses, three servants, a tent, the British flag flying over his head, cooking-stoves, medicine-chests, writing-desks, and type-writers. He carried letters from prime ministers, and he lunched with the young princes daily. And I have seen a boy, named Sammy, who acted as a courier for the New York *Herald*, eighteen years of age, who had a keener scent for news than the War Eagle ever possessed, who better knew what was going to happen before it happened, and who was in every way more alert, intelligent, and suited to the work in hand.

Whigham, with his two years' residence in America, made, in my opinion at least, a much better war correspondent than the War Eagle with his record of twelve campaigns. And his outfit was limited to a canteen and a bottle of Scotch whiskey. The War Eagle's despatches are intelligible, and probably of great interest to a drill-sergeant; Whigham's letters were equally interesting to the military expert and to the civilian. Whigham came from Oxford to America to lecture in the university extension series, but he is better known in this country as the ex–golf champion of the United States, and as a dramatic critic. He arrived at Key West during the earliest days of the war, and that same night was dropped on the coast of Cuba, where he was promptly made prisoner by the Spaniards, but was later set at liberty in Havana. Immediately on his release he went to Guantanamo, where the marines had landed, and while trying to find their firing-line, walked into a Spanish picket and received a Mauser bullet across the forehead. Later he joined the army at Daiquiri, and was one of the half-dozen correspondents who scaled the San Juan hills immediately after they were charged by the regulars. Later he was invalided home with a fever, which attacked him in a most serious form. His must certainly be considered a full and creditable record, and his only experience of war was gathered on the golf-links of Chicago. It is impossible to designate one correspondent as being better than another, because what is important to one does not seem important to his rival, and their ideas as to their duty differ. One may prefer to stand on the firing-line in order to see what is going forward close at hand, but while he is in greater personal danger, another who watches the battle from an elevation in the rear can obtain a much better view, and a much more correct idea of what is being done in all parts of the field. So the presence of a correspondent on the firing-line, or his absence from it, does not prove that he is not doing his full duty to his paper. The best correspondent is probably the man who by his energy and resource sees more of the war, both afloat and ashore, than do his rivals, and who is able to make the public see what he saw. If that is a good definition, Stephen Crane would seem to have

Theodore Roosevent and Richard Harding Davis.
(Library of Congress)

distinctly won the first place among correspondents in the late disturbance. John Fox, Sylvester Scovel, Caspar Whitney, Howard Thompson, and Mr. Millard of the New York *Herald* are close seconds. Of these gentlemen, Mr. Fox and Mr. Whitney were hampered by the fact that they were not writing for a daily paper.

Near the close of the war, a group of correspondents in Puerto Rico made out a list of the events which, in their opinion, were of the greatest news value during the campaign, and a list of the correspondents, with the events each had witnessed credited to his name. Judged from this basis, Mr. Crane easily led all the rest. Of his power to make the public see what he sees it would be impertinent to speak. His story of Nolan, the regular, bleeding to death on the San Juan hills, is, so far as I have read, the most valuable contribution to literature that the war has produced. It is only necessary to imagine how other writers would have handled it, to appreciate that it could not have been better done. His story of the marine at Guantanamo, who stood on the crest of the hill to "wigwag" to the war-ships, and so exposed himself to the fire of the entire Spanish force, is also particularly interesting, as it illustrates that in his devotion to duty, and also in his readiness at the exciting moments of life, Crane is quite as much of a soldier as the man whose courage he described. He tells how the marine stood erect, staring through the dusk with half-closed eyes, and with his lips moving as he counted the answers from the war-ships, while innumerable bullets splashed the sand about him. But it never occurs to Crane that to sit at the man's feet, as he did, close enough to watch his lips move and to be able to make mental notes for a later tribute to the marine's scorn of fear, was equally deserving of praise.

Crane was the coolest man, whether army officer or civilian, that I saw under fire at any time during the war. He was most annoyingly cool, with the assurance of a fatalist. When the San Juan hills were taken, he came up them with James Hare, of *Collier's*. He was walking leisurely, and though the bullets passed continuously, he never once ducked his head. He wore a long rain-coat, and as he stood peering over the edge of the hill, with his hands in his pockets and smoking his pipe, he was as unconcerned as though he were gazing at a cinematograph.

The fire from the enemy was so heavy that only one troop among the entire line of the hills was returning it, and all the rest of our men were lying down. General Wood, who was then colonel of the Rough Riders, and I were lying on our elbows at Crane's feet, and Wood ordered him also to lie down. Crane pretended not to hear, and moved farther away, still peering over the hill with the same interested expression. Wood told him for the second time that if he did not lie down he would be killed, but Crane paid no attention. So, in order to make him take shelter, I told him he was trying to impress us with his courage, and that if he thought he was making me feel badly by walking about, he might as well sit down. As soon as I told him he was trying to impress us with his courage, he dropped on his knees, as I had hoped he would, and we breathed again.

After that, in Puerto Rico, we agreed to go out together and take a town by surprise and demand its surrender. At that time every town in Puerto Rico surrendered to the first American who entered it, and we thought that to accept the unconditional surrender of a large number of foreigners would be a pleasing and interesting experience. But Crane's business manager, who guarded him with much the same jealousy as that with which an advance-agent guards the prima donna, did not want anyone else to share the glory of the surrender, and sent Crane off by himself. He rode into Juana Diaz, and the town, as a matter of course, surrendered, and made him welcome. He spent the day in establishing an aristocracy among the townspeople, and in distributing largesse to the hungry. He also spent the night there, sleeping peacefully beyond our lines and with no particular interest as to where the Spaniards might happen to be. The next morning, when he was taking his coffee on the sidewalk in front of the only cafe, he was amused to see a "point" of five soldiers advance cautiously along the Ponce road, dodging behind bushes, and reconnoitering with both the daring and skill of the American invader. While still continuing to sip his coffee he observed a skirmish-line following this "point," and finally the regiment itself, marching bravely upon Juana Diaz. It had come to effect its capture. When the commanding officer arrived, his sense of humor deserted him, and he could not see how necessary and proper it was that any town should surrender to the author of the *Red Badge of Courage*.

A week later, Millard of the New York *Herald*, "El" Root of the New York *Sun*, Howard Thompson, and myself, with some slight assistance from four thousand soldiers, captured a much larger city than the one Crane attacked; but as we stumbled into the town first, under the impression that it was filled with American cavalry, the town of Coamo surrendered to us. The question is, whether it is more creditable to take a town of five thousand people with three other correspondents, supported by four thousand soldiers, or to take a town of two thousand soldiers single-handed. I fear that in the eyes of history Crane's victory will be ranked higher than that of Millard, Root, Thompson, and myself.

One of the most amusing and daring acts of the correspondents was that of Burr W. MacIntosh, of *Frank Leslie's*. When the troops arrived at Daiquiri, a general order was issued forbidding any of the correspondents to accompany the soldiers when they made their first landing. The men on the press-boats of course promptly disobeyed this order; but the correspondents on the transports were forced to obey it, or run the risk of losing their credentials. Mr. MacIntosh was the one exception. He was most desirous of obtaining a photograph, taken on the shores of Cuba, which would show the American soldiers making their first hostile landing on that shore. To this end he gave his camera into the hands of a sergeant in one of the shore-boats, and hid his clothes under the cross-seats of another. When these boats started, MacIntosh dived from the stern of the transport, and after swimming a quarter of a mile through a heavy surf, reached the coast of Cuba in time to recover his camera and perpetuate the first landing of our Army of Invasion.

The correspondents might be divided into three classes—the men who gathered the news, the descriptive writers, and those who collected names. Some of them did all of these three things. There was also a fourth class of correspondent, who accompanied a volunteer regiment and told only of what was done by the particular regiment he accompanied, without touching on the war at all, except when the regiment took a part in it. These young gentlemen unconsciously did a very great injury to the men of the regular army, in persuading the public at home that the volunteer is an effective fighting-machine, instead of making it clear that he is an "amateur," and, as such, is a menace and a danger to the safety of the country.

The points of view of these several correspondents were entirely different. Writers like Stephen Crane, John Fox, Caspar Whitney, and Stephen Bosnal were interested in what was most dramatic and picturesque. The fact that the Rough Riders sang "Fair Harvard" in the rifle-pits, within easy ear-shot of the enemy, was of as much value to them as the movements of Sampson's squadron or the terms of the surrender.

But the men in the news-gathering class, although they possessed as quick an eye for what was striking and human as did the magazine-writers, found that their duty led them in another direction. It was their part to treat the whole campaign as a series of events, to describe it as they would a political convention, to ascertain exactly what orders were given and exactly who carried them into effect. The best of these, as a rule, were the representatives of the *Associated Press*, and they entered into the work in the same impersonal spirit with which they would have handled an annual encampment of the G.A.R., or the first night of a new play. They looked on the thing broadly and from all sides. They wanted the news, all the news, but nothing but the news. The last words of a dying soldier were not important to them. His name, spelled correctly, and the letter of his troop, were to their employers of the highest value. These correspondents were ubiquitous. They were in Jamaica one day, and the next ploughing through heavy seas, and a few hours later back on the firing-line. They were anonymous, and their work, which was at times both brilliant and of historic value, was sunk and lost under the levelling head-line of a press bureau, a machine which would make all men equal, and for which writers sell their

birthright of originality and humor and point of view. Howard Thompson, the Washington correspondent of the *Associated Press*, and E. R. Johnstone, managing editor of the Minneapolis *Times*, are perhaps the two men who, by their individuality, have risen above the anonymity of the bureau they serve. In them the personal element predominates. They are young men who would be conspicuous on a sinking ship or at a dinner table. They are the confidants of Presidents and would-be Presidents, Senators and their "bosses," and they are equally at home in an Indian uprising or at a Presidential convention.

Lyman, of the *Associated Press*, paid the penalty of serving at Siboney, by dying a month after the war of fever.

It is a difficult thing for a correspondent to praise the work of his comrades. Such expression of appreciation would come with more weight from some of the officers of the army, except that these latter could not be free from prejudice, as not a few of them owe much to the young men who made their victories conspicuous. But there are some of the correspondents of whose courage and regard for duty a correspondent can speak more fully, because he knows them more intimately than can the men of the army.

Caspar Whitney and John Fox were distinctly among the most earnest, honest, and brilliant. If each of them had not been well known before the war, one as a novelist, the other as an explorer, their conduct during it would have made their reputations. But there were many others who had never written books in covers, nor explored unknown lands, nor tried themselves by facing unknown dangers. There were so many of these that it would be unfair to mention one before another, but the one who appealed to me the most was Frank Collins, the correspondent of the Boston *Journal.* Only his nearest friends really know how much that young man risked losing when he offered to represent his paper at the front. He was a reporter of the law courts, and he accompanied the Second Massachusetts Regiment. There was no press-boat belonging exclusively to his paper, and while in Cuba he was unable to obtain a horse, so that in order to file his despatches he was forced to go on foot to Siboney, and trust to the kindness of his comrades to see that his copy was taken to Jamaica. He worked by day, and by night tramped through the jungle. A more gentle, courteous, and manly man I have seldom met. He nursed the sick and bandaged the wounded, wrote letters for the dying, and acted as postman for the living. He was always at the front, and he never complained or grumbled. The first time I met him he was gathering flowers to place on the body of a volunteer who had died at Lakeland, and the last time was before the battle of San Juan, when I was unable to walk, and he persuaded a mule-driver to give me a lift in his wagon. Two weeks later, racked with fever and worn out with lack of food, he died, as much a martyr to the war as the men in uniform who were killed by Mauser bullets. We could not have better spared a better man, because better men than Frank Collins are very few.

If the correspondents on land encountered hardships, their condition in comparison was preferable to that of the correspondents who followed the fleet. Their days and nights were spent in dirty tugboats, tossing and turning in heavy seas.

They were sick for sleep, wet to the skin, and sometimes seasick as well. The crews of their boats were always in a state of active or threatened mutiny, and they were engaged in constant struggles with censors, cable companies, and the authorities of the different ports. John R. Spears, of *Scribner's* and the New York *Sun*, Harry S. Brown, of the *Herald*, Walter Howard, of the *Journal*, and Charles H. Diehl are perhaps the four men who most successfully battled with the waves, eluded the cannon balls from the warships, and overcame the difficulties which the censors and the officials of the cable companies placed in the way of their duty. It is impossible to give too much credit to the men who manned the press-boats. They were not able to take anything for granted, and soon learned that they could depend upon no one save themselves. They were forced to learn navigation, geography, diplomacy, and finance. In time each man knew just how many motions of the wheel would carry his tug to Jamaica, how much coal was needed to feed her fires, and how much his crew would drink before they would scramble on deck and demand an increase of wages before deserting in a body. He was captain, engineer, supercargo, and deck hand. With a salary of forty dollars a week, he was responsible for thousands of dollars. One cable alone to the New York *Herald* cost five thousand dollars. He also had to pay for boat hire, port dues, and salaries. These many responsibilities were carried out by young men who were, for the most part, under thirty years of age, who had previously never been farther from New York City than Coney Island, and with an experience as executives which was limited to guessing at the insurance on a fire and reporting Dr. Depew's speeches. Yet with all these duties pressing upon them they were forced to sit in a choking cabin and write accurate and dramatic pictures of bombardments, engagements with shore batteries, and races after blockade-runners, while the cabin table was at an angle of forty-five degrees, and the cabin lamp swung in complete somersaults. Their reward was a hastily written cable-gram of congratulation from the "chief," or a precise and detailed message of instruction from the same source, which, if followed, would have left the paper without news. There is apparently nothing which the "chief" in the home office finds so difficult to comprehend as the fact that the man on the spot must be a better judge of what is needed there than any one else, no matter how clever he may be, two thousand miles away.

The great proportion of correspondents sent home ill was out of all proper relation to their numbers. One reason for this was that too many of them selected to live at Siboney, and made their headquarters in the former huts of the Cubans. These huts were little better than ill-kept dog-kennels, and reeked with fever, which, with the lack of proper food and the hot sun, incapacitated over thirty of the newspaper representatives. It is also true that almost all of the other correspondents who were at the front suffered from fever; in fact, I know of but one or two who escaped it. With but few exceptions, the employers at home made but little effort to preserve the health of their correspondents in the field, which they might easily have done by forwarding them food, tents, and clothing by the press-boats from Jamaica. An occasional cable-gram of congratulation, while grati-

fying to the pride, is not so effective a preventive against fever as quinine or a rubber "poncho." One of the best known of the correspondents, who was on the firing-line at Guantanamo, Guasimas, and San Juan, was sent home, desperately ill with fever, in the same clothes he had been forced to wear for over three weeks. He had forded streams in them, slept on the bare ground in them, and sweated in them from the heat and from fever, and when he reached Fortress Mountain he bought himself a complete new outfit at the modest expenditure of twenty-four dollars. For this his paper refused to pay. This was the same paper that discharged Sylvester Scovel for telling the truth about the Seventy-First New York Volunteers and for returning a blow.

The correspondents who suffered from wounds were four in number—Edward Marshall, who was shot through the body near the spine, and who, after he had been told he could not live, wrote his despatch to his paper as he lay bleeding on his blanket; James Whigham; James F. J. Archibald; and James Creelman. Archibald was one of the "fighting" correspondents, who rendered as effective service as many of the junior officers. He was attached to the First Regiment, and was in command of a squad of men at the time of the landing of the *Gussie* expedition. He was shot through the arm at that time, and was the only man wounded.

There has been no attempt made in this article to describe the acts of every correspondent who acquitted himself well, and there were many whose work was as conspicuous as that of those mentioned here; but what has been said of one is deserved by nearly all. The "water-front" correspondents, as those were called who remained at Siboney, were perhaps the only men who did not perform their whole duty. At that place, thirteen miles from the "side lines," it was impossible, obviously, to obtain any knowledge of the operations of the army, except as it was carried to the rear by stragglers or by the wounded, who were in no fit mental condition to give an accurate account of what had occurred. But the information furnished by these men formed the basis for the news sent out by "water-front" correspondents, and owing to the fact that they were thirteen miles nearer the press-boats than the correspondents with the army, their alarming and visionary accounts were usually the first to reach the American people. This was not only unfair to the reading public, but to the men who were gathering the facts at the front at some personal risk and with some hardships. When the despatches of these latter, which were complete and accurate, reached Jamaica, the wires were already choked with the premature and sensational stories of their less adventurous brothers. It was an instance of "he who is first shall be last." Of the men, besides those already mentioned, who acquitted themselves most notably, and who in the event of another war would be of the first value to any newspaper, are Millard of the *Herald*, Root and Armstrong of the *Sun*, Henry Roberts of the *Eagle*, and John F. Bass, of *Harper's Weekly*. C. E. Akers, of the London *Times*, Phil Robinson, and Seppings Wright were easily the most able and distinguished among the English correspondents. Among the artists and photographers, Frederic Remington, Wilson of the *Herald*, Christy, Floyd Campbell, Dinwiddie, Burton, and James Hare are of the greatest prominence. These are the men to whom the public owe a debt of gratitude. They kept the American people informed of what their countrymen—their brothers, fathers, and friends were doing at the front. They cared for the soldiers when they were wounded, and, as Americans, helped Americans against a common enemy by reconnoitering, scouting, and fighting. They had no uniform to protect them; they were under sentence to be shot as spies if captured by the Spaniards, and they were bound, not by an oath as were the soldiers, but merely by a sense of duty to a newspaper, and by a natural desire to be of service to their countrymen in any way that offered.

WORLD WAR I

THE WAR TO END ALL WARS

1914–1918

THE **FIRST WORLD WAR VIOLENTLY** and precisely reminded Americans that, however romantic and heroic, war exacted a high price in blood and lives. By 1918 the two generations born after the Confederate surrender at Appomattox were too willing to ignore the lessons of the Civil War. In part this was because of the quick, resounding success of the Spanish-American War.

At first, Americans did not want to plunge into the remote European conflict that exploded in summer of 1914. For the people of Sinclair Lewis's fictional Gopher Prairie in *Main Street*, the war brought "the delight of shuddering, then, as the war settled down to a business of trench-fighting, they forgot." The horror and slaughter of the early battles on the eastern and western fronts astonished Americans and strengthened the desire of isolationists to keep the United States at a distance from the European conflict.

Though the people of Gopher Prairie had little interest in events so far removed from their everyday lives, nothing was more newsworthy than the "Great War." President Woodrow Wilson secured passage of socially progressive bills in his first two years in office, but the European war ultimately shouldered aside the era of reform. The war was front-page news, from the success of German U-boats and the ugliness of trench warfare to the actions of opposing leaders and the viciousness of the new weapons.

The war was more than romanticized conflict. Angering, infuriating accounts of German atrocities fueled the passion of a generation. Then came the sinking of the Cunard liner *Laconia*. The very thought of innocent American women and children being torpedoed without warning in the frigid waters of the North Atlantic by German U-boat captains whetted the nation's appetite for vengeance. Who could disagree with the heated words of the Louisville *Courier-Journal* in February 1917: "To hell with the Hohenzollerns and Hapsburgs! The world must be made safe for democracy!"

When it was time to save democracy from the grip of German aggressors, Americans eagerly joined the fight "over there." George M. Cohan, Charles Chaplin, Mary Pickford, and Douglas Fairbanks sold $18 billion in Liberty Bonds. Troops shipped out to France singing "Goodbye Broadway, Hello France!" and promising "sweethearts, wives and mothers" that it would not take too long to defeat the Kaiser. Indeed, the troops would start coming home within two years. But, as in the case of the American Civil War, the shocking reality of war would take even less time to hit home and to forever alter the lives of those who survived the Great War.

Not that soldiers heading across the Atlantic had no prior warning. Reports from the battlefield had warned that European warfare had changed dramatically. A dispatch from United Press correspondent Karl H. von Wiegand described the "new sound" of war—"the staccato rattle of machine guns"—and told how squads of men charging the lines ended up "melting" in a "grotesque manner." The New York *Tribune* reported in April 1915, that the Germans were using poison gas. The vapor with a strange odor induced nausea and death. Technology, the promise borne of the nineteenth-century Industrial Revolution, had become the hallmark of twentieth-century war. Even before the Americans arrived, three years of artillery bombardments had ravaged the European landscape and countless machine-gun turrets had created millions of human casualties. As Barbara Tuchman would write in *The Guns of August*, "The lamps are going out all over Europe, we shall not see them lit again in our lifetime. The sun of the old world is in a dying blaze of splendor never to be seen again."

Correspondents traveled with the "doughboys" across the Atlantic and into battle. From the trenches of northeastern France, as two million of the nation's sons were introduced to the horrors of modern warfare, reporters relayed the grim news. Many journalists saw in the war a great opportunity, and the competition between newspapers and news services to get the scoop reached a new level. Most of the war correspondents were young men who had never witnessed warfare. Both experienced and inexperienced American war correspondents had crossed the Atlantic at the outbreak of World War I. Old hands found covering the war frustrating, as censors kept a close watch on what they had written. Reporters had to work hard to get good stories. Green reporters quickly learned to adapt to covering a war that soon proved to be the most deadly in history. At times, the reporters seemed to flock together, but they never lost the spirit of competition. All strove to get the story first and relay it as quickly as possible to their newspaper or news service.

With America's entrance into the war in April 1917, a second wave of American reporters crossed the Atlantic to offer their perspective on the Great War. Among the new batch of newsmen were soldiers in uniform who put together a newspaper for the large number of American soldiers in the Allied Expeditionary Force. The participation of American forces in the European battles during the spring, summer, and fall of 1918 raised the public's demand for news to a new peak. The reports from the battlefield, the

Yanks leave for France in 1917. *(National Archives)*

maps, photographs, lists of casualties, political cartoons, and editorials could never quite satisfy the appetite for information on the progress of the American effort.

For all the mechanization of the war—the machine guns, railroads, poison gas, airplanes, and submarines—the war still contained a measure of a personal conflict. The story of Verdun Belle, a canine companion to a marine unit, tears at the emotions when the wounded marine and his dog are reunited. Indeed, as *Stars and Stripes* reported, to the busy medical workers, the marine was just a number. But to Belle, and to the soldier's family back home, the young marine was much more than that.

By 1918 the stagnant battle lines and the mounting casualties wore American passions thin. The death by firing squad of the spy Mata Hari, Henry G. Wales of the International News Service soberly told readers, was not as Hollywood would depict it. Rather, when the executioners' volley struck her, she simply collapsed and "lay prone, motionless with her face to the sky." Ernest Hemingway's somber narrative of a farewell dance for troops who had trained at Leavenworth lacked the dazzle Broadway might give it. Reality set in. As A. A. Milne argued, "Once more I beg you all . . . tear away the veil of sentimental mysticism through which you have looked at war, and try to see it as it really is." Indeed, the war ended not with a resounding cheer of victory but with a terse midnight statement released to straggling newspapermen at the State Department.

Despite claims that the conflict had dealt a decisive loss to Germany and that German acquiescence to the armistice meant the enemy accepted the loss, history would prove otherwise.

For war correspondents, World War I advanced the progressively greater recognition of their public service. The first Pulitzer Prize for reporting went to Herbert Bayard Swope for his dispatches from the western front. Many other newspapermen would win the award for their work during subsequent wars. When the war ended on Armistice Day, November 11, 1918, war correspondents became foreign correspondents, but war-related news kept coming. It came from the peace conference that drafted the Treaty of Versailles. It came when the United States dedicated the Tomb of the Unknown Soldier. And it continued to come as veterans founded the American Legion and attempted to perpetuate the camaraderie they had known in uniform. As for so many wars, the end of the war was not the end of the war story.

RICHARD HARDING DAVIS

"SAW GERMAN ARMY ROLL ON LIKE FOG"

NEW YORK *TRIBUNE*, AUGUST 23, 1914

The August day that Great Britain declared war on Germany, Richard Harding Davis sailed aboard the Lusitania *for Liverpool. Fifty years of age, Davis had covered the Spanish-American War and the Russo-Japanese War, so he was no stranger to the battlefield. And he was not the only seasoned war correspondent aboard the Cunard liner. Gerald Morgan and Frederick Palmer had also established reputations. The three correspondents would compete for scoops in the new conflict.*

The seat of the war was Belgium, where the kingdom's forces were trying to stop the advancing German tide. Davis quickly made his way to Brussels, from which he made day trips to seek out the military action. On August 20, the war came to the reporter in the Belgian capital. The American watched as a corps of General Alexander von Kluck's First Army marched through Brussels, not even stopping to occupy the city. The reporter was reminded of an event a quarter century earlier, the 1889 Johnstown flood in which thousands died—his first big story.

Another reporter might have admired a model army, flowing with a precision and speed that would have awed soldiers in any army. Another reporter might have admired the harmony of the German men as they sang of their fatherland. Another reporter might have seen the German army not as a fog or a flood but as the product of kultur. But Davis had already judged the invading force, and it frightened him.

Within days after von Kluck's army passed through Brussels, Davis was arrested by the Germans and nearly executed as a British spy. Later he would be arrested by the French. The obstacles to reporting on the war by both sides eventually prompted Davis to observe: "The day of the war correspondents is over." Just over eighteen months after he saw the German army move like a fog through Brussels, he died of a heart attack at his home in Westchester County, New York.

BRUSSELS, Friday, Aug. 21, 2 P.M.

THE ENTRANCE OF THE GERMAN army into Brussels has lost the human quality. It was lost as soon as the three soldiers who led the army bicycled into the Boulevard du Regent and asked the way to the Gare du Nord. When they passed the human note passed with them.

What came after them, and twenty-four hours later is still coming, is not men marching, but a force of nature like a tidal wave, an avalanche or a river flooding its banks. At this moment it is rolling through Brussels as the swollen waters of the Concemaugh Valley swept through Johnstown.

At the sight of the first few regiments of the enemy we were thrilled with interest. After three hours they had passed in one unbroken steel gray column [and] we were bored. But when hour after hour passed and there was no halt, no breathing time, no open spaces in the ranks, the thing became uncanny, inhuman. You returned to watch it, fascinated. It held the mystery and menace of fog rolling toward you across the sea.

The gray of the uniforms worn by both officers and men helped this air of mystery. Only the sharpest eye could detect among the thousands that passed the slightest difference. All moved under a cloak of invisibility. Only after the most numerous and severe tests at all distances, with all materials and combinations of colors that give forth no color could this gray have been discovered. That it was selected to clothe and disguise the German when he fights is typical of the German staff striving for efficiency to leave nothing to chance, to neglect no detail.

After you have seen this service uniform under conditions entirely opposite you are convinced that for the German soldier it is his strongest weapon. Even the most expert marksman cannot hit a target he cannot see. It is a gray green, not the blue gray of our Confederates. It is the gray of the hour just before daybreak, the gray of unpolished steel, of mist among green trees.

I saw it first in the Grand Place in front of the Hotel de Ville. It was impossible to tell if in that noble square there was a regiment or a brigade. You saw only a fog that melted into the stones, blended with the ancient house fronts, that shifted and drifted, but left you nothing at which you could point.

Later, as the army passed below my window, under the trees of the Botanical Park, it merged and was lost against the green leaves. It is no exaggeration to say that at a hundred yards you can see the horses on which the Uhlans ride, but cannot see the men who ride them.

If I appear to overemphasize this disguising uniform it is because of all the details of the German outfit, it appealed to me as one of the most remarkable. The other day, when I was with the rear guard of the French Dragoons and Curassiers and they threw out pickets, we could distinguish them against the yellow wheat or green course at half a mile, while these men passing in the street, when they have reached the next crossing, become merged into the gray of the paving stones and the earth swallows them. In comparison the yellow khaki of our own American army is about as invisible as the flag of Spain.

Yesterday Major General von Jarotzky, the German Military Governor of Brussels, assured Burgomaster Max that the German army would not occupy the city, but would pass through it. It is still passing. I have followed in campaigns six armies, but, excepting not even our own, the Japanese or the British, I have not seen one so thoroughly equipped. I am not speaking of the fighting qualities of any army, only of the equipment and organization. The German army moved into this city as smoothly and as compactly as an Empire State Express. There were not halts, no open places, no stragglers.

This army has been on active service three weeks, and so far there is not apparently a chinstrap or a horseshoe missing. It came in with the smoke pouring from cookstoves on wheels, and in an hour had set up postoffice wagons, from which mounted messengers galloped along the line of column distributing letters and at which soldiers posted picture postcards.

The infantry came in in files of five, two

The New York *Tribune* reports the declaration of war. The *Tribune* was founded by Horace Greeley in 1841. Such leading correspondents as Richard Harding Davis and Will Irwin were notable contributors.

hundred men to each company; the Lances in columns of four, with not a pennant missing. The quick fire guns and field pieces were one hour at a time in passing, each gun with its caisson and ammunition wagon taking twenty seconds in which to pass.

The men of the infantry sang "Fatherland, My Fatherland." Between each line of song they took three steps. At times two thousand men were singing together in absolute rhythm and beat. When the melody gave way the silence was broken only by the stamp of iron-shod boots, and then

again the song rose. When the singing ceased the bands played marches. They were followed by the rumble of siege guns, the creaking of wheels and of chains clanking against the cobble stones and the sharp bell-like voices of the bugles.

For seven hours the army passed in such solid column that not once might a taxicab or trolley car pass through the city. Like a river of steel it flowed, gray and ghostlike. Then, as dusk came and as thousands of horses' hoofs and thousands of iron boots continued to tramp forward, they struck tiny sparks from the stones, but the horses and the men who beat out the sparks were invisible.

At midnight pack wagons and siege guns were still passing. At 7 this morning I was awakened by the tramp of men and bands playing jauntily. Whether they marched all night or not I do not know; but now for twenty-six hours the gray army has rumbled by with the mystery of fog and the pertinacity of a steam roller.

KARL H. VON WIEGAND

"EASTERN FRONT DISPATCH"

UNITED PRESS, OCTOBER 8, 1914

Newspaper correspondents already in Europe in August 1914 were present to witness and testify to a more deadly warfare than ever before seen. One of the first reporters to describe the horrors of the new war to Americans was German-born Karl H. von Wiegand, who had begun his newspaper career in Arizona and California. Since 1911 he had served the United Press in Berlin. While a correspondent like Richard Harding Davis was decidedly anti-German, von Wiegand was more sympathetic to the Central European power.

The Berlin-based reporter covered both the eastern and western fronts. In the first few days of the war, he witnessed the German attack on Liège, sending out his dispatches to The Hague for transmittal to the United States. Soon afterward his report of an interview with a witness of the first air battle of the war was a sensation. Shifting to the eastern front, von Wiegand witnessed the following battle near Wirballen, about a hundred miles to the east of Konigsberg—where Immanual Kant had taught philosophy more than a century earlier. The war was barely over a month old.

Von Wiegand continued to cover World War I, winning lasting renown for his conversations with German leaders and his reports from the German side of the war's fronts. After the war von Wiegand was in Munich to cover Hitler's "putsch."

WIRBALLEN, RUSSIAN POLAND (ON THE FIRING LINE, VIA THE HAGUE AND LONDON) October 8 (UP)

AT SUNDOWN TONIGHT AFTER four days of constant fighting, the German Army holds its strategic and strongly entrenched position east of Wirballen. As I write this in the glare of a screened automobile headlight several hundred yards behind the German trenches, I can catch the occasional high notes of a soldier chorus. For days, these soldiers have lain cramped in these muddy ditches, unable to move or to stretch except under cover of darkness. And still they sing. They believe they are on the eve of a great victory.

Today I saw a wave of Russian flesh and blood dash against a wall of German steel. . . .

From the outset of the advance the German artillery began shelling the on-rushing mass with wonderfully timed shrapnel.

On came the Slave swarm—into the range of the German trenches, with wild yells and never a waver. Russian battle flags, the first I had seen, appeared in the front of the charging ranks.

Then came a new sound. First I saw a sudden, almost grotesque melting of the advancing line. It was different from anything that had taken place before. The men literally went down like dominoes in a row. Those who had kept their feet were hurled back as though by a terrible gust of wind. Almost in the second that I pon-dered, puzzled, the staccato rattle of machine guns reached us. My ear answered the query of my eye.

For the first time, the advancing lines here hesitated, apparently bewildered. Mounted officers dashed along the line urging the men forward. Horses fell with the men. I saw a dozen riderless horses dashing madly through the lines, adding a new terror. . . . Then with the withering fire raking them even as they faltered, the lines broke. Panic ensued.

WILL IRWIN

"GERMANS USE BLINDING GAS TO AID POISON FUMES"

NEW YORK *TRIBUNE*, APRIL 27, 1915

A little over two weeks after the outbreak of the Great War, Will Irwin, together with three journalist friends, hired a taxi to take them to the battle raging near Louvain, Belgium. The four had no knowledge of Belgium, and only Irwin had an elementary knowledge of France. Like Richard Harding Davis, whose path they crossed, the four eager but inept war correspondents soon found themselves behind the advancing German lines.

Irwin quickly recovered from this fumbling start. While censorship left the public in the dark on much of what was going on in the war, Irwin pieced together an account approved by censors that told of an October 1914 battle in which "Europe lost as many men as the North lost in the whole Civil War." Irwin's "The Splendid Story of Ypres" appeared in the Tribune *in February 1915, and although it appeared months after the battle, the news was fresh. The report was one of the principal scoops in the war and was an immediate sensation.*

Not long after the publication of "The Splendid Story of Ypres," Irwin again had a remarkable story. When the Second Battle of Ypres exploded in April 1915, he was nearby to cover it. Irwin reported in a dispatch dated April 24 that the Germans had used "asphyxiating bombs, which will doubtless become famous in this war." Irwin did not know what gas was used but noted that it was not ordinarily fatal. The American reporter followed up his short remarks on gas warfare in this first dispatch, with a lengthier account in a second dispatch two days later. Both pieces made the front page of the New York Tribune. *After writing the first story, Will Irwin made his way to the front to further investigate the gas attack. There he himself became a victim of gas.*

Fresh troops from the Yorkshire Regiment move up to an advanced position on a French battlefield. *(Library of Congress)*

THE GERMAN TROOPS, WHO FOL-
lowed up this advantage with a direct attack, held inspirators in their mouths, these preventing them from being overcome by the fumes.

The effect of the noxious trench gas seems to be slow in wearing away. The men come out of their violent nausea in a state of utter collapse. Some of the rescued have already died from the after effects. How many of the men left unconscious in the trenches when the French broke died from the fumes it is impossible to say, since those trenches were at once occupied by the Germans.

This new form of attack needs for success a favorable wind. Twice in the day that followed the Germans tried trench vapor on the Canadians who made on the right of the French position a stand which will probably be remembered as one of the heroic episodes of this war. In both cases the wind was not favorable, and the Canadians managed to stick through it. The noxious, explosive bombs were, however, used continually against the Canadian forces and caused some losses.

HERBERT BAYARD SWOPE

"ON THE SOMME: ORDEAL BY BATTLE"

INSIDE THE GERMAN EMPIRE (NEW YORK WORLD, 1917)

On assignment to cover a transatlantic air flight for the New York World, *Herbert Bayard Swope arrived in Europe just as the First World War was about to begin. The experienced reporter, like Ralph Pulitzer, son of Joseph and owner of the* World, *had German roots and was anxious to offer a sympathetic treatment of the Germans. Swope sent his accounts from the German side of the lines in 1914 and then again in 1916.*

While American newspapers were filled with numerous reports from correspondents covering the war from the Allied side of the Western front, Swope and Karl von Wiegand were among a much smaller number who viewed the war from the German side of the lines. After the expulsion from the United States of Franz von Papen, the German military attaché, in December 1915, the Germans had become increasingly antagonistic toward Americans and their correspondents. Swope met von Papen at the Somme front and found him still "friendly" toward the United States. Swope's dispatches from the less covered side of the western front were published early in 1917 in a single volume, Inside the German Empire. *His insightful reporting won him a Pulitzer Prize, the first Pulitzer awarded for reporting.*

In September 1916 General Karl von Wenninger hosted a group of neutral army observers and correspondents, including Swope and James O'Donnell Bennett of the Chicago Tribune, as they took a look at a portion of the Somme front near Thiepval. The following account gives Swope's remarks on his visit to this unquiet part of the front.

THE SOMME REPRESENTS WAR raised to the nth power.

At different times one can see and hear every phase of activity, drumfire, light field pieces, machine guns, hand grenades, mine-throwers, infantry attacks, mine explosions, liquid fire gas, observation balloons, anti-aircraft cannon, while aeroplane observation and flights are so common that they fail to stir up any excitement even among visitors. I counted as many as sixty machines aloft in half an hour a few weeks ago. The large majority of them were French and English, for the German machines are heavily outnumbered, so much so that their value as observers is sharply curtailed.

Where before a division covered about three miles of front, the fighting is so intensive on the Somme that it now holds less than one mile. This is true on both sides.

In one day the Third (German) Division, standing opposite the Courcelette-Martinpuich line, shot away 160 heavy truck loads of ammunition. This is a fair example of the tremendous drain on supplies. The reserve men and supplies are brought up at night. That is why the roads on both sides are generously sprayed with cannon-fire after sunset.

The Germans have pushed the railroad

Gun crew from regimental headquarters company, 23rd Infantry, fire a 37 mm gun during an advance against German entrenched positions. *(National Archives)*

construction right up to the firing lines to facilitate replenishment of supplies. It is rather incongruous to see locomotives puffing away, with harvesters at work on one side (the Germans till the ground right up to the volcano's edge) and heavy guns shooting on the other.

One of the proudest boasts the Germans make is that at the Hohenzollern redoubt their hand-grenade men outthrew in distance and accuracy the English, who should have excelled through their cricket practice. Some English prisoners admitted this claim. "We didn't know how to handle the things at first, and they did, but you ought to see us now."

Pigeon-posts are much used at the Somme. The birds are taken into the front lines, and when communications are broken, they are released, two at a time, each carrying the same message, and they fly back to headquarters.

As you pass through the villages in the line of fire you notice that every house has a sign on it indicating how many soldiers can find place in the cellar when bombardment begins.

Bapaume, one of the greatest objectives of the British just now, is under almost constant fire, yet many French villagers still stay there. They no longer live in the houses; they live entirely in the cellars and the improvised chimneys stick up along the street in a weird manner.

In going down the roads and across fields under fire, the reserves go single file and several paces apart. So do the correspondents, and the precaution is not calculated to heighten one's feeling of safety, especially when fountains of earth are kicked up by exploding nine-inch shells only eighty or one hundred yards away.

One finds himself thinking that if the gunner had deflected only two points, well, as Bennett of the Chicago *Tribune* and I were leaving a 21-centimeter position opposite Pozihres a shot scythed through a tree not ten yards from us. A new world's record for the 880-yard run was made from then and there. Bennett is fat, so I beat him, but I could have beaten a real champion under the same conditions.

FLOYD GIBBONS

"THE SINKING OF THE *LACONIA*"

CHICAGO *TRIBUNE*, FEBRUARY 26, 1917

When the Chicago Tribune's *Floyd Gibbons set sail for Europe in February 1917, he hoped to have a story even before he set foot in Great Britain. In January, Germany had resumed unrestricted submarine warfare in its war zone around the British Isles. Gibbons could have taken passage aboard the* Frederik VIII, *which sailed in mid-February carrying German ambassador Count Johann Heinrich von Bernstorff, who was leaving the country after the United States broke diplomatic ties with Germany. The passengers aboard the* Frederik VIII *did not have to worry about German submarines. But Floyd Gibbons chose to take his chances on a British Cunard liner, the* Laconia. *The ambitious war correspondent hoped the ship would be attacked by a U-boat, as had three sunken Cunard passenger liners—the* Lusitania, *the* Franconia, *and the* Alaunia. *That would be a story.*

The Laconia *was the largest ship in the British merchant service to be attacked by a German submarine since the* Lusitania *in 1915. With the sinking of the* Laconia, *the Cunard lost its fourth large passenger ship and had only five remaining. February 1917 was by far the worst single month of the war to date in terms of Allied and neutral tonnage lost to submarines.*

The journalistic ardor of Floyd Gibbons was not dampened by the sinking of the Laconia. *What did dampen his spirit was the strict censorship of reporters' dispatches. He confided his sentiments to a colleague, Ring Lardner: "I'm getting sick of it. My* Laconia *experience has convinced me that all that is left me to do is to pull some sensational stunt, and I'm going to do it. I'm going over the top with the boys at the first opportunity." Gibbons was with American forces as they went into one of their first actions at Belleau Wood. On June 6, 1918, while he was attempting to cross a field with a marine officer, the two were hit by German machine-gun fire. One shot shattered the correspondent's arm, while another passed through his left eye. His wounded eyeball dangling from its socket, Gibbons and the wounded officer were pinned down by machine-gun fire for three hours before darkness made possible their escape. France later honored Gibbons for his valor.*

After the war, Gibbons, wearing a patch over his missing eye, was a foreign correspondent for the Chicago Tribune *for several years.*

QUEENSTOWN, February 26 (VIA LONDON)—

I HAVE SERIOUS DOUBTS WHETHER this is a real story. I am not entirely certain that it is not all a dream and that in a few minutes I will wake up back in stateroom B19 on the promenade deck of the Cunarder *Laconia* and hear my cockney steward informing me with an abundance of "and sirs" that it is a fine morning.

It is now a little over thirty hours since I stood on the slanting decks of the big liner, listened to the lowering of the lifeboats, heard the hiss of escaping steam and the roar of ascending rockets as they tore lurid rents in the black sky and cast their red glare over the roaring sea.

I am writing this within thirty minutes after stepping on the dock here in Queenstown from the British mine sweeper which picked up our lifeboat after an eventful six hours of drifting and darkness and bailing and pulling on the oars and of straining aching eyes toward the empty, meaningless horizon in search of help. But, dream or fact, here it is:

The Cunard liner *Laconia*, 18,000 tons' burden, carrying seventy-three passengers; men, women, and children, of whom six were American citizens, manned by a mixed crew of 216, bound from New York to Liverpool, and loaded with foodstuffs, cotton, and raw material, was torpedoed without warning by a German submarine last night off the Irish coast. The vessel sank in about forty minutes.

Two American citizens, mother and daughter, listed from Chicago and former residents there, are among the dead. . . .

The first cabin passengers were gathered in the lounge Sunday evening, with the exception of the bridge fiends in the smoke room.

"Poor Butterfly" was dying wearily on the talking machine, and several couples were dancing.

About the tables in the smoke room the conversation was limited to the announcement of bids and orders to the stewards. Before the fireplace was a little gathering which had been dubbed the Hyde Park corner—an allusion I don't quite fully understand. This group had about exhausted available discussion when I projected a new bone of contention.

"What do you say are our chances of being torpedoed?" I asked.

"Well," drawled the deliberative Mr. Henry Chetham, a London solicitor, "I should say four thousand to one."

Lucien J. Jerome, of the British diplomatic service, returning with an Ecuadorian valet from South America, interjected: "Considering the zone and the class of this ship, I should put it down at two hundred and fifty to one that we don't meet a sub."

At this moment the ship gave a sudden lurch sideways and forward. There was a muffled noise like the slamming of some large door at a good distance away. The slightness of the shock and the meekness of the report compared with my imagination were disappointing. Every man in the room was on his feet in an instant.

"We're hit!" shouted Mr. Chetham.

"That's what we've been waiting for," said Mr. Jerome.

"What a lousy torpedo!" said Mr. Kirby in typical New Yorkese. "It must have been a fizzer."

I looked at my watch. It was 10:30 P.M.

Then came the five blasts on the whistle. We rushed down the corridor leading from the smoke room at the stern to the lounge, which was amidship. We were running, but there was no panic. The occupants of the lounge were just leaving by the forward doors as we entered. . . .

The torpedo had hit us well astern on the starboard side and had missed the engines and the dynamos. I had not noticed the deck lights before. Throughout the voyage our decks had remained dark at night and all cabin portholes were clamped down and all windows covered with opaque paint. . . .

Steam began to hiss somewhere from the giant gray funnels that towered above. Suddenly there was a roaring swish as a rocket soared upward from the captain's bridge, leaving a comet's tail of fire. I watched it as it described a graceful arc in the black void overhead, and then, with an audible pop, it burst in a flare of brilliant colors.

There was a tilt to the deck. It was listing to starboard at just the angle that would make it necessary to reach for support to enable one to stand upright. In the meantime electric floodlights—large white enameled funnels containing clusters of bulbs—had been suspended from the promenade deck and illuminated the

dark water that rose and fell on the slanting side of the ship. . . .

A hatchet was thrust into my hand and I forwarded it to the bow. There was a flash of sparks as it crashed down on the holding pulley. One strand of the rope parted and down plunged the bow, too quick for the stern man. We came to a jerky stop with the stern in the air and the bow down, but the stern managed to lower away until the dangerous angle was eliminated.

Then both tried to lower together. The list of the ship's side became greater, but, instead of our boat sliding down it like a toboggan, the taffrail caught and was held. As the lowering continued, the other side dropped down and we found ourselves clinging on at a new angle and looking straight down on the water.

Many feet and hands pushed the boat from the side of the ship, and we sagged down again, this time smacking squarely on the pillowy top of a rising swell. It felt more solid than mid-air, at least. But we were far from being off. The pulleys stuck twice in their fastenings, bow and stern, and the one ax passed forward and back, and with it my flashlight, as the entangling ropes that held us to the sinking *Laconia* were cut away.

Some shout from that confusion of sound caused me to look up, and I really did so with the fear that one of the nearby boats was being lowered upon us. . . .

As we pulled away from the side of the ship, its receding terrace of lights stretched upward. The ship was slowly turning over. We were opposite that part occupied by the engine rooms. There was a tangle of ears, spars, and rigging on the seat and considerable confusion before

World War I–era
recruiting poster.
(National Archives)

four of the big sweeps could be manned on either side of the boat. . . .

We rested on our oars, with all eyes on the still lighted *Laconia*. The torpedo had struck at 10:30 P.M., according to our ship's time. It was thirty minutes afterward that another dull thud, which was accompanied by a noticeable drop in the hulk, told its story of the second torpedo that the submarine had dispatched through the engine room and the boat's vitals from a distance of two hundred yards.

We watched silently during the next minute, as the tiers of lights dimmed slowly from white to yellow, then to red, and nothing was left but the murky mourning of the night, which hung over all like a pall.

A mean, cheese-colored crescent of a moon revealed one horn above a rag bundle of clouds in the distance. A rim of blackness settled around our little world, relieved only by general leering stars in the zenith, and where the *Laconia*'s lights had shone there remained only the dim outline of a blacker hulk standing out above the water like a jagged headland, silhouetted against overcast sky.

The ship sank rapidly at the stern until at last its nose stood straight up in the air. Then it slid silently down and out of sight like a piece of disappearing scenery in a panorama spectacle.

HENRY G. WALES

"DEATH COMES TO MATA HARI"

INTERNATIONAL NEWS SERVICE, OCTOBER 19, 1917

Henry G. Wales's account of Mata Hari's execution dispelled much of the myth that surrounded the seductive spy's life and death. Wales, the staff correspondent for the International News Service, was simply at the right place at the right moment to record the shooting. He was there when Mata Hari was awakened and accompanied her and the military escorts to the Vincennes barracks, where he witnessed the firing squad. In fine detail, he dutifully jotted down the simple facts. When pieced together in the correspondent's account, these facts dispelled the aura of mystery that enveloped the spy—and indeed made her look as human as the private in the trenches.

Wales's straightforward account of the informant's shooting lacked the flair and intrigue that Hollywood, or a more fanciful writer, might have added. The story belied the tale that in her last moment she opened her coat to bare her body to her executioners. But the reporter's account was rich in its austerity.

PARIS, October 18, 1917

MATA HARI, WHICH IS JAVANESE for Eye-of-the-Morning, is dead. She was shot as a spy by a firing squad of Zouaves at the Vincennes Barracks. She died facing death literally, for she refused to be blindfolded.

Margaretha Geertruida Zelle, for that was the real name of the beautiful Dutch-Javanese dancer, did appeal to President

Poincare for a reprieve, but he refused to intervene.

The first intimation she received that her plea had been denied was when she was led at daybreak from her cell in the Saint-Lazare prison to a waiting automobile and then rushed to the barracks where the firing squad awaited her.

Never once had the iron will of the beautiful woman failed her. Father Arbaux, accompanied by two sisters of charity, Captain Bouchardon, and Maitre Clunet, her lawyer, entered her cell, where she was still sleeping—a calm, untroubled sleep, it was remarked by the turnkeys and trusties.

The sisters gently shook her. She arose and was told that her hour had come.

"May I write two letters?" was all she asked.

Consent was given immediately by Captain Bouchardon, and pen, ink, paper, and envelopes were given to her.

She seated herself at the edge of the bed and wrote the letters with feverish haste. She handed them over to the custody of her lawyer.

Then she drew on her stockings, black, silken, filmy things, grotesque in the circumstances. She placed her high-heeled slippers on her feet and tied the silken ribbons over her insteps.

She arose and took the long black velvet cloat, edged around the bottom with fur and with a huge square fur collar hanging down the back, from a hook over the head of her bed. She placed this cloak over the heavy silk kimono which she had been wearing over her nightdress.

Her wealth of black hair was still coiled about her head in braids. She put on a large, flapping black felt hat with a black silk ribbon and bow. Slowly and indifferently, it seemed, she pulled on a pair of black kid gloves. Then she said calmly:

"I am ready."

The party slowly filed out of her cell to the waiting automobile.

The car sped through the heart of the sleeping city. It was scarcely half-past five in the morning and the sun was not yet fully up.

Clear across Paris the car whirled to the Caserne de Vincennes, the barracks of the old fort which the Germans stormed in 1870.

The troops were already drawn up for the execution. The twelve Zouaves, forming the firing squad, stood in line, their rifles at ease. A subofficer stood behind them, sword drawn.

The automobile stopped, and the party descended, Mata Hari last. The party walked straight to the spot, where a little hummock of earth reared itself seven or eight feet high and afforded a background for such bullets as might miss the human target.

As Father Arbaux spoke with the condemned woman, a French officer approached, carrying a white cloth.

"The blindfold," he whispered to the nuns who stood there and handed it to them.

"Must I wear that?" asked Mata Hari, turning to her lawyer, as her eyes glimpsed the blindfold.

M. Clunet turned interrogatively to the French officer.

"If Madame prefers not, it makes no difference," replied the officer, hurriedly turning away.

Mata Hari was not bound and she was

not blindfolded. She stood gazing stead-fastly at her executioners, when the priest, the nuns, and her lawyer stepped away from her.

The officer in command of the firing squad, who had been watching his men like a hawk that none might examine his rifle and try to find out whether he was destined to fire the blank cartridge which was in the breach of one rifle, seemed re-lieved that the business would soon be over.

A sharp, crackling command, and the file of twelve men assumed rigid positions at attention. Another command, and their rifles were at their shoulders; each man gazed down his barrel at the breast of the woman which was the target.

She did not move a muscle.

The underofficer in charge had moved to a position where from the corners of their eyes they could see him. His sword was extended in the air.

It dropped. The sun—by this time up—flashed on the burnished blade as it de-scribed an arc in falling. Simultaneously the sound of the volley rang out. Flame and a tiny puff of grayish smoke issued from the muzzle of each rifle. Automati-cally the men dropped their arms.

At the report Mata Hari fell. She did not die as actors and moving-picture stars would have us believe that people die when they are shot. She did not throw up her hands nor did she plunge straight for-ward or straight back.

Instead she seemed to collapse. Slowly, inertly, she settled to her knees, her head up always, and without the slightest change of expression on her face. For the fraction of a second it seemed she tot-tered there, on her knees, gazing directly at those who had taken her life. Then she fell backward, bending at the waist, with her legs doubled up beneath her. She lay prone, motionless, with her face turned towards the sky.

A noncommissioned officer, who ac-companied a lieutenant, drew his revolver from the big, black holster strapped about his waist. Bending over, he placed the muzzle of the revolver almost—but not quite—against the left temple of the spy. He pulled the trigger, and the bullet tore into the brain of the woman.

Mata Hari was surely dead.

ALEXANDER WOOLLCOTT

"VERDUN BELLE, MARINE'S PAL FINDS HER OWN"

STARS AND STRIPES, JUNE 14, 1918

Alexander Woollcott was an unlikely war correspondent. In the same year the First World War broke out in Europe, the young reporter became the dramatic critic for the New York Times *and made a name for himself with his column "Second Thoughts on First Nights" in the next few years. When the United States entered the European war, Woollcott enlisted in the army. Initially he served as a hospital orderly in France, but later he was transferred to the staff of* Stars and Stripes, *the wartime newspaper for enlisted men. Bespectacled and overweight, Woollcott stood out prominently in a number of Albian A. Wallgren's cartoons in the soldiers' newspaper. The reporter, despite his appearance, was able to get good stories from the more soldierlike officers and enlisted men with whom he talked.*

In the spring of 1918, Woollcott and John T. Winterich, another Stars and Stripes *correspondent, visited an American field hospital in the country villa of a Paris business-man. Winterich struck up a conversation with a wounded marine who had a dog. Moments later, Woollcott arrived on the scene and quickly recognized a good story in the marine and his faithful dog, whose name was Belle. By all rights the story should have been Winterich's, but Woollcott insisted on writing it.*

Discharged several months after the end of the war, Alexander Woollcott returned to his position as dramatic critic for the New York Times *in August 1919.*

THIS IS THE STORY OF VERDUN Belle, a trench dog who adopted a young leatherneck, of how she followed him to the edge of the battle around Chateau-Thierry, and was waiting for him when they carried him out. It is a true story.

Belle is a setter bitch, shabby white, with great splotches of chocolate brown in her coat. Her ears are brown and silken. Her ancestry is dubious. She is undersize and would not stand a chance among the haughtier breeds they show in splendor at Madison Square Garden back home. But the marines think there never was a dog like her since the world began.

No one in the regiment knows whence she came, nor why. When she joined the outfit in a sector near Verdun, she singled out one of the privates as her very own and attached herself to him for the duration of the war. The young marine would talk long and earnestly to her, and everyone swore that Belle could "compree" English.

She used to curl up at his feet when he slept, or follow silently to keep him company at the listening post. She would sit hopefully in front of him whenever he set-

tled down with his laden mess kit, which the cooks always heaped extra-high in honor of Belle.

Belle was as used to war as the most weather-beaten poilu. The tremble of the ground did not disturb her, and the whining whir of the shells overhead only made her twitch and wrinkle her nose in her sleep. She was trench-broken. You could have put a plate of savory pork chops on the parapet, and nothing would have induced her to go up after them.

She weathered many a gas attack. Her master contrived a protection for her by cutting down and twisting a French gas mask. At first this sack over her nose irritated her tremendously, but once, when she was trying to claw it off with her forepaws, she got a whiff of the poisoned air. Then a great light dawned on Belle, and after that, at the first *alerte*, she would race for her mask. You could not have taken it from her until her master's pat on her back told her everything was all right.

In the middle of May, Belle presented a proud but not particularly astonished regiment with nine confused and wriggling puppies, black and white or, like their mother, brown and white, and possessed of incredible appetites. Seven of these were alive and kicking when, not so very many days ago, the order came for the regiment to pull up stakes and speed across France to help stem the German tide north of the troubled Marne.

In the rush and hubbub of marching orders, Belle and her brood were forgotten by everyone but the young marine. It never once entered his head to leave her or her pups behind. Somewhere he found a market basket and bumbled the litter into that. He could carry the pups, he explained, and the mother dog would trot at his heels.

Now the amount of hardware a marine is expected to carry on the march is carefully calculated to the maximum strength of the average soldier, yet this leatherneck found extra muscle somewhere for his precious basket. If it came to the worst, he thought, he could jettison his pack. It was not very clear in his mind what he would do with his charges during a battle, but he trusted to luck and Verdun Belle.

For forty kilometers he carried his burden along the parched French highway. No one wanted to kid him out of it, nor could have if they would. When there followed a long advance by camion, he yielded his place to the basket of wriggling pups, while he himself hung on the tailboard.

But then there was more hiking, and the basket proved too much. It seemed that the battle line was somewhere far off. Solemnly, the young marine killed four of the puppies, discarded the basket, and slipped the other three into his shirt.

Thus he trudged on his way, carrying those three, pouched in forest green, as kangaroo carries its young, while the mother dog trotted trustingly behind.

One night he found that one of the black and white pups was dead. The road, by this time, was black with hurrying troops, lumbering lorries jostling the line of advancing ambulances, dust-gray columns of soldiers moving on as far ahead and as far behind as the eye could see. Passing silently in the other direction was the desolate procession of refugees from the invaded countryside. Now and then a herd of cows or a little cluster of fugitives from some desolated village, trundling their most cherished possessions in wheelbarrows and babycarts, would cause an eddy in the traffic.

Somewhere in this congestion and confusion, Belle was lost. In the morning there was no sign of her, and the young marine did not know what to do. He begged a cup of milk from an old Frenchwoman, and with the eyedropper from his kit he tried to feed the two pups. It did not work very well. Faintly, the veering wind brought down the valley from far ahead the sound of the cannon. Soon he would be in the thick of it, and there was no Belle to care for the pups.

Two ambulances of a field hospital were passing in the unending caravan. A lieutenant who looked human was in the front seat of one of them, a sergeant beside him. The leatherneck ran up to them, blurted out his story, gazed at them imploringly, and thrust the puppies into their hands.

"Take good care of them," he said. "I don't suppose I'll ever see them again."

And he was gone. A little later in the day, that field hospital was pitching its tents and setting up its kitchens and tables in a deserted farm. Amid all the hurry of preparation for the big job ahead, they found time to worry about those pups.

The problem was food. Corned willy was tried and found wanting.

Finally, the first sergeant hunted up a farm-bred private, and the two of them spent that evening chasing four nervous and distrustful cows around a pasture, trying vainly to capture enough milk to provide subsistence for the new additions to the personnel.

Next morning the problem was still unsolved. But it was solved that evening.

For that evening a fresh contingent of marines trooped by the farm, and in their wake—tired, anxious, but undiscouraged—was Verdun Belle. Ten kilometers back, two days before, she had lost her master and, until she should find him again, she evidently had thought that any marine was better than none.

The troops did not halt at the farm, but Belle did. At the gate she stopped dead in her tracks, drew in her lolling tongue, sniffed inquiringly the evening air, and like a flash—a white streak along the

A shattered church in the ruins of Neurilly furnishes a temporary shelter for American wounded being treated by the 110th Sanitary Train, 4th Ambulance Corps. *(National Archives)*

drive—she raced to the distant tree where, on a pile of discarded dressings in the shade, the pups were sleeping.

All the corps men stopped work and stood around and marveled. For the on-looker it was such a family reunion as warms the heart. For the worried mess sergeant it was a great relief. For the pups it was a mess call, clear and unmistakable.

So, with renewed faith in her heart and only one worry left in her mind, Verdun Belle and her puppies settled down on detached service with this field hospital. When, next day, the reach of the artillery made it advisable that it should move down the valley to the shelter of a fine hillside chateau, you may be sure that room was made in the first ambulance for the three casuals.

This was the Chateau of the Guardian Angel, which stands on the right of the Paris-Metz road, just north of La Ferti as you hike toward Chateau-Thierry.

In a grove of trees beside the house the tents of the personnel were pitched, and the cots of the expected patients ranged side by side. The wounded came—came hour after hour in steady streams, and the boys of the hospital worked on them night and day. They could not possibly keep track of all the cases, but there was one who did. Always a mistress of the art of keeping out from underfoot, very quietly Belle hung around and investigated each ambulance that turned in from the main road and backed up with its load of pain to the door of the receiving room.

Then one evening they lifted out a young marine, listless in the half stupor of shell shock. To the busy workers he was just Case Number Such-and-Such, but there was no need to tell anyone who saw the wild jubilance of the dog that Belle had found her own again at last.

The first consciousness he had of his new surroundings was the feel of her rough pink tongue licking the dust from his face. And those who passed that way on Sunday last found two cots shoved together in the kindly shade of a spreading tree. On one the mother dog lay contented with her puppies. Fast asleep on the other, his arm thrown out so that one grimy hand could clutch one silken ear, lay the young marine.

Before long they would have to ship him to the evacuation hospital, on from there to the base hospital, on and on and on. It was not very clear to anyone how another separation could be prevented. It was a perplexing questions, but they knew in their hearts they could safely leave the answer to someone else. They could leave it to Verdun Belle.

ERNEST HEMINGWAY

"MIX WAR, ART, AND DANCING"

KANSAS CITY *STAR*, 1918

In October 1917 an eighteen-year-old midwesterner stepped off the train in Kansas City, Missouri. Though his parents had hoped he would attend college, he was not interested. If he had wanted to enlist in the United States armed forces, he knew his eyesight would probably cause his rejection. The young man, who had a flair for writing, went to work for the Kansas City Star *as a reporter. Though he remained in Kansas City for only a little more than seven months, Ernest Hemingway's experience working for a newspaper started to shape his unique writing style.*

The United States had entered the war six months before Hemingway arrived in Kansas City. Hemingway, who wanted to do his part during the war, joined the National Guard after less than a month in Kansas City. While the reporter served part time in uniform, tens of thousands of army draftees and recruits underwent their basic training at Camp Funston, located on the Fort Riley military reservation about a hundred miles from Kansas City. Fort Leavenworth, about twenty-five miles up the Missouri River, was much closer to the city. The young men who were still learning to be soldiers at the two army posts were part of the story of the Great War.

Hemingway left the city at the beginning of May 1918. He responded to Italian recruiters passing throughout the city, joined the Italian Red Cross Ambulance Service, and by the middle of June was on duty in Italy. About a month later, he was wounded. Still not yet twenty, Hemingway sent reports of the war to the Toronto *Star.*

OUTSIDE A WOMAN WALKED along the wet street-lamp sidewalk through the sleet and snow.

Inside in the Fine Arts Institute on the sixth floor of the Y.M.C.A. Building, 1020 McGee Street, a merry crowd of soldiers from Camp Funston and Fort Leavenworth fox trotted and one-stepped with girls from the Fine Arts School while a sober faced young man pounded out the latest jazz music as he watched the moving figures. In a corner a private in the signal corps was discussing Whistler with a black haired girl who heartily agreed with him. The private had been a member of the art colony at Chicago before the war was declared.

Three men from Funston were wandering arm in arm along the wall looking at the exhibition of paintings by Kansas City artists. The piano player stopped. The dancers clapped and cheered and he swung into "The Long, Long Trail Awinding." An infantry corporal, dancing with a swift moving girl in a red dress, bent his head close to hers and confided something about a girl in Chautauqua, Kas. In the corridor a group of girls surrounded a tow-headed young artilleryman and applauded his imitation of his pal Bill chal-

Soldiers being mustered out at Camp Dix, New Jersey, 1918. *(National Archives)*

lenging the colonel, who had forgotten the password. The music stopped again and the solemn pianist rose from his tool and walked out into the hall for a drink.

A crowd of men rushed up to the girl in the red dress to plead for the next dance. Outside the woman walked along the wet lamp lit sidewalk.

It was the first dance for soldiers to be given under the auspices of the War Camp Community Service. Forty girls of the art school, chaperoned by Miss Winifred Sexton, secretary of the school, and Mrs. J. F. Binnie were the hostesses. The idea was formulated by J. P. Robertson of the War Camp Community Service, and announcements were sent to the commandants at Camp Funston and Fort Leavenworth inviting all soldiers on leave. Posters made by the girl students were put up at Leavenworth and on the interurban trains.

The first dance will be followed by others at various clubs and schools throughout the city according to Mr. Robertson.

The pianist took his seat and the soldiers made a dash for partners. In the intermission the soldiers drank to the girls. The girl in red, surrounded by a crowd of men in olive drab, seated herself at the piano, the men and the girls gathered around and sang until midnight. The elevator had stopped running and so the jolly crowd bunched down the six flights of stairs and rushed waiting motor cars. After the last car had gone, the woman walked along the wet sidewalk through the sleet and looked up at the dark window of the sixth floor.

KIRKE L. SIMPSON

"BUGLES SOUND TAPS FOR WARRIOR'S REQUIEM"

ASSOCIATED PRESS, NOVEMBER 11, 1921

Nations were determined not to forget the men who died during the Great War. On Friday, November 11, 1921, the United States dedicated the Tomb of the Unknown Soldier at Arlington Cemetery. The body of an unidentified American soldier was selected from those buried at Romagne Military Cemetery in France and brought to the United States aboard the Olympia. *Before the dedication of the tomb, thousands of visitors passed by the casket as it rested in state in the Capitol's rotunda.*

The ceremonies at Arlington Cemetery brought together a collection of notables. President Warren G. Harding delivered the dedicatory address, while the two living former presidents—William Howard Taft and Woodrow Wilson—were in attendance. Among others present were presidents-to-be Calvin Coolidge and Herbert Hoover.

The dedication not only drew a huge crowd to Arlington Cemetery, it also attracted large audiences in other cities. The ceremony was transmitted by telephone wires and then amplified so that thousands could listen in at New York's Madison Square Garden and at San Francisco's civic center.

Kirke L. Simpson, who had years of experience as a reporter in Washington, covered the ceremony for the Associated Press. His stories describing the arrival in the United States of the remains of the unknown soldier, the observance in the rotunda of the Capitol, and the reinterment at the new monument in Arlington Cemetery appeared in Associated Press newspapers on November 9, 10, and 11, 1921. The following if from the third and last of these stories.

Though historians have paid little attention to the dedication of the Tomb of the Unknown Soldier, it was one of the leading news stories of the year. Simpson's story so impressed newspaper editors that they insisted on a byline—the first time an Associated Press piece provided a byline. Simpson won the Pulitzer Prize for reporting in 1922, his story being judged one of the "best examples of a reporter's work during 1921, the test being strict accuracy, terseness and the accomplishment of some public good commanding public attention and respect."

UNDER THE WIDE AND STARRY skies of his own homeland America's unknown dead from France sleeps tonight, a soldier home from the wars.

Alone, he lies in the narrow cell of stone that guards his body; but his soul has entered into the spirit that is America. Wherever liberty is held close in men's hearts, the honor and the glory and the pledge of high endeavor poured out over this nameless one of fame will be told and sung by Americans for all time.

Scrolled across the marble arch of the memorial raised to American soldier and sailor dead, everywhere, which stands like a monument behind his tomb, runs this legend: "We here highly resolve that these dead shall not have died in vain."

The words were spoken by the martyred Lincoln over the dead at Gettysburg. And today with voice strong with determination and ringing with deep emotion, another President echoed that high resolve over the coffin of the soldier who died for the flag in France.

Great men in the world's affairs heard that high purpose reiterated by the man who stands at the head of the American people. Tomorrow they will gather in the city that stands almost in the shadow of the new American shrine of liberty dedicated today. They will talk of peace; of the curbing of the havoc of war.

They will speak of the war in France, that robbed this soldier of life and name and brought death to comrades of all nations by the hundreds of thousands. And in their ears when they meet must ring President Harding's declaration today beside that flag-wrapped, honor-laden bier:

"There must be, there shall be, the commanding voice of a conscious civilization against armed warfare."

Far across the seas, other unknown dead, hallowed in memory by their countrymen, as this American soldier is enshrined in the heart of America, sleep their last. He, in whose veins ran the blood of British forebears, lies beneath a great stone in ancient Westminster Abbey; he of France, beneath the Arc de Triomphe, and he of Italy under the altar of the fatherland in Rome. . . .

And it seemed today that they, too, must be here among the Potomac hills to greet an American comrade come to join their glorious company, to testify their approval of the high words of hope spoken by America's President. All day long the nation poured out its heart in pride and glory for the nameless American. Before the first crash of the minute guns roared its knell for the dead from the shadow of Washington Monument, the people who claim him as their own were trooping out to do him honor. They lined the long road from the Capitol to the hillside where he sleeps tonight; they flowed like a tide over the slopes about his burial place, they choked the bridges that lead across the river to the fields of the brave, in which he is the last comer. . . .

As he was carried past through the banks of humanity that lined Pennsylvania Avenue a solemn, reverent hush held the living walls. Yet there was not so much of sorrow as of high pride in it all, a pride beyond the reach of shouting and the clamor that marks less sacred moments in life.

Out there in the broad avenue was a simpler soldier, dead for honor of the flag. He was nameless. No man knew what part in the great life of the nation he had died as Americans always have been ready to die, for the flag and what it means. They read the message of the pageant clear, these silent thousands along the way. They stood in almost holy awe to take their own part in what was theirs, the glory of the American people, honored here in the honors showered on America's nameless son from France.

Soldiers, sailors, and marines—all played their part in the thrilling spectacles as the cortege rolled along. And just behind the casket, with its faded French flowers on the draped flag, walked the President, the chosen leader of a hundred million, in whose name he was chief mourner at his bier. Beside him strode the man under whom the fallen hero had lived and died in France, General Pershing, wearing only the single medal of Victory that every American soldier might wear as his only decoration.

Then, row on row, came the men who lead the nation today or have guided its destinies before. They were all there, walking proudly, with age and frailties of the flesh forgotten. Judges, Senators, Representatives, highest officers of every military arm of government, and a trudging little group of the nation's most valorous sons, the Medal of Honor men. Some were gray and bent and drooping with old wounds; some trim and erect as the day they won their way to fame. All walked gladly in this nameless comrade's last parade.

Behind these came the carriage in which rode Woodrow Wilson, also stricken down by infirmities as he served in the highest place in the nation, just as the humble private riding in such state ahead had gone down before a shell of bullet. For the dead man's sake, the former President had put aside his dread of seeming to parade his physical weakness and risked health, perhaps life, to appear among the mourners for the fallen.

There was handclapping and a cheer here and there for the man in the carriage, a tribute to the spirit that brought him to honor the nation's nameless hero, whose commander-in-chief he had been.

After President Harding and most of the high dignitaries of the government had turned aside at the White House, the procession, headed by its solid blocks of soldiery and the battalions of sailor comrades, moved on with Pershing, now flanked by secretaries Weeks and Denby, for the long road to the tomb. It marched on, always between the human borders of the way of victory the nation had made for itself of the great avenue; on over the old bridge that spans the Potomac, on up the long hill to Fort Myer, and at last to the great cemetery beyond, where soldier and sailor folk sleep by the thousands. There the lumbering guns of the artillery swung aside, the cavalry drew their horses out of the long line and left to the foot soldiers and the sailors and marines the last stage of the journey.

Ahead, the white marble of the amphitheater gleamed through the trees. It stands crowning the slope of the hills that sweep upward from the river, and just across was Washington, its clustered buildings and monuments to great dead who have gone before, a moving picture in the autumn haze.

People in thousands were moving about the great circle of the amphitheater. The great ones to whom places had been given in the sacred enclosure and the plain folk who had trudged the long way just to glimpse the pageant from afar, were finding their places. Everywhere within the pillared enclosure bright uniforms of foreign soldiers appeared. They were laden with the jeweled order of rank to honor an American private soldier, great in the majesty of his sacrifices, in the tribute his honors paid to all Americans who died.

Down below the platform placed for the casket, in a stone vault, lay wreaths and garlands brought from England's King and guarded by British soldiers. To them came the British Ambassador in the full uniform of his rank to bid them keep safe against that hour.

Above the platform gathered men whose names ring through history—Briand, Foch, Beatty, Balfour, Jacques, Diaz, and others—in a brilliant array of place and power. They were followed by others, Baron Kato from Japan, the Italian statesmen and officers, by the notables from all countries gathered here for tomorrow's conference, and by some of the older figures in American life too old to walk beside the approaching funeral train.

Down around the circling pillars the marbled box filled with distinguished men and women, with a cluster of shattered men from army hospitals, accompanied by uniformed nurses. A surpliced choir took its place to wait the dead.

Faint and distant, the silvery strains of a military band stole into the big white bowl of the amphitheater. The slow cadences and mourning notes of a funeral march grew clearer amid the roll and mutter of the muffled drums.

At the arch where the choir awaited the heroic dead, comrades lifted his casket down and, followed by the generals and the admirals, who had walked beside him from the Capitol, he was carried to the place of honor. Ahead moved the white-robed singers, chanting solemnly. Carefully, the casket was placed above the banked flowers, and the Marine Band played sacred melodies until the moment the President and Mrs. Harding stepped to their places beside the casket; then the crashing, triumphant chorus of The Star Spangled Banner swept the gathering to its feet again.

A prayer, carried out over the crowd over the amplifiers so that no word was missed, took a moment or two, then the sharp, clear call of the bugle rang "Attention!" and for two minutes the nation stood at pause for the dead, just at high noon. No sound broke the quiet as all stood with bowed heads. It was much as though a mighty hand had checked the world in full course. Then the band sounded, and in a mighty chorus rolled up in the words of America from the hosts within and without the great open hall of valor.

President Harding stepped forward beside the coffin to say for America the thing that today was nearest to the nation's heart, that sacrifices such as this nameless man, fallen in battle, might perhaps be made unnecessary down through the coming years. Every word that President Harding spoke reached every person through the amplifiers and reached other thousands upon thousands in New York and San Francisco.

Mr. Harding showed strong emotion as his lips formed the last words of the address. He paused, then with raised hand and head bowed, went on in the measured, rolling periods of the Lord's Prayer. The response that came back to him from the thousands he faced, from the other thousands out over the slopes beyond, perhaps from still other thousands away near the Pacific, or close-packed in the heart of the nation's greatest city, arose like a chant. The marble arches hummed with a solemn sound.

Then the foreign officers who stand highest among the soldiers or sailors of their flags came one by one to the bier to place gold and jeweled emblems for the brave above the breast of the sleeper. Already, as the great prayer ended, the President had set the American seal of admiration for the valiant, the nation's love for brave deeds and the courage that defies death, upon the casket.

Side by side he laid the Medal of Honor and the Distinguished Service Cross. And below, set in place with reverent hands, grew the long line of foreign honors, the Victoria Cross, never before laid on the breast of any but those who had served the British flag; all the highest honors of France and Belgium and Italy and Rumania and Czechoslovakia and Poland.

To General Jacques of Belgium it remained to add his own touch to these honors. He tore from the breast of his own tunic the medal of valor pinned there by the Belgian King, tore it with a sweeping gesture, and tenderly bestowed it on the unknown American warrior.

Through the religious services that followed, and prayers, the swelling crowd sat motionless until it rose to join in the old, consoling Rock of Ages, and the last rite for the dead was at hand. Lifted by his hero-bearers from the stage, the unknown was carried in his flag-wrapped, simple coffin out to the wide sweep of the terrace. The bearers laid the sleeper down above the crypt, on which had been placed a little soil of France. The dust his blood helped redeem from alien hands will mingle with his dust as time marches by.

The simple words of the burial ritual were said by Bishop Brent; flowers from war mothers of America and England were laid in place.

For the Indians of America Chief Plenty Coos came to call upon the Great spirit of the Red Men, with gesture and chant and tribal tongue, that the dead should not have died in vain, that war might end, peace be purchased by such blood as this. Upon the casket he laid the coupstick of his tribal office and the feathered war bonnet from his own head. Then the casket, with its weight of honors, was lowered into the crypt.

A rocking blast of gunfire rang from the woods. The glittering circle of bayonets stiffened to a salute to the dead. Again the guns shouted their message of honor and farewell. Again they boomed out; a loyal comrade was being laid to his last, long rest.

High and clear and true in the echoes of the guns, a bugle lifted the old, old notes of taps, the lullaby for the living soldier, in death his requiem. Long ago some forgotten soldier-poet caught its meaning clear and set it down that soldiers everywhere might know its message as they sink to rest:

> Fades the light;
> And afar
> Goeth day, cometh night,
> And a star,
> Leadeth all, speedeth all,
> To their rest.

———

The guns roared out again in the national salute. He was home, The Unknown, to sleep forever among his own.

IN RETROSPECT

DOUGLAS D. MARTIN AND OTHERS

"MILLIONS WATCH LEGION VETERANS MARCH FOR HOURS"

DETROIT *FREE PRESS*, SEPTEMBER 23, 1931

The idea of creating an association for veterans had its origins while Americans were still fighting in Europe and came to fruition in the early months of 1919. The newly established American Legion held its first convention in Minneapolis a year after the end of the war. The annual conventions became opportunities for those who had served in the Great War to come together, enjoy a revival of wartime camaraderie, and show off to the rest of the nation. The parades held in the convention cities became an important means for the American Legion to show their large numbers and their unity.

The Legion held its thirteenth annual meeting in Detroit in 1931. Fifty thousand Legionnaires participated in the parade, while half a million watched the parade in the hot summer streets of Detroit. It was the largest parade the city had ever seen.

This story, written by several reporters from the Detroit Free Press, *won the Pulitzer Prize for reporting in 1932. Douglas D. Martin, one of the reporters who wrote the prizewinning story, went on to become managing editor of the Detroit* Free Press *and to teach journalism at the University of Arizona.*

THE LEGION MARCHED

THE YANKS CAME—THOUSANDS UPON thousands of them who have been sung about always as coming. Pulses quickened. Tempo moved up. The pendulum flew faster. And those who thought they had lain away the World War in a cobwebby file felt again a familiar throbbing.

The crowd that watched was estimated at a million. The number of marchers was put at 85,000 by the National Commander Ralph T. O'Neil. Other estimates, among them that of Maj. Gen. Guy Wilson, field marshal, were as high as 100,000.

Still, this was nothing new. Men have marched so down the ages. They marched in Athens and Nineveh and Marathon fighting their various Armageddons; and, when these were over, they marched behind their Hannibals and Alexanders and Caesars before those they had fought for.

HOUR AFTER HOUR THEY MARCHED ON AND ON

THEY, LIKE THESE, FARED OFF TO wars inspired by ideals and buoyed by ladies' prayers and kudos. Men of war the length of time differ only in quests and instruments.

Up Woodward Avenue they swept, the men of our civilization, in lush impressiveness. They came out, hour after hour, a part of the force which barged out in '17 when folly took the world by the hand and led it out on a sanguinary holiday to fill the meadows of France with dead.

All kinds of men, and the women they left behind them, filled the prideful, clicking columns. There were men who saw none of it and there were men who saw it all and played the string out. There were men too late at the final push, and men who made, in America, household names and tourist spots of tiny French villages previously unknown, unvisited, unhonored, unawakened.

There were men who never reached an outbound gang-plank and men who knew full well the green fumes rising off the long stretches of mustard, the bitterness of Archangel and the streaked sky of Belleau, clipped by lead and stumps standing like gallows-trees against the sky-line.

NO PACKS ON SHOULDERS

GAY WERE THESE INTERMINABLE columns. One realized that this, because of that gayness, was a censored photograph. This day they needed no khaki to blend inconspicuously into the landscape. They were not going up at night into the line and toward an unknown. This could be a lark in all a lark's pretty accouterment.

No awkward packs on the shoulders. Nothing of fear and solitude. Nothing of corruption and men crushed in mud, moaning ones masked with dust and calling to stretcher-bearers, men living and dying in dirty trenches—and away off beyond a broad sea, a quaint commingling of preachment about mercy, in one breath, and the glorifications of barbarity, in the next.

THOUSANDS UPON THOUSANDS

SO THE THOUSANDS UPON THOUsands marched, swinging down E. Jefferson Avenue and turning North at Woodward into the roaring canyon. It was only occasionally one could forget the magnificence of helmets, the tranquility of faces, the hilarity of bugles, and tailor for the paraders the garb in which they journeyed shipward more than a decade ago and finally, on some star-lit night when clover scented the air, heard for the first time the whine of shell and saw, perhaps, no house where one had been only a second before.

But it was no effort at times, for all we know that guns no longer grumble from the Alps to the Channel, to throw around this host its war-day aura and see its units vividly—the sappers and bombers, tank men and machine gunners, signal men, fliers, brass hats, artillerymen and all the myriad others the war casts for its shows.

Old songs strengthened old memories. Band after band blared the whistled airs of war; men came singing the tunes that lightened their packs a bit 13 years ago when their boots dragged:

Oh, Mademoiselle from Armentieres.
You might forget the gas and shell.
You'll never forget the Mademoiselle.

Up past the reviewers they came. "It's a Long, Long Trail A-Winding," the pipes of kilties skirling, drums pounding, fifes shrill and martial. Kipling's boots, boots, boots. Men from every state, every territory, every distant island, generals, top-sergeants and buck-privates.

Welcome home: a parade of returned fighters passes the public library, New York City, 1919. *(National Archives)*

GRAND STAND GLITTERS

PAGEANTS SUCH AS THIS MUST HAVE epaulettes, of course, and the reviewing stand sparkled with celebrities, but it was the doughboy's show; and the high stand, after all, was just a place where hands came up briskly to salute and came down again to continue their work of making it a grand, care-free holiday as well as display of might.

Those who looked on, packing themselves into the smallest of spaces, began to gather shortly after 7 o'clock; and when the Legion entered Woodward Avenue at Jefferson at 12:10 P.M. o'clock in all its display of man power, downtown Detroit held room only for those with endurance and stout shoulders. Campus ropes, the police and volunteer gendarmes had all they could do to restrain the surging crowds, and the skyscrapers forming the perpendicular sides of the picture framed at their windows an additional army of watchers.

Shortly after noon, a sudden hush fell. Away in the distance rolled the drums. Police lines strained more than they had before. Hundreds of police struggled in efforts to control the pressing thousands. The Yanks were coming.

THE MARCHING YANKS

AND AROUND THE CORNER THEY DID —those marching men who after reading history went out for themselves in 1917 and wrote some.

With mounted police and four companies of U.S. regulars from Fort Wayne, the Second Infantry, and Company I, of the 106th Cavalry, U.S.A., before them, the Yanks came with Ralph T. O'Neil, their national commander; Newton D. Baker, secretary of war for America in Woodrow Wilson's cabinet; Theodore Roosevelt, the son of a famous father and swinging along on foot; Gen. Charles S. Summerall, former chief of staff, and numerous envoys of foreign governments in the van.

Twenty-seven planes from Selfridge roared overhead filling the air with the clamorous staccato of their engines as the Regular Army men ushered in the Legion.

Behind the infantry rolled three floats of rare beauty—one wholly covered with oak leaves and pretty girls depicting a French village, another with a mammoth Liberty Bell accompanied by a battalion of girls, and a third on which were massed young women in the dress of the various nations of the world. . . . Like a roll-call of the Republic, the states and every possession of America followed in the wake of the Legion champion band of Electric Post 228, Milwaukee, gorgeous in blue and gold and playing the song of the football field, "On, Wisconsin!"

The Yanks had arrived!

They gave the place of honor, behind the distinguished guests, to the Canadian Legion, to Hawaii, the Philippines and Puerto Rico, and a single Alaskan trudging along magnificently with his shirt-tail out.

BURRO FROM PHOENIX

THEY CAME FROM ARIZONA, PROUD leader of all state departments. By virtue of their championship standing in percentage of membership gains, the men from the land of buttes and deserts marched first. The Phoenix Post band in silver helmets and blouses of horizon blue set the cadence. Their mascot was a shambling burro.

Next came Mississippi. Then the orange trench caps of Florida waved down the avenue. North Dakota, swinging close behind, mustered half a hundred in her first contingent of Legionnaires. Flashing scarlet and white, the uniform colors of the Grand Forks Drum Corps drew a burst of applause from the grand stands.

From the Golden West, 20 standards were sent to lead the men of California. Their black bear mascot lolled in a broiling sun. White was the costume, appropriate to the day and circumstances.

Nebraska followed its band in rapid tempo. Vermont, led by the Montpelier Post band, forced a path in the same avenue. The crowd, over anxious to glimpse the columns yet to come, had closed in toward the car tracks. No longer could 16 men march abreast. Police waged a losing battle. . . . At 1:40 P.M., the crowd broke through police lines at Fort Street, holding up the marchers nearly five minutes while the lines were reestablished. At the Campus and Woodward, the crowd forged half way out into Woodward and stayed there—another zigzag in the line.

La Porte, with a drum and bugle corps of 40 men, was followed by Lafayette, led by its 40 and 8 locomotive firing intermittently. An old gray mare trailed them. Logansport, Ind., in bright blue, came along with Michigan City in gorgeous purple.

FORCE LINE BACK

THE INDIANAPOLIS OUTFIT WAS headed by its crack drum and bugle corps followed by a host of Legionnaires, from the National Headquarters city. It was succeeded in the line of march by Colum-
bus, Ind., veterans and the brass band of Valparaiso, whose deployed drummers and bugler were forced to close in as the crowds pressed farther out into Woodward Avenue. As this contingent of the parade passed, police made a concerted "attack" on the crowd, forcing the line back.

Richmond, Ind., represented by a band which has been seen many times on the streets of Detroit, preceded in the line of march the huge Polar Bear Float of Gimco Post 87 of Alexandria, Inc. Airplanes continued to roar overhead as the parade neared its second hour.

Post 46 of Tipton, Ind., representing themselves as farmers and as such, made a favorable showing which was applauded by the agriculturally minded of the crowd. They were followed by a float representing a huge ear of corn. . . .

ILLINOIS MARCHES PROUDLY

THEN CAME ILLINOIS, LEADING THE 10th Division. Illinois represents the largest of all American Legion State divisions.

They were the boys who formed the Prairie Division. They fought with the British at Chipilly Woods, and left their dead at the Meuse. They were the pivot of the Third Army Corps in the Argonne and faced the German shellfire at St. Milhiel.

They marched proudly—with reason. Among them were eight Congressional Medals of Honor, 110 Distinguished Service Crosses, 51 British crosses and 47 French decorations.

A lot they cared. They went by singing "Illinois, My Illinois," with massed flags and a business looking color guard of a dozen rifles at right shoulder and looking neither right nor left.

As far as the eye could see the street was filled with Illinois Legionnaires. Two hours and a half had passed since the parade opened and still the waves of color rolled up Woodward Avenue to be lost in the black mobs along the line of march.

A note of music spoke of the changing pace of the day. A band from Illinois struck up "America," the first time other than old army airs had crashed out.

The tempo of the crowd changed. The carnival spirit had struck a deeper note. The measured tread of thousands, pounding on interminably, the beat, beat, beat of thousands of drums, echoing and re-echoing through the deep canyons of the city street, fostered a realization that back of the color and the play and the music, there was the strongest organization in America. . . .

CHEER WILDLY FOR NEW YORK

A SHOUT WENT UP FROM THE CROWD about the reviewing stand as a large drum and bugle corps dressed in gray and marching like cadets, swung into view. It was the vanguard of New York. Just as their colors passed the stand and the Legion standards dipped, the street lamps flashed on through their veils of red and yellow decorations, lending a touch of fresh beauty to the scene.

The crowd was cheering wildly for almost the first time as the Buffalo Drum and Fife Corps walked on at a quick step. Here was a sight to remember.

There were silver bands on the regimental flags of some of those units, and the crowd knew it. Who could forget the old 27th Division of the National Guard—the Yankee Division? Thrown into battle with strange comrades in arms—beside the British—they fought their fight for freedom. Their Armageddon was a bitter place known as Vierstandt Ridge, one of those ridges that the Germans swept with killing fire. Read the roll call of their dead and injured if you would know the stuff of which these men were made. Eleven thousand casualties. That's the record.

Some of them had been with the Yankee Division. They had shared the glory of that body of troops which, thrown into battle unprepared and untrained, to save the cause of the Allies, had stood like an iron brigade at Soudaine and then, re-attacking, had driven the enemy back 15 kilometers for good Yankee measure.

Overhead the red aerial beacon of the Penobscot Tower became a brilliant ball of light. The windows in the great office buildings which had been black all day, began to turn yellow, and momentarily the street lights glowed brighter as the darkness deepened.

Corps after corps of the boys from New York came swinging up the street. The roll call of the drums was punctuated minute by minute by exploding bombs.

HERE COME MICHIGAN

AT 7 O'CLOCK CAME MICHIGAN, LED by Gov. Brucker and Mayor Murphy. Marching behind the color guard came the State's standards—50 beautiful American flags, followed by an equal number of Legion banners in blue and gold.

One thought of the words "Like an Army with Banners," as they swept up the street. And of an Army which has earned its banners, if any ever won its standards in battle!

Gay and brave and colorful they looked last night and, in the kindly light, very young. They might have been the National Guard of old marching away for Waco. Surely they were not the hard-bitten veterans of the fighting Red Arrow Division which came back to Detroit loaded with citations and medals of honor.

WHAT A RECORD

YET THEIR RECORD RUNS THAT WAY. These are the home boys who went over and smashed the Hindenburg line at the Aisne-Marne, making a total advance of 19 kilometers.

They fought with the French at Soissons and outflanked the Germans at Chemin des Dames. The French gave them a love term for that. They called them Les Terribles. These boys! Out there in tricky uniforms, and with the smiles of youth on their faces!

Nor was that all. They swept over the Meuse-Argonne front; and for three weeks, they attacked and attacked again. Three weeks of hell, that was. Then east to the Meuse; and when the Armistice came, they were still in the front-line shock troops of the Nation, ready for the attack.

Three thousand eight hundred and ninety-eight dead they left in France. Eleven thousand wounded.

They marched again in the Big Parade and received an ovation. Virtually in close order formation, the men of this state swung between the lines of spectators, the most imposing in number, of the entire procession.

CROWDS BEGIN TO SHIFT

AS DAY SLIPPED OVER INTO NIGHT the crowd began to change. Many who had lined the streets since early in the day surrendered to hunger and went home to eat. Their places were taken by Legionnaires who had been near the head of the parade and who came back to watch their buddies. The Michigan detachment marched through rows in which the uniforms of their fellow Legionnaires were well sprinkled.

Michigan bands were given to the gay reckless tunes of the war. "Hinkey Dinkey Parley Vous." "You're in the Army Now." The crowd lost its weariness, and voices which they thought were gone came back. They could cheer. Those who could not applauded.

"Hail, hail, the gang's all here.
What the hell do we care?"

The 23rd Engineers went by. A roar went up from the crowds that would have done well on Armistice Day.

APPLAUD POLAR BEARS

SILENCE FELL, AND THEN APPLAUSE came from the crowd as the white form of a huge polar bear, mounted on a float, rolled through the lighted streets.

Behind the symbol of the strangest war ever fought by American troops marched a pitiful handful of that glorious regiment, the 339th Infantry, known as "Detroit's Own." First of the men in the national draft, they were. They came from the benches, the lathes, the counters and the offices of the city.

How they fought and died is an epic which needed no retelling Tuesday night and needs none now.

There were no great gaps between the Michigan units. Grand Rapids was only a few steps removed from Sault St. Marie. All moved at a lively tempo, bolstered by the gay airs. The crowd grew merrier and merrier. The Mardi Gras spirit seemed to emanate from the Michigan troops. Their comedians seemed just a little funnier, possibly because of their anticipation that the long day was nearing an end.

As the Michigan march proceeded and the skyline signs of the city blazed out overhead, it became evident that something of the Mardi Gras spirit was creeping back over the crowd and the marchers.

STRICT FOR HOME BOYS

THE MICHIGAN LEGIONNAIRES, BEing at home, where parades mean nothing to them, showed less military discipline than those of the preceding states. In fact, discipline would have been impossible with groups along the line of march shrieking wildly for "Jerry" or "Bill" or "Hank."

After the Polar Bears came the Second Division. The crowds, which had thinned shortly after 6:30, again swelled until there no longer was walking room on the sidewalks. The pedestrians who attempted to cross Woodward Avenue were entirely isolated. The Michigan sections came so close at the heels of each other that there was no crossing from the east to the west side of the street.

Each distinct group could be recognized, however, by the ripple of cheering that accompanied it. The flag which marked the head of each unit was the signal for greetings.

CARRY BUNYAN'S AX

THERE WAS SOMETHING NEW EVERY minute. A huge load of logging wheels, wheels on which the hubs were as high as the tallest man in the crowd, rolled by. On it was a huge ax sticking from a stump. That ax, the Grayling Post would have you understand, once was Paul Bunyan's, that legendary logging man.

A man and woman drum major led a lively band. The applause was spontaneous. Neither of the drum majors ever knew who was the favorite. Toward the close of the parade, the bands came closer and closer together. Their tunes merged. Sometimes their tempos clashed. But it was a case of who cares. The spirit of pageantry was in the crowd. Everything was grand.

Michigan's floats: Doughboys in a dugout and pretty Miss Liberty, on a pedestal behind her protectors. Another float— this one carried a queen, Michigan's peach queen.

For the first time since the Michigan posts swept into Woodward Avenue, there was a distraction. The crowd took its eyes from the parade. An airplane, whirring loudly, swung low until its wings were perpendicular with the earth and cut past the Penobscot Building. How the pilot missed it was a mystery that the crowd forgot in a burst of applause that greeted the Michigan company of Zouaves which widened into a company front as it passed the reviewing stand.

The maneuver of the Zouaves, intentional or otherwise, forced the crowd back again, widening a lane, comfortable for marching.

DARKNESS SET IN

AT 7:45 O'CLOCK IT WAS IMPOSSIBLE to distinguish numerals on the Legion banners or to read the names of their posts. The crowd, assured that Michigan was passing, cheered every unit without impartiality.

The Fifth Division was headed by a "German" band. Weird musicians dressed in ill-fitting uniforms! Their tunes did not fit any horn. It made little difference, for their music was lost in the laughter their antics earned.

The laugh was followed by a louder one. A boxcar passed; and on its roof was, of all things, a hula dancer going through gyrations.

The clock in the City Hall tower struck eight just as the last of the parade passed the reviewing stand. The parade lacked 12 minutes of being as long as the Boston parade. It was exactly eight hours long.

A DAY OF DRAMA

IT WAS A DAY THAT NONE WHO SAW it will forget. Yet it was a day that memory can never reconstruct. One will not forget the rolling thunder of drums, beating, beating, until they seemed to shake the brick and granite walls of the city's canyons. None will forget that steady tread of marching feet, going on hour after hour, nor the shrill, brass calls of the bugles. But these are only highlights. The picture itself can never be adequately redrawn.

The sheer drama of it! The patient, pleasant but determined throng. The flashing waves of color rolling up the avenue hour after hour, like the endless wash of some mighty human stream.

The blue sky, across which drifted white streamers like "the trailing robes of God." A glorious sun throwing each flash of color into bold brilliance.

The endless passing of the hours with the crowd growing larger each minute. The inexorable forward movement which defeated every effort to hold it in check.

The encroachment on the street, the imperceptible movement which finally filled the pavements until the Legion marched a path no wider than the car tracks.

QUIET BUT DETERMINED

THE QUIET, SO UNLIKE THAT OF other throngs Detroit has seen. There were no fears, no flaunted grief. There were no long continued, uncontrolled bursts of enthusiasm. The crowds were determined to see the faces of the marching Legionnaires, and having seen them, they were satisfied.

Long shadows creeping across the streets. Early dusk—the coming of the first lights. Great red signs bursting into permanent explosion and throwing their crimson over the passing columns.

Marching into the dusk the great parade rolled on. Every downtown light went on, and the whole scene was transformed.

Each member of the division carried a football, tucked in his arm, much after the manner of Herb Joesting.

GIRL LEADS CORPS

THE GIRL DRUM MAJOR OF THE Duluth Drum and Bugle Corps was a high stepper. She wore a beautiful red uniform which matched her complexion. She kicked even with her head in directing her musicians.

The drum and bugle corps marched on. There seemed no end of this particular form of martial music, despite the 150 bands.

It was too much for one Negro drummer from Charles Young Post of Charlotte, N.C. Swinging his drum to his shoulder, he dropped out of line, mopping a wet brow. He craned his neck at the Selfridge Field plans, and with a sigh, sank to a resting position on his instrument. The crowd swallowed him.

The crowd throughout the early afternoon was noticeably quiet. Occasionally scattering applause greeted bands or bugle corps of special distinction, or a particular funny float or Legionnaire-actor would elicit a laugh or hand clap.

Cheers in most cases were reserved for outfits.

"Yoo Hoo Charlies" frequently brought eyes right from "Charlie." Other than this, the crowd made no recognition of special outfits or men.

MARCHED IN SOLID RANK

THE MASSACHUSETTS MEN marched in solid rank; and for the first time since the parade started, the marching Legionnaires could be seen coming north from Jefferson Avenue in extended rank.

No wonder these men marched well.

They are remnants of the old Yankee Brigade. They had bitter training and discipline over there on the Western front. They were at St. Mihiel, the Aisne-Marne and Chemin des Dames. Fifteen thousand casualties was the price they paid for their valor and their victories.

Not until 3:30 o'clock did the parade really open up and march in anything resembling a quick step. The sun, sinking behind the skyscrapers, threw shadows grateful alike to marchers and crowd over Woodward Avenue.

It is a ditty they sung in the old days, revived for Detroit's carnival. They sung it well, in the Massachusetts parade, the boys from Lynn.

Like a corps of British grenadiers, whom their forefathers beat back at Bunker Hill, the Westboro, Mass., Drum and Bugle Corps swept up the streets at a typical British tempo.

This was their song:

Oh, I don't have to fight like the Infantry,
  Fight like the Calvary,
  Fight like the Artillery,
Oh, I don't have to fly over Germany,
For I'm a Q.M.C.—

REVERE, WITHOUT HORSE

PAUL REVERE—WITHOUT HIS HORSE —swaggered up the avenue in the Massachusetts line. Malden, Mass., sent greetings to the citizens of Detroit on a banner so wide that the standard-bearers had to walk sideways to get through the lane between the crowds.

Lexington, Lowell, Watertown, Boston, Concord, all names inseparably linked with another day in American history, were blazoned for the parade. It was a wordless testimonial that Massachusetts keeps the faith.

South Boston's Auxiliaries, rejecting the Princess Eugenia styles of the day, went back to the three-cornered hats of early times and wore them with a jauntiness which set women in the crowd a-twitter.

Mrs. Edith Nourse Rogers, congresswoman from Massachusetts, rode in the state commander's car in the Massachusetts Division.

The Jamaica Plains, Mass., drum and bugle corps evidently grew hungry along about 4 o'clock. It gave vent to its sentiments by playing the mess call all the way up Woodward Avenue. The words ran:

Porky, porky, porky, without a single
   bean.
Soupy, soupy, soupy, the weakest ever
   seen.

Massachusetts Legionnaires staged what was heralded as a "tea party" behind the grilled panels of a yellow patrol wagon.

Shadows crept over the street, and a freshening breeze unfurled decorative banners fixed to lamp posts and buildings. Drum majors seemed to revive as the sun was slipping in the West. The crowd was quiet.

WEAR YELLOW SLICKERS

CAPE COD WENT BY WEARING YELlow oilskin slickers. It was followed by a Gloucester outfit in a large lifeboat.

Salem was represented by a delegation of Legionnaires dressed as witches car-

rying brooms. East Lynn proved it had not forgotten how to drill.

To late afternoon arrivals on Woodward Avenue, it seemed like a Massachusetts parade, the column of troops from the Bay State continuing for nearly two hours.

The first of the Massachusetts Legionnaires passed the reviewing stand at 3:20. Their last marchers trailed up Woodward at 4:45 o'clock.

Some humorous spectator in a window high up in the Majestic Building thought to give Legionnaires some of their own hotel medicine and a shower of water, whipped by the wind into a fine mist, floated down on the paraders.

SHOWER PAPER ON PARADE

UNUSUAL DETACHMENTS WERE greeted from this building by showers of paper as they swung up the avenue. Fragments revealed there will be a shortage of telephone books in the building today.

Texans went in for hand organs in their musical presentation to Detroiters. The buddies from Port Arthur, Tex., put such an instrument at the head of their paraders. A milk-white horse led another Texas contingent.

ROAR WELCOME TO OHIO

OHIO SWUNG INTO VIEW. THESE were neighbor boys. The Michigan crowd felt it knew them, and it gave them a roaring welcome.

Not so many years ago it seemed that homes in Michigan were reading of these boys, members of the 37th Division (National Guard), fighting in the trenches of

France, even as Michigan's own sons in the 32nd Division fought there.

It was not too long to remember that the Buckeyes, who marched in such gay panoply, in purple and gold and red and silver, and who cheered back at the crowd with youthful abandon, won their service stripes in some of the most severe fighting American troops have ever seen.

They threw themselves into the Argonne to hold the line—and they held it. Pershing rushed them across country to Belgium, where the Buckeyes stormed across the Escaut River and ripped the German defense to bits. The white crosses which mark the graves of their comrades are to be found in every American cemetery from Roumain to Flanders Field. They were soldiers over there, and they stepped like soldiers Tuesday.

MARTIAL AIRS CATCH

THEIR TOTAL ADVANCES IN THE FACE of enemy resistance totaled 31 kilometers, but great as that progress was in wartime, they out-distanced it Tuesday in their march into the hearts of their neighbors of Michigan.

Perhaps it was the fact that the men from the first state south marched to the strains of particularly martial music, an abundance of bands having accompanied the 12,000 Legionnaires from this state.

Put your head down, Fritzie boy,
Put your head down, Fritzie boy,
We were out last night in the pale
   moonlight,
We saw you—.

The crowd was exuberant as the strains of the war song came from a 60-piece band in the line of the march.

DISPLAY 'LEGION-HEIRS'

ONE OHIO POST MADE A PLAY ON the name of Legionnaires. On a well-decorated float they placed a dozen small boys in uniform and surmounted them all with a giant sign which read: "Legion-Heirs." It got a hand and a shower of confetti from the crowd.

The first Boy Scout band in the parade followed the banner of Cleveland. More than 50 boys were in the organization.

As the Ohio organizations passed, crowd scenes were being enacted. Tired spectators ambled off to side streets for rest and refreshment, only to return to a new point of vantage. The crowd had moved so far into the streets that room was available on Woodward Avenue sidewalks and pedestrian traffic moved north and south without much difficulty. It was harder for the Legionnaires, however, who were confined to the narrow lane bounded by Woodward Avenue street car tracks.

The drum and bugle corps of Galion, O., was the 100th to have passed in the parade while 44 bands had completed the march. This was at 5:15 o'clock.

LINE SPEEDS UP

THE COLUMBUS, O., BAND SWUNG past the reviewing stand playing something that sounded much like "Beautiful Katy" but swung into a military march of quick beat. The parade moved at an accelerated pace.

It was followed, however, by a hearse of the Lorraine Post, which failed to give the exact number of "hommes" accommodated. "Worst Aid Station" was the name given this vehicle. It was occupied by Lorraine Legionnaires.

Paper water-bags thrown from an eight-story window of the First National garage at E. Congress and Bates Streets became a counter attraction at this point. Groups gathered at the corner, waiting to see someone hit.

COLORADO UNITS FOLLOW

THE OHIO STATE DEPARTMENT WAS followed in the line of march by Colorado, whose Victory Post No. 4 led the contingent.

Notwithstanding that boys had climbed to their barrelled lenses, traffic lights along Woodward Avenue continued to operate as though the Legion's Big Parade were a thousand miles away. It was one-way traffic.

The Department of Pennsylvania, headed by a distinctive drum and bugle corps from Uniontown, stopped at the reviewing stand to pay its respects to officialdom. The throng cheered this unusually military outfit, dressed after the manner of Pennsylvania State Troopers, when they saluted the Governor and the National Commander.

PENNSYLVANIA STIRS CROWD

THE BOYS OF THE KEYSTONE STATE aroused exceptional enthusiasm.

"Keep away from the engineers,
"Keep away from the engineers,
"They'll break your back—
"With a shovel and pack—
"Keep away from the engineers."

Perhaps it was a veteran of the Second engineers from Marne 12 years ago, who shouted the verse from among the Pennsylvanians. He sang it alone but with the courage that made him an engineer, as he marched forward with his companions.

One of the most striking outfits was the green-clad marchers of Greensburg, Pa., in Trojan uniform of green, topped with a black-plumed broad-brimmed hat. Jeanette, Pa., bore out their reputation of "Red Devils."

Greensville, Pa., another snappy unit in powder blue uniform, clicked with the crowd. The brassy helmets and cardinal uniforms of James Zindell Post, of Mt. Pleasant, Pa., were distinctive.

Tarentum Post No. 85, of Tarentum, Pa., in white, proceeded floats with the inevitable locomotive of Forty and Eight. Quite a large detachment preferred riding in Pennsylvania buses to stepping off the long line of march.

The Quaker State was followed by Connecticut, arriving at the reviewing stand at 6 o'clock with a Police Post from New Haven at its head in uniform with black clubs.

SILK HATS GRACE DANBURY

HARTFORD, NEW LONDON, AND New Haven were numerically strong. Danbury produced a float and a silk-hatted contingent. All alone at Danbury's rear came a still spry veteran in a G.A.R. uniform who asked no odds on the tiring march and received a tremendous hand from his buddies of 1917.

Two bands of Detroit Citadel of the Salvation Army reminded the veterans of its war work.

Georgia Department stepped snappily into line in their shirt-sleeves and wearing blue field hats behind the Georgia Peach float bearing Peach Queens as well. There were four posts.

Jefferson Post, Louisville, Ky., introduced the Kentucky contingent to the spectators. In blue hats, red coats and white cross belts, the precision and rhythm of the marching bugle corps won generous attention.

The strains of "Old Kentucky Home" floated out from the band as Jesse M. Dykes Post, of Richmond, marched by.

COLORS BECOME RADIANT

GROUPS OF AMERICAN AND LEGION colors became moving clusters of jewels. Radiant colors of the marcher's uniforms were whipped into a riotous rainbow, through which unreal lines of moving men kept pressing.

Out of the yellow mist far down the street came the last of the Legionnaires. And out of the black night skies overhead there echoed the last roll of the fading drums. With one movement the tremendous crowd surged free.

For nine hours, all through the day and into the night, the police had battled them back. Trucks, motorcycles, cavalry and men afoot had charged against the pressure of the crowding thousands. Inch by inch they had been forced back. Then with the last tap of the last drum, the gates swung open.

The long thin line of open space that had been so valiantly fought for by the guards through nine long hours was obliterated in a second. A swarming mass of humanity swirled under the dancing lights of the night.

Many fought their way to waiting cars and buses to go home to eat after a day in which hunger had been forgotten. But the greater number, like children released at recess, turned to play.

Gone was the martial spirit of discipline. King Carnival reigned, and far into the night the revelry ran.

The Legion had marched.

Its day was done.

WORLD WAR II

MAKING THE WORLD SAFE
FOR DEMOCRACY

1941–1945

THE **"ROARING TWENTIES"** ended with the advent of the Great Depression, replacing gaiety with gloom. Bewildered by international developments such as the rise of fascism, most Americans wanted to insulate the United States from the rest of the world's troubles. The rise of Hitler in Germany, Mussolini in Italy, and the powerful military leadership in Japan troubled the people of the United States, but they were not prepared to use military power to change the situation. And because of the nation's traditional antimilitarism, its army in 1930 did not even rank among the top ten national armies in the world.

The thirties, however, brought a revolution to the world of news. Radio had appeared during World War I, but as a means of transmitting news it did not come into its own until the 1930s. Radio offered commentators such as Floyd Gibbons the opportunity to render their interpretation of events. It also created broadcast journalism, which could bring eyewitness accounts to Americans hours before they could read it in the morning newspaper. Radio journalists described events as they were actually happening.

American's international innocence and legal neutrality came to an abrupt, numbing end on a sun-soaked morning in Oahu. In a matter of hours, carrier-based Japanese planes crushed the battleships USS *Arizona, Oklahoma, California, Nevada,* and *West Virginia* moored in Pearl Harbor. The demolition of the U.S. Pacific fleet in Pearl Harbor had enormous impact. No American family would be untouched by the forty-five months of United States involvement in World War II. "GI Joe," the symbol of the nation's fighting men, represented the real-life brothers, uncles, fathers, and sons of millions. For the first time in its history, America also inducted entire corps of women into the armed forces. A total of 16.4 million men and women served in uniform, a number equal to the entire population of the country in 1835. Those who did not fight on the front lines worked around the clock in factories. Thousands of "Rosie the Riveters" served the country on the home front. The federal government mobilized the country's resources and labor to provide the tools that would turn the tide in Asia and Europe. For four years the nation's attention focused exclusively on the war.

With the outbreak of World War II, correspondents crossed the Atlantic to report on the conflict using new technology. Via newsprint, radio, and newsreel, the press cooperated fully with the Federal Office of War Information, keeping the home front up to date on events overseas. Civilians relied on the daily radio broadcasts from Europe, growing familiar with the smoky-voiced Edward R. Murrow, the smooth-toned Eric Severeid, and others. Hundreds of newspaper correspondents followed the American armies into the battles for North Africa, Italy, France, and finally Germany itself. Usually these civilian reporters donned the uniforms of officers and relayed events from that privileged perspective. The most notable exception was Ernie Pyle, who preferred to bunk, eat, walk, and brave the front lines with the enlisted soldiers. His dispatches' sober outlook was borne of this experience and directly linked the common folk in the United States to the common soldier fighting abroad. The average GI served sixteen months. Many, like reporter Pyle, never returned: deaths exceeded 405,000; total wounded, 670,000. The cost of World War II in American lives was second only to the Civil War.

Reports from the European and Pacific theaters highlighted, more than in any other conflict, the paradox of war: that the early morning pride and the desire to rescue fellow human beings must give way to a grisly afternoon of casualties. From Dorothy Thompson's spirited appeal on behalf of Herschel Thompson to Ernie Pyle's reporting from Normandy, the following passages are woven with just such complex emotion. The Holocaust, the sunken passenger vessels, the Battle of Britain, D day—all were reported with stirring sympathy. A shopkeeper told Edward Murrow that his store had been in business for one hundred years and would remain open despite the Luftwaffe blitz. A battleship captain at Pearl Harbor, after being mortally wounded by shrapnel, "disdained attempts to lift him to safety" and "continued to command until the bridge went up in flames." John Gunther told of the heroics of Judge Dimitrov, who in his role as magistrate and investigator of the Reichstag fire, "unerringly asked just those questions most damaging." Ernie Pyle meticulously detailed the assembly-line process of resupplying troops and equipment to Normandy Beach as the bodies of soldiers floated along the coast and slept in the sand. Homer Bigart reported on the last bombing raid on Japan. Mark Watson's account from liberated Paris told of French Resistance fighters and their return to a city relatively unscathed by German occupation, where grateful French men and women kissed and hugged their liberators. Such accounts restored the sense of justice among the Allied ranks.

But, as at the end of all conflicts, there was anxiety and uneasiness. Larry Newman

In one of the most famous images of the war, Marines hoist "Old Glory" atop Mt. Suribachi on Iwo Jima. *(Joe Rosenthal/AP)*

quoted George Patton, "What the hell is all the mourning about? This is the end of a beginning." Most servicemen reflected, along with the *Yank*'s correspondent at the Japanese surrender ceremony, when a peace treaty was signed on the deck of the USS *Missouri*, "Brother, I hope those are my discharge papers."

But unlike the American Revolution, which left a philosophical legacy, World War II bequeathed two frightening heirs: the atomic bomb and the revelation and remembrance of Nazi concentration camps, both vividly described by correspondents. Thus the journalism of World War II has reverberated through the decades since 1945. The war itself left the legacy of the cold war and the iron curtain. That curtain would not be raised for nearly half a century.

DOROTHY THOMPSON

RADIO BROADCAST, NOVEMBER 14, 1938

"I am willing to die for political freedom, for the right to give loyalty to ideals above a nation or above a class." Dorothy Thompson, who wrote those words in Dorothy Thompson's Political Guide, *published in the summer of 1938, expressed her passion for freedom in regular columns in the New York* Herald Tribune *and* Ladies Home Journal, *in speeches, and on the radio. Thompson began her journalistic career in Europe, where in 1925 she became the first woman to head an overseas news bureau for a major American newspaper and where, in 1928, she married novelist Sinclair Lewis. After interviewing Adolf Hitler in 1931, she wrote a book in which she discounted the possibility that this seemingly insignificant man would ever rise to power. She was wrong. Thompson's continued criticism of the new reichsführer soon led to her expulsion from Germany. By 1938 she was a constant and passionate critic of nazism, both in print and on the radio.*

On November 7, 1938, Herschel Grynzspan, a seventeen-year-old German-born Jew, mortally wounded a German embassy official in Paris. The murder was an angry protest against the poor treatment of Jews in the country from which his parents had just been deported. Kristallnacht, a rampage of German anti-Semitic violence, followed in the wake of the assassination. Dorothy Thompson was inspired to defend Grynzspan's murderous action in her regular Monday evening radio commentary. Millions of radio listeners listened to her analysis just one week after the murder.

Grynzspan never stood trial in a French court. After war broke out between France and Germany in 1939, Grynzspan appealed to be permitted to join the French army so he could "kill some more Germans." That request was denied, and later the Vichy government handed him over to the Germans. Some believe that Grynzspan survived the war and lived in later years under an alias. Firmer evidence suggests he died toward the end of the conflict.

Dorothy Thompson's career continued to rise after her radio commentary on Herschel Grynzspan. Describing her as "something between a Cassandra and a Joan of Arc," Time put Dorothy Thompson on its cover seven months after her defense of Herschel Grynzspan.

A WEEK AGO TODAY AN ANAEMIC-looking boy with brooding black eyes walked quietly into the German embassy in the rue de Lille in Paris, asked to see the ambassador, was shown into the office of the third secretary, Herr von Rath, and shot him. Herr von Rath died on Wednesday.

I want to talk about that boy. I feel as though I knew him, for in the past five years I have met so many whose story is the same—the same except for this unique desperate act. Herschel Grynzspan was one of the hundreds of thousands of refugees whom the terror east of the Rhine has turned loose in the world. His permit to stay in Paris had expired. He could not leave France, for no country would take him in. He could not work because no country would give him a work permit. So he moved about, hoping he would not be picked up and deported, only to be deported again, and yet again. Sometimes he found a bed with another refugee. Sometimes he huddled away from the wind under the bridges of the Seine. He got letters from his father, who was in Hanover, in Germany. His father was all right. He still had a little tailoring shop and managed honorably to earn enough for food and shelter. Maybe he would have sent his son money, but he was not allowed to send any out of Germany. Herschel read the newspapers, and all that he could read filled him with dark anxiety and wild despair. He read how men, women and children, driven out of the Sudetenland by a conquering army—conquering with the consent of Great Britain and France—had been forced to cross the border into Czechoslovakia on their hands and knees—and then had been ordered out of that dismembered country, that, shorn of her richest lands and factories, did not know how to feed the mouths that were left.

He read that Jewish children had been stood on platforms in front of classes of German children and had had their features pointed to and described by the teacher as marks of a criminal race. He read that men and women of his race, amongst them scholars and a general decorated for his bravery had been forced to wash the streets, while the mob laughed. There were men of his race, whom he had been taught to venerate—scientists and educators and scholars who once had been honored by their country. He read that they had been driven from their posts. He heard that the Nazi government had started all this because they said the Jews had made them lose the World War.

But Herschel had not even been born when the World War ended. He was seventeen years old.

Herschel had a pistol. I don't know why he had it. Maybe he had bought it somewhere thinking to use it on himself, if the worst came to the worst. Thousands of men and women of his race had killed themselves in the last years, rather than live like hunted animals. Still, he lived on. Then, a few days ago, he got a letter from his father. His father told him that he had been summoned from his bed, and herded with thousands of others into a train of box cars, and shipped over the border, into Poland. He had not been allowed to take any of his meager savings with him. Just fifty cents. "I am penniless," he wrote to his son.

This was the end. Herschel fingered his pistol and thought: "Why doesn't someone do something! Why must we be chased around the earth like animals!" Herschel was wrong. Animals are not chased around the world like this. In every country there are societies for the prevention of cruelty to animals. But there are none for the prevention of cruelty to people. Herschel thought of the people responsible for this terror. Right in Paris were some, who were the official representatives of these responsible people. Maybe he thought that assassination is an honorable profession in these days. He knew, no doubt, that the youths who murdered the Austrian Chancellor Dollfuss are heroes in Nazi Germany, as are the murderers of Rathenau. Maybe he remembered that only four years ago the Nazi Leader himself had caused scores of men to be assassinated without a trial, and had justified it simply by saying that he was the law. And so Herschel walked into the German embassy and shot Herr von Rath. Herschel made no attempt to escape. Escape was out of the question anyhow.

Herr von Rath died on Wednesday. And on Thursday every Jew in Germany was held responsible for this boy's deed. In every city an organized and methodical mob was turned loose on the Jewish population. Synagogues were burned; shops were gutted and sometimes looted. At least four people were put to death. Many, many more were beaten. Scores killed themselves. In cold blood, the German government imposed a fine of four hundred million dollars on the entire Jewish community, and followed it by decrees which mean total ruin for all of them. A horrified world was stunned. In the United States nearly every newspaper protested. A former governor, Thomas Dewey, protested with unusual eloquence.

But in Paris, a boy who had hoped to make some gesture of protest which would call attention to the wrongs done his race burst into hysterical sobs. Up to then he had been apathetic. He had been prepared to pay for his deed with his own life. Now he realized that half a million of his fellows had been sentenced to extinction on the excuse of his deed.

I am speaking of this boy. Soon he will go on trial. The news is that on top of all this terror, this horror, one more must pay. They say he will go to the guillotine, without a trial by jury, without the rights that any common murderer has.

The world has endured for five years unheard-of things. The fortunes of American citizens have been all but confiscated in Germany. We have protested, and no attention has been paid. What could we do? Some weeks ago two hundred Ameri-

can citizens of Jewish blood were ordered to close their businesses and depart from Italy as undesirable aliens. Our State Department protested, but the protest has been all but ignored. What could we do? Every country in the world has had a refugee problem to add to all its others, as a result of a system which cares nothing for what happens to other countries, and we among them. What could we do?

We could, of course, do many things. There are half a million non-naturalized Germans in the United States, and as many Italians. We might have loaded them on boats, confiscated their property and shipped them home. There are hundreds of thousands of dollars in German and Italian fortunes in this country. We might have confiscated them as reprisals for the confiscated fortunes of American citizens and for unpaid debts. Why don't we do it? We don't do it because we refuse to hold people responsible for crimes that others commit. We don't do it because our sense of justice is still too strong to answer terror with terror. We don't do it because we do not want to add to the hatred and chaos which are already making this world intolerable. We fear that violence breeding violence will destroy us all, in the long run.

When the dictators commit what to the rest of the world are crimes, they say there is a higher justice—they claim the justification of national necessity and emergency. We do not think that such justice is higher. We think it low and cannot therefore answer it in its own language.

But is there not a higher justice in the case of Herschel Grynzspan, seventeen years old? Is there not a higher justice that says that his deed has been expiated with four hundred million dollars and half a million existences, with beatings, and burnings, and deaths, and suicides? Must the nation, whose Zola defended Dreyfus until the world rang with it, cut off the head of one more Jew without giving him an open trial?

Who is on trial in this case? I saw we are all on trial. I say the Christian world is on trial. I say the men of Munich are on trial, who signed a pact without one word of protection for helpless minorities. Whether Herschel Grynzspan lives or not won't matter much to Herschel. He was prepared to die when he fired those shots. His young life was already ruined. Since then his heart has been broken into bits by the result of his deed.

They say a man is entitled to trial by a jury of his peers, and a man's kinsmen rally around him, when he is in trouble. But no kinsman of Herschel's can defend him. The Nazi government has announced that if any Jew, anywhere in the world, protests at anything that is happening, further oppressive measures will be taken. They are holding every Jew in Germany as a hostage.

Therefore, we who are not Jews must speak, speak our sorrow and indignation and disgust in so many voices that they will be heard. This boy has become a symbol, and the responsibility for his deed must be shared by those who caused it.

WILLIAM L. SHIRER

ENTRY FOR SEPTEMBER 1, 1939, IN *BERLIN DIARY* (KNOPF, 1941)

In 1934 William L. Shirer arrived in Berlin as a correspondent first for the Universal News Service and later for Columbia Broadcasting Service. Berlin was a good beat for a reporter in the late 1930s. Louis P. Lochner of Associated Press and Otto D. Tolischus of the New York Times, *winners of Pulitzer Prizes in international reporting in 1938 and 1939, were both based in Berlin. Nevertheless, the German capital was not a comfortable place for an American reporter. The United States withdrew its ambassador from Berlin in November 1938 in protest of the officially sanctioned violence against Jews following Herschel Grynzspan's murder of a German official in Paris.*

As World War II broke out on September 1, 1939, Shirer's "only competitor" for journalistic scoops in Berlin was European-born Max Jordan of NBC. While their broadcasts had to meet with the approval of strict German censors, Shirer kept a diary in which he recorded the thoughts and observations that he could not send out over the airways. The following is his entry in that diary on the first day of what was to be the Second World War.

Shirer remained in Berlin as a CBS broadcaster for over a year after the start of the war. Returning to the United States in December 1940, his unbroadcasted thoughts were published as Berlin Diary *a few months later. This inside view of Hitler's Germany became America's number-one nonfiction best-seller in 1941. Nearly two decades later Shirer's weighty* Rise and Fall of the Third Reich *was also high on the best-seller charts.*

The *New York Times,* founded by Henry J. Raymond in 1851, was rescued from bankruptcy in 1896 by Adolph Ochs. It set its course as America's leading newspaper under the leadership of Arthur Hayes Sulzberger, who promised to include "All the News That's Fit to Print."

IT'S A "COUNTER-ATTACK"! AT DAWN this morning Hitler moved against Poland. It's a flagrant, inexcusable, unprovoked act of aggression. But Hitler and the High Command call it a "counter-attack." A grey morning with overhanging clouds. The people in the street were apathetic when I drove to the Rundfunk for my first broadcast at eight fifteen A.M. Across from the Adlon the morning shift of workers was busy on the new I. G. Farben building just as if nothing had happened. None of the men bought the Extras which the newsboys were shouting. Along the east-west axis the Luftwaffe

were mounting five big anti-aircraft guns to protect Hitler when he addresses the Reichstag at ten A.M. Jordan and I had to remain at the radio to handle Hitler's speech for America. Throughout the speech, I thought as I listened, ran a curious strain, as though Hitler himself were dazed at the fix he had got himself into and felt a little desperate about it. Somehow he did not carry conviction and there was much less cheering in the Reichstag than on previous, less important occasions. Jordan must have reacted the same way. As we waited to translate the speech for America, he whispered: "Sounds like his swan song." It really did. He sounded discouraged when he told the Reichstag that Italy would not be coming into the war because "we are unwilling to call in outside help for this struggle. We will fulfill this task by ourselves." And yet Paragraph 3 of the Axis military alliance calls for immediate, automatic Italian support with "all its military resources on land, at sea, and in the air." What about that? He sounded desperate when, referring to Molotov's speech of yesterday at the Russian ratification of the Nazi-Soviet accord, he said: "I can only underline every word of Foreign Commissar Molotov's speech."

Tomorrow Britain and France probably will come in and you have your second World War. The British and French tonight sent an ultimatum to Hitler to withdraw his troops from Poland or their ambassadors will ask for their passports. Presumably they will get their passports.

HELEN KIRKPATRICK

"LONDON STILL STOOD THIS MORNING"

CHICAGO *DAILY NEWS*, SEPTEMBER 9, 1940

While Edward R. Murrow's reports on the London Blitz are the best known, the CBS correspondent was far from the only journalist on the scene. Helen Kirkpatrick, the lone female on the international staff of the Chicago Daily News, *also dodged the Luftwaffe's raids to tell readers what it was like to weather the bombardments. The following chronicle by Kirkpatrick differs in style and substance from Murrow's accounts, which focused more on how Londoners coped with the Nazi air attacks. Kirkpatrick's is a more personal story of how she managed to survive the blitz.*

LONDON STILL STOOD THIS MORNing, which was the greatest surprise to me as I cycled home in the light of early dawn after the most frightening night I have ever spent. But not all of London was still there, and some of the things I saw this morning would scare the wits out of anyone.

When the sirens first shrieked on Saturday, it was evident we were in for something, but dinner proceeded calmly enough. It was when the first screaming bomb started on its downward track that we decided the basement would be healthier.

The whole night was one of moving from the basement to the first floor, with occasional sallies to make sure that no incendiaries had landed on the rooftop.

That was perhaps more frightening than the sound of constant bombs punctuated by guns near and far. For the London air was heavy with the burning smell. The smoke sometimes brought tears to the eyes, and the glow around the horizon certainly looked as though the entire city might be up in flames any minute.

On one occasion I dropped off to sleep on a basement floor and slept probably forty-five minutes, when two screamers sounding as though they had landed right next door brought me, startled, to my

Helen Kirkpatrick.
(National Archives)

feet. A few minutes later a couple of incendiaries arrived just around the corner, but the fire equipment came within seconds.

Most of the time we felt that the entire center of the city had probably been blasted out of existence and we ticked off each hit with "That must be Buckingham Palace—that's Whitehall." It was staggering, to say the least, to cycle for a mile through the heart of London and fail to see even one pane of glass shattered and eventually to find one's own house standing calm and in one piece.

A later tour, however, showed that while none of the bombs hit any objectives we had picked out, they had landed squarely on plenty of places. I walked through areas of rubble and debris in southeastern London this morning that made it seem incredible that anyone could be alive, but they were, and very much so. Fires for the most part were put out or were well under control by early morning.

It was a contrast to find one section of "smart London" that had as bad a dose as the tenement areas. Near one of many of Sir Christopher Wren's masterpieces, houses were gutted structures with windowpanes hanging out, while panes in a church were broken in a million pieces.

It is amazing this morning to see London traffic more like New York theater traffic than the slow dribble it had been during past months, but it is most amazing to see that there is any London to have traffic at all. it is pretty incredible, too, to find people relatively unshaken after the terrific experience.

There is some terror, but nothing on the scale that the Germans may have hoped for and certainly not on a scale to make Britons contemplate for a moment anything but fighting on.

Fright becomes so mingled with a deep almost uncontrollable anger that it is hard to know when one stops and the other begins. And on top of it all London is smiling even in the districts where casualties must have been very heavy.

EDWARD R. MURROW

"A REPORT DURING THE BLITZ"

SEPTEMBER 13, 1940

Known for his broadcast opener "This is London . . . ," Edward R. Murrow was not yet thirty years old when he became European director for CBS in 1937. In this capacity he hired William L. Shirer, Eric Sevareid, Howard K. Smith, and other correspondents whose names would become household words to Americans. These radio newsmen offered the American public accounts of the latest developments hours before the words of print journalists could appear in the newspapers. Perhaps no reporting brought out the character of radio news broadcasting better than Murrow's accounts of the Battle of Britain, the German bomb attacks on London and other targets in the summer and fall of 1940. The following report came just over a month after the first bombing raid on London.

THIS IS LONDON AT 3:30 IN THE morning. This has been what might be called a "routine night"—air-raid alarm at about 9 o'clock and intermittent bombing ever since. I had the impression that more high explosives and few incendiaries have been used tonight. Only two small fires can be seen on the horizon. Again the Germans have been sending their bombers in singly or in pairs. The antiaircraft barrage has been fierce but sometimes there have been periods of twenty minutes when London has been silent. Then the big red busses would start up and move on till the guns started working again. That silence is almost harder to bear. One becomes accustomed to rattling windows and the distant sound of bombs and then there comes a silence that can be felt. You know the sound will return—you wait, and then it starts again. That waiting is bad. It gives you a chance to imagine things. I have been walking tonight—there is a full moon, and the dirty-gray buildings appear white. The stars, the empty windows, are hidden. It's a

Edward R. Murrow (*right*)
with radio technician. *(Murrow
Center/Tufts University)*

beautiful and lonesome city where men and women and children are trying to snatch a few hours' sleep underground.

In the fashionable residential districts I could read the **TO LET** signs on the front of big houses in the light of the bright moon. Those houses have big basements underneath—good shelters, but they're not being used. Many people think they should be.

The scale of this air war is so great that the reporting is not easy. Often we spend hours traveling about this sprawling city, viewing damage, talking with people, and occasionally listening to the bombs coming down, and then more hours wonder-

ing what you'd like to hear about these people who are citizens of no mean city. We've told you about the bombs, the fires, the smashed houses, and the courage of the people. We've read you the communiqués and tried to give you an honest estimate of the wounds inflicted upon this, the best bombing target in the world. But the business of living and working in this city is very personal—the little incidents, the things the mind retains, are in themselves unimportant, but they somehow weld together to form the hard core of memories that will remain when the last "all-clear" has sounded. That's why I want to talk for just three or four minutes about the things we haven't talked about before; for many of these impressions it is necessary to reach back through only one long week. There was a rainbow bending over the battered and smoking East End of London just when the "all-clear" sounded one afternoon. One night I stood in front of a smashed grocery store and heard a dripping inside. It was the only sound in all London. Two cans of peaches had been drilled clean through by flying glass and the juice was dripping down onto the floor.

There was a flower shop in the East End. Nearly every other building in the block had been smashed. There was a funeral wreath in the window of the shop—price: three shillings and sixpence, less than a dollar. In front of Buckingham Palace there's a bed of red and white flowers—untouched—the reddest flowers I've ever seen.

Last night, or rather early this morning, I met a distinguished member of Parliament in a bar. He had been dining with Anthony Eden and had told the Secretary for War that he wouldn't walk through the streets with all that shrapnel falling about, and as a good host Eden should send him home in a tank. Another man came in and reported, on good authority, that the Prime Minister had a siren suit, one of those blue woolen coverall affairs with a zipper. Someone said the Prime Minister must resemble a barrage balloon when attired in his siren suit. Things of that sort can still be said in this country. The fact that the noise—just the sound, not the blast—of bombs and guns can cause one to stagger while walking down the street came as a surprise. When I entered my office today, after bombs had fallen two blocks away, and was asked by my English secretary if I'd care for a cup of tea, that didn't come as much of a surprise.

Talking from a studio with a few bodies lying about on the floor, sleeping on mattresses, still produces a strange feeling but we'll probably get used to that. Today I went to buy a hat—my favorite shop had gone, blown to bits. The windows of my shoe store were blown out. I decided to have a haircut; the windows of the barbershop were gone, but the Italian barber was still doing business. Someday, he said, we smile again, but the food it doesn't taste so good since being bombed. I went on to another shop to buy flashlight batteries. I bought three. The clerk said: "You needn't buy so many. We'll have enough for the whole winter." But I said: "What if you aren't here?" There were buildings down in that street, and he replied: "Of course, we'll be here. We've been in business here for a hundred and fifty years."

But the sundown scene in London can never be forgotten—the time when people pick up their beds and walk to the shelter.

JOHN GUNTHER

INSIDE EUROPE

(HARPER AND BROTHERS, 1940)

Gunther contributed numerous stories as a freelance correspondent in Europe, but his greatest contribution was a series of books titled Inside Europe, *published between 1933 and 1940. The works gave readers an "insider's" view of the political events and international happenings on the continent. The popularity of the series was obvious—Gunther wrote and published seven volumes at the rate of one a year between 1933 and 1938, with the last arriving on library shelves in 1940.*

The following selection is from the author's reports on the Reichstag fire trial. The 1933 blaze was a Nazi trap carried out to taint the Communist party as one of saboteurs in hopes of improving Nazi chances in the upcoming elections. It might have worked if not for the persistence of the Bulgarian-born presiding judge Dimitrov. Rather than rubber-stamping the proceedings, the magistrate assumed the role of investigator, and by trial's end, the Nazi scheme had been revealed and a furious Göring had ordered Dimitrov's removal from the bench.

Years after the Reichstag incident and the subsequent trial, Gunther reportedly claimed that he believed that his reporting on the matter was his claim to fame. After all, the uncovering of the plot behind the inferno exposed the lengths to which Hitler and the Nazis would go. Gunther allegedly told an associate, "My God, suppose I hadn't written it."

THE FIRE PRODUCED EXACTLY what the Nazis hoped for.

The one hundred Communist deputies were arrested. A state of virtual siege was proclaimed. The provisions of the Constitution guaranteeing individual liberty were suppressed. Plans for a Communist outbreak were "revealed." Germany rose with a roar. There was intense public excitement. The Nazis stormed the country, and Hitler was able to maneuver himself into a dictatorship for four years, affix himself to power immovably.

The true story of the fire is not so well known today as it might be. The Nazis did their job so well that, whereas everyone well informed instantly suspected them of complicity, there was much puzzlement as to details. Even today there are mysteries, subsidiary mysteries, not entirely clear. Let us deal with them.

During the night of the fire a Dutch half-wit named Marinus van der Lubbe was arrested when police found him in the burning ruins. There were no witnesses except the police to his arrest. The first statements about the Dutchman, issued by Goring, were false. It was said that he had a membership card of the Communist party on his person, a leaflet urging common action between Socialists and Communists, several photographs of himself, and a passport. Obliging fellow! He did possess the passport, but not the other documents, as the trial subsequently proved.

His career and movements were closely traced. He had set three other fires—minor ones—in Berlin just before the Reichstag fire. In 1929 he had joined something called the Dutch Communist Youth Organization, a secessionist group. Two years later he was expelled from this as a worthless and stupid fellow. He never belonged to the Communist party itself. Van der Lubbe's itinerary the few days before the fire was well established. As late as the night of February 17–18 he slept at Glinow, near Potsdam. He could not have got to Berlin before the nineteenth or twentieth. Yet inside a week he, an unknown hobo, either (a) so insinuated himself into the graces of the rigidly articulated Communist party as to be given the dangerous and delicate job of firing the Reichstag, or (b) was hired to do it by someone else.

When it became clear, even in Germany, that the van der Lubbe explanation simply would not hold water, the mystery thickened. The police got to the point of having to admit that van der Lubbe had confederates. But how, carrying incendiary material, could enough of them possibly have penetrated the Reichstag walls, doorways, or windows in the middle of Berlin without being seen?

The German authorities themselves let the cat out of the bag, and an astounding cat it proved to be. It was announced that the incendiaries had presumably entered and escaped form the building by means of an underground tunnel leading from the Reichstag basement to the palace of the speaker of the Reichstag—Goring—across the street. Originally this tunnel was part of the Reichstag's central heating system. Until an official communique revealed its existence not a dozen persons in Berlin had ever heard of it. So one aspect of the mystery was solved. The incendiaries, whoever they were, got in and out of the Reichstag building—through Goring's back yard. Incredible information!

An ostrich sticks its head in the sand—well-meaning but stupid ostrich. There is an obverse of the ostrich process. A man may naively and stridently call attention to something he wishes to conceal, hoping thereby to lessen interest in it. A squirrel hides a nut under a tree. Then he squats and points at it, showing where it is. Disingenuously a man may reveal what is embarrassing to him, hoping to modify the terms of the embarrassment.

Long before the trial opened the accusation that the Nazis themselves had burned the building had impressed the world. A mock trial was held in London. The Brown Book, telling part of the story—but inaccurately—was published by emigres and widely circulated. Moreover, a secret nationalist memorandum, written to the order of a prominent deputy named Oberfohren, was passed from hand to hand. Oberfohren was a nationalist, a Junker, one of Papen's men. He asserted flatly that the Nazis were the incendiaries. In June, a Nazi detachment searched his flat; mystery for some time surrounded Oberfohren's whereabouts. Then it was announced that he had "shot himself."

The half-wit van der Lubbe was not the only person arrested. Ernst Torgler, chairman of the Communist bloc in the Reichstag, gave himself up to the police when he heard the announcement incredible to his ears that he was accused of complicity; subsequently three Bulgarian Communists, Dimitrov, Popov, and Tanev, were arrested, when a waiter who had served them in a Berlin cafe told the police that their activities had been "suspicious." Dimitrov was in Munich, not Berlin, on the night of the fire, as an incontrovertible alibi proved; nevertheless, he was held for five months until the trial, without a scrap of evidence against him.

I covered the trial in Leipzig and Berlin during its first six weeks. The court sat for fifty-seven days, and provided superlative drama. The trial was neither a farce nor a frame-up. The behavior of the police and judicial authorities before the trial was outrageous, but once the proceedings reached the courtroom there was a difference. The court got itself into a curious dilemma, of having to pretend to be fair even while exercising the greatest animus against the defendants, and little by little this necessity—caused mostly by the pressure of foreign opinion—to simulate justice led to some modicum of justice in the courtroom.

When the trial opened, I think, the judges like many people in Germany genuinely thought that van der Lubbe was a Communist and that the Communists were guilty. The prosecution thought so too and, assuming that the trial would be quick and easy, it made no serious effort to fabricate a "good" case. As the hearings went on it became evident even to the judges that there was no case at all. The evidence of the prosecution was a mystifying confusion of inaccuracies, contradictions, and plain lies. But once the trial started, it couldn't be stopped. With dreadful pertinacity, with true Teutonic thoroughness, the court plodded on, deeper every day in a morass of evidence that ineluctably proved just what it didn't want proved—the innocence of the accused. The prosecution, panicky, began to produce incredible cranks as witnesses, whom even the judges couldn't stomach; the judge, nervous, threw Dimitrov out of court whenever his questions became too intolerably pointed—which was often.

No one, of course, counted on the brilliant gallantry of Dimitrov. This Bulgarian revolutionary had, moreover, brains. Unerringly he picked every flaw in the testimony of a dishonest witness; unerringly he asked just those questions most damaging to the prosecution. He turned the trial into a public forum. The trial started as an attempt to pin the guilt of the Reichstag arson on the defendants. Dimitrov turned it before long into an action precisely opposite: one seeking to clear the Nazis of the same charge.

Once the court was forced into calling every relevant witness, like porters and workmen in the Reichstag building, the floodgates were open. Hot little clues dodged out. Lubbe, inert, apathetic, testified—in one of his few lucid moments— that he had been "with Nazis" the night before the fire. A gateman testified that a Nazi deputy, Dr. Albrecht, left the burning building, in great excitement, as late as ten P.M. A servant in Goring's house, Aldermann, testified that he heard, on several night before the fire, mysterious sounds in the underground tunnel. Thus the fire—got hot.

CECIL BROWN

"ALL HANDS ON DECK, PREPARE TO ABANDON SHIP. MAY GOD BE WITH YOU!"

COLUMBIA BROADCASTING SYSTEM, DECEMBER 11, 1941

Cecil Brown, who served as CBS's reporter in Singapore, witnessed the first firefights in Asia. The following broadcast was Brown's account of the sinking of the British battlewagons Prince of Wales *and* Repulse. *Like the U.S. ironclads overwhelmed days earlier in Pearl Harbor, the British warships were the target of a swarm of Japanese fighter planes and were sunk after putting up a fierce battle.*

The sinking of the ships was another in a line of unnerving defeats for the Allies in the last, dark days of 1941. But the tales of heroism overshadowed the costly losses. And like the sailors on the English vessels, Brown did not lose his sense of humor. Upon receipt of a camouflaged note congratulating him on doing a "grand job," Brown exclaimed that he'd gotten a thousand-dollar bonus for his reporting.

HERE'S THE EYEWITNESS STORY of how the *Prince of Wales* and the *Repulse* ended their careers in the South China Sea, fifty miles from the Malaya coast and a hundred and fifty miles north of Singapore.

I was aboard the *Repulse* and with hundreds of others escaped. Then, swimming in thick oil, I saw the *Prince of Wales* lie over on her side like a tired war horse and slide beneath the waters. I kept a diary from the time the first Japanese high-level bombing started at 11:15 until 12:31, when Captain William Tennant, skipper of the *Repulse* and senior British captain afloat, shouted through the ship's communication system, "All hands on deck, prepare to abandon ship. May God be with you!"

I jumped twenty feet to the water from the up end of the side of the *Repulse* and smashed my stop watch at thirty-five and a half minutes after twelve. The sinking of the *Repulse* and the *Prince of Wales* was carried out by a combination of high-level bombing and torpedo attacks with consummate skill and the greatest daring. I was standing on the flag deck slightly forward amidships when nine Jap bombers approached at ten thousand feet strung in a line, clearly visible in the brilliant sunlit sky. They flew directly over our ship, and our antiaircraft guns were screaming constantly.

Just when the planes were passing over, one bomb hit the water beside where I was standing, so close to the ship that we were drenched from the waterspout. Simultaneously another struck the *Repulse* on the catapult deck, penetrating the ship and exploding below in a marine's mess and hangar. Our planes were subsequently unable to take off. At 11:27 fire is raging below, and most strenuous efforts are under way to control it. All gun crews are replenishing their ammunition and are very cool and cracking jokes. There are a couple of jagged holes in the funnel near where I am standing.

It's obvious the Japs flew over the length of the ship, each dropping three bombs so that twenty-seven bombs fell around us at first in their attack. Brilliant red flashes are spouting from our guns' wells. The *Prince of Wales* is half a mile away. Destroyers are at various distances, throwing everything they have into the air. A splash about two miles off our port beam may be antiaircraft, but we are uncertain. At 11:40 the *Prince of Wales* seems to be hit. She's reduced her speed. Now they're coming to attack us. The communication system shouts, "Stand by for barrage." All our guns are going. We are twisting and snaking violently to avoid torpedoes. The Japs are coming in low, one by one in single waves. They're easy to spot. Amid the roar from the guns aboard the *Repulse* and the pom-poms of antiaircraft fire, we are signaled, "We've a man overboard."

Two Jap aircraft are approaching us. I see more of them coming with the naked eye. I again count nine. They're torpedo bombers and are circling us about a mile and half or two miles away. Eleven forty-five—now there seem to me more bombers but they are circling like vultures at about one-thousand-feet altitude. The guns are deafening. The smell of cordite is almost suffocating and explosions are ear-shattering and the flashes blinding. The officer beside me yells, "Here comes a tin fish."

A Jap torpedo bomber is heading directly for us, two hundred yards above the water. At 11:48 he's less than five hundred distant, plowing onward. A torpedo drops, and he banks sharply and his whole side is exposed to our guns, but instead of driving away he's making a graceful dive toward the water. He hits and immediately bursts into flame in a gigantic splash of orange against the deep-blue sky and the robin's-egg blue water. Other planes are coming, sweeping low in an amazing suicide effort to sink the *Repulse*.

Their daring is astonishing, coming so close you can make out the pilot's outline. One coming in at 11:48 to our starboard just dropped a torpedo. A moment later I hear shouts of joy indicating that he was brought down, but I didn't see that. We also claim we brought down two high-level bombers previously, but I didn't see these crash. At least, for the moment I have no recollection of seeing them.

At 12:01 another wave of torpedo bombers is approaching. They are being met with everything we've got except our fourteen inchers. Beside me the signal officer flashes word from Captain Tennant to the *Prince of Wales:* "We eluded all torpedoes this second attack." It's fascinating to watch our tracer bullets speeding toward the Jap bombers. 12:03: we've just shot down another torpedo bomber who is about four hundred yards away, and we shot it out. All of its motors are afire, and disintegrating pieces of the fuselage are flying about. Now it disappears over the surface of the water into scrap. The brilliant orange from the fire against this blue sky is so close it's startling. All the men are cheering at the sight. It's so close it seems you could almost reach out and touch the remains of this Jap bomber.

At 12:15 the *Wales* seems to be stopped definitely. I've been too busy to watch the attacks against her, but she seems in utmost difficulty. Her guns are firing constantly and we are both twisting. One moment the Wales is at our starboard, the next it's at our port. I'm not watching the destroyers, but they have not been subjected to air attacks. The Japs are throwing everything recklessly against the two capital ships.

There's fire aboard us; it's not out. I just saw some firemen and fire-control parties. The calmness of the crews is amazing. I have constantly roved from one side of the flag deck to the other during the heavy firing and attacks, and the cool precision of all hands has seemed unreal and unnatural. Even when they are handing up shells for the service guns, each shell is handed over with a joke. I never saw such happiness on men's faces. This is the first time these gun crews have been in action in this war, and they are having the time of their lives. Twelve-twenty: I see ten bombers approaching from a distance. It's impossible to determine whether this will be a high-level attack or another torpedo-bomber attack. "Stand by for barrage" comes over the ship's communication system.

One plane is circling around; it's now at three or four hundred yards, approaching us from the port side. It's coming closer, head on, and I see a torpedo drop. It's streaking for us. A watcher shouts, "Stand by for torpedo," and the tin fish is streaking directly for us. Someone says: "This one got us." The torpedo struck the side on which I was standing about twenty yards astern of my position. It felt like the ship had crashed into a well-rooted dock. It threw me four feet across the deck, but I did not fall and I did not feel any explosion. Just a very great jar. Almost immediately we began to list, and less than a minute later there was

another jar of the same kind and the same force, except that it was almost precisely on the starboard side.

After the first torpedo, the communication system coolly announced: "Blow up your life belts." I was in this process when the second torpedo struck, and the settling ship and the crazy angle were so apparent I didn't continue blowing my belt.

That the *Repulse* was doomed was immediately apparent. The communication system announced, "Prepare to abandon ship. May God be with you!" Without undue rush we all started streaming down ladders hurrying but not pushing. It was most difficult to realize I must leave the ship. It seemed so incredible that the *Repulse* could or should go down. But the *Repulse* was fast keeling over to port and walking ceased to become a mode of locomotion. I was forced to clamber and scramble in order to reach the side. Men were lying dead around the guns. Some were half hidden by empty shell cases. There was considerable damage all around the ship. Some of the men had been machine-gunned. That had been unquestioned fact.

All around me men were stripping off their clothes and their shoes and tossing aside their steel helmets. Some are running alongside the three-quarter-exposed hull of the ship to reach a spot where they can slide down the side without injuring themselves in the jagged hole in the ship's side. Others are running to reach a point where they have a shorter dive to the water. I am reluctant to leave my new portable typewriter down in my cabin and unwilling to discard my shoes, which I had made just a week before. As I go over the side, the *Prince of Wales* half a mile away seems to be afire, but her guns are still firing the heaviest. It's most obvious she's stopped dead and out of control due to her previous damage.

The air attack against the *Prince of Wales* carried out the same scheme directed against the *Repulse*. The Japs were able to send two British capital ships to the bottom because of, first, a determined air torpedo attack and, second, the skill and efficiency of the Japanese operations. It's apparent that the best guns and crews in the world will be unable to stem a torpedo-bombing attack if the attackers are sufficiently determined.

According to the best estimate obtainable, the Japs used in their operations against both the *Wales* and the *Repulse* eighty-six bombers; eighteen high-level bombers and approximately twenty-five torpedo bombers against the *Repulse* and probably an equal number against the *Prince of Wales*. In the case of the *Wales*, however, the Japs started the torpedo bombing instead of initial high-level bombing. In the first attack, one torpedo hit the Wales in the after-part. Some survivors believe the *Wales* was hit twice in the initial attack, then followed two more torpedo attacks, both successful. The final attack on the *Wales* was made by high-level bombers around ten thousand feet. When that attack came, the *Wales* was sinking fast and everyone threw himself down on deck.

Most of the guns were unmanageable as a result of the list and the damage. I jumped into the water from the *Repulse* at 12:35. While I was in the water, the *Wales* continued firing for some time. The *Wales* suffered two direct hits by bombs on the deck. Like the attack on the *Repulse*, the Japs flew across the length of the *Wales* in a single line, each bomber dropping a stick. One officer said a child of six could see some of them were going to hit us. During the entire action Admiral Tom Phillips, Commander-in-Chief of the Far East Fleet, and Captain Leech, skipper of the *Prince of Wales*, were on the bridge.

While the torpedo bombers were rushing in toward the *Wales*, dropping ten fish and machine-gunning the decks, Phillips clambered up on the roof of the bridge and also atop the gun turrets to see better and to direct all phases of the action.

When it was apparent that the *Wales* was badly hit, the Admiral issued an order to the flag officer for the destroyer then lying alongside close by. "Signal to Singapore to send tugs to tow us." Evidently up to that moment, Phillips was not convinced that the *Wales* was sinking. The last order issued by Phillips came at approximately 1:15. It said, "Blow up your life boats."

Later the ship was underwater. Phillips and Leech were the last from the *Wales* to go over the side, and they slid into the water together. It's probable that their reluctance to leave the ship until all possible men had left meant their death, since it's most likely they were drawn down by the suction when the *Wales* was on her side and then settled at her stern with her bow rising into the air.

Swimming about a mile away, lying on top of a small stool, I saw the bow of the *Wales*. When Phillips signaled to ask Singapore to send tugs, the *Wales* already had four torpedoes in her. Like the *Repulse*, the *Wales* gun crews were very cool, and although many guns were no longer effective the crew stood beside them. When the final high-level-bombing attack came, only three guns were capable of firing, except the fourteen-inchers, which naturally did not go into action. I did not meet Phillips, but last week when I visited the *Wales* at the naval base I had a long talk with Captain Leech. He's a jovial, convivial, smiling officer who gave me the impression of the greatest kindness and ability. The *Wales* carried a complement of seventeen hundred; the *Repulse* twelve hundred and fifty officers and ratings. When the *Wales* sank, the suction was so great it ripped off the life belt of one officer more than fifty feet away. A for-tunate feature of the sinking of both the *Repulse* and the *Wales* was that neither blew up.

Since the tide was strong and there was an extremely powerful suction from both ships, it was extremely difficult to make any progress away from the ship in the thick oil. The gentle, quiet manner in which these shell-belching dreadnoughts went to their last resting place without ex-ploding was a tribute of gratitude from two fine ships for their fine sailors.

RAYMOND GRAHAM SWING

"ANNIVERSARY OF NAZI BOOK-BURNING"

MAY 10, 1943

On May 10, 1933, Nazis organized book burnings throughout Germany. Goebbels, Hitler's propaganda minister, proclaimed "the soul of the German people can again express itself. These flames not only illuminate the final end of an old era; they also light up the new." Among the authors whose works were thrown into the flames were Sigmund Freud, Erich Maria Remarque, and Thomas Mann. Among those who watched as forty thousand assembled to watch the book burning in Berlin was Frederick T. Birchall of the New York Times. *His report on another fire that destroyed the Reichstag just weeks earlier would help him win the Pulitzer Prize for international reporting in 1934.*

Raymond Graham Swing was a foreign correspondent in Europe at the time of the book burning. Years earlier Swing had covered the First World War from Germany before America's entry into the war. By 1933 Swing's longtime German friend, Dr. Rudolf Breitscheid, had seen his political and diplomatic career ruined by Hitler's rise to power. Not only had he been a member of the Reichstag, but he had also been part of the German delegation to the League of Nations. Swing spoke to him shortly after the book burning. In the decade since, Dr. Breitscheid had gone into exile, seen Marburg University strip him of the doctorate that it had awarded him in 1899, and been nabbed by German authorities in 1941.

Swing's long service abroad as a foreign correspondent came to an end in the mid-1930s. Returning to the United States, he soon began broadcasting a nightly commentary and soon became the most respected of commentators on world affairs. Swing's broadcasts in 1943 were heard on BBC, the Mutual Broadcasting System, and American Broadcasting Company. The following is one of those broadcasts.

THE ANNIVERSARY OF MAY 10, 1933, gives perspective in still greater clarity. For on that day the world had its warning and should have known what was in the making. But the world hadn't been training ears to hear warnings or eyes to see such beacons as were lit in the Berlin bonfire of books. And here I shall repeat something about this event which I said a year ago, and do so at the request of the Council of Books in Wartime and the OWI.

I know I didn't appreciate the full portent of the warning of that event in Berlin. But it came to me shortly, and on this anniversary I see again vividly the figure of the man who taught me. He was an unusually tall, an unusually narrow man, with legs as long as Lincoln's, a rounded stoop of the shoulders, and a long, gaunt face. He had been chairman of the Social-Democratic party in the Reichstag of the Weimar Republic, and his name was Dr. Rudolf Breitscheid. In my newspaper days in Germany I had come to know him well. And after Hitler seized power I knew that he had managed to escape to France. Then he came to London, and I was deeply moved to hear that I should be allowed to have an hour with him alone at the home of a member of the House of Commons.

I found him in that home, slumped and, it seemed, almost collapsed, in a big chair. He looked up at me with large eyes filled with the pain one sees during a mortal illness. The first glance at him told its story: here was a man whose life-work was in ruins, who had lost not only his country but all possibilities of serving his country or himself, a man bereft and broken.

I expected him to tell me, in that hour, about himself and his escape, and to give me the news of our personal friends in Germany, many of whom, I knew, had been tortured by the Nazis. I was keyed up to withstand the shock of the brutality our friends had suffered. But I was stopped short by his tragic appearance and was unable to start the conversation. I hoped he would begin without prompting, in his own way.

He was silent for quite a time, then he looked up with an expression of utter helplessness in his face, and he said weakly, but with horror: "Swing, they're burning books."

I was startled, and for a moment I thought that he was being irrelevant. I was expecting news of persecution, torture, and terrible personal disasters, and he began by mentioning what I already knew, that in Berlin they were burning books. But he was a true messenger of tragedy, for that was in the furthermost depth of the tragedy, the burning of books. That was the symbol of it. . . .

That fire has not died, and it will not have died until Germans themselves have free minds again and no power remains on the face of the earth to deny the liberty of man's mind. And when the history of this awful war is written, there is a description of it that would be fitting. It was the war to put out the fire which Hitler lighted in Berlin ten years ago today.

SA troops parade past Adolf Hitler in Nuremberg. *(National Archives)*

JOHN HERSEY

"MAJOR RINGS A BELL IN LICATA"

LIFE, AUGUST 23, 1943

AMGOT it was called—the Allied Military Government of Occupied Territory. The first task of the American and British armies as they fought their way up the peninsula was to strike down the enemy. The second was to set up a military government to administer Italian soil under joint Anglo-American supervision. For this purpose American and British officers were sent to govern the Italian villages and cities as long as they remained in the military theater. For some of these officers the assignment was a sinecure important only in terms of wine, women, and song. Others of a more conscientious mold appreciated the critical nature of the experiment—a heaven-sent opportunity to teach Italy self-government. In unhappy Sicily, as occupation troops soon discovered, the spirit of Garibaldi was quite dead.

The story of one of these officers with a mission and of the magnificent job he performed was told by a young journalist soon to be acclaimed as one of the outstanding writers of World War II. "Major Rings a Bell in Licata" was the genesis of John Hersey's Pulitzer Prize–winning novel about the American occupation of a Sicilian town, **A Bell for Adano** *(1944). One of the most popular books published during World War II, it sold some 100,000 copies within a year. A highly successful stage version was produced on Broadway by Leland Hayward, and a suitably colossal film adaptation came from the studios of Twentieth Century–Fox.*

"I THANK YOU AND I KISS YOUR HAND"

ARMY DESK JOBS ARE FAMOUS for dullness. And yet one of the most exciting things you can do in Sicily right now is to sit for a day by the desk of the Major who runs the town of Licata in the name of the Allies.

For a long time we have taken pleasure in the difficulties met by Germany and Japan in organizing the conquered lands. Here at the Major's desk you see difficulties, hundreds of them, but you see shrewd action, American idealism and generosity bordering on sentimentality, the innate sympathy of common blood that so many Americans have to offer over here. You see incredible Italian poverty, you see the habits of Fascism, you see a little duplicity and a lot of simplicity and many things which are comic and tragic at one time. Above all you see a thing succeeding—and it looks like the future.

First look at the desk. It is no ordinary Army desk. It is oak and it is vast. Underneath it there is a little wooden scrollwork footstool. On each end of the desk are fasces and inscription ANNO XV—for the fifteenth year of Fascism, 1937, when the desk must have been made. It sits at the end of a huge marble-floored room in the Palazzo Dicitta or Town Hall—a room obviously copied from the famous room of the recent Number One boy. Sitting at the desk you see pictures of King Victor Emmanuel, his Queen, Prince Umberto and his Princess, and scenes of the King driving through the town after it was bombed some time ago. Approaching the desk you see a huge and violent painting which the Major's fawning interpreter will tell you represents Columbus discovering American but actually is a scene from Sicilian Vespers, the bloody revolt against a previous invader.

The Major comes in at 7:45. His assistant, Corporal Charles Nocerini of Franklin, Kansas, is already at his improvised table at the opposite end of the huge room from the Major's desk. The corporal goes to a closet against the wall, takes out a big tin of orange juice, pokes holes in it with a bayonet, and pours out breakfast for the Major, which he takes at his desk. He is already deep in his account book, balancing fines and incomes from sales of seized equipment against home-relief payments and repair costs. Bent over his work, the Major appears furiously energetic in a La Guardia kind of way. His skin is dark. He has a mustache which he says he grew "because it makes me look more fitted for the job." His dark-brown eyes are clear and quick in spite of the fact that he didn't sleep very well last night because he had so many things to think about for today.

After balancing his books he writes a couple of brief reports, and then the process begins which makes his day both killing and fascinating—a stream of visitors bring their problems to him. First come two women dressed in black. For some reason the women always come in pairs. The younger of these two has a baby in

her arms. The Major sits them down. As the older one starts explaining trouble in fine circumlocutions the younger one pulls out a tit and starts nursing the baby, which is pathetically thin. It seems the family had nine goats, eight of which were killed by the bombing. It seems that the roof leaks. The girl's husband is in the Italian Army. Her brother deserted but is in Palermo. The family has always been against Fascism. There is much malaria in Sicily . . . and so the tale of woe rambles on until the Major says sharply, "You wish?"

"We wish," says the old lady, "permission to go to Palermo to find the brother of my daughter here, my son who fought for his country but still does not work for his family."

The Major politely explains that there is a war going on, that trains are not now carrying civilians, that everything is being done to hurry the war but that one must have patience.

Next visitor is a lawyer, an unctuous man in a white suit and blue glasses who out of habit raises his hand in the Fascist salute and then, remembering, slides it over his forehead. With gestures which beggar description he describes the unhappy lot of an old man who is a client of his and who owns a five-room house. Three of the rooms the old man has sold. He is dying. He wants permission to sell the other two rooms at once so that he will not die intestate still owning the rooms. Major grants permission.

An old fisherman comes in. His face is like the hills of Sicily and his hands are like good rope, though he is over sixty. He is very sad. The Major brought it about that Licata was the first Sicilian town to send out civilian fishing boats, for in the first days after the invasion people almost starved. Yesterday one of the seven boats hit a stray mine and all but one of the crew were killed. The old man tells what is known of the accident. The Major asks if the others are willing to go out today. The old man straightens himself up and says, "Yes, Mr. Major, we will go because our people are hungry."

A prosperously dressed man comes in complaining that he has perfectly good draft notes on the Bank of Sicily but that no one will advance cash against them. The Major explains that the Allies had to close the banks for a few days because it was feared that a panic might develop which would break all the banks. Allied funds, he says, will soon be forwarded to the banks, which will then be able to give out cash in controlled amounts. Meanwhile the man must get along as best he can.

An MP breaks into the room. He salutes snappily and says, "A problem for you, sir. We have here a diseased whore." The Major orders her brought in. A sorry procession comes in: a forty-five-year-old woman, in a pink blouse and black polka-dotted skirt, with the mouth of a mackerel, a scarecrow of a man in green slacks and white shirt, a soldier who caught the clap from this mockery of womankind and a witness. The evidence is clear and frank. The sick and frightened boy says, "I seen a GI who says he had a piece off this whore in a pink shirt and I says to him, 'She's the one who dosed me, Mac.' We had her took in by the MP's." The Major then asks the thin man if he is a pimp. He acts most offended and denies it. Major says, "I am a lover of truth. If you speak truly you will merely be a man in trouble, but if you speak lies you will go

to jail." The Major has somehow made the truth seem an admirable thing to this thin, contemptible man, and he tells it— he pimped for this girl and three others whose names were . . . "Never mind," says the Major, "this is a case for the Carabinieri," and he turns the pair over to the local police, all of whom the Major has continued in office.

A merchant comes in. His shirt is buttoned, but he has no tie. He is a man who was recommended to the Major as honest. He says (as does everyone, including the notorious Squadristi, or Fascist thugs, in Licata) that he has been against the Fascists for many years and if there is anything he can do to help he will be glad. The Major says that his men have found certain clothing and stuffs which have been impounded by the Fascists and which he wishes now to sell since the people have had no new clothes for a long time. Will the merchant please prepare him a list of really fair prices on the understanding that all the merchants in town will be allowed to sell the goods at a small commission, proceeds to go to the town government for home relief? The merchant waves his hand from habit and says he will gladly do so.

It is time for lunch. As the Major leaves his office and makes his way through the big crowd of waiting beseechers outside you can hear the whisper, "Kiss your hand . . . kiss your hand . . . kiss your hand . . ." This is a vestigial expression of respect left over from times when hands really were to be kissed. It embarrasses the Major, and he says he is going to pass the word that the expression ought not to be used any more.

You lunch in a little restaurant where for breakfast, lunch, and dinner the menu is *pasta* and eggplant, fried fish, red wine, and grapes. During lunch the Major tells you his own story, which is a thoroughly American history. His parents were peasants from Parma who went to the States when they were sixteen. His father has always worked in hotels and now is assistant steward in the Merchants Club in New York. Frank went to school through high school. When he was fourteen he began working nights. When he was sixteen he lied and said he was eighteen so that he could get a driver's license and a truck driver's job. For two years he drove trucks and lifted terrible weights—until they ruptured him. When he was well a friend suggested a job with the city. He was afraid he hadn't enough education, but on his exams he came out 177th out of 1100. They gave him a job as clerk in the Markets Department. When La Guardia was elected he was laid off. He married a daughter of one of the owners of a big trucking firm, borrowed money, bought a grocery store in the Bronx, and made out all right for two years. Then he sold out and went back to the city, where he worked up to be a second-class clerk in the Sanitation Department at forty-two dollars a week. Then he went into the Army.

He says, "I can't tell you how anxious I was to get on shore to see what this was all about. At first I looked around all the time at these people, their mannerisms, their expressions, their dress. I saw them barefooted and didn't believe white people could be in that state. I am the son of an immigrant. I have seen what I thought was poverty. But now I can just picture my father's family and how poor they were. I want to help these people out as much as possible, I don't want to see

them suffer that way." Then he adds, "But we've got to go now. I'm holding trials this afternoon."

Back at the office the Major finds a note from Arturo Verdirami, eighty-two-year-old eccentric who owns most of Licata's sulphur business and has for many years been agent there for Lloyd's of London. He writes the Major many notes in an English for which he apologizes "because it is Shakespearean, I am sorry." The letter says:

I beg to notify for the necessary steps: since four months the small people of Licata does not receive the Italian *razione tesspata* of olive oil or other fats, but the officials both of commune civil and military staff have been largely provided for the families and personal friends.

I am informed that the small population is therefore compelled to pay at the black market any price up to lire 80 per liter equal to 800 grammes. The price fixed by the Fascist government for the supply is lire 15 1/2 per kilo of 1000 grammes.

You cannot allow any longer this tyranny against the poors. You should therefore stop this tyrannical sufferance for the poor inhabitants by giving dispositions on the subject of the Commissario at the municipality *dokt sapio*, inviting him to notify his guards that any preference for anyone in the distribution of ailments [sic] will be punished inexorably and any official civil or communal is not allowed to take the quantity to which his family has a right before the poors have received their rations. Respectfully signed Arturo Verdirami.

The Major is acutely aware of the black market and he has already taken the steps which the ancient Verdirami suggests. He called all the municipal employees together one day. Most of them were in the same jobs they had held under the Fascists. The Major said to them, "Now that the Americans are here, Licata is a democracy. Democracy is this—it is that the people in its government are no longer the masters of the people. How are the government people paid? They are paid out of taxes which come from the people. And so the people are really masters of the government, not the government of the people. You are now servants of the people of Licata." And he warned them about standing in line for rations, among many other things.

Now the trials begin. The chief of the Carabinieri reads off the accusations and practically acts out the crime, so acute is his sense of drama. The culprits stand before the desk and all without exception give an absentminded Fascist salute, then the first is led in.

The first case is of a man who refused to take American dollars but, much worse, refused to sell bread on credit to the local people. His plea, supported by the unctuous lawyer in white suit and blue glasses, is ignorance. He says he never had time to read the proclamations. The Major is stern as he says that ignorance of the law is no defense, and he fines the man a stiff penalty.

The second case also concerns bread. A loaf is produced in evidence to show that it was badly baked of inferior flour. Major points at the baker's hands and tells him that filth is as great a crime as cheating, and he fines the man.

Next comes a pathetic old man who stole some clothing from an Italian military storehouse. He pleads guilty and says he can't read but hates Fascists. He is so patently poor that the Major sentences him to three months' suspended sentence and gives him a lecture on honesty.

Next, six peasants are brought forward. They are very slow of speech and mind and heartbreaking to look at. They are accused of having taken some hay from an abandoned warehouse. Again the Major gives only a warning.

The last case is both the funniest and saddest. The accused is an old cartman. He stands before the desk with his cloth cap clutched in his hand and as defiant as if his accusers are Fascists, whom he says he hates. The chief of the Carabinieri starts to read the accusation. It appears that the old cartman was driving through town when a train of American amphibious trucks approached. The old man was drowsing at his reins and blocked their way. Leaping about the room and roaring, the chief of Carabinieri describes how one of his men grasped at the reins of the horse and with towering strength got the cart aside and saved the honor of Licata. The old man stays silent.

The chief now describes how the old man jumped down from his cart and charged the Carabinieri and tried to fight with him. Finally the old man speaks.

He speaks slowly about the death of his wife and the number of his children and grandchildren with malaria. He describes in detail how the Fascists once took away a horse. Then he himself begins to act out the scene in question, and it really turns out after much swooping and shouting and another near fight that the reason he charged the Carabinieri was that he who loved his horse could not bear to see this rider of motorcycles attack his old animal. The Major dismissed the case.

After the trials an embarrassment walks up to the desk in the person of Signor Giuseppe Santi, owner of the house at Number 29 Piazzi San Sebasiano. Signor Santi's house had been requisitioned for billets. This, he says, pleased him because he hated the Fascists. But it did not please him, he says, to go into the house and find drawers broken open, glasses broken, and door panels split. The Major tells the man that the soldiers were not willfully destructive but that war had given them rough habits. The Major's explanation is a masterpiece of tact. He tells Signor Santi to file a claim for damages.

Now a girl comes in who is quite pretty but very frightened-looking. She says her sweetheart is in the Army and she has heard that he was captured by the Americans. The Major asks his name. He calls up the prison-of-war enclosure and asks if the man is there. He is able then to tell the girl that her man is indeed a prisoner. Tears come into her eyes. "Mr. Major, I thank you, I thank you and I kiss your hand," she says.

The Major says, "I think I'll go home. I like to end each day on a happy note if I can because there are so many unhappy ones." But before he leaves, if you ask him, he will tell you the ways in which the people of Licata are already, after only a handful of days, better off than they were under the Fascists, whom they say with varying degrees of honesty that they hated.

"Sure, they're better off," he says. "For one thing they can congregate in the streets any time they want and talk about whatever they want to. They can listen to the radios. They came to me and asked if they could keep their receiving sets. I said sure. They were surprised. They asked what stations they could listen to. I said any stations. They said, 'Can you mean it?' Now they prefer the English news to the Italian, and today a crowd of them laughed and whistled at an Italian propaganda broadcast saying Sicilians were being oppressed by Americans. They can come to the City Hall and talk to the Mayor at any time they want. The Fascist Mayor had office hours from twelve to one each day, and you had to apply for an interview weeks in advance. Their streets are clean for the first time in centuries. I have forty-five men with a water truck and eight wagons cleaning up the place. Oh, there are lots of ways and there will be lots more."

And then he adds, "We have a big job to do here. You see, I can't stop imagining what it must have been like for my father and his family."

ERNIE PYLE

"THE DEATH OF CAPTAIN WASKOW"

WASHINGTON *DAILY NEWS*, JANUARY 10, 1944

When Ernie Pyle finished his column on the death of Captain Waskow, he handed it over to a fellow reporter with the comment, "This stuff stinks. I just can't seem to get going again." In fact, his tribute to Waskow was among the most moving pieces of reportage to come out of the war, and the editors at the Washington Daily News *thought well enough to devote the entire front page to it.*

AT THE FRONT LINES IN ITALY,
Jan. 10 (By Wireless)

IN THIS WAR I HAVE KNOWN A LOT of officers who were loved and respected by the soldiers under them. But never have I crossed the trail of any man as beloved as Capt. Henry T. Waskow of Belton, Tex.

Capt. Waskow was a company commander in the 36th Division. He had been in this company since long before he left the States. He was very young, only in his middle twenties, but he carried in him a sincerity and gentleness that made people want to be guided by him.

"After my own father, he comes next," a sergeant told me.

"He always looked after us," a soldier said. "He'd go to bat for us every time."

"I've never known him to do anything unkind," another one said.

I WAS AT THE FRONT OF THE MULE trail the night they brought Capt. Waskow down. The moon was nearly full, and you could see far up the trail, and even part way across the valley. Soldiers made shadows as they walked.

Dead men had been coming down the mountain all evening, lashed onto the backs of mules. They came lying belly down across the wooden pack-saddle, their heads hanging down on the left side of the mule, their stiffened legs sticking awkwardly from the other side, bobbing up and down as the mule walked.

The Italian mule skinners were afraid to walk beside dead men, so Americans had to lead the mules down that night.

Even the Americans were reluctant to unlash and lift off the bodies, when they got to the bottom, so an officer had to do it himself and ask others to help.

The first one came early in the morning. They slid him down from the mule, and stood him on his feet for a moment. In the half light he might have been merely a sick man standing there leaning on the other. Then they laid him on the ground in the shadow of the stone wall alongside the road.

I don't know who the first one was. You fell small in the presence of dead men, and you don't ask silly questions. . . .

We left him there beside the road, that first one, and we all went back in to the cowshed and sat on the watercans or lay on the straw, waiting for the next batch of mules.

Somebody said the soldier had been dead for four days, and then nobody said anything more about him. We talked for an hour or more; the dead man lay all alone, outside in the shadow of the wall.

THEN A SOLDIER CAME INTO THE cowshed and said there were some more bodies outside. We went out into the road. Four mules stood there in the moonlight, in the road where the trail came off the mountains. The soldiers who led them stood there waiting.

"This one is Capt. Waskow," one of them said quickly.

Two men unlashed his body from the mule and lifted it off and laid it in the shadow beside the stone wall. Other men took the other bodies off. Finally, there were five lying end to end in a long row. You don't cover up dead men in the combat zones. They just lie there in the shadows until somebody else comes after them.

The uncertain mules moved off to their olive groves. The men in the road seemed reluctant to leave. They stood around, and gradually I could sense them moving, one by one, close to Capt. Waskow's body. Not so much to look, I think, as to say something in finality to him and to themselves. I stood close by and I could hear.

One soldier came and looked down, and he said out loud:

"God damn it!"

Another one came, and he said, "God damn it to hell anyway!" He looked down for a few last moments and then turned and left.

Another man came. I think he was an officer. It was hard to tell officers from men in the dim light, for everybody was grimy and dirty. The man looked down into the dead captain's face and he spoke directly to him, as tho he were alive.

"I'm sorry, old man."

Then a soldier came and stood beside the officer and bent over, and he too spoke to his dead captain, not in a whisper but awfully tender, and he said:

"I sure am sorry, sir."

Then the first man squatted down, and he reached down and took the Captain's hand, and he sat there a full five minutes holding the dead hand in his own and looking intently into the dead face. And he never uttered a sound all the time he sat there.

Finally, he put the hand down. He reached up and gently straightened the points of the Captain's shirt collar, and then he sort of rearranged the tattered edges of his uniform around the wound, and then he got up and walked away down the road in the moonlight, all alone.

The rest of us went back into the cowshed, leaving the five dead men lying in a line, end to end, in the shadow of the low stone wall. We lay down on the straw in the cowshed, and pretty soon we were all asleep.

ERNIE PYLE

"THIS IS THE WAY IT WAS . . ."

WASHINGTON *DAILY NEWS*, JUNE 16, 1944

While commentators interpreted the "Big Picture" of the Second World War and many war correspondents stayed close to the generals, Ernie Pyle chose the company of the ordinary soldier. Weighing not much more than one hundred pounds, he might have naturally favored the little guy in the ranks. He covered the war in North Africa and Italy, and for his reports on the Allied forces' invasion of France, Pyle received a Pulitzer Prize. The D-day landing in early June 1944 was one of the most startling sights the reporter had witnessed. Ernie Pyle did not witness the horror of the landing, but as he walked the beach the next day, his imagination could re-create the event.

From Coast Guard–manned "Sea-horse" landing craft, American troops leap forward to storm a North African beach during final amphibious maneuvers in 1944. *(National Archives)*

NORMANDY BEACHHEAD, June 16, 1944

I TOOK A WALK ALONG THE HIS-toric coast of Normandy in the country of France.

It was a lovely day for strolling along the seashore. Men were sleeping on the sand, some of them sleeping forever. Men were floating in the water, but they didn't know they were in the water, for they were dead.

The water was full of squishy little jelly fish about the size of your hand. Millions of them. In the center each of them had a green design exactly like a four-leaf clover. The good-luck emblem. Sure. Hell yes.

I walked for a mile and a half along the water's edge of our many-miled invasion beach. You wanted to walk slowly, for the detail on that beach was infinite.

The wreckage was vast and startling. The awful waste and destruction of war, even aside from the loss of human life, has always been one of its outstanding features to those who are in it. Anything and everything is expendable. And we did expend on our beachhead in Normandy during those first few hours.

For a mile out from the beach there were scores of tanks and trucks and boats that you could no longer see, for they were at the bottom of the water— swamped by overloading, or hit by shells, or sunk by mines. Most of their crews were lost.

You could see trucks tipped half over and swamped. You could see partly sunken barges, and the angled-up corners of jeeps, and small landing craft half submerged. And at low tide you could still see those vicious six-pronged iron stakes that helped snag and wreck them.

On the beach itself, high and dry, were all kinds of wrecked vehicles. There were tanks that had only just made the beach before being knocked out. There were jeeps that had burned to a dull gray. There were big derricks on caterpillar treads that didn't quite make it. There were half-tracks carrying office equipment that had been made into a shambles by a single shell hit, their interiors still holding their useless equipage of smashed typewriters, telephones, office files.

There were LCT's turned completely upside down, and lying on their backs,

and how they got that way I don't know. There were boats stacked on top of each other, their sides caved in, their suspension doors knocked off.

In this shoreline museum of carnage there were abandoned rolls of barbed wire and smashed bulldozers and big stacks of thrown-away lifebelts and piles of shells still waiting to be moved.

In the water floated empty life rafts and soldiers' packs and ration boxes, and mysterious oranges.

On the beach lay snarled rolls of telephone wire and big rolls of steel matting and stacks of broken, rusting rifles.

On the beach lay, expended, sufficient men and mechanism for a small war. They were gone forever now. And yet we could afford it.

We could afford it because we were one, we had our toehold, and behind us there were such enormous replacements for this wreckage on the beach that you could hardly conceive of their sum total. Men and equipment were flowing from England in such a gigantic stream that it made the waste on the beachhead seem like nothing at all, really nothing at all.

A few hundred yards back on the beach is a high bluff. Up there we had a tent hospital, and a barbed-wire enclosure for prisoners of war. From up there you could see far up and down the beach, in a spectacular crow's-nest view, and far out to sea.

And standing out there on the water beyond all this wreckage was the greatest armada man has ever seen. You simply could not believe the gigantic collection of ships that lay out there waiting to unload.

Looking from the bluff, it lay thick and

clear to the far horizon of the sea and on beyond, and it spread out to the sides and was miles wide. Its utter enormity would move the hardest man.

As I stood up there I noticed a group of freshly taken German prisoners standing nearby. They had not yet been put in the prison cage. They were just standing there, a couple of doughboys leisurely guarding them with tommy guns.

The prisoners too were looking out to sea—the same bit of sea that for months and years had been so safely empty before their gaze. Now they stood staring almost as if in a trance.

They didn't say a word to each other. They didn't need to. The expression on their faces was something forever unforgettable. In it was the final horrified acceptance of their doom.

If only all Germans could have had the rich experience of standing on the bluff and looking out across the water and seeing what their compatriots saw.

LARRY NEWMAN, INTERNATIONAL NEWS SERVICE

"WHAT THE HELL IS ALL THE MOURNING ABOUT?"

NEW YORK *JOURNAL-AMERICAN*, DECEMBER 24–29, 1944

Larry Newman knew General George S. Patton well by the time this piece appeared in U.S. newspapers. The International News Service correspondent had traveled a long road with the salty, contentious general. The account that follows is from Newman's chronicles of the general during the decisive moments of the Battle of the Bulge. The German offensive during Christmas 1944 threatened to force the Allies' eastward push into a retreat and prolong the war, if not stall it into a World War I–like stalemate. The story is part of a feature on the commander and includes one of Patton's memorable and controversial "prayers."

THE GERMANS' INITIAL GAINS were staggering. The snow-covered forests of the Ardennes were soaked with the blood of American boys who never had a chance to fight.

Our forces were scattered, confused. [Seven thousand men of the 106th Infantry Division became captives.]

Tiny groups of men stood out against the Germans. Held out miles behind the most advanced Nazi units. Refused to yield even though ammunition was scarce, food supplies impossible to obtain.

Meanwhile, General Eisenhower and all his commanding generals met at Verdun to decide what had to be done.

After hours of discussion a decision was reached. Bedell Smith, Eisenhower's chief of staff, said to the assembled generals:

"Montgomery will contain them to the north.

"General Hodges [commander of the U.S. First Army] will hold them at the Meuse River.

"Georgie [General Patton], can hold them on the south flank?"

A burning body bears ghastly witness to the horror of the V-2 rocket. The missile hit this portion of the Holland-Belgium supply line in Antwerp on November 27, 1944. *(National Archives)*

Patton stood up, looking about the room, then said:

"Hold them! Why, I'll take von Rundstedt and ram him right down Montgomery's———!"

Patton's Third Army was fighting the Germans in the Saar at the time and was taking a pasting from them. He wanted nothing more than to let go of the lion's tail and instead take a crack at von Rundstedt. When he got his orders to move north, he traveled personally to the command post of the Fifth (Red Diamond) Division and ordered its commander, General Irwin, to break contact with the enemy.

All day long on December 19 he drove his men. Then he shot the Fifth north. They traveled ninety miles and attacked the German flank. All within twenty-four hours.

Bastogne was surrounded by Germans who predicted over their radios that the arrogant 101st Airborne Tenth Division would be annihilated unless they gave up.

Everything favored the Germans for a while. But Patton never was disheartened. In the midst of the battle—perhaps the most desperate a U.S. Army ever had to fight—Patton called a conference of correspondents. As we filed into the war room, the tenseness was depressing. But

ROBERT CAPA, 1913–1954

In 1936 a young Hungarian émigré named Andre Friedman was working as a news photographer in Paris. In his early twenties, he was beginning to do pretty well as a freelancer. But he was anxious to do better, and after giving the problem some thought, he came up with a scheme that involved posing as the assistant of a famed but purely fictitious American photographer named Robert Capa. He would sell his own pictures to the press under the allegedly brilliant American's name. With his girlfriend serving as Capa's agent, the plot worked like a charm. Soon Friedman's work was selling at a substantially healthier clip and for higher fees as well. Friedman became thoroughly enamored with the glamorous and internationally acclaimed figment of his imagination. When an editor caught on to his deception, rather than letting Capa die, Friedman decided it was time to make Capa a reality. From that moment on, Andre Friedman was Robert Capa.

The new flesh-and-blood Capa quickly measured up to his fabricated billing. By the summer of 1936, he was in Spain photographing the civil war there. It was there that he discovered the subject matter that would make him even more celebrated than his fictional counterpart might ever have dreamed of becoming. For in turning his camera on that struggle, Capa found he had a special knack for capturing military action. He was soon turning out a series of pictures that, for the first time in the history of photography, seemed to depict war in all its momentary and tragic immediacy.

Several years later, writing about his work as a recorder of war, Capa noted: "Slowly I am feeling more and more like a hyena. Even if you know the value of your works, it gets on your nerves. Everybody suspects that you . . . want to make money at the expense of other people's skins." By late 1938 he was being hailed in both European and American press circles as the "Greatest War-Photographer in the World."

Given his credentials, it would seem natural that once World War II broke out, Capa should have been there in the thick of it. Instead circumstances kept him at the war's periphery in its initial stages, and his early war-related photo stories for various publications were focused on such things as the effects of German air bombing on Great Britain.

Not the least of Capa's problems in getting close to the war was his national origin. Although he moved to New York City in 1939, he nevertheless remained a citizen of Hungary, which by late 1940 had entered the Axis fold. When the United States finally declared war on the Axis powers, Capa was categorized as an enemy alien. It was not until March 1943 that the "Greatest War-Photographer in the World" was finally on his way to cover the final stages of the Allied drive to push the Germans from North Africa.

Late starter though he was, Capa ultimately produced some memorable pictures of the war. Transferring from *Collier's* to *LIFE* shortly before joining the Allied invasion of Sicily in mid-1943, he was on hand to record newsworthy military actions in the Italian campaign and the invasion of France.

Capa said of photographing combat: "if your pictures aren't good enough, you aren't close enough." Capa lived by those words; for example, joining the first invasion wave into Normandy as well as a paratroop drop behind enemy lines in Germany.

"Watching for Snipers," Robert Capa's famous photograph of a fallen American soldier in the house-to-house battle for Leipzig, Germany. *(Robert Capa/ Magnum Photos)*

Capa spent the last weeks of the war in Europe witnessing the final death throes of Nazi Germany. As German surrender became ever more certain, *LIFE* asked him and its other photographers in Europe to produce a picture that would be appropriate for the cover of its issue marking that event, whenever it came. It is not known whether Capa had this request in mind when he rode into Nuremburg in April 1945 and met up with Corporal Hubert Strickland, who had been his jeep driver at the liberation of Paris the previous summer. In any case, the fortuitous reunion of the photographer and his driver yielded precisely the pictorial epigraph on the war in Europe that *LIFE* was looking for. On the cover of its first issue following the German surrender on May 7, 1945, the magazine featured Capa's picture of Strickland, standing before the huge swastika at Nuremburg's sports stadium and jubilantly offering a mock Nazi salute. Another Capa picture in the same issue, however, sounded a decidedly more somber note. Taken shortly before the one at Nuremburg, it showed an American soldier lying dead in his own blood on an apartment balcony in Leipzig, the victim of a German sniper.

when Patton strode into the room, smiling, confident, the atmosphere changed within seconds. He asked:

"What the hell is all the mourning about? This is the end of the beginning. We've been batting our brains out trying to get the Hun out in the open. Now he is out. And with the help of God we'll finish him off this time—and for good."

He talked of his plans. Then he said:

"I have a little Christmas card and prayer for all of you."

On one side of a piece of paper was a simple Christmas greeting with his signature. On the other side this prayer was printed:

"Almighty and most merciful Father, we humbly beseech Thee, of Thy great goodness, to restrain these immoderate rains with which we have had to contend. Grant us fair weather for battle. Graciously hearken to us as soldiers who call upon Thee that, armed with Thy power, we may advance from victory to victory, and crush the oppression and wickedness of our enemies, and establish justice among men and nations. Amen."

He said he had called Major General Otto P. Weyland, commanding general of the Nineteenth Tactical Air Force, and told him to be ready to throw everything at the Germans when the weather broke.

The following day the sun broke through. And then came nine perfect flying days.

Our air forces shuttled over and smashed the German tanks, riddled their infantry columns, left the roads littered with dead and dying.

Patton told us the following Friday:

"The war is all but over. The God of battles always stands on the side of right when the judgment comes."

In the meantime, the paratroopers and tankers turned infantry had held Bastogne and received the plaudits of the Allied world. The 101st Airborne and Bastogne took place alongside Valley Forge, Anzio, Cassino.

But the Fourth Armored fighting up the road from Arlon to Bastogne had suffered more grievously than the paratroopers.

When Patton finally stood in the division Command Post of the 101st Airborne Division, he told correspondents to remember:

"It's a helluva lot easier to sit on your rear end and wait than it is to fight into a place like this.

"Try to remember that when you write your books about this campaign.

"Remember the men who drove up that bowling alley out there from Arlon."

ED KENNEDY

"NEW BEAT OR UNETHICAL DOUBLE CROSS?"

NEW YORK TIMES, MAY 8, 1945

Ed Kennedy was stationed in Paris as bureau chief for the New York Times *during the last days of the war in Europe. Rumors abounded that the German fighting machine was de-*

feated, but no one dared to make the announcement or to send the news until confirmation was at hand. Even though Berlin had been seized, there were still questions about where the United States and the Russians actually stood, and who in the Nazi hierarchy was still around to offer the white flag. Finally the AP London bureau received a call from Kennedy, who uttered the long-awaited words reprinted below.

Kennedy's transmission was passed through London and relayed to New York. Within hours after the news began spreading, wild celebrations erupted in American cities—none larger than in New York, where at least one sailor was caught embracing a nurse. The Allied High Command, however, was not in the mood for a party. The news leak that Kennedy picked up and sent off forced the military to make an announcement much earlier than had been anticipated. In retribution, they cancelled the transmitting capabilities of AP reporters at the scene (within hours the ban was lifted). But the subservience of the press was gone forever.

THE WAR IN EUROPE IS ENDED! SURRENDER IS UNCONDITIONAL V-E WILL BE PROCLAIMED TODAY

REIMS, FRANCE, May 7

GERMANY SURRENDERED UN-conditionally to the Western allies and the Soviet Union at 2:41 A.M. French time today. [This was at 8:41 P.M. Eastern war time, Sunday, May 6, 1945.]

The surrender took place at a little red schoolhouse that is the headquarters of General Dwight D. Eisenhower.

The surrender was signed for the Supreme Allied Command by Lieutenant General Walter Bedell Smith, chief of staff for General Eisenhower.

It was also signed by General Ivan Susloparov of the Soviet Union and by General Francois Sevez for France.

General Eisenhower was not present at the signing, but immediately afterward General Jodl and his fellow delegate, General Admiral Hans Georg Friedeburg, were received by the Supreme Commander.

They were asked sternly if they understood the surrender terms imposed upon Germany and if they would be carried out by Germany.

They answered yes.

Germany, which began the war with a ruthless attack upon Poland, followed by successive aggressions and brutality in concentration camps, surrendered with an appeal to the victors for mercy toward the German people and armed forces.

After having signed the full surrender, General Jodl said he wanted to speak and received leave to do so.

"With this signature," he said in soft-spoken German, "the German people and armed forces are for better or worse delivered into the victor's hands.

"In this war, which has lasted more than five years, both have achieved and suffered more than perhaps any other people in the world."

NORMAN CORWIN

"ON A NOTE OF TRIUMPH"

MAY 8, 1945

Even before the outbreak of the Second World War, Norman Corwin had made a name as a radio writer and director for CBS. When victory over Germany seemed to be imminent in late 1944, CBS requested that Corwin put together a program to celebrate the triumph when it eventually came. May 8, 1945, was V-E Day, and that day CBS broadcast Corwin's "On a Note of Triumph." With Martin Gabel as narrator and with original music composed by Bernard Herrmann, the live broadcast began at eight o'clock that Tuesday evening.

The already jubilant American public responded enthusiastically to "On a Note of Triumph." Variety praised the broadcast, asserting that "it should take its place in the halls of fame accorded literary, dramatic and canvas creations." So favorable was the response that the participants reassembled for a second broadcast the following Sunday evening. An excerpt follows.

Music: Broad introduction. It comes down behind:

NARRATOR. So they've given up.

They're finally done in, and the rat is dead in an alley back of the Wilhelmstrasse.

Take a bow, G.I.,

Take a bow, little guy.

The superman of tomorrow lies at the feet of you common men of this afternoon.

This is it, kid, this is The Day, all the way from Newburyport to Vladivostok.

You had what it took and you gave it, and each of you has a hunk of rainbow round your helmet.

Seems like free men have done it again!

Music: Bells ring, horns blow, and we rejoice. After a good strong tutti, the strings go down like a crowd quieting, and they stay behind:

NARRATOR. Is Victory a sweet dish or isn't it?

And how do you think those lights look in Europe after five years of blackout, going on to six?

Brother, pretty good. Pretty good, sister.

The kids of Poland soon will know what an orange tastes like.

And the smell of honest-to-God bread, freshly made and sawdust-free, will create a stir in the streets of Athens.

There's a hot time in the old town of Dnepropetrovsk tonight,

And it is reasonable to assume the same goes for a thousand other cities, including some Scandinavian.

It can at last be said without jinxing the campaign:

Somehow the decadent democracies, the bungling Bolsheviks, the saps and softies,

Were tougher in the end than the brown-shirt bullyboys, and smarter, too;

For without whipping a priest, burning

a book or slugging a Jew, without corraling a girl in a brothel or bleeding a child for plasma,
Far-flung ordinary men, unspectacular but free, rousing out of their habits and their homes, got up early one morning, flexed their muscles, learned (as amateurs) the manual of arms, and set out across perilous plains and oceans to whop the bejesus out of the professionals.
This they did. . . .

WILLIAM L. LAURENCE

"A REPORTER DESCRIBES A MUSHROOM CLOUD"

NEW YORK TIMES, SEPTEMBER 3, 1945

William L. Laurence well deserved the nickname "Atomic Bill," for no reporter was more closely associated with the discovery of nuclear fission and the work culminating in the successful use of the atomic bomb to induce Japan to surrender.

Born in Lithuania of Jewish parents, Laurence came to America with his family as a teenager. After obtaining a law degree from Boston University, he headed to New York to find a job. There he met Herbert Bayard Swope, who hired him to work for the New York World. *A few years later he moved to the* New York Times, *where he was assigned to report on scientific matters. From 1939, when he wrote an article on splitting the atom, Laurence followed the scientific explorations into nuclear energy. No other reporter was so successful in clearly explaining the complicated physics of fission.*

In 1944 Major General Leslie R. Groves, head of the Manhattan Project, asked Laurence to become the project's historian. Though sworn to secrecy at the time, Laurence was offered the inside view as the nation's most brilliant physicists worked to create an atomic bomb. He was present at Alamogordo, New Mexico, when the first atomic bomb was tested. Though not at Hiroshima to see the first use of the bomb in war, he was aboard a B-29 to see the destruction of Nagasaki three days later.

Laurence won his second Pulitzer Prize for the following account of the bombing of Nagasaki.

WE FLEW SOUTHWARD DOWN the channel and at 11:33 crossed the coastline and headed straight for Nagasaki, about one hundred miles to the west. Here we again circled until we found an opening in the clouds. It was 12:01 and the goal of our mission had arrived.

We heard the prearranged signal on our radio, put on our arc welder's glasses, and watched tensely the maneuverings of the strike ship about half a mile in front of us.

"There she goes!" someone said.

Out of the belly of *The Great Artiste* what looked like a black object went downward.

Captain Bock swung around to get out of range; but even though we were turning away in the opposite direction, and despite the fact that it was broad daylight in our cabin, all of us became aware of a giant flash that broke through the dark barrier of our arc welder's lenses and flooded our cabin with intense light.

We removed our glasses after the first flash, but the light still lingered on, a bluish-green light that illuminated the entire sky all around. A tremendous blast wave struck our ship and made it tremble from nose to tail. This was followed by four more blasts in rapid succession, each resounding like the boom of cannon fire hitting our plane from all directions.

Observers in the tail of our ship saw a giant ball of fire rise as though from the bowels of the earth, belching forth enormous white smoke rings. Next, they saw a giant pillar of purple fire, ten thousand feet high, shooting skyward with enormous speed.

By the time our ship had made another turn in the direction of the atomic explosion the pillar of purple fire had reached the level of our altitude. Only about forty-five seconds had passed. Awe-struck, we watched it shoot upward like a meteor coming from the earth instead of from outer space, becoming ever more alive as it climbed skyward through the white clouds. It was no longer smoke, or dust, or even a cloud of fire. It was a living thing, a new species of being, born right before our incredulous eyes.

At one stage of its evolution, covering millions of years in terms of seconds, the entity assumed the form of a giant square totem pole, with its base about three miles long, tapering off to about a mile at the top. Its bottom was brown, its center was amber, its top white. But it was a living totem pole, carved with many grotesque masks grimacing at the earth.

Then, just when it appeared as though the thing had settled down into a state of permanence, there came shooting out of the top a giant mushroom that increased the height of the pillar to a total of forty-five thousand feet. The mushroom top was even more alive than the pillar, seething and boiling in a white fury of creamy foam, sizzling upward and then descending earthward, a thousand Old Faithful geysers rolled into one.

It kept struggling in an elemental fury, like a creature in the act of breaking the bonds that held it down. In a few seconds it had freed itself from its gigantic stem and floated upward with tremendous speed, its momentum carrying it into the stratosphere to a height of about sixty thousand feet.

But no sooner did this happen when another mushroom, smaller in size than the first one, began emerging out of the pillar. It was as though the decapitated monster was growing a new head.

As the first mushroom floated off into the blue it changed its shape into a flowerlike form, its giant petals curving downward, creamy white outside, rose-colored inside. It still retained that shape when we last gazed at it from a distance of about two hundred miles. The boiling pillar of many colors could also be seen at that distance, a giant mountain of jumbled rainbows, in travail. Much living substance had gone into those rainbows. The quivering top of the pillar was protruding to a great height through the white clouds, giving the appearance of a monstrous prehistoric creature with a ruff around its neck, a fleecy ruff extending in all directions, as far as the eye could see.

A mushroom cloud from the atomic bomb. *(National Archives)*

HOMER BIGART

"HOPE THIS IS THE LAST ONE, BABY"

NEW YORK *HERALD TRIBUNE*, AUGUST 16, 1945

The conventional bombing of Japan continued even as a first atomic bomb was dropped on Hiroshima on August 6 and a second on Nagasaki on August 9, 1945. When the Japanese agreed to surrender unconditionally on August 14, B-29 Super Fortresses out of Guam were already on their way to bomb Kumagaya and Isesaki. This was the final bombing raid of the war.

Flying aboard one of the B-29s was Homer Bigart of the New York Herald Tribune, *one of the most noted correspondents of the war and one often compared to Ernie Pyle. Bigart was a World War II version of Floyd Gibbons. A fellow war correspondent warned another to steer clear of Bigart: "He's always trying to build his reputation at the cannon's mouth." He had covered campaigns in Sicily, Italy, and France before he moved to the Pacific theater. His experience in Europe included flying on bombing raids over Germany. He was no novice to dangerous missions when he went on the last strategic bombing raid of the war.*

IN A B-29 OVER JAPAN, Aug. 15

THE RADIO TELLS US THAT THE war is over but from where I sit it looks suspiciously like a rumor. A few minutes ago—at 1:32 A.M.—we fire-bombed Kumagaya, a small industrial city behind Tokyo near the northern edge of Kanto Plain. Peace was not official for the Japanese either, for they shot right back at us.

Other fires are raging at Isesaki, another city on the plain, and as we skirt the eastern base of Fujiyama Lieutenant General James Doolittle's B-29s, flying their first mission from the 8th Air Force base on Okinawa, arrive to put the finishing touches on Kumagaya.

I rode in the *City of Saco* (Maine), piloted by First Lieutenant Theodore J. Lamb, twenty-eight, of 103-21 Lefferts Blvd., Richmond Hill, Queens, N.Y. Like all the rest, Lamb's crew showed the strain of the last five days of the uneasy "truce" that kept Superforts grounded.

They had thought the war was over. They had passed most of the time around radios, hoping the President would make it official. They did not see that it made much difference whether Emperor Hirohito stayed in power. Had our propaganda not portrayed him as a puppet? Well, then, we could use him just as the war lords had done.

The 314th Bombardment Wing was alerted yesterday morning. At 2:20 P.M., pilots, bombardiers, navigators, radio men, and gunners trooped into the briefing shack to learn that the war was still on. Their target was to be a pathetically small city of little obvious importance, and their commanding officer, Colonel Carl R. Storrie, of Denton, Texas, was at pains to convince them why Kumagaya, with a population of 49,000, had to be burned to the ground.

There were component parts factories of the Nakajima aircraft industry in the town, he said. Moreover, it was an important railway center.

No one wants to die in the closing moments of a war. The wing chaplain, Captain Benjamin Schmidke, of Springfield, Mo., asked the men to pray, and then the group commander jumped on the platform and cried: "This is the last mission. Make it the best we ever ran."

Colonel Storrie was to ride in one of the lead planes, dropping four 1,000-pound high explosives in the hope that the defenders of the town would take cover in buildings or underground and then be trapped by a box pattern of fire bombs to be dumped by eighty planes directly behind.

"We've got 'em on the one yard line. Let's push the ball over," the colonel exhorted his men. "This should be the final knockout blow of the war. Put your bombs on the target so that tomorrow the world will have peace."

Even after they were briefed, most of the crewmen hoped and expected that an official armistice would come before the scheduled 5:30 take-off. They looked at their watches. Two and a half hours to go.

You might expect that the men would be in a sullen, almost mutinous, frame of mind. But morale was surprisingly high.

"Look at the sweat pour off me," cried Major William Marchesi, of 458 Baltic Street, Brooklyn. "I've never sweated out a mission like this one."

A few minutes earlier the Guam radio had interrupted its program with a flash and quoted the Japanese Domei Agency announcement that Emperor Hirohito had accepted the peace terms.

Instantly the whole camp was in an uproar. But then a voice snapped angrily over the squawk box: "What are you trying to do? Smash morale? It's only a rumor."

So the crews drew their equipment—parachutes, Mae Wests, and flak suits—and got on trucks to go out to the line. We reached the City of Saco at about 4:30 P.M., and there was still nearly an hour to go before our plane, which was to serve as a pathfinder for the raiders, would depart.

We were all very jittery. Radios were blaring in the camp area but they were half a mile from us and all we could catch were the words "Hirohito" and "Truman." For all we knew, the war was over.

Then a headquarters officer came by and told Lieutenant Lamb that the take-off had been postponed thirty minutes in expectation of some announcement from Washington.

By that time none of us expected to reach Japan, but we knew that unless confirmation came soon the mission would have to take off, and then very likely salvo its bombs and come home when the signal "Utah, Utah, Utah," came through. That was the code agreed upon for calling off operations in the event of an announcement of peace by President Truman.

Lamb's crew began turning the plane's props at 5:45, and we got aboard. "Boy, we're going to kill a lot of fish today," said Sergeant Karl L. Braley, of Saco, Maine.

To salvo the bombs at sea is an expensive method of killing fish.

We got San Francisco on the radio. "I hope all you boys out there are as happy as we are at this moment," an announcer was saying. "People are yelling and screaming and whistles are blowing."

"Yeah," said one of the crewmen disgustedly, "they're screaming and we're flying."

We took off at 6:07.

We saw no white flags when we reached Japanese territory. Back of the cockpit Radioman Staff Sergeant Rosendo D. del Valle Jr., of El Paso, Texas, strained his ears for the message, "Utah, Utah, Utah." If it came on time, it might save a crew or two, and perhaps thousands of civilians at Kumagaya.

The message never came. Each hour brought us nearer the enemy coast. We caught every news broadcast, listening to hours of intolerable rot in the hope that the announcer would break in with the news that would send us home.

The empire coast was as dark and repellent as ever. Japan was still at war, and not one light showed in the thickly populated Tokyo plain.

Lamb's course was due north to the Kasumiga Lake, then a right angle, turning west for little Kumagaya. It was too late now. There would be bombs on Kumagaya in a few minutes.

Kumagaya is on featureless flats five miles south of the Tone River. It is terribly hard to pick up by radar. There were only two cues to Kumagaya. Directly north of the town was a wide span across the Tone, and a quarter of a mile south of it was a long bridge across the Ara River.

The radar observer, Lieutenant Harold W. Zeisler, of Kankakee, Ill., picked up both bridges in good time and we started the bomb run.

An undercast hid the city almost completely but through occasional rifts I could see a few small fires catching on from the bombs dropped by the two preceding pathfinders.

The Japanese were alert. Searchlights lit the clouds beneath us and two ack-ack guns sent up weak sporadic fire. Thirty miles to the north we saw Japanese searchlights and ack-ack groping for the bombers of another wing attacking Isesaki.

Leaving our target at the mercy of the eighty Superforts following us, we swerved sharply southward along the eastern base of Fujiyama and reached the sea. At one point we were within ten miles of Tokyo. The capital was dark.

Every one relaxed. We tried to pick up San Francisco on the radio but couldn't. The gunners took out photos of their wives and girl friends and said: "Hope this is the last, baby."

This postscript is written at Guam. It was the last raid of the war. We did not know it until we landed at North Field.

The results of the raid we learned from the pilots who followed us over the target. General conflagrations were devouring both Kumagaya and Isesaki. Japan's tardiness in replying to the peace terms cost her two cities.

SERGEANT DALE KRAMER

"THE JAPANESE DRINK BITTER TEA ABOARD THE USS *MISSOURI*"

YANK, OCTOBER 5, 1945

"The war situation had developed not necessarily to Japan's advantage." In this masterpiece of understatement, Emperor Hirohito informed his people on August 14, 1945, that they would have to endure what was unavoidable and to suffer what was "unsufferable" in order "to pave the way for a grand peace for all the generations to come." Atom bomb three had helped Hirohito make up his mind.

On September 2, 1945, representatives of the Japanese Imperial General Headquarters signed the instrument of surrender aboard the USS Missouri in Tokyo Bay. Sergeant Dale Kramer, staff correspondent for Yank, witnessed the ceremonies and enlivened his account with a grand GI punch line.

ABOARD THE USS MISSOURI, TOKYO BAY

FOR A WHILE IT LOOKED AS though the proceedings would go off with almost unreasonable smoothness. Cameramen assigned to the formal surrender ceremonies aboard the battleship Missouri arrived on time and although every inch of the turrets and housings and life rafts above the veranda deck where the signing was to take place was crowded, no one fell off and broke a collarbone.

The ceremonies themselves even started and were carried on according to schedule. It took a Canadian colonel to bring things back to normal by signing the surrender document on the wrong line.

No one had the heart to blame the colonel, though. A mere colonel was bound to get nervous around so much higher brass.

The other minor flaw in the ceremonial circus was that it was something of an an-ticlimax. Great historic events probably are always somewhat that way, and this one, to those of us who had taken off three weeks before with the Eleventh Airborne Division from the Philippines, was even more so. We had started out thinking in terms of a sensational dash to the Emperor's palace in Tokyo, only to sweat it out on Okinawa and later off Yokohama.

When it did come, the signing aboard the Missouri was a show which lacked nothing in its staging. A cluster of microphones and a long table covered with a green cloth had been placed in the center of the deck. On the table lay the big ledger-size white documents of surrender, bound in brown folders.

The assembly of brass and braid was a thing to see—a lake of gold and silver sparkling with rainbows of decorations and ribbons. British and Australian Army officers had scarlet stripes on their garrison caps and on their collars. The French were more conservative, except for the acres of vivid decorations on their breasts. The stocky leader of the Russian delegation wore gold shoulder boards and red-striped trousers. The Dutch had gold-looped shoulder emblems. The British admirals wore snow-white summer uniforms with shorts and knee-length white stockings. The olive-drab of the Chinese was plain except for ribbons. The least decked-out of all were the Americans. Their hats, except for Admiral Halsey's go-to-hell cap, were gold-braided, but their uniforms were plain suntan. Navy regulations do not permit wearing ribbons or decorations on a shirt.

Lack of time prevented piping anyone over the side, and when General MacArthur, Supreme Commander for the Allied powers, came aboard he strode quickly across the veranda deck and disappeared inside the ship. Like the other American officers, he wore plain suntans. A few minutes later, a gig flying the American flag and operated by white-clad American sailors putted around the bow of the ship. In the gig, wearing formal diplomatic morning attire, consisting of black cutaway coat, and striped pants and stovepipe hat, sat Foreign Minister Mamoru Shigemitsu, leader of the Japanese delegation.

Coming up the gangway, Shigemitsu climbed very slowly because of a stiff left leg, and he limped onto the veranda deck with the aid of a heavy, light-colored cane. Behind him came ten other Japs. One wore a white suit, two more wore formal morning attire, the rest were dressed in pieced-out uniforms of the Jap Army and Navy. They gathered into three rows on the forward side of the green-covered table. The representatives of the Allied powers formed on the other side. When they were arranged, General MacArthur entered and stepped to the microphone.

His words rolled sonorously: "We are gathered here, representatives of the major warring powers, to conclude a solemn agreement whereby peace may be restored." He emphasized the necessity that both victors and vanquished rise to a greater dignity in order that the world may emerge forever from blood and carnage. He declared his firm intention as Supreme Commander to "discharge my responsibility with justice and tolerance while taking all necessary dispositions to insure that the terms of surrender are fully, promptly, and faithfully complied with."

The Japanese stood at attention during the short address, their faces grave, but otherwise showing little emotion. When the representatives of the Emperor were invited to sign, Foreign Minister Shigemitsu hobbled forward, laid aside his silk hat and cane, and lowered himself slowly into a chair. The wind whipped his thin, dark hair as he reached into his pocket for a pen, tested it, then affixed three large Japanese characters to the first of the documents. He had to rise and bend over the table for the others.

The audience was conscious of the historic importance of the pen strokes, but it watched for something else, too. General MacArthur had promised to present General Wainwright, who had surrendered the American forces at Corregidor and until only a few days before had been a prisoner of war, with the first pen to sign the surrender. Shigemitsu finished and

Margaret Bourke-White's acclaimed *LIFE* photograph of Buchenwald prisoners, taken in April 1945. *(Margaret Bourke-White)*

MARGARET BOURKE-WHITE, 1904–1971

Among the best poised for World War II was *LIFE* photographer Margaret Bourke-White. In her youth Bourke-White had harbored ambitions for a career in biology. But in college she took up photography more or less as a sideline, and during her final undergraduate years at Cornell University, armed with a secondhand camera, she helped to defray tuition expenses by taking and selling pictures of Cornell's campus.

In 1935 Bourke-White joined the staff of *LIFE* while it was still in its formative stages. When the magazine finally made its appearance late the following year, her picture essay on the construction of a New Deal dam in Montana was the main story.

At the end of the war in Europe, Bourke-White photographed many scenes in German concentration camps that revealed the horrors of those places far more explicitly than her pictures of newly liberated inmates at Buchenwald. Nevertheless, she managed to capture in this picture a haunting joylessness that makes it one of her most compelling and often-reproduced wartime images.

closed his pen and replaced it in his pocket. There could be no objection. He had needed a brush-pen for the Japanese letters.

When the big surrender folders were turned around on the table, General Mac-Arthur came forward to affix his signature as Supreme Commander. He asked General Wainwright and General Perci-val, who had surrendered the British forces at Singapore, to accompany him. General MacArthur signed the first document and handed the pen to General Wainwright. He used five pens in all, ending up with one from his own pocket.

Sailors have been as avid souvenir collectors in this war as anyone else, but when Admiral Nimitz sat down to sign for the U.S. he used only two pens. After that the representatives of China, the United Kingdom, Russia, Australia, Canada, France, the Netherlands, and New Zealand put down their signatures.

As the big leather document folders were gathered, a GI member of a sound unit recorded a few historic remarks of his own. "Brother," he said, "I hope those are my discharge papers."

IN RETROSPECT

A. M. ROSENTHAL

"THERE IS NO NEWS FROM AUSCHWITZ"

NEW YORK TIMES MAGAZINE, AUGUST 31, 1958

World War II ended in Europe in May 1945, but reminders of the conflict linger even to the present. The war helped to create the continent divided by an "iron curtain" from Stettin to Trieste. East of that curtain were the nations dominated by the Soviet Union. To the west were the democratic nations that became closely allied with the United States. On the far side of the line was censorship and thought control, while on the near side was freedom of speech and of the press. On the far side the state dictated what the media could report. On the near side the press was so powerful in its own right that it was often referred to as the Fifth Estate.

In 1958 the New York Times *posted A. M. Rosenthal to Poland on the far side of the iron curtain. Canadian-born and of Russian-Jewish origins, Rosenthal soon noted another lingering reminder of World War II. Poles had been known for their anti-Semitism long before the war, but the Nazis had carried out a systematic program against the Jews that dwarfed all earlier programs. Rosenthal had not been in Poland many weeks when he made a pilgrimage to the site of the Nazi concentration camp at Auschwitz.*

Political authorities may have applauded Rosenthal's report on Auschwitz, but they constantly complained of his reporting on national affairs. They did not contest the accuracy of his dispatches but rather that they reflected ill on Poland. The police bugged his phone and watched his house. In November 1959 Rosenthal wrote a series of articles for the New York Times *that included candid remarks on Polish leader Władysław Gomułka and the part of the Soviet Union in suppressing dissent in the country. Rosenthal could not have been surprised when he was ordered to leave Poland. Nevertheless, his stories from behind the iron curtain won him the Pulitzer Prize for international reporting in 1960.*

BRZEZINKA, POLAND

THE MOST TERRIBLE THING OF all, somehow, was that at Brzezinka the sun was bright and warm, the rows of graceful poplars were lovely to look upon and on the grass near the gates children played.

It all seemed frighteningly wrong, as in a nightmare, that at Brzezinka the sun should ever shine or that there should be light and greenness and the sound of young laughter. It would be fitting if at Brzezinka the sun never shone and the grass withered, because this is a place of unutterable terror.

And yet, every day, from all over the world, people come to Brzezinka, quite possibly the most grisly tourist center on earth. They come for a variety of reasons—to see if it could really have been true, to remind themselves not to forget, to pay homage to the dead by the simple act of looking upon their place of suffering.

Brzezinka is a couple of miles from the better-known southern Polish town of Oswiecim. Oswiecim has about 12,000 inhabitants, is situated about 171 miles from Warsaw and lies in a damp, marshy area at the eastern end of the pass called the Moravian Gate. Brzezinka and Oswiecim together formed part of that minutely organized factor of torture and death that the Nazis called Konzentrationslager Auschwitz.

By now, fourteen years after the last batch of prisoners was herded naked into the gas chambers by dogs and guards, the story of Auschwitz has been told a great many times. Some of the inmates have written of those memories of which sane men cannot conceive. Rudolf Franz Ferdinand Hoess, the superintendent of the camp, before he was executed wrote his detailed memoirs of mass exterminations and the experiments on living bodies. Four million people died here, the Poles say.

And so there is no news to report about Auschwitz. There is merely the compulsion to write something about it, a compulsion that grows out of a restless feeling that to have visited Auschwitz and then turned away without having said or written anything would somehow be a most grievous act of discourtesy to those who died here.

Brzezinka and Oswiecim are very quiet places now; the screams can no longer be heard. The tourist walks silently, quick at first to get it over with and then, as his mind peoples the barracks and the chambers and the dungeons and flogging posts, he walks dragging by. The guide does not say much either, because there is nothing much for him to say after he has pointed.

For every visitor, there is one particular bit of horror that he knows he will never forget. For some it is seeing the rebuilt gas chamber at Oswiecim and being told that this is the "small one." For others it is the fact that at Brzezinka, in the ruins of the gas chambers and the crematoria the Germans blew up when they retreated, there are daisies growing.

There are visitors who gaze blankly at the gas chambers and the furnaces because their minds simply cannot encompass them, but stand shivering before the great mounds of human hair behind the plate-glass window or the piles of babies' shoes or the brick cells where men sentenced to death by suffocation were walled up.

One visitor opened his mouth in a silent scream simply at the sight of boxes—great stretches of three-tiered wooden boxes in the women's barracks. They were about six feet wide, about three feet high, and into them from five to ten prisoners were shoved for the night. The guide walks quickly through the barracks. Nothing more to see here.

A brick building where sterilization experiments were carried out on women prisoners. The guide tries the door—it's locked. The visitor is grateful that he does not have to go in, and then flushes with shame.

A long corridor where rows of faces stare from the walls. Thousands of pictures, the photographs of prisoners. They are all dead now, the men and women who stood before the cameras, and they all knew they were to die.

They all stare blank-faced, but one picture, in the middle of a row, seizes the eye and wrenches the mind. A girl, 22 years old, plumply pretty, blond. She is smiling gently, as at a sweet, treasured thought. What was the thought that passed through her young mind and is now her memorial on the wall of the dead at Auschwitz?

Into the suffocation dungeons the visitor is taken for a moment and feels himself strangling. Another visitor goes in, stumbles out and crosses herself. There is no place to pray at Auschwitz.

The visitors look pleadingly at each other and say to the guide, "Enough."

There is nothing new to report about Auschwitz. It was a sunny day and the trees were green and at the gates the children played.

THE COLD WAR AND
THE KOREAN WAR

A FRAGILE PEACE

1945–1990

EVERYBODY GET DOWN. HERE WE GO."** Those words launched the Fifth Marine Division's charge onto the shores of Inchon's Red Beach and the escalation of the Korean War. No sooner had World War II ended on the deck of the USS *Missouri*—and a return to civilian calm begun—when yet another confrontation emerged between the United States, its allies, and an enemy nation.

However, the cold war was unlike the other wars that America had fought. For the most part it was a war of stand-offs and eyeball-to-eyeball staredowns. The threat of "massive retaliation" meant that men in olive green and armaments of war often stood on the sidelines while policy makers in suits played a chess game with stakes higher than ever before: the threat of nuclear holocaust. The cold war battlefields thus would be a mixed bag of nerve-racking confrontations and "hot" engagements in places such as Inchon, Pork Chop Hill, the skies over Cuba, and even space, with manned and unmanned rockets.

The enemy during the cold war often changed, and it often became unidentifiable. At first the antagonist was an obvious and clear one: the International Communist movement headquartered in Moscow. Like Hitler's Nazis, the Communist menace was seen as an especially wicked foe. Almost overnight, Uncle Joe Stalin became public enemy number one. He died in 1953, but the ruthlessness and aggressiveness of the Kremlin was not buried with him, as exemplified in Harrison Salisbury's reporting on the power struggle sparked by Lavrenti Beria's attempted coup. In a Pulitzer Prize–winning story, Salisbury succinctly summed up Beria's objectives—and the empire he wished to lead—and demonstrated the dangers found wherever Marxist-Leninists took power. "It was an individual. A powerful, ruthless man of extraordinary ability named Lavrenti Beria," he wrote. "And it was Beria's troops and Beria's tanks and Beria's trucks that had accomplished this small miracle and taken over the city of Moscow while the radios were still blaring out the news of Stalin's death to the startled citizenry."

Even though Beria's effort failed, there were others to worry about and fight against. In 1956 Nikita Khrushchev reaffirmed the Red Army's grip on Eastern Europe with the crushing of the Hungarian Revolution. The UPI's Russell Jones was there and he experienced the invasion almost as if he were a Hungarian. He reported walking the streets searching for food and "crying for the first time since I was a boy." "Believe none of the stories that this was a misguided uprising fomented to restore the great estate owners of the Horthy regency or the industrial magnates," he wrote in indignation. "I saw with my own eyes who was fighting and heard with my own ears why they fought."

The cold war was fought at home, too. Americans were riveted by the allegations and charges revolving around Communist infiltration. The Alger Hiss trial found a wide audience and Wisconsin's Joseph McCarthy began his inquisitions. What would happen if America relaxed its defenses? One needed only to read Relman Morin's account of what happened in a Korean village after a Communist takeover for a frightening reminder. To be prudent, President Truman ordered the Atomic Energy Commission to develop the hydrogen bomb and America seemingly felt a measure of reassurance—maybe that would sober the Communists into reconsidering their plans. But as long as the cold war remained one of threat and mercenaries, Americans could afford a measure of detachment—and wealth. Corporate giants such as General Motors announced massive profits in 1949—and the affluent 1950s began.

The fragile peace was shattered when the cold war turned hot in Korea. Frustration over the inability to roll back communism in Europe fueled the desire to end it in the Asian peninsula. When Red North Korea invaded the free South, the United States, under aegis of the United Nations, faced its first military encounter since World War II. Eager to flex their muscle, the GIs hit the beach at Inchon—and Marguerite Higgins went along. Despite surging enthusiasm and confidence among the marine divisions, Higgins's reporting foreshadowed the difficulties that the Korean War would present. Against the impressive firepower the U.S.-led assault rifled at the North Koreans, the enemy put up a fight that amazed the U.S. fighting force. Higgins quoted a surprised marine lieutenant who exclaimed, "My God, there are still some left!" Indeed, there would be more of a resistance than the marines, or their compatriots back home, cared to believe.

But the cause seemed just. Morin told the story of a Korean village that refused to submit to Communist control. "Only weeks ago in the region around Seoul and Inchon," Morin told readers, "people were being killed, dispossessed of land and homes, left to starve, or driven away from all they held dear—because they were not Communists and refused to act like Communists."

By 1951 the scene and attitude in Korea had changed abruptly. The Chinese entry into the war in December 1950 ruined the Christmas that lay just ahead. Gene Symonds of the UP reported that there were no "tousled-haired kids" looking for Santa's presents. "Christmas Eve here is a machine gun sitting on the edge of your foxhole with the bolt back ready to go," Symonds wrote. The Chinese troop avalanche overwhelmed both the fighting men and their leaders. Keyes Beech quoted marine hero Chesty Puller's insistence that "whatever you write, this was no retreat." By the time Jim Lucas's account was written in early 1953, the war had become a stalemate. "Our Town's business is war," he wrote. "It produces nothing but death." The message was clear. The Korean War was no longer about victory or liberation as had taken place in Paris and Berlin. Neither was it about making the enemy drink a bitter tea on the USS *Missouri*. It was an open-ended commitment where the goal was not to win but simply to avoid losing.

But the struggle against communism continued even after the truce at the thirty-eighth parallel. Walter Lippman's interview with Nikita Khrushchev in 1961 made clear that both sides remained distanced and irreconcilable. "If it comes to war," the Soviet leader told the American newsman, "we shall use only the biggest weapons." At Guantánamo, Cuba, the cooks and laundry workers, like the troops in the foxholes, were "learning to hold a gun." And when war became too dangerous on Earth, it was taken into space in the race for the moon and the stars.

MARGUERITE HIGGINS

"MY GOD! THERE ARE STILL SOME LEFT"

NEW YORK *HERALD TRIBUNE*, SEPTEMBER 18, 1950

Marguerite Higgins, one of the few female war correspondents, had plenty of experience covering the male-dominated art of battle when she waded onto Red Beach with the marines in the fall of 1950. Riding with U.S. forces as they crisscrossed Germany, she was with the GIs as they occupied Berlin and was among the first to see the death camp at Dachau. She not only dodged enemy bullets but had to overcome male biases. The report that follows is her account of the invasion of Inchon in September 1950. Higgins washed ashore with the marines on a landing craft and then ducked gunfire along the beach to get her story.

Higgins's reports from the front helped her win the Pulitzer Prize for International Reporting in 1951. Like the men in fatigues whom she wrote about, Higgins was used to recording American military triumphs—and Inchon was not much different. The spectacular victory overwhelmed the North Korean army, relieved the pressure on allied forces at Seoul, and led to a furious charge toward the Manchurian border as the enemy forces collapsed in retreat. Yet Higgins's writings also contained an undercurrent of concern. Like the marines, she seemed surprised by the resiliency of the enemy and the fact that the landing was far from a "pushover." The exact magnitude of the challenge in Korea would not be known, however, until after the entry of Chinese forces into the campaign.

WITH THE U.S. MARINES AT INCHON, KOREA, September 15 (Delayed)

HEAVILY LADEN U.S. MARINES, in one of the most technically difficult amphibious landings in history, stormed at sunset today over a ten-foot sea wall in the heart of the port of Inchon and within an hour had taken three commanding hills in the city.

I was in the fifth wave that hit "Red Beach," which in reality was a rough, vertical pile of stones over which the first assault troops had to scramble with the aid of improvised landing ladders topped with steel hooks.

Despite a deadly and steady pounding from naval guns and airplanes, enough North Koreans remained alive close to the beach to harass us with small-arms and mortar fire. They even hurled hand grenades down at us as we crouched in trenches, which unfortunately ran behind the sea wall in the inland side.

It was far from the "virtually unopposed" landing for which the troops had hoped after hearing of the quick capture of Wolmi Island in the morning by an earlier Marine assault. Wolmi is inside Inchon harbor and just off "Red Beach." At H-hour minus seventy, confident, joking Marines started climbing down from the transport ship on cargo nest and dropping into small assault boats. Our wave commander, Lieutenant R. J. Schening, a veteran of five amphibious assaults, including Guadalcanal, hailed me with the comment, "This has a good chance of being a pushover."

Because of tricky tides, our transport had to stand down the channel and it was more than nine miles to the rendezvous point where our assault waves formed up.

The channel reverberated with the ear-splitting boom of warship guns and rockets. Blue and orange flames spurted from the "Red Beach" area and a huge oil tank, on fire, sent great black rings of smoke over the shore. Then the fire from the big guns lifted and the planes that had been circling overhead swooped low to rake their fire deep into the sea wall.

The first wave of our assault troops was speeding toward the shore by now. It would be H-hour (5:30 P.M.) in two minutes. Suddenly, bright-orange tracer bullets spun out from the hill in our direction.

"My God! There are still some left," Lieutenant Schening said. "Everybody get down. Here we go!"

It was H-hour plus fifteen minutes as we sped the last two thousand yards to the beach. About halfway there the bright tracers started cutting across the top of our little boat. "Look at their faces now," said John Davies of the Newark News. I turned and saw that the men around me had expressions contorted with anxiety.

We struck the sea wall hard at a place where it had crumbled into a canyon. The bullets were whining persistently, spattering the water around us. We clambered over the high steel sides of the boat, dropping into the water and, taking shelter beside the boat as long as we could, snaked on our stomachs up into a rock-strewn dip in the sea wall.

In the sky there was good news. A bright, white star shell from the high ground to our left and an amber cluster told us that the first wave had taken their initial objective, Observatory Hill. But whatever the luck of the first four waves, we were relentlessly pinned down by rifle and automatic-weapon fire coming down on us from another rise on the right.

There were some thirty Marines and two correspondents crouched in the gouged-out sea wall. Then another assault boat swept up, disgorging about thirty more Marines. This went on for two more waves until our hole was filled and Marines lying on their stomachs were strung out all across the top of the sea wall.

An eerie colored light flooded the area as the sun went down with a glow that a newsreel audience would have thought a fake. As the dusk settled, the glare of burning buildings all around lit the sky.

Suddenly, as we lay there intent on the firing ahead, a sudden rush of water came up into the dip in the wall and we saw a huge LST (Landing Ship, Tank) rushing at us with the great plank door half down. Six more yards and the ship would have crushed twenty men. Warning shouts sent every one speeding from the sea wall, searching for escape from the LST and cover from the gunfire. The LST's huge bulk sent a rush of water pouring over the sea wall as it crunched in, soaking most of us.

The Marines ducked and zigzagged as they raced across the open, but enemy bullets caught a good many in the semi-darkness. The wounded were pulled aboard the LSTs, six of which appeared within sixty-five minutes after H-hour.

As nightfall closed in, the Marine commanders ordered their troops forward with increasing urgency, for they wanted to assure a defensible perimeter for the night.

In this remarkable amphibious operation, where tides played such an important part, the Marines were completely isolated from outside supply lines for exactly four hours after H-hour. At this time the outrushing tides—they fluctuate thirty-one feet in twelve-hour periods—made mud flats of the approaches to "Red Beach." The LSTs bringing supplies simply settled on the flats, helpless until the morning tides would float them again.

At the battalion command post the news that the three high-ground objectives—the British Consulate, Cemetery Hill, and Observatory Hill—had been taken arrived at about H-hour plus sixty-one minutes. Now the important items of business became debarking tanks, guns, and ammunition from the LSTs.

Every cook, clerk, driver, and administrative officer in the vicinity was rounded up to help in the unloading. It was exciting to see the huge M-26 tanks rumble across big planks onto the beach, which only a few minutes before had been pro-

tected only by riflemen and machine gunners. Then came the bulldozers, trucks, and jeeps.

It was very dark in the shadow of the ships, and the unloaders had a hazardous time dodging bullets, mortar fire, and their own vehicles.

North Koreans began giving up by the dozens by this time and we could see them, hands up, marching across the open fields toward the LSTs. They were taken charge of with considerable glee by a Korean Marine policeman, Captain Woo, himself a native of Inchon, who had made the landing with several squads of men who were also natives of the city. They learned of the plan to invade their home town only after they had boarded their ship.

Tonight, Captain Woo was in a state of elation beyond even that of the American Marines who had secured the beachhead. "When the Koreans see your power," he said, "they will come in droves to our side."

As we left the beach and headed back to the Navy flagship, naval guns were booming again in support of the Marines. "This time," said a battalion commander, "they are preparing the road to Seoul."

RELMAN MORIN

"HATRED TO STAY"

ASSOCIATED PRESS, SEPTEMBER 25, 1950

Morin won two Pulitzer Prizes for war coverage in the 1950s. The piece that follows is not so much about combat but about what battle and conflict do to a community. His account depicts the friction and enmity between the Communist and non-Communist members of a Korean village liberated shortly after Inchon. The struggle was not just on the front lines but in civilian life as well, as seemingly ordinary people tried to bring their lives back to order and reestablish their sense of homeland. For those who had forgotten what the bloodshed was all about, Morin's work served as a reminder. This piece won him the first of his two Pulitzers.

LONG AFTER THE LAST SHOT IS fired, the weeds of hatred will be flourishing in Korea, nourished by blood and bitter memories.

This is the heritage of the short weeks during which most of South Korea was learning Communism.

Only weeks ago in the region around Seoul and Inchon, people were being killed, dispossessed of land and homes, left to starve, or driven away from all they held dear—because they were not Communists and refused to act like Communists.

EXPECT TO REMAIN RED

TODAY, IN THAT SAME REGION, the same things are still happening—because some Koreans are Communists and propose to remain so.

Hidden in the hills a mile off the road to Seoul, there is a village of twenty-four mud-stone huts with thatched roofs. The people raise rice and corn. Once they had a few cattle.

There were no rich here and, by Koreans standards, no poor either.

Even before the North Korean military invasion last June, nine of the men in the village were Communists.

The headman didn't know why. He simply said they belonged to a Red organization, and frequently went to meetings in Inchon at night.

They talked of the division of land and goods.

"It made trouble," the headman told an American intelligence officer through an interpreter.

She says the lectures talked about life in Russia, how things are done there, and how good everything is. She says it was convincing, and people believed what they heard.

"But she is not a Communist. She went because she was hungry."

BEAT THE COMMUNISTS

AS A RESULT, THE HEADMAN SAID, some of the other villages banded together and beat the Communists.

"There was always trouble and fighting," said the headman, "and we talked of driving the Reds away."

Then the North Korean army swept southward over this little village. The nine Communists suddenly appeared in uniforms.

They killed some of their neighbors and caused others to be put in jail at Inchon. The headman himself fled to safety in the south. One of the villagers went with him.

"He did not want to go," said the headman. "He was to be married. The girl stayed here. She is 18 and a grown woman, but she did not know what to do."

Back in the village the nine Communists began putting theory into practice. First they confiscated all land. Then they summoned landless tenant farmers from nearby villages and told them the land would be given to them if they became Communists.

A Korean soldier
surrenders.
(National Archives)

CONFORMED TO GET LAND

"THE FARMERS ARE IGNORANT OF these things," the headman said. "They were very glad, and they accepted the land and said they were Communists."

Next the nine Reds went to the homes of all the men who had fought with them before.

"They took away all the furniture, even the pots and kettles, and put all these things into one house," the headman related. "Then they said the people who were Communists could come and take whatever they wanted.

"Even the people who were robbed in this way were permitted to come. If they agreed to be Communists they could take back some of their things. Most of them did that."

The parents of the engaged girl were among those who fled. She stayed. Maybe she was waiting for the man who escaped to the south with the headman.

PROMISED FOOD BY REDS

"SHE WAS HUNGRY MOST OF THE time," the headman said. "The Communists told her that if she would attend some cultural classes they would give her food." So she went to the school.

Then, ten days ago, the Americans attacked Inchon. Before the Communists left they herded thirty-three men into a large cell in the Inchon jail and locked the doors. Then the thirty-three were shot to death.

As soon as possible the headman came back to his village. Soon the man who had fled with him came back too.

The landowners took back their own

fields and furniture. Some of the newly made "Communists" were bewildered, and tried to resist. Some were injured.

The American officer asked: "What would you do if the nine Communists came back?"

The headman and the others listening burst into hearty laughter.

"Kill them, naturally," the headman said.

KEYES BEECH

"THIS WAS NO RETREAT"

CHICAGO *DAILY NEWS*, DECEMBER 11, 1950

A reporter for the Chicago Daily News, *Beech witnessed the Chinese entrance into the war in December 1950. Barely three months after the victorious landing at Inchon, the Marines were on a sure path to a quick, triumphant ending of the Korean War. But when "at least 60,000" Chinese troops overwhelmed the Marines not far from the Chinese border, the character of the fighting changed dramatically. Beech's reports probed the deepest emotions and revealed the damaged dignity of the proud Marines. The mere evacuation of the region by the Marines was a heroic episode—they left neither wounded nor dead behind. Yet, as Beech notes, it was a retreat for a unit that was unaccustomed to being pushed back or vanquished.*

YONPO AIRSTRIP, KOREA

"REMBEMBER," DRAWLED COLonel Lewis B. "Chesty" Puller, "whatever you write, that this was no retreat. All that happened was we found more Chinese behind us than in front of us. So we about-faced and attacked."

I said "so long" to Puller after three snowbound days with the 1st Marine Division, 4,000 feet above sea level in the sub-zero weather of Changjin Reservoir. I climbed aboard a waiting C-47 at Koto Airstrip and looked around.

Sixteen shivering Marine casualties—noses and eyes dripping from cold—huddled in their bucket seats. They were the last of more than 2,500 Marine casualties to be evacuated by the U.S. Air Force under conditions considered flatly impossible. Whatever this campaign was—retreat, withdrawal, or defeat—one thing can be said with certainty. Not in the Marine Corps' long and bloody history has there been anything like it. And if you'll pardon a personal recollection, not at Tarawa or Iwo Jima, where casualties were much greater, did I see men suffer as much.

The wonder isn't that they fought their way out against overwhelming odds but that they were able to survive the cold and fight at all. So far as the Marines themselves are concerned, they ask that two things be recorded:

1. They didn't break. They came out of Changjin Reservoir as an organized unit with most of their equipment.

2. They brought out all their wounded. They brought out many of their dead. And most of those they didn't bring out they buried.

It was not always easy to separate dead from wounded among the frozen figures that lay strapped to radiators of jeeps and trucks. I know because I watched them come in from Yudam to Hagaru, 18 miles of icy hell, five days ago.

That same day I stood in the darkened corner of a wind-whipped tent and listened to a Marine officer brief his men for the march to Koto the following day. I have known him for a long time but in the semidarkness, with my face half-covered by my parka, he didn't recognize me. When he did the meeting broke up. When we were alone, he cried. After that he was all right.

I hope he won't mind my reporting he cried, because he's a very large Marine and a very tough guy.

He cried because he had to have some sort of emotional release; because all his men were heroes and wonderful people; because the next day he was going to have to submit them to another phase in the trial by blood and ice. Besides, he wasn't the only one who cried.

In the Marines' twelve-day, forty-mile trek from Yudam to the "bottom of the hill," strange and terrible things happened.

Thousands of Chinese troops—the Marines identified at least six divisions totaling 60,000 men—boiled from every canyon and rained fire from every ridge. Sometimes they came close enough to throw grenades into trucks, jeeps, and ambulances.

Whistles sounded and Chinese ran up to throw grenades into Marine foxholes. Another whistle and the Chinese ran back.

Then mortar shells began to fall. The 3rd Battalion of the 5th Marine Regiment was reduced to less than two companies but still was ordered to attack "regardless of cost."

"We had to do it," said Lieutenant Colonel Joe Stewart, of Montgomery, Alabama. "It was the only way out."

Fox Company, 7th Regiment, was isolated for three or four days—nobody seems to remember dates or days—but held at terrible cost.

One company killed so many Chinese the Marines used their frozen bodies as a parapet. But for every Chinese they killed there were five, ten, or twenty to take his place.

"What 'n hell's the use in killing them," said one Marine. "They breed faster 'n we can knock 'em off."

The Chinese had blown bridges and culverts behind the Americans. The Marines rebuilt them or established bypasses under fire.

No part of a division escaped, including headquarters sections composed of file clerks, cooks, and bakers. Bullets plowed through a Korean house in Hagaru occupied by General O. H. P. Smith.

Always the infantry had to take high ground on each side of the road to protect the train of vehicles that sometimes stretched ten miles.

When the Chinese attacked a train the artillerymen unhooked their guns from their vehicles and fired muzzle bursts from between trucks at the onrushing foe. This was effective, but rather rough on Marine machine gunners who had set up their guns on the railroad tracks fifteen or twenty yards in front of the artillery.

If there was an occasional respite from the enemy there was none from the cold. It numbed fingers, froze feet, sifted through layers of clothing, and crept into the marrow of your bones. Feet sweated by day and froze in their socks by night. Men peeled off their socks—and the soles of their feet with them.

Among the men of the 5th Marines, Lieutenant Commander Chester M. Lessenden, Jr., of Lawrence, Kansas, a Navy doctor, became a hero.

"Lessenden is the most saintly, Godlike man I've ever known," said Stewart. "He never seemed to sleep. He was always on his feet. He never said it can't be done. And yet he was suffering from frostbite worse than most of the men he treated."

In their struggle to keep from freezing, the Marines wrapped their feet in gunny-sacks or pieces of old cloth scrounged from the countryside. When they could, they built fires, but this wasn't often, because fire gave away their positions.

When they came to Koto before the final breakthrough to the sea, they made tents of varicolored parachutes used by the Air Force to drop supplies. The red, white and green chute tents looked like Indian wigwams.

Some covered themselves with Japanese quilts dropped from the air. But they were warmest when they were fighting. Combat was almost welcome because they forgot about the cold.

The cold did strange things to their equipment. Because of sub-zero temperatures, artillery rounds landed as much as 2,000 yards short. Machine guns froze up. Men tugged frantically at their frozen

Pfc. Roman Prauty (*crouching foregound*), a gunner with 31st RCT, and his gun crew fires a 75mm recoilless rifle near Oetlook-tong, Korea, in support of infantry units directly across the valley. *(National Archives)*

bolts. The M-1 rifle generally held up but the Marines cursed the lighter carbine.

Communications gear broke down because equipment, like men, can stand only so much. Canteens burst as water froze inside them.

Despite all these things, the Marines who walked down from Changjin Reservoir still could laugh.

"It was impossible for us to get out, because we were surrounded, encircled, and cut off," said one lieutenant. "But we never got the word, so we came on out. That's us—we never get the word."

JOHN M. HIGHTOWER

"MACARTHUR TRIES TO TAKE OVER U.S. POLICY IN WARZONE"

ASSOCIATED PRESS, MARCH 26, 1951

Although John M. Hightower's reporting did not come from the front, his dispatches had all the fierceness of combat news. From behind the scenes he detailed the widening rift between the commander on the scene, General Douglas MacArthur, and the commander in chief, President Harry Truman. The rupture between the two leaders mirrored the debate over American foreign policy—was it to be containment or rollback of communism? Hightower was well equipped to handle this story. A veteran reporter in the area of high-level policy making, he had covered plenty of high-stakes diplomatic episodes. Among the highlights were the Roosevelt-Churchill summit in Canada, the early United Nations meetings, and the birth of NATO and the Marshall Plan. His accounts on the battles between the president and the general won him a Pulitzer in 1952.

The battle between the two men spoke volumes about the war—and the U.S. role in it. Not certain about the importance of the Korean peninsula in terms of global security, the United States had become involved in the Korean crisis only after the North's invasion of the South. Washington was undecided on how deep a commitment it wanted to make. Truman resolved the debate by firing MacArthur after the latter spoke publicly of their disagreement. In doing so, Truman upheld the supremacy of the executive. But it was a costly point, and U.N. forces stalled on the front while support for the conflict sagged at home.

T HE DISPUTE THAT RAGES BE-tween General Douglas MacArthur and the Truman administration over how to win the Korean war has reached fever heat again. The administration may shortly ask the general to clear with Washington anything he says involving broad foreign policy issues.

This may or may not prove acceptable to MacArthur, but State Department officials as well as some others with great influence at the White House privately say something must be done to prevent a repetition of last week's exchange of shocks and harsh words between Tokyo and Washington.

President Truman circulated last December a firm, government-wide directive declaring that any statement on foreign policy by any official or employee of the government in a speech, article or other public utterance, should be cleared with the State Department. Informants said today that order was called to MacArthur's attention at that time.

Friday night, Washington time, MacArthur left Tokyo for the Thirty-eighth Parallel area of Korea to order United Nations forces to cross into North Korea as tactical requirements made necessary. Before leaving Tokyo he issued a statement to the press.

MADE PEACE BID

IN THIS STATEMENT HE MADE A bid for peace talks with his opposite number on the Communist side, said the Chinese Reds were licked and incapable of waging modern war and warned that if the United Nations launched attacks on Chinese bases and coastal area the Red nation would probably suffer military collapse.

This statement, a check showed, caught the State Department completely unawares. It apparently also caught President Truman without advance notice. After several hours of parleying, including a talk between Secretary of State Acheson and Mr. Truman, a rather meaningless statement was issued, designed to say on Saturday that Washington had nothing to do with what MacArthur had declared Friday night.

The statements said MacArthur had authority to conduct military operations but that political issues which "he has stated are beyond his responsibilities are being dealt with in the U.N. and by the governments having troops in Korea."

The key MacArthur clause which set off the alarm here was that the United Nations could probably succeed in forcing a military collapse of Red China by a limited coastal attack and base-bombing war. A Tokyo dispatch yesterday suggested MacArthur probably was trying to divert the Chinese Reds' attention from Korea to the danger of a coastal attack.

Whatever his objective, any statement he makes—even mingled in with "ifs"— about extending the war in the Far East always sends huge shudders among the Canadian, French, British and other friendly governments. When the Europeans come in to the State Department wanting to know "what does MacArthur propose to do," Acheson and his aides get upset about the problems of holding together the political side of the coalition of which MacArthur is military commander.

JIM LUCAS

"OUR TOWN'S BUSINESS IS WAR"

SCRIPPS HOWARD, JANUARY 3, 1953

Jim Lucas's account from Pork Chop Hill became symbolic of the Korean War. Pork Chop Hill and, specifically, "Our Town" epitomized the stalemate and loss of perspective that enveloped the war by 1953. The only business in Our Town, as Lucas noted, was war. War for the sake of war and maintained only by war. In fact, by the time this piece was written, the war had bogged down across the thirty-eighth parallel and the fiercest of fighting yielded only inches of territory. For many others, the pace of life at Our Town must have been unnerving, but not for Lucas. During World War II he had served as a military officer and correspondent and had accompanied marines through eight bloody campaigns. At one point, during the furious fighting on the island of Tarawa, Lucas was listed as MIA. He not only emerged alive days later but he won a Bronze Star for his accounts. Perhaps the earlier experiences allowed him to spice grim reality with a dash of black humor. The Korean War might later become the "Forgotten War" to many, but surely not to those who lived Our Town in person or from the pages of the morning newspaper.

Readers were given a clear view of what it was what like to fight on a front that rarely moved backward or forward. That was not a feeling Americans—or Lucas—were accustomed to after the victorious drive through Western Europe and Asia. Had the Korean War ended in a tie? The reports, written in January 1953, arrived just as Dwight Eisenhower prepared to assume the presidency. Six months later an armistice was signed in Panmunjom, codifying the stalemate.

PORK CHOP HILL, KOREA

OUR TOWN ATOP PORK CHOP HILL is in a world of its own.

Its contacts with the outside world are few—but imperative. Its immediate concern is the enemy on the next ridge. That's "His Town." Our Town gives grudging respect. But, if possible, "His Town" is going to be wiped out.

Our Town's business is war. It produces nothing but death. To exist, therefore, it must rely on others. Food, mail, clothing—even the weapons of destruction—are shipped in.

These items are sent in from that part of the outside world which the men of Our Town call "rear." As often—and far more passionately—they are at war with "rear" as they are with the enemy. "Rear," which includes anything beyond the foot of Pork Chop, is populated, Our Town is convinced, by idiots and stumblebums.

Physically, Our Town—while hardly attractive—is not uncomfortable. Much municipal planning went into it.

The streets are six to eight feet deep. At times after dark, Our Town's streets are invaded by men from His Town. The citizens of Our Town invariably expel these interlopers. To assist in maintaining law

American soliders wait in the trenches. *(National Archives)*

and order on such occasions, the shelves along the streets of Our Town are liberally stocked with hand grenades.

There are thirty to fifty houses in Our Town. They are referred to as bunkers. Each street and each bunker is numbered. After a few days it's comparatively easy to find one's way.

Half of Our Town's bunkers are living quarters. The others are stores—storage bunkers, that is. From these you can obtain a wide assortment of ammunition, sandbags, candles, charcoal, or canned rations.

Our Town's buildings are sturdy. The typical building is at least six feet underground. It is made of four-by-ten inch logs to which are added many sandbags. It's almost impervious to enemy shelling.

Our Town is not without its social life.

I went visiting this morning at 19 Third Street in Our Town. Entering No. 19, one gets down on his hands and knees. The front door is low.

My hosts were First Lieutenant Pat Smith of Hollywood, California, Corporal Joe Siena of Portland, Connecticut, Private First Class Eddie Williams of Brooklyn, New York, and Private Don Coan of Anadarko, Oklahoma.

Don had coffee brewing in an old ration can. He opened a can of sardines. Eddie was heading for the rear on a shopping trip. His list included candles, a coffeepot (which he's had on order for a month already), and a reel of communications wire. He also was taking a field telephone for repairs.

Our Town, like others, enjoys small talk. Over coffee, the group discussed what a man should do if a grenade-wielding Chinese suddenly appeared at the door. There was no unanimous decision.

Our Town has its own banker—Warrant Officer James W. Cherry of Jackson, Tennessee. He came up the other afternoon. Within three hundred yards of the enemy, he distributed $23,411.

Many men didn't want their money, really. Money is an almost valueless commodity up here. Three days from now, the postal officer will come up the hill, selling money orders.

If money has no value, other things do. Things like candles, fuel, toilet tissue. There's never enough charcoal for the stoves which heat the bunkers. To stay warm you can climb into your sleeping bag—if you're a fool. The men refer to sleeping bags as "coffins." Too many soldiers have been killed before they could unzip their sleeping bags.

Our Town's Mayor is a tall, gangling Texan—Captain Jack Conn of Houston. He's company commander. The Vice Mayor is his executive officer—First Lieutenant Bill Gerald, also of Houston. Bill Gerald is a Negro.

The battalion commander, Lieutenant Colonel Seymour Goldberg of Washington, D.C., is convinced Our Town's residents think Colonel Goldberg is a martinet.

Colonel Goldberg always arrives in a foul mood, to be expected, since high-up officials usually are blind to local problems. The Colonel expects miracles overnight. (Privately, he concedes this is an act—"If I didn't raise hell, they wouldn't take me seriously.")

Our Town endures this outsider stoically. The Colonel says the men need haircuts. "When would they have time to get haircuts?" say Our Town's citizens. He says the bunkers need cleaning. "They look all right to us," fume Our Towners. "We live here." He says ammunition isn't stored properly. "Let up on these all-night patrols and we'll store it right," retorts Our Town—not to the Colonel's face, of course.

Invariably the Colonel corrals a hapless private and demands he be court-martialed for one thing or another. Our Town's Mayor dutifully notes the boy's name and then throws away the notes when the Colonel leaves.

But the Colonel expects this.

There was much glee the other day when the Colonel issued an order that any man found outside a bunker without a bulletproof vest be punished. A moment later, the Colonel left the bunker—and forgot his vest.

There's method in the Colonel's madness. He deliberately sets out to make Our Town hate him. "If I didn't," he says, "it would go to pot."

You see, the Colonel once was a company commander who hated "rear." He knows he must prod the men up front, so that their outfit will remain—despite the presence of death itself—a proud, disciplined, organized Army fighting unit.

An "Extra" edition of the *St. Paul Pioneer Press* proclaims the end of the Korean War.

HARRISON E. SALISBURY

"BERIA'S TROOPS HELD MOSCOW BUT HE HESITATED AND LOST"

NEW YORK TIMES, SEPTEMBER 21, 1954

It is hard to appreciate the skill and insight that it took to piece together the following story that appeared in the New York Times. *Few places have been as inaccessible as the Kremlin and the policy-making apparatus in the former Soviet Union. Yet the veteran correspondent was able to penetrate Moscow's most secretive bastion to get the details on a failed coup that would have altered the course of history. In stunning and proficient detail, Harrison E. Salisbury noted how Beria's men attempted to seal off the Kremlin to make himself its ruler. That Salisbury was able to report the following account is remarkable—that he was able to do so at the height of cold war maneuvering by figures as ruthless as Beria makes the feat all the more incredible.*

What makes this piece so engrossing is its detail, which seemingly places the reader in Moscow at the height of the scheming and plotting. Readers could feel the mix of somber feelings with the chilling prospect of a Beria takeover. And yet, as Salisbury notes, the collapse of his coup revealed his inherent weakness and inability to muster significant support, whether through fear or perhaps through promises of liberalization.

FOR ABOUT SEVENTY-EIGHT HOURS in March of last year, Lavrenti Pavlovich Beria held Russia in the hollow of his pudgy hand. He was supreme. There was no one who could challenge him—not Malenkov, not Khrushchev, not Molotov, not the Army.

At any moment within those fateful hours, Beria might have proclaimed himself dictator, all-supreme ruler of Russia, heir of Stalin.

He did not do so, and in that failure to act he sealed his own fate. The life that came to an end last Christmas Eve, probably in the blood-stained cellars of the Lubyanka Prison, was doomed from that moment when Beria did not act.

The story of the March days of 1953, just before and just after the death of Stalin, has never been publicly told. Much of it was concealed and suppressed by Moscow censorship. Many details are not yet and possibly never will be known outside the tight little circle of men in the Kremlin who were the chief actors in one of the great dramas of modern times.

Enough is known, however, so that the factors that led to Beria's removal and execution can be traced with almost crystal clarity, in an otherwise Florentine labyrinth of intrigue and counter-intrigue, plot and counter-plot.

These factors were so obvious at the time that this correspondent could confidently note in his private correspondence that a showdown over Beria's power was inevitable.

To see why this was so, it is necessary to turn back to the story of the events of Stalin's death in March, 1953—the real story, not the emasculated one that was all that fearful censors permitted correspondents to cable at that time.

The first announcement of Stalin's fatal illness was made in Moscow about 8 A.M. on March 4, 1953. It said the Generalissimo had suffered a massive cerebral hemorrhage early Monday morning, March 2, two days previously. It was apparent to everyone in Moscow that the question was how long the end would be in coming. It did not seem likely to be long.

This anticipation proved correct. At 4 A.M. on March 6, the Moscow radio, in its shortwave broadcasts overseas and to provincial newspapers within Russia, announced that Stalin had died at 9:50 the previous evening.

This correspondent was at the Central Telegraph Office in Moscow at the time the flash on Stalin's death came through. The office is in Gorky Street, just two blocks from the Kremlin. At frequent intervals that night I circled the Kremlin by car and toured central Moscow. All was quiet in the city. There were lights burning late in the Kremlin, but that was not unusual.

About 1 A.M. a number of Kremlin limousines pulled into the Kremlin garages, as if returning from taking home the participants in some midnight conference. About 3 A.M. three big limousines parked in front of the Moscow City Soviet building. This was the first indication of anything unusual. A few minutes later a woman at the Izvestia distribution desk said the papers would be "very, very" late.

LINK TO WORLD SEVERED

THESE DETAILS ARE CITED TO show how quiet was the center of Moscow on the night of Stalin's death. Nor was there much drama in the way the news reached the Moscow correspondents. My chauffeur, sitting at the car radio tuned to the Tass dictation-speed broadcast, heard the announcement at 4 A.M. He chambled in and whispered in my ear. I filed a bulletin I had already prepared, and within a few minutes the other correspondents had filed theirs.

But there the matter ended. An iron censorship clamped down. The cables about Stalin were not passed. Neither was a message about office accounts that this correspondent tried to file.

Not only were no messages passed, but a telegraph clerk flipped all the jack cords out of the switchboard through which international calls are placed. While the switchboard lighted up and correspondents frantically shouted to be connected with London and Paris and Stockholm, the operator sat quietly with folded hands. The censors ordered her not even to touch the board. A few minutes later a sleepy mechanic hurried in, ripped open the back of the switchboard and yanked the main cable.

It was three and a half hours before communications were resumed from Moscow. The world got its first news of Stalin's death, not from Moscow correspondents but from London pickups of the Soviet radio.

However, thanks to the hiatus imposed by the censors, this correspondent is in possession of an almost complete picture of what occurred in Moscow in the hours immediately after the official announcement of Stalin's death. And that account is the key to the Beria story.

Seeing that no copy was likely to be passed for hours, I got into my car and made several tours of the city. As late as 5 A.M. the center was absolutely quiet. Outside of the City Soviet, where obviously some arrangements connected with the death were going forward, there was no sign of unusual activity. No more militia (as the Russians call their police) were on duty. Only a few lights dimly burned in the Kremlin. Nothing extraordinary.

BERIA'S FORCES APPEAR

BUT SHORTLY BEFORE 6, A DIFference became apparent. Whereas before that hour traffic was sparse, possibly even sparser than is customary in those pre-dawn hours, smooth-running, quiet convoys of trucks began converging on the center of the city. They rolled quietly down Gorky Street. They slipped noiselessly down Lubyanka Hill. More appeared from beyond the Moscow River and slowly crossed through the Red Square.

In each of these trucks, sitting silently, arms folded, on wooden cross-benches, was a detachment of twenty-two soldiers of the special battalions of the M.V.D., or to translate its initials, the Ministry of Internal Affairs, Beria's ministry.

For the first hour or so the disposition of these troops was not apparent. The truck convoys crossed and recrossed the center of the city without obvious pattern. Slowly little knots of trucks congregated at various intersections and began to accumulate in the enormous open squares that are so numerous in the heart of Moscow.

Around 7:30 A.M. the censorship on Stalin's death was lifted, and it was about 9 o'clock before I again emerged from the telegraph office. Vast changes met my eyes. By that time there were thousands of troops in the central part of the city and great lines of trucks. Columns of tanks had also made their appearance on upper Gorky Street. All the trucks, all the tanks, all the troops bore the familiar red-and-blue insignia of the Ministry of Internal Affairs. They were Beria's force.

I went over into Red Square. The way was still open, and a curious spectacle was revealed. A thousand or two thousand persons were standing in a cigar-shaped crowd toward the main Spassky Gate of the Kremlin. The crowd was quiet and well-mannered and had not yet been interfered with by the police. Obviously these people expected (correctly, as it turned out) that Stalin's body would be brought out through this gate.

It was extraordinary to see a crowd freely collected right in the middle of Red Square. I had never seen such a thing before. While I watched, however, freedom of movement into and within Red Square gradually was brought to an end by a giant pincers operation of the M.V.D.

First, light lines were thrown across the streets giving access to the Square.

Persons were allowed out, but not in. Then, rapidly growing bodies of troops were introduced into the lower end of Red Square and began to press the crowds back away from the Spassky Gate toward the State Historical Museum end.

Drifting back with the crowds, I saw that the troops intended to clear not only Red Square but Manezhny Square and Theatre Square, the big adjacent open spaces, as well. During the next hour, this great pincers operation continued and the movement of both pedestrians and traffic in the heart of the city was brought to a total halt.

Moscow is constructed like a series of expanding rings. The Kremlin is the innermost ring. About a mile out is the second ring, a tree-lined boulevard constructed on the site of an old city wall. Perhaps half a mile farther out is a second broad asphalted boulevard, the Sadavaya Circle, built on the base of another old wall. Avenues radiate through these circles, like the spokes of a wheel, giving access to the heart of the city.

IRON BAND ON CITY'S HEART

THE MILITARY MOVEMENT THAT HAD occurred clamped an iron band on each of these circles and spokes. Not only were thousands of troops deployed across all these streets and along their sides to form cordons, but tens of thousands of trucks were brought into Moscow and formed bumper-to-axle and tailboard to radiator, into impenetrable barricades. At all key points the truck and troop barricades were reinforced by phalanxes of tanks drawn up three deep.

There was an iron collar around Moscow's heart; and from about 10 or 11 A.M.

of March 6, 1953, until 4 P.M. on March 9 it was not removed.

During those hours not one person entered or left the center of Moscow without leave of the M.V.D. command, Beria's command.

There was literally no traffic movement in the center of the city. The *New York Times* offices were right in the heart of this dead area, in the Hotel Metropole. Since the *Times* car was operating on the morning of March 6, it was within this area; and, by one of those strange quirks of fate, it continued to operate within the closed ring during all those hours, molested and threatened repeatedly by the M.V.D., but somehow continuing to pass through the seven police lines that barred the way from the Metropole through Theatre and Manezhny Squares and the back door of Gertzen Street to the telegraph office.

This fantastic military operation had steel tentacles that rammed their way back through the city to its outskirts. Nor was this the limit of the M.V.D.'s grip on Moscow.

On Sunday, March 8, this correspondent decided to investigate rumors that thousands of persons were arriving in Moscow from all over the country to view Stalin's body, which was then lying in state. There were reports that the trains were so crowded that persons had ridden the roofs of trains all the way from Leningrad in sub-freezing weather.

There was no way of getting to the railroad stations, all of which lie at or beyond the second circle, except by walking through the countless military barricades. The metro (subway) system was working, but not to the sealed-off center of the city.

Not long after dawn, I left the Metropole Hotel and made my way past sleepy sentry lines, past curbside campfires where some troops were whiling away the hours, playing accordions and stamping out tunes with their soft leather boots, to the Kursk railroad station. There the true state of affairs was considerably different from the rumor. Notices, hand-written, were posted at the ticket offices. All trains out of Moscow were running, but no trains into Moscow within the suburban radius or other near-by points.

Moscow was a city truly sealed off— not only on the inside, but from without as well.

Later that day, by dint of simply walking past the sentry posts with an absolute air, I strolled right into Red Square. It was a strange feeling. The huge square was deserted. Troops were on guard at all the entrances to keep everyone out. But in the center, at the famous Mausoleum, there were power cables running out from inside the Kremlin, and power chisels and hammers were busy. Fifteen or twenty workmen were busy chiseling the name of Stalin into the stone beds beside that of Lenin and making arrangements in the tomb's inner chamber.

A colonel of the M.V.D. was supervising the work. Beria's colonel. I strolled over and watched idly. No one paid any attention. It probably seemed to them that I had a right to be there, otherwise the sentries would not have admitted me.

It was deathly quiet in Red Square except for the intermittent sound of hammers and chisels. The quiet must have been noticeable to the men inside the Kremlin walls. It was then that the thought struck home so sharply.

PROOF OF BERIA'S POWER

WHAT TROOPS WERE THESE THAT held the city? M.V.D. troops. Were there any other troops in the city? No. Could any other troops enter the city? No. The closest military camps were all M.V.D. camps. Other troops could enter only with M.V.D. permission or by fighting their way street by street through the barricades. What of the Air Force? Perfectly useless. Even if it bombed the whole city to rubble, it could not break the grip of the M.V.D. upon every strategic position in Moscow.

And what of the Kremlin? The men who were there were there because the M.V.D. permitted them to pass through the lines. Or, if they wished to leave the Kremlin, they could leave only by M.V.D. permission.

It was not likely that the men in the Kremlin had failed to note that they were, in effect, the prisoners of the M.V.D. They were men trained to think in military terms, and, particularly, in terms of civil war and street fighting. To the military leaders the realization of their position must have been even more forcible.

Because the M.V.D. was not just a group of initials. It was not just a department of the Government. It was an individual. A powerful, ruthless man of extraordinary ability named Lavrenti Pavlovich Beria. And it was Beria's troops and Beria's tanks and Beria's trucks that had accomplished this small miracle and taken over the city of Moscow while the radios were still blaring out the news of Stalin's death to the startled citizenry.

Using the basic movement plans that twice a year for many years had been employed on May Day and on Nov. 7 to control traffic movement in the center of the city, and simply extending the plan back to control the whole city and its environs, Beria had with the smoothness of clockwork put Moscow into his grasp.

It was too smooth and too complete and too good.

STRONG HAND OVERPLAYED

NO MILITARY MAN COULD SEE that exhibition and feel a moment's safety—unless he trusted Beria completely or unless Beria was the top boss. It was too plain and too obvious that Beria had a machine that, before dawn any morning, could take over the Kremlin, take over Moscow, and, having done this, have a crack at making Beria master of all Russia.

There is not much doubt that Beria himself was fully aware of his power at that moment. It is also likely that he had only in the final hours of Stalin's life regained full and unchallenged control over the M.V.D. He and his command of this vast police army had been one of the targets of machinations that generally are described as the so-called "doctors' plot," which had a vital role in the events leading up to Stalin's death.

But in the coalition of forces that occurred at or about the time of Stalin's death, Beria got back his M.V.D. Perhaps that is why he overplayed his hand so badly at a moment when he was not prepared to strike for full mastery of Russia. Perhaps he did not fully realize the impression he would make on his colleagues. Whatever the explanation, on the next day, Monday, when Stalin was formally laid to rest beside Lenin, Beria spoke at the funeral bier along with

Georgi M. Malenkov and Vyacheslav M. Molotov. There was an undercurrent in Beria's speech that could have flowed only from his knowledge of his power.

He sounded just a little more condescending toward Mr. Molotov and Mr. Malenkov—perhaps more in his delivery than in his language. What was more interesting, he sought to convey without exactly saying so that he spoke for the Army as well as the police.

It took only three and a half months to demonstrate that condescension was not exactly called for on Beria's part and that he had shown the Army, only too plainly, the power and danger of his position. There can be no shadow of a doubt that, from the moment Beria sealed off the Kremlin and Moscow with his troops he signed his own death warrant.

He was not strong enough to rule. But he was too dangerous to any other ruler or rulers. In the unstable coalition of party, police and Army, Beria had too much sheer military power that could be too quickly applied at the center. He was too big for the triumvirate, but not big enough to be dictator.

The only real surprise about Beria's end was that it came so soon. It was a measure of the real weaknesses of his position (once his troops were out of Moscow) that his colleagues were able to deliver the coup de grace so quickly and with hardly a ripple on the surface of the Moscow waters.

A legend has arisen in some quarters outside Russia in the months since Beria's downfall that he was a great "liberal." It is recalled that the announcement of the exposure and reversal of the so-called "doctors' plot" was made in the name of his ministry. It is said that he advocated more liberal measures for Russia's multitudinous and usually mistreated minority nationalities.

Some color, perhaps, is lent to such tales by the fact that Beria was a minority man himself, coming from Georgia and being partly of Jewish ancestry and from the small mountain area known as Mingrelia. While he bossed Georgia before going up to Moscow in 1938 at the end of the purge period he did a good deal for the Georgian Jews, sponsoring a charitable Jewish aid society, various trade and farm schools and even opening a museum of Jewish culture, which still survives.

LIBERAL LABEL BELIED

HOWEVER, AS STALIN'S POLICE chief he was the man who carried out the deportation of hundreds of thousands of minority nationals from their home places, Balts to Central Asia, Byelorussians to Siberia, Jews to the Far North, and so on. It is hard to find in his record as M.V.D. chief any trace of "liberalism." Nor did I ever hear anyone in Russia suggest that the chief of the secret police was really a kind and liberal man.

One piece of so-called evidence that was cited to bolster the case for Beria's "liberalism" was the fact that, whereas the man he installed as chief of special investigations of the M.V.D. after the reversal of the doctors' case in April, 1953, was executed along with Beria last December, the previous chief inquisitor, a man named Ryumin whom Beria had blamed for fabricating the doctor's plot evidence, had not, apparently, been punished.

Six weeks ago, however, a brief announcement in the Soviet press revealed that Ryumin had been executed for his role in the notorious conspiracy. That demolished about the only remaining pin supporting the case of "Beria the liberal."

Naturally, hardly a word of any of the foregoing was ever permitted to pass the Moscow censorship.

RUSSELL JONES

"FOR THE FIRST TIME SINCE I WAS A BOY I WEPT"

UNITED PRESS INTERNATIONAL, OCTOBER 29–DECEMBER 3, 1956

Before arriving in Eastern Europe, Russell Jones had a distinguished reporting career as a U. S. Army correspondent in World War II. He joined the service in 1941 and was sent to follow the Allied advance through Europe, first joining the combatants during the campaigns in North Africa. A founder of the European edition of Stars and Stripes, *Jones stayed with the publication after his discharge in 1945. Four years later he became a UPI correspondent in London and later was sent to manage the wire service's bureau in Prague. Inside Budapest when Red Army tanks came rolling through, Jones was the only U.S. correspondent to remain in the country during and after the occupation. For these stories about the rise and fall of the Hungarian Revolution, Jones was awarded a Pulitzer.*

The crushing of the Hungarian revolt, like the smashing of the Prague Spring a dozen years later, heightened the sense of futility among Americans with their inability to win the cold war. As in Korea, Hungary represented a country that yearned for freedom and national liberation—but U.S. policy makers were seemingly powerless to help. Instead Americans could do little more than stand back and read about the despair and vain valor of the Hungarian freedom fighters—and were wont to shed tears for the shattered hopes in Hungary.

BUDAPEST, November 15

LIFE AS THE ONLY AMERICAN correspondent left in shattered Budapest is sometimes frightening, sometimes amusing. But mostly it is a continuous feeling of inadequacy both as an American and as a reporter who helplessly watched the murder of a people.

For the first time since I was a boy I wept.

I saw a former British soldier break down completely. The situation was worse than the Warsaw uprising into which he was parachuted in 1944.

None of us are Hemingways and it needs a Hemingway to tell this story adequately.

Since a convoy of other newsmen left Budapest under Russian guard last weekend there have been five Western journalists left to tell the world what happens here. There are two British reporters, a Frenchman, a stateless person, and myself.

Except for the stateless person, who has continued to live in the shelter of the British legation, all of us are gathered in the Duna Hotel on the east bank of the Danube.

In the last few days our life has settled

down to a routine struggle—checking with Western diplomats for their reports on the situation, futile attempts to interview the puppet regime of Janos Kadar, endless wandering through the city to find out what is going on, and hours-long struggles for telephone connections with the outside world.

Our average day: Sleeping in hotel rooms—unheated in near freezing weather—then rushing for a bath before the hot-water supply is cut off at 9 A.M. Then down to the hotel lobby where everyone is sitting family-style at two long tables. The dining room itself is unusable, since Russian shells have knocked out two of the huge windows.

The food—bread and bad coffee for breakfast—comes from the basement, as the kitchen was destroyed by a Soviet attack.

After a quick check of the situation we start our morning struggle to telephone. Sometimes we find ourselves with a story written but no telephone, and other times with a connection but no news.

Our tours of the town are punctuated by frequent checks by Soviet soldiers or Hungarian AVO—secret police.

Treatment at the checkpoints can vary from a polite salute and waving hands to the suspicious examination of all papers by an AVO man apparently unable to read. As the evening curfew at 7 P.M. local time nears, the checks become more rigorous—and more frightening. One correspondent was killed and three others wounded in the early stages of the revolt, and none of us is anxious to join the casualty list.

Walking through the city is made more difficult by masses of Hungarians streaming along in their search for food and wandering aimlessly through the wreckage, determined to continue their general strike until the Russians leave. They have nothing else to do.

Our meals are shared by a handful of prostitutes, elderly "class enemies" who returned from deportation after the revolt, a Swiss Red Cross man, a Czech businessman whose faith in Communism has been shaken, and a few ordinary Hungarians bombed out of their homes.

A strange multilingual community has been established, with the Hungarians watching for news, the prostitutes washing the correspondents' laundry, and correspondents completing less eagerly the normal work of the newsman.

One of the few bright spots in the city is the Grand Hotel on Margaret Island, isolated from the rest of the city by the Danube River. The Island might be a thousand miles away from the scene of death and destruction.

Yesterday I lunched there with Mrs. Tanya Rahmann, wife of the Indian charge d'affaires in Budapest, and rarely have I had a more pleasant meal. But it was a brief interlude.

On leaving, as on entering the Island, I made a sharp right turn literally under the guns of a huge Soviet tank, which stood at a Soviet checkpoint on Margaret Island, and drove back to the tangle of fallen street-car wires, piles of rubble, and crowds of hopeless, desperate people.

BUDAPEST, November 21 (UP)

THEY ASK THE SAME WHISPERED questions in the hurried conversations that spring up wherever the only American goes in search of news in Budapest.

"How do I get out?" . . . "What are the borders like?"

"How many times do the Russians check you before the borders?"

The news has come to this battletorn city that President Eisenhower will allow 5,000 Hungarian refugees to enter the United States. Hungarians want to know how to get out, and this reporter is a busy man.

Already the U.S. legation has been besieged by dozens of Hungarians seeking visas under the "Eisenhower Plan."

While the fighting was going on, many a newspaperman received tearful pleas for help, for moral support from the freedom fighters—both men and women. Now there are the whispers, and the notes. Dozens and dozens of times, in three weeks in Budapest, you have found the notes.

You come back to your car and find a note stuck under the windshield wiper. You find them under your plate at lunch. They are slipped into your hand as you pass by.

Sometimes they want you to get word to relatives in America. At the Csepel Island Steelworks south of Budapest yesterday, a hand reached out of the crowd and pressed a dirty scrap of paper into my hand.

"To Louis Menyhert, 34-54 89th St., Jackson Heights (New York City)," a scratchy pencil had written. "We are all living. I also have uncles in San Diego and Detroit. We miss them."

It was signed "Louis."

To the Louis in Long Island, I can only say: Your friend or relative is safe. I did not see him, only the hand, but there is his message and God bless him.

LONDON, December 10

THE GREATEST SHOCK TO THE Hungarian Communists and their Russian masters must have been the type of people who fought the hardest.

Believe none of the stories that this was a misguided uprising fomented to restore the great estate owners of the Horthy regency or the industrial magnates. I saw with my own eyes who was fighting and heard with my ears why they fought.

The first armed resistance came from students of the schools and universities, the youth who had been so carefully selected as the party elite of the future.

The fiercest fighters were the workers, the proletarians in whose name Communism had ruled. Even the Hungarian army, purged and repurged a dozen times, joined the battle for freedom or sat on the sidelines.

The two big names that came out of the revolt were Communist—Imre Nagy, a lifelong Party member, and Lieutenant Colonel Pal Maleter, who had deserted to the Russians in World War II and returned as a Red partisan.

Wherever came the spark, it found its tinder among the common people. The areas of destruction, the buildings most desperately defended and the dead themselves are the most eloquent proof of this. It was the workers' tenements that Soviet siege guns smashed, factory buildings that became forts and the tired shabby men with broken shoes and horny hands of the laborer who died by the thousands. The women with their hair bound with kerchiefs and the cheap and tawdry dresses of working people.

A seventeen-year-old girl, twice wounded at Corvin Theatre, told me she fought because "it isn't right that my father, with four children to feed, should get only nine hundred forints ($80) a month."

The chairman of the Workers' Council at the Csepel Iron and Steel plant with 38,000 workers, biggest in the country, said, "These are our factories. We will fight to the death to hold them. But we will continue plant maintenance because we want to work here again."

In Dorog, one of the coal centers, miners continued to work despite the general strike. But not to produce coal. They didn't want their mines ruined by flooding.

The same attitude is true in the country. The farmers want to get out of the collectives but they do not want the restoration of the landlords. They think everyone should have the right to own and till his own land. Something like 100 acres a family would be fair, they think.

It was for these simple, basic things that the Hungarian people fought. These and the right to speak and think freely, to elect men of their own choice, and to raise their children in their own way.

They will go on fighting for them.

PRESTON GROVER

"RUSSIAN DOWNERS OF PLANE RECEIVE MEDAL REWARDS"

ASSOCIATED PRESS, MAY 7, 1959

The admission on May 19, 1960, that the Soviet Union had shot down a U.S. U-2 spy plane and captured its pilot, Francis Gary Powers, was a jolting revelation for the American public and press. Both had accepted the official U.S. government version of the incident, which claimed the aircraft was a weather plane that accidentally strayed over Soviet territory. But when Moscow produced Powers and aircraft wreckage, the lie was revealed and a humbled White House could no longer continue the coverup. The following piece wired to U.S. newspapers by the AP's Preston Grover was a bitter pill. It conveyed not only Khrushchev's statements but also illustrated the premier's gloating at having caught his rivals in a trap.

K. SAYS PILOT CONFESSES SPYING; U.S. TO DEMAND TALK WITH HIM

**Premier Indicates Trial,
Show Deputies 'Proof'
Jet Sought Red Targets**

THE UNITED STATES ADMITTED last night that "an unarmed civilian" aircraft probably made an information-gathering flight over the Soviet Union.

A statement cleared by President Eisenhower and released by the State Department in effect conceded the accuracy of much of Soviet Premier Nikita S. Khrushchev's charge that a plane shot down in Russia last Sunday was on a spy mission.

MOSCOW, May 7 (AP)

PREMIER NIKITA S. KHRUSHchev said today that Francis G. Powers, pilot of a United States high-altitude jet plane shot down by rocket in the Urals Sunday, is safe in Soviet hands and has confessed he was spying. The Premier submitted film, money, weapons and an unused suicide kit as proof and indicated the flier will be tried.

Khrushchev waved pictures before a shouting, applauding Supreme Soviet—the Soviet version of a parliament—in support of his charge that the 30-year-old pilot was photographing Soviet military bases and industrial installations for the United States Central Intelligence Agency.

"This time the thief was caught red-handed," he said. ". . . We are going to decorate those soldiers who shot down this plane. We are proud of the fact that they fulfilled their duty."

PLANE TRAPPERS HONORED

DECORATIONS WERE REPORTED awarded promptly by the Supreme Soviet to 18 officers and men for destruction of the plane. . . .

This is the way Khrushchev hinted that the American airman, who he said escaped by parachute when his speedy Lockheed U2 was hit, may be tried for espionage:

"I think that it will be correct to pose a question about the bringing of this pilot before a court in order that the public itself may become convinced of the actions undertaken by the United States, provoking the Soviet Union with a view to inflaming the atmosphere, brushing aside even the successes which had been achieved in the easing of international tension."

REJECTS U.S. CLAIM

KHRUSHCHEV DISMISSED AS A fabrication the United States' State Department report that Powers, Lockheed test pilot for Pound, Va., was on a weather research mission from Adana, Turkey, when his plane vanished. . . .

(T)he Soviet Premier gave this account:

Powers flew from Turkey April 27 to Peshawar, then took off Sunday for a flight across Soviet territory toward a United States base at Bodo, Norway.

He was flying at an altitude of 20,000 meters—more than 12 miles—when he was downed near Sverdlovsk in the Urals, deep in Soviet territory.

Both the pilot, "alive and well," and the wreckage of the plane were reported brought to Moscow. Khrushchev announced earlier this week that the plane had been brought down by a remarkable rocket.

PREMIER QUOTES PILOT

KHRUSHCHEV QUOTED POWERS AS saying:

"I had to take off from the airdrome at Peshawar in Pakistan to cross the state frontier of the U.S.S.R. and to fly across Soviet territory to Norway to the airdrome at Bodo. I had to fly over definite points in the U.S.S.R. Of them, I remember Murmansk and Archangel. During the flight over Soviet territory I had to switch some apparatus on and off over definite landmarks which were shown on a map. I think my flight over Soviet territory was for the collection of information on Soviet guided missiles and radar stations."

Khrushchev told the deputies the plane was rigged with a demolition charge that should have been triggered by a catapult ejection device when the pilot bailed out, but that Powers avoided the ejector and jumped in taking to his parachute.

Powers also was equipped with a poison needle, Khrushchev said, and had been "told that he should not fall alive into hands of Soviet authorities."

TELLS OF SPY EQUIPMENT

THE PLANE WAS NOT FITTED FOR weather study at all, he declared, "it was just an ordinary military reconnaissance aircraft equipped with various instruments for gathering espionage information." Its camera, he said, was good.

Of the poison needle, the Premier said Powers did not use it because "living things want to go on living."

The pilot also carried a silenced pistol, a dagger and a penknife, Khrushchev said.

He said Powers was also carrying 7500 rubles, some French gold francs and other foreign money, two gold watches in addition to Power's own and seven gold bracelets for women.

The Premier said "we have not only the instruments found on the aircraft, but also a developed film consisting of several places on our territory."

"Here, look at this. Here is the airfield, here. Fighters in position on the ground. Two little white strips. Here you see another airfield. Here also a single line you see a long belt. They are our fighters in position on the ground. Again an airfield

photographed. And again an airfield photographed. This is their film and we have developed it. Again an airfield photographed. Well, this will suffice. . . ."

He passed out the pictures for inspection by the deputies.

Khrushchev said he had delayed announcing capture of the pilot in order to expose "fabrications in the official American version."

WARNS OTHER NATIONS

HE SUGGESTED THAT TURKEY, PAKistan and Norway take a second look at American use of bases on their soil.

By Khrushchev's account, Powers said he went to work for an "American spy organization" in 1956 for $2500 a month. That was the year Powers signed up as a Lockheed test pilot.

Khrushchev also said, "I think it would be expedient to hold a press conference and to show during it all the (plane's) means for the exploration of the atmosphere." He did not specify when this might be held.

The Premier said he got a very favorable impression from his talks with Americans last September, "but apparently militarists in the Pentagon . . . continue to work for war purposes."

Warningly he said:

"A nuclear bomb can be dropped (by plane) in such a way, but such an aggressor can get back a more powerful nuclear bomb. . . .

"What kind of morality are these people following if they consider themselves Christian?"

WALTER LIPPMAN

"KHRUSHCHEV TO LIPPMAN—FACE TO FACE NO. 1"

NEW YORK *HERALD TRIBUNE*, APRIL 17, 1961

A master columnist and influential opinion-maker, Walter Lippman scored a coup with this interview. Lippman had advocated a softer approach toward the Soviet Union back in the early days of the Truman administration. Now, roughly fifteen years later, with two new leaders at the helm in Washington and Moscow, the interviewer hoped to relay an olive branch from Moscow, especially since a summit between Khrushchev and Kennedy lay only months ahead in Vienna. But the moment chosen for this chat was one rife with anxiety, since both leaders were talking a tough public line.

Unknown to both men as their conversation took place, the United States was aiding the landing of an exile force at Cuba's Bay of Pigs. The humiliating defeat for Brigade 2506 held severe ramifications for both Washington and Moscow. Having supported the brigade's target, the government of Fidel Castro, the Soviet Union was now in keen focus: aid Castro with its considerable might or stand accused of being a paper tiger. For the Kennedy team, Cuba would be a failure that would need rectification. Thus, even as Lippman and Khrushchev sat down to discuss ways to ease the strain between the missile empires, events were making such an accomplishment impossible.

O N THIS, OUR SECOND VISIT, MY wife and I were taken on a long journey by plane and auto to Mr. Khrushchev's country place in Sochi on the Black Sea. Before we left Moscow, accompanied by two interpreters and an official of the Press Department, there was much mystery about all the details of the coming visit, such as when and where we were to see the great man. In fact, as it turned out, he had no other appointments after half past eleven in the morning, when he met us in the pinewoods near the entrance of his place. Eight hours later, a bit worn by much talk and two large meals, we insisted on leaving in order to go to bed.

I would not like to leave the impression that all eight hours were devoted to great affairs of the world. Perhaps, all told, three and a half hours were spent in serious talk. The rest of the time went into the two prolonged meals at which Mr. Khrushchev, who is on what appears to be a non-fattening diet, broke the rules, saying joyously that the doctor had gone to Moscow for a day or two. The talk was largely banter between Mr. Khrushchev and Mikoyan (First Deputy Premier), who joined us for lunch, and the banter turned chiefly on Armenian food and Armenian wine and Armenian customs, which include the compulsion to drink all glasses to the end at each toast. Though we all drank a bit more than we wanted, Mikoyan chose to regard us as American ascetics who only sipped their wine. Finally Mr. Khrushchev took pity on us by providing a bowl into which we could pour the wine as fast as Mikoyan filled our glasses.

Between this heroic eating and drinking we walked around the place, which is large, met Mr. Khrushchev's grandson and Mikoyan's granddaughter, inspected the new and very gadgety swimming pool and, believe it or not, played badminton with Mr. Khrushchev.

In the serious talks, I might say that my wife made fairly full notes, I made a few jottings, but there was no transcript and the translating was done very ably by Mr. Victor M. Sukhodrev, who is an official in the Foreign Ministry. It was understood that I was free to write what I liked when I had left Russia and to quote Mr. Khrushchev or not to quote him as seemed desirable. I shall set down my own understanding and interpretation of the most important and interesting points that he made.

For an opening I reminded him that we had last seen him in October 1958, nearly a year before his visit to the United States. Much has happened in these two and a half years and would he tell me what seemed to him the most important events for good or evil?

After a moment or two of hesitation, he replied that during this period the two main forces in the world—the Capitalist, and the Socialist—have concluded that it was useless to "test" the backing of their political aims by the threat of war.

In contrast with 1958 when he professed to believe that the United States and Germany might attack him, he spoke with confidence that, because of the growing strength of the Communist orbit, the threat of war from our side was dying down. As a result, the United States was abandoning the "Dulles doctrine" that the neutrality of small states is "immoral." He himself welcomed President Kennedy's proposals for a neutral Laos.

You think then, I asked him, that there has been a change in United States policy? To this he replied that while there were some signs of a change, as for example in Laos, it was not a "radical" change, as could be seen in the United States attitude toward disarmament. What, I asked him, is wrong with the United States attitude? We cannot see, he replied, that any change is imminent when the subject of disarmament is put in the hands of such a believer in armaments as Mr. McCloy. We think well of Mr. McCloy and during his time in Germany we had good relations with him. But asking him to deal with disarmament is a case of asking the goat to look after the cabbage patch.

I interjected the remark that the final decisions would be made by the President. But Mr. Khrushchev insisted that the forces behind the President would determine his policy. These forces behind the Kennedy administration he summed up in the one word "Rockefeller." The view that he is running the Kennedy administration will be news to Gov. Rockefeller. I should add that Mr. Khrushchev considers me a Republican, which will be news to Mr. Nixon.

Then we got onto the subject of nuclear testing. He said that the Western powers were not ready to conclude an agreement and that this was shown, among other things, by the demand for twenty-one or perhaps nineteen inspections a year.

He had been led personally to believe that the West would be satisfied with

The New York *Herald Tribune* covers the Cuban crisis.

about three "symbolic" inspections. Nineteen inspections, our present demand, were nothing but a demand for the right to conduct complete reconnaissance of the Soviet Union.

I asked him about his attitude towards underground testing. He replied that the U.S.S.R. has never done any underground testing and never will. I asked why? Because, he said, we do not see any value in small, tactical atomic weapons. If it comes to war, we shall use only the biggest weapons. The smaller ones are very expensive and they can decide nothing.

The fact that they are expensive doesn't bother you because you don't care what you spend and what is more many of your generals are connected with big business. But in the U.S.S.R. we have to economize, and tactical weapons are a waste. I report this without having the technical expertise to comment on it.

Then we went on to say that the second reason why he had no great hopes of an agreement was that the French are now testing and are unlikely to sign the agreement. It is obvious, he said, that if the French are not in the agreement, they will do the testing for the Americans. To which, I said, and the Chinese will do the testing for you. He paused and then said that this was a fair remark. But, he added, while China is moving in the direction where she will be able to make tests, she is not yet able to make them. When the time comes that she can, there will be a new problem. We would like all states to sign a nuclear agreement.

Finally, he came to his third reason why an agreement may not be possible. It turns on the problem of the administrator of the agreement. Here, he was vehement and unqualified. He would never accept a single neutral administrator. Why? Because, he said, while there are neutral countries, there are no neutral men. You would not accept a Communist administrator and I cannot accept a non-Communist administrator. I will never en-

trust the security of the Soviet Union to any foreigner. We cannot have another Hammarskjold, no matter where he comes from among the neutral countries.

I found this enlightening. It was plain to me that here is a new dogma, that there are no neutral men. After all the Soviet Union had accepted Trygve Lie and Hammarskjold. The Soviet Government has now come to the conclusion that there can be no such thing as an impartial civil servant in this deeply divided world and that the kind of political celibacy which the British theory of the civil service calls for is in international affairs a fiction. This new dogma has long consequences. It means that there can be international co-operation only if, in the administration as well as in the policy-making, the Soviet Union has a veto.

IN RETROSPECT

Americans had barely finished defeating the Axis powers on European fields and Pacific islands when a slew of anxieties took root. Inflation, spurred by postwar demobilization, and a momentary spurt in unemployment rekindled bitter memories of the Great Depression. And the inability to come to peacetime terms with the erstwhile Soviet ally divided the West and hardened attitudes. Just as World War II followed World War I, was it not only a matter of time before World War III summoned Americans to the battlefield? But rather than another global conflagration, the cold war was fought both at home and abroad in a series of skirmishes as deadly and precarious as ever witnessed. For the next forty-five years, the cold war's ebb and flows, crises, and détentes shaped and reshaped American commitments and values. Korea, Vietnam, oil shocks, malaise, ICBMs. At times a confused population could barely keep up with events.

In fact, the bombing of Pearl Harbor and the declarations of war had not healed the U.S.-Soviet rift but, simply, iced it for a handful of years. The Soviet refusal to clear out of occupied Eastern Europe, its aiding of insurgents in Greece, and its support of Mao and his Communist forces in China reconfirmed Moscow's intent on world conquest. At first America responded with dollars for European reconstruction and guns for combatants in Greece and Turkey. The results were encouraging—the Red tide in

Europe and the Mediterranean was stemmed without U.S. troop commitments. Given a breather, former GIs went back to work and a corps of riveting Rosies returned to their homes. The baby boom and the American century of suburban growth and prosperity had begun.

By 1950, however, the future appeared as dark as a bomb shelter. Inexplicably, Washington had lost China and the Soviets had the bomb. Initial good news from Korea turned bad faster than it took a horde of Chinese infantrymen to cross the Korean border. Incredulous Americans agreed that the Koreans had only themselves to blame—more precisely, Communist traitors. The Red Scare had begun. From Washington to Hollywood, the nation cleansed itself. The Rosenburgs were executed, Alger Hiss faced a jury, and the electorate sent Ike to resolve the Korean "police action." In the American backyard, Guatemalan Communists were kicked out of power. With suburbia spreading west and interstates paving roads to Disneyland and Dodger Stadium, the country breathed easier. By the mid-1950s, Americans could afford to tune out world politics and tune in to "Ozzie and Harriet."

The calm and turbulent phases of the cold war continued in the 1960s. Americans had grown accustomed to the roller-coaster nature of mid-twentieth-century life. What they did not understand was that as the pendulum swings gravitated farther and farther from the center, a serious rupture lay ahead. Early on that looked unlikely to occur. The 1960s saw the culmination of the consumer society. The Ford Mustang and the proliferation of household appliances heralded the modern age. The Soviet backpedaling at the Cuban Missile Crisis trumpeted the might of American resolve and firepower as well. In nearly twenty years of cold war, Washington retained its containment perimeter, pacified Europe and Asia, spurred unprecedented prosperity at home, and beat the Russians to the moon.

Yet fissures appeared on the American landscape. In the North and the South, restless black Americans sought equal rights and protection under the law. The orphans of the New Deal, an impoverished underclass, continued to struggle. In Selma, Alabama, the confrontations between civil rights activists and southern segregationists turned ugly—as it had in plenty of other places. Race riots and the plight of the poor raised questions about the American dream. Suddenly the white hat America wore in the cold war looked grayer and grayer. Meanwhile, the violence that Americans had avoided overseas was present at home. Political assassinations, race riots, and shootings at college campuses nauseated the nation. Television, the mark of the affluent society, now beamed images of Americans dying not only in Vietnam but in Watts, at Kent State, and in suburban America, too, as the crime rate skyrocketed. The young—the children of the American dream—turned to the counterculture of sex, drugs and rock'n roll. A Great Society? Far from it. The cold war abroad had become a hot war on American streets.

In a desperate measure to regain its dreams, America turned, first, to a law-and-order stalwart and, after, to a quasi-religious revivalist. Richard Nixon promised peace with honor and a return to sensibility. His declaration of détente with the Soviets and his trip to China eased pressure at home. By calling a time-out in the U.S.-Soviet competition, Nixon hoped to buy the time necessary to cool passions at home. But frustrated by the complexity of wage and price controls, a free-floating dollar, and Vietnamization, the president's mood grew dark and bleak. His appeal to rule of law became hollow as the silent majority came to believe he was a crook. His born again successor, Jimmy Carter, held the country's trust but fared little better in solving its crisis of confidence and energy. Carter planned to use Nixon's détente to patch up oil shortages and Middle East quarrels. But domestic inflation, recession, and hostages befuddled the Georgian and malaise set in. The Soviet invasion of Afghanistan closed the window on détente, and on the Carter presidency as well.

It took the last of the revivalists, Ronald Reagan, to fight the final battles of the cold war—and claim victory while assuring his place in history. Reagan reasserted the cold war as the nation's top priority. He raised defense spending to astronomical levels and sent mercenaries. Focused on domestic problems for over a decade, Americans had not realized that behind the iron curtain, the Soviet economy was on life support. Forty years of military budgets, inefficient central planning, and propping of client regimes had permanently sapped its strength. When Reagan and his counterpart, Mikhail Gorbachev, met during a series of summits in the mid-1980s, arms control was on the agenda. In retrospect, the two men were discussing terms of conditional surrender— terms that would collapse the Berlin Wall and yank the hammer-and-sickle banner from Kremlin flagpoles. Gorbachev sought glasnost and perestroika. He got McDonald's and IBM in Red Square.

Paradoxically, while the forty years of cold war scared an anxious population, it also had the converse effect of soothing its frayed nerves. In a tumultuous world of brinkmanship and limited wars, the cold war offered simple answers to complex problems. The Soviets and their Communist allies were easy to blame for all that was wrong in the world. In the post cold war world, the maladies and afflictions of the past remain. What is gone, then, is the simple answer. In some ways, that is more unsettling.

THE VIETNAM WAR

"A NEW KIND OF WAR"

1960–1975

JOHN F. KENNEDY USED TO TELL a story about the outbreak of World War I. After diplomatic negotiations during the long summer of 1914 deteriorated into war, German chancellor Bethmann-Hollweg was approached by his predecessor, Prince von Bülow. "How did it all begin?" Von Bülow asked. Bethmann-Hollweg answered slowly, "If only one could say." So it was with Americans throughout the 1960s as they debated over a war in which victory seemed unattainable and defeat unacceptable. No one could say how it happened, but as they looked back at the end most could say it shouldn't have.

From the Truman and Eisenhower regimes, President Kennedy had inherited a commitment to preventing a Communist takeover in South Vietnam. The small, weak Southeast Asian country had been formed in 1954 from a coastal strip of the former French colony of Indochina. To keep this tiny ally from going down "the Red drain," Kennedy increased aid to the South Vietnamese government. Where President Truman had sent thirty-five military advisers and President Eisenhower had sent some five hundred more, Kennedy sent sixteen thousand.

No roars of protest went up from the public; no eyebrows rose in Congress; no editorialists thundered as the United States suffered its first casualties and increased its aid in materiel and in men. For the American presence in Vietnam was completely in line with Truman's popular policy, established in 1947, of stopping cold any Communist advances anywhere in the world, from Korea to Berlin.

The United States crept into the war and then found it could neither duck nor run from it. Presidents Truman, Eisenhower, and Kennedy sent advisers to help the South Vietnamese fight their war. Next, President Lyndon Johnson, who in the end was blamed for the loss, sent American airmen to assist South Vietnamese infantry assaults, then U.S. Marines to protect U.S. airstrips. Before Americans knew it, Vietnam was their war.

At home, Americans were stumbling through a labyrinth of change. Many were forever stunned by the murder of John Kennedy. The Supreme Court ruled that reading the Lord's Prayer in schools was unconstitutional. *The Feminine Mystique* disputed notions of traditional American home and gender roles. The War on Poverty and the British rock invasion challenged America's leadership.

In the midst of the Tet offensive, John S. Carroll of the Baltimore *Sun* surveyed the effects of the battle on the U.S. embassy. After reporting the carnage on the building's front lawn, Carroll quoted a marine who succinctly summed up the victory: "We kept them out. They did not get into the building." Most stories depicted the bravery of the GIs fighting a difficult battle. Lee Lescaze wrote of the fighting that Bravo Company faced in the city of Hue: "The street fighting in Hue is terrifying. There is cover everywhere and nowhere. Walk into a street and a sniper may kill you. . . . Run into a building and you may find an enemy soldier there, waiting."

Vietcong prisoners on the Mekong Delta, 1962. *(Larry Burrows/LIFE © Time, Inc.)*

But other news dispatches reflected an uneasiness with the behavior of the American troops. Reporter Charles Mohr told how U.S. Marines looted the homes of Vietnamese civilians after retaking a section of Hue. "Under such circumstances," Mohr explained, "some looting was inevitable." But this was not what Americans had read about in earlier wars. In 1969, hearing of the March 1968 My Lai massacre, many Americans stopped supporting the troops and the cause.

The mounting losses and lack of progress in Vietnam gnawed away at U.S. confidence. In 1970 the escalation of domestic protest against the war exploded at Kent State. The report on that tragedy from Al Thompson of the Cleveland *Press* read almost like a dispatch from the front. He wrote: "I hit the dirt as the bullets flew, but I saw the students' faces frozen with utter disbelief as they were shot and fell—wounded or dead." In the televised and written reports arriving from Vietnam—and from American campuses—war lost its heroic, romantic, and adventurous luster. It never actually had any of the above, but now Americans on the homefront were seeing it too.

Even critics who accepted the idea that America must fight assailed the conduct of the war. William F. Buckley, Jr., expressed the frustration of watching the thrashing that the seemingly inferior ranks of Vietnamese jungle fighters inflicted on America's mighty forces. "We need to hit back with such weapons as we are in a position to use to spare us the most precious commodity we have, the American soldier," he wrote vehemently.

President Johnson sent more and more young men and women to battle, but the war dragged on. Americans were fed up and university campuses became centers of opposition to the war. Unlike in other American conflicts, opponents to the war gained the upper hand. Protests, sit-ins and love-ins gained the attention of the press and the televised media. Johnson's successor, Richard Nixon, promised "peace with honor" but could attain neither. Nor could he quell demands by the vocal opposition to get America out of Vietnam.

Finally, a settlement allowed Washington to exit the conflict with a modicum of dignity in 1973. But that dignity collapsed in April 1975, when the last marines and embassy personnel scrambled out of Saigon in ignominious fashion. Peter Arnett, who witnessed the frenzied evacuation of Saigon, noted that it "pointed up the failure of the whole war effort as dramatically as any military defeat."

Perhaps the most important lesson of Vietnam was summed up by a POW named Daly. The war, he said, was fought "without understanding anything about the country beyond a few cliches." That was the key to the American failure in Vietnam. Affluent Americans had misjudged and underestimated the Vietnamese in their "black pajamas." The harder Washington attempted to fight the war, the more injury, disruption, and chaos it brought to a peasant society long used to repelling foreign invaders. Americans seemed unable to make sense of the complexities; when frustration set in, they simply demanded to get out.

ROBERT P. MARTIN

"JUNGLE WAR FROM THE INSIDE: AN EYEWITNESS REPORT"

U.S. NEWS & WORLD REPORT, OCTOBER 30, 1961

In the fall of 1961, while the U.S. role in Vietnam was still that of "adviser," Robert P. Martin wandered through the villages of South Vietnam to get a firsthand view of what President Kennedy's man on the scene, Maxwell Taylor, was up against. Kennedy had entered the White House nine months before, promising to "pay the price" and to meet the Communist challenge in every village and hut on the globe. On the heels of the defeat at the Bay of Pigs, U.S. forces were now trying to enforce the containment line in Vietnam. At the time, most Americans, like Martin, understood little about the Southeast Asian republic, except that it was the scene of a firefight between freedom and the "Reds."

The nuance within this account vividly portrayed the challenge. In fact, the United States was not only going to help defend the Vietnamese from Communist aggression but also to begin the process of "nation building." Beyond providing arms and protection, it was the duty of Americans to provide the basic structures of civilization. Thus, Vietnam became the ideal test case for Kennedy's best and brightest—a place to defeat communism and mold a nation. But in this quest, as Martin noted, the United States had better get busy. The Communists had been building support and, as elsewhere, the United States was playing catch-up in Vietnam.

I N THIS VILLAGE OF 500 PEOPLE, more or less, you can see and feel the jungle war that is slowly strangling South Vietnam.

Lac Tien is a place few Americans ever heard of. It sits on the edge of a beautiful lake in the heart of what must be one of the richest rice-growing areas in all of Asia.

Most of the villagers are lowlanders, Vietnamese from coastal areas who were resettled here by the Government in an effort to fill a vacuum that the Communists could exploit.

Outside Lac Tien are clusters of straw-thatched "long houses"—the homes of the primitive mountain people known by the French name of *montagnards,* or "mountaineers." They consider this their land, just as the American Indians once regarded the vast expanse of mountains and prairies as their own.

A few miles distant is the edge of the lush, nearly impenetrable jungle. In the jungle are tigers, elephants, boars and—most dangerous of all—the Viet Cong, or South Vietnamese Communists.

From their jungle bases the Reds are trying to build the skeleton of a "liberated area" which can be transformed into a government that will take over all of South Vietnam.

A MISSIONARY AND A RED.

IN LAC TIEN AT THIS MOMENT ARE two men of interest to Americans. One is Henry F. Blood, a 42-year-old Pennsylvanian who lives here with his wife, Evangeline. The other is Ybang, a tribesman who thinks he is "about 20." He can neither read nor write. He knows nothing about Communism or Leninism. But, until he was captured recently, Ybang was an armed Viet Cong guerrilla, fighting on the side of the Communists.

"This was a peaceful place when we first came here," says Mr. Blood. "We could take our bikes and ride 10 miles or more in any direction. Now we must stay inside Lac Tien, and who knows when we'll have to evacuate from here."

Mr. Blood's job is to develop a written language for the *montagnards*, and, in the process, produce a Bible they can read. He has lived on the high plateau for 16 months.

The Bloods, with their 20-month-old daughter, Cindy, were in Lac Tien when the Communists hit.

The Reds came in the middle of the night, screaming and shooting. The Bloods hid in their back room and knelt behind a half dozen oil drums. They could hear the Communists ransacking the village. They prayed: "The name of the Lord is a strong tower; the righteous runneth into it, and is safe."

The Communists left just before dawn. Their band—about 100 men—burned seven Government buildings, ransacked the village of food, killed two home guards and captured the weapons of the others. The Communists took 30 villagers and five home guards with them, releasing all but two within 48 hours. Those two decided to stay with the guerrillas.

The Bloods and others familiar with the high plateau do not think the mountaineers are pro-Communist. But the available evidence indicates that the sim-

ple tribesmen do not trust their Government.

Promises of money and jobs have not been kept. Appointed local officials are all Vietnamese, most of whom do not speak the tribal dialects.

Also, the Communists kill a few people, but mostly district chiefs whom the tribesmen call "bad people." On the other hand, the loyal Air Force recently dropped napalm bombs on a nearby village suspected of harboring Communists, and killed 37 *montagnards*. The raid can be justified as a military necessity, but it also enraged the tribesmen.

The story told by Ybang, the captured guerrilla, shows how the Communists operate among the mountain people.

Ybang belonged to a unit of 50 men, 30 of them mountaineers. They slept in the jungle, using nylon hammocks made in China, and had about three bowls of rice a day, plus whatever fish or game they could catch.

Military training was meager. Ybang was given a World War I–type French rifle. He was not permitted to practice with live ammunition because bullets were scarce. Going on a raid, he was issued two pouches containing 30 rounds of ammunition.

Leaders of the unit, far better armed than Ybang, had been trained in Communist North Vietnam. When not training their unit, or marching it through the jungle, the leaders gave the men indoctrination lectures. The men were expected to return to their villages and spread the word.

Ybang did not hear the word "Communism" used, ever. He was told that when Vietnam was unified, the tribesmen would be given back their land and would have their own government. Over and over, he and the others heard the declaration: "This is a difficult life now, but we are working for a new and happy life in the future."

The Communists live in the jungle, protected by its cover and secure from Government attacks through a network of spies and agents who report movements of every Government force, large or small. The Reds attack only when the time, place and conditions are weighted in their favor. If they miscalculate and find the defenses stronger than they expect, they merely melt into the jungle and wait for another time.

". . . UNTIL THEY STRIKE."

OUR GOVERNMENT FORCES ARE better armed. But officers admit the Communists have them running in circles. Maj. Nguyen Bang, the 34-year-old chief of Darlac Province, points wearily at his maps and says: "Not even half the trails are shown. We almost never know where the Viet Cong are until they strike. By the time we get our forces there they are gone."

A regimental commander with his headquarters in Banmethuot is responsible for the security of an area covering thousands of square miles. His platoons are scattered across three provinces. Day after day, they are in the jungle trying to track down guerrillas.

"It's an impossible job," he says. "Com-munist intelligence is so much better than ours that they know every move we make just as we make it."

Lately, the Communist units have been getting bigger. A few months ago the Reds used platoons for their attacks. Now they are able to group platoons into companies and even battalions, which means many Army bases are not as secure as they once were. Recently, an attacking force of 1,200 hit a resettlement village, overpowered the local guard and captured quantities of food and American equipment.

POISON-DART WARFARE.

ONLY THE HARD-CORE COMMU-nists—and nobody knows how many there really are—have up-to-date weapons. The bulk of their forces are tribesmen, many of whom wear only loincloths and who hunt with crossbows and poison darts. Often, in raids, they are armed only with spears and machetes.

But, as you travel across the high plateau, it is easy to see why the Government is waging a losing battle here.

Without the support, active or passive, of more than half a million mountain-dwelling tribesmen, the Communists could get nowhere.

The fact is that they have the support. And with it they have won control of the countryside in three provinces and are threatening to seize control of six more.

DAVID HALBERSTAM

"THE FACE OF THE ENEMY IN VIETNAM"

HARPER'S MAGAZINE, FEBRUARY 1965

As a correspondent for the New York Times, *David Halberstam was one of the first American reporters to challenge the official version of events in Vietnam and to write what he saw—disasters misrepresented as victories. In 1964 he shared a Pulitzer Prize for reporting of the Vietnam War with Malcolm W. Browne of the Associated Press; in 1965 he published an influential evaluation of U.S. policy in Vietnam,* The Making of a Quagmire *(Harper's Weekly).*

When President Kennedy tried nudging Arthur Ochs Sulzberger into reassigning Halberstam, the Times *publisher not only refused but delayed a two-week vacation Halberstam had scheduled. Sulzberger wanted to make clear that the* Times *would not bow to Kennedy's pressure. Later Halberstam's reporting would be proven accurate. On at least one occasion, even the State Department would admit that its official version was wrong and that Halberstam's version was essentially right.*

He was tough, indoctrinated, and ready to die, and in this endless relentless war of revolution the misery of the people was his constant source of strength.

BY MID-1962 THE AMERICAN MILItary assistance command in Vietnam was basking in its own optimism. It was a time when, in high levels of the American government, guerrilla warfare was becoming fashionable. In Saigon the first stage of our new and increased American commitment to South Vietnam had begun. Helicopters, new rifles, armored personnel carriers, and first-rate young American advisers had arrived. Top officials of our mission in Saigon, ordered by their superiors to be optimistic about the outcome of the war, remained excessively faithful.

The American high command had an exaggerated opinion of its own understanding of the type of war going on, and an insufficient awareness of the toughness and patience of the enemy. Yet for a reporter traveling regularly in the Mekong delta at that time, going on operations and talking with American field advisers, it was very hard to be optimistic about anything—particularly the enemy.

We never saw much of the enemy. We saw his handiwork—the ravaged outposts, the defenders with their heads blown off, their women lying dead beside them—but more often than not, the enemy only showed himself when he had superior strength. The first lesson that an American adviser in Vietnam learned was that the enemy was good; then if he stayed on a little longer, he learned that this was wrong; the enemy was very good. He learned that the Vietcong did very few things, but that they did them all well; they made few mistakes, and in sharp contrast to the government forces, they rarely repeated their mistakes. The American officers also learned that the enemy had a reason—political, psychological, or military—for almost everything he did. Even when he appeared to be doing nothing, we learned belatedly and bitterly that this did not mean that he was inactive, only that he was content to *appear* inactive.

If they paid attention, Americans also learned that the enemy was absolutely sincere; he was willing to pay the price for the difficult task he had set for himself, and he had a far better sense of these difficulties than the authorities in Saigon. If he was underrated in Saigon, this was certainly not the case in the field. There it was widely known that we were fighting the war on his terms.

The Vietcong had no illusions about the type of war in which they were engaged. It was a war of revolution, and they knew their own strengths and the weaknesses of the government. The Americans thought of them as men carrying weapons, but the fact was that they were most effective when they carried no weapons and wore no uniforms—at night when they indoctrinated the peasants. The misery of the people was their great ally, and they knew how to play on it.

Where Americans often parroted slogans about improving the world of the Vietnamese peasant, the Vietcong, who had risen from this misery themselves, knew that lip service was not enough. To them the war was entirely political; its military aspects were simply a means to permit them to practice their political techniques. They made every grievance theirs; long-standing historical grievances, whether against Asians or Caucasians, became *their* grievances, as were

economic inequities, the division of land, the whimsical system of tax collection, and even the ravages of disease.

GUERRILLA ARTISTS

AS THE VIETCONG ACHIEVED MILI- tary success through their political techniques, the government and the Americans responded with increased weaponry and more troops. But this did not mitigate the grievances; indeed, the increased number of troops often meant more bombings, more deaths, and more grievances.

The Vietcong's predecessors had developed their style of guerrilla fighting against the Chinese Nationalists, and a previous generation of their own countrymen had refined it in the war against the French. Guerrilla warfare is virtually an art form, and the Vietcong were more than craftsmen at their trade; they were artists. So knowledgeable and successful were the Vietcong that when American officers prepared for their tour in Vietnam, they read not the writings of the French or American tacticians, but the writings of the enemy. We were there because he had proven stronger than our allies; we were fighting a war on his soil, among his people, where he had been successful for twenty years.

The Vietcong, of course, were not the Vietminh [the group that fought the French during the Indochina War]; it was not that simple. For one thing, the American role was not comparable to the French; we were, after all, fighting to get out, whereas the French had fought to stay on. Yet to the enemy the heritage and the legacy were very much the same. To much of the peasantry the Vietcong was the same as the Vietminh; it dressed the same way, and it used exactly the same tactics and techniques.

Just as the Vietcong looked like the Vietminh, the government troops too often acted like the troops in the same uniforms who had fought during the days of the French: around the hamlets during the day, village chickens for lunch, and gone after 6:00 P.M., so that if some villager might be inclined to help the government, he would have no protection at night when the Vietcong arrived.

Inevitably, the government troops frequently played into the Communists' hands. The Vietcong would prophesy that the government troops would come, that they would be led by Americans, that this would mean bombings from planes piloted by Americans, and that this would mean the deaths of villagers. Sooner or later there would be a battle, there would be strafings of the village, and of course there would be troops with American advisers. That night or the next the Vietcong cadre in the area would arrive in the village and give out medical aid, and of course they would gain more recruits.

The Vietcong had prepared for this war long in advance. At the end of the Indochina war they had carefully set to work developing cadres, gathering ammunition and preparing weapon-storage points, digging secret cave-like hideaways and tunnels, and training cadres to take over the schools. They had had another advantage, for in the embryo years of a new nation they were the dissenters. It was the government's job to deliver; their job was only to sit by and criticize. In underdeveloped countries a new government starts out with a tiny number of trained people and must somehow develop a competent administrative staff. It cannot meet (at least no new government has met) the vast hopes of a newly independent people—expectations in education, standard of living, reforms, agriculture, or health.

Such new governments are inevitably clumsy; the Diem government was no worse than most. But in South Vietnam the problems were greater than in most other newly independent states. The French had left behind a civil service system based on corruption; Diem himself was a poor administrator; what little talent there was in the country was quickly siphoned off to the military—where if it was really outstanding it was ignored. Too often, all that the villagers saw were corrupt local officials who showed up often enough to collect taxes, but never long enough to provide services.

In addition, the Vietcong had years of experience behind them. As one American intelligence officer told me, "The trouble with this war is that everywhere in the countryside they have some political commissar who's been fighting revolutionary warfare on the winning side for twenty years, with all the training and professionalism that means, and up against him we've got someone who, if he's trained at all, was trained by the Americans or the French, and who has been on the losing side." Because competent officials who were a threat to the Vietcong soon were murdered, there was a tendency toward fence-straddling on the part of local officials. While sending in enthusiastic progress reports, they tried not to see what the enemy was do-ing; in effect they had come to a gentle-man's agreement, and thus provided a vacuum in which the Vietcong could work.

THE CALL OF GRIEVANCE

THE VIETCONG STARTED WITH THEIR people when they were very young—the younger the better. They offered them ad-venture and excitement. They advertised themselves as the enemies of oppression, as the heralders of a better world, but they always did it at the most basic level. If land were the grievance in one commu-nity, their appeal was based on land re-form; if bad local government was the source of unhappiness, the Vietcong would murder the government leader publicly while the peasants watched. To a young boy growing up in the total depri-vation of an Asian backland, dimly aware of the discrepancy between his life and that of other wealthier Asians, the ene-my's call had great appeal—particularly when a member of the Vietcong ran the local school. Soon the youngsters would be involved as bearers for the troops or as messengers, earning advancement only on merit, and fully committed every step of the way. There was a thoroughness in their political indoctrination which was completely missing on the government side. Before a youth could hold a Vietcong rifle he would have first undergone long political and psychological training. He *believed;* his, he was sure, was a righteous cause. He was liberating his people, the government was cruel and was owned by the Americans, his war was to liberate his countrymen from the Americans, just as his father had liberated half of the coun-

try from the French. Even the capturing of weapons had a twofold purpose, it was part of the mystique that they were the poor robbing the rich. For this reason the Vietcong often went to great lengths to capture weapons when they could more easily have smuggled them into the coun-try; it gave them an intense pride and sense of self-reliance.

This, then, was the human raw mate-rial: tough, indoctrinated, willing, and ready to die; men of great physical endur-ance who had known few softening dis-tractions in a lifetime of hardship. The leadership was equally good. The battal-ion commanders were usually men who had fought in the Indochina war. Though they were Southerners, and usually from the specific area in which they would serve, they had been given additional training in the North. The best of a good army, they had fought for twenty years and had risen on the ability to get along—and they knew that they would lose their jobs if they made mistakes. They also had a sense of military cunning that few Americans took into account. During these twenty years they had fought con-stantly against an enemy which had supe-rior weaponry, machinery, and air power. To survive was to be wily; to be careless, sloppy, or indifferent meant sure death. They could never rely on an air strike or on armored personnel carriers to bail them out of trouble; rather, there would be air strikes to wipe them out and am-phibious armored carriers to crush them. They had to be elusive; "Their command-ers," an American captain once told me, "have a sixth sense about their flanks. It is almost impossible to surround them."

In this war where commanders exer-cised their resources carefully, the ambush was a vital ingredient; it risked relatively little manpower and it often gained much. Always there were preordained escape routes. In addition to killing government troops and capturing weapons, the ambush had a psychological advantage. It scared government troops, made them less anxious to leave their bases, and it slowly helped to dry up government access to the countryside, thus allowing the Vietcong to move around that much more freely. Frequently an attack was made only to set up an ambush; thus, the attack might be a minor part of the operation, the major Vietcong objective being to ambush the relief columns. For this reason there was little enthusiasm on the part of government troops to come to the aid of their less fortunate colleagues under attack.

By nature the Vietnamese are afraid of the night and of the jungle. Very early in a young man's career the Vietcong broke his fear of the night. Instead, the guerrillas were taught that the night was their friend, the enemy of the white man and his airplanes. The dark became a way of life with the Vietcong: they lived, taught, traveled, and fought at night. The same was true with the jungle. The Vietcong came to know and use the tropical forests as their countrymen under the government flag never would.

The Vietcong's military commanders were completely under the control of their political commissars. Every decision was based first on political needs, only secondarily on military ones. "If we give them a licking in a certain area," said one American officer, "we can expect almost certainly within ten days or so that they'll knock off a pretty good-sized outpost in the same neighborhood, just to show the flag and let the peasants know they're still in business."

WAR FROM A HELICOPTER

THE FIRST TIME ONE SEES A MEMber of the Vietcong there is a sharp sense of disappointment. He is not, it turns out, very different; he is simply another Vietnamese. Generally when you see him he is either kneeling and firing at you, or he has just been captured, or, more often than not, he is dead. The bodies of enemy dead are always lined up, feet all in an orderly row. The guerrilla wears little, perhaps a simple peasant pajama suit, perhaps only shorts. He is slim and wiry, and his face could be that of your interpreter or of the taxi driver who drove you to My Tho. Only the haircut is different, very thin along the sides and very long on top and in front. It is a bad haircut and, like the frailness of the uniform and the thin wallet with only a few pictures of some peasant woman, it makes the enemy human. But one's sympathy does not last long; this is the same face which has been seen by the outnumbered defenders of some small outpost before it was overrun.

There were not many operations in which Vietcong were caught; there were few prisoners in this war. One of the rare exceptions to this that I ever observed took place in April 1963, when I accompanied the new armed-helicopter units in the upper Camau peninsula on what were known as Eagle flights. An Eagle flight is risky business; it means that a small number of elite troops circle above the paddies in the choppers looking for likely targets. When an objective is sighted the helicopters drop out of the sky, virtually on top of hamlets, and the troops make a quick search, probing and scouting. If the enemy is there, other regular units, waiting in the rear with other helicopters, will be thrown in quickly. But dropping swiftly out of the sky and exploring the unknown with a handful of troops is sometimes terrifying. The helicopters have the visibility of a press box, but one is watching a war instead of a football game. When you drop out of the sky, little men rush to different positions, kneel, and start firing at the press box while your own tracers seek them out.

On that day in April 1963, the 21st Recon company, a particularly good company made up largely of troops who had fought with the Vietminh during the Indochina war, was with us. We were scouting a hard-core Vietcong battalion, moving along a line of villages which we thought the battalion had been using as its main line of communication in that region—the upper Camau peninsula was a notorious enemy stronghold.

At about 8:30 A.M. we saw some movement in a village below, followed by a few light crackles around us. It was ground fire; the bait had been taken. We came in low once over the village and saw some men scurrying to positions. Three of the helicopters, including our own, dropped their troops while the others circled and strafed some of the positions. We were making our advance on the tree line under fire when we saw one man in a black suit desperately running across the open field. It was the dry season and the fields were of sun-caked mud. Suddenly a helicopter descended almost on top of the man, and he stopped and held up his hands. The Vietnamese commander ran over to him. There was no weapon on this Vietcong; neither was there any of the

bowing or scraping that local guerrillas who posed as farmers sometimes employed.

This enemy was angry and defiant, and at first a little scared as well—until he saw me and spit at me. The commander slapped his face very hard and said something in Vietnamese. Later I was told that the captain had said to the prisoner, "The Americans are very kind. They do not kill, and they are always telling us not to kill you, but I am not so kind and I will kill you. You will see." The interpreter thought this was very funny. "You know, the enemy takes these young boys and they tell them how fierce you Americans are, and so they are all convinced that the Americans will eat their hearts for breakfast as soon as they are captured. The captain is right; you have no real taste for this war." The Vietnamese commander said that the captured guerrilla was well indoctrinated. "They are taught well to hate," he said, a little apologetically.

The captain said that the guerrilla was probably a squad leader from an elite battalion operating in the area. Then the officer turned and spoke briefly and intensely to the guerrilla. He was telling the prisoner that they would kill him unless he talked—and perhaps they would kill him by throwing him out of the helicopter. "The captain is very smart," the interpreter said. "It will be the guerrilla's first helicopter ride and he will be very scared." They tied up the guerrilla and placed him in the helicopter, and the captain and I walked back across the open field to the village. We could hear a good deal of firing, and as always I hunched over as much as I could, but the Vietnamese officer strolled casually. He carried a small swagger stick, and he looked as if he were a large landowner making an inspection of the plantation. I was impressed.

By the time we reached the village the troops had rounded up two more guerrillas. There was no pretense on their part that they were farmers; they had fought until they began to take fire not only from the ground but from some of the nine other helicopters in the area. They had surrendered. One, about nineteen years old, gave the captain a look of defiance and turned away from him. But the other, who might have been twenty-five, gave him a curious look. "Maybe," the captain said later, "he is a little more tired of the war and propaganda. We shall see. The other will not talk." He was right, the next morning the older one confessed that they were members of a battalion which had hit two outposts in the Camau the week before and had come here to rest. This guerrilla was tired; he had been fighting too long, for seven years, and he wanted to leave the army.

At the appointed minute, the troops were back. They had found an American carbine, and the captain was surprised because it was more than he had expected. The weapon had been found in a false thatch in a roof. The captain was pleased. "Good troops," he told me. "When they search they want to find something, and when they fight they want to kill." Then the helicopters returned and we all jumped in and prepared for the next assault.

The next two villages produced only some homemade grenades made by an old farmer. "The local guerrilla," said the Vietnamese captain. These were the lowest of the three types of Vietcong. They farmed in the day and fought at night,

and they had the worst weapons. When I first came to Vietnam their arms were all homemade, but by the time I left they were using French equipment and even some American M-1s. But even in April 1963, in a village where there were no other weapons, a homemade grenade or rifle has great power.

DEATH IN THE PADDY

THE LOCAL GUERILLAS WERE A vital part of the communist apparatus. They gave a village a sense of communist continuity, they could provide intelligence on government activities, serve as a local security force for a traveling commissar, or they could guide the hard-core Vietcong troops. This last was particularly important to the success and mobility of the guerrillas; everywhere they went they had trained local guides to steer them through seemingly impenetrable areas. Because of these local men, the enemy's elite could often move twenty-five miles in five hours, which meant that a raiding force attacking at night was almost impossible to find by daylight. These local guerrillas were also part of the propaganda network, for in a village they might be the only ones with a radio. Sometimes it was only the shell of a radio, but the local man would pretend he could hear news and would give out information of Vietcong victories.

We flew back to the base to refuel, and then returned to the area. Suddenly out of one village came a flock of Vietcong, running across the paddy, and intense fire came from the tree line. While five of our ships emptied their troops, the rest of the choppers strafed the area. We bore down on one fleeing Vietcong. The paddy's surface was rough and his run was a staggered one, like that of a good but drunken broken-field runner against imaginary tacklers. We came closer and closer; inside the helicopter I could almost hear him gasping for breath, and as we bore down I could see the heaving of his body. It was like watching a film of one of your own nightmares, but in this case we were the pursuers rather than the pursued. The pilot fired his machine guns, but he missed and the man kept going. Then came a flash of orange and a blast of heat inside the ship, and the helicopter rocked with the recoil of its rockets. As they exploded the man fell, and he lay still as we went over him. But as we turned he scrambled to his feet, still making for the canal, now only about fifty yards away. As we circled and swept toward him again, he was straining for the bank, like a runner nearing the finish line. We had one last shot at him. The guerrilla made a desperate surge and our copilot fired one last burst of the machine gun. The bullets cut him down as he reached the canal, and his body skidded on the hard bank as he collapsed.

We turned and circled again. All over the paddy field, helicopters were rounding up Vietcong soldiers. It was like a rodeo. We landed near the village which members of the Recon company were searching. The troops were gentler with the population than most of the government soldiers I had seen. In front of one hut a medic was treating a wounded guerrilla.

"I have never taken this many prisoners before," the captain said. There were sixteen of them. He turned to one of his men. "Show the American the poor little farmer," he said. They brought in a wiry

young man. "This one says he is a farmer," the officer said. He pushed the young man in front of me and flipped the prisoner's palms over. "He has very soft hands for a farmer," the captain said. "He has the hands of a bar girl in Saigon. He is not a very good soldier yet. In a few months, though, he might have been very good."

The prisoner was beginning to tremble. The conversation in a foreign language obviously frightened him, and I was sure that this was why the captain was using English. I asked the captain what kind of enemy we had surprised. "Territorial," he said. This was the middle rank of Vietcong guerrillas; we called them provincial guerrillas. They operated in groups of up to one hundred and were often attached to the hard-core units to beef up their strength for a major attack; they also hit smaller outposts. "The leadership was not very good," the captain said. "There were many prisoners. If it had been a hard-core unit I think there would have been more fighting and more dying. I think we surprised them."

ENDLESS AND WITHOUT RULES

WE HIT ONE MORE VILLAGE AND drew minimal resistance. But as I was walking toward the tree line I suddenly heard shouts and cries all around me. I was terrified, for I was about fifty yards from the nearest soldier and I had no weapon. Suddenly from deep bomb shelters all around me about thirty women and children stood up; they were crying and pointing at me and wailing. Clearly they were scared. Judging from its defensive preparations this was a Vietcong village, and for years these people had heard propaganda about vicious Americans like me. As far as I was concerned they were dangerous too, and we stood looking at each other in mutual fear.

I yelled out to Major James Butler and asked him what to do. Butler suggested that I try to give a good impression of Americans. "Protect our image," he said. Later he congratulated me on being the first *New York Times* correspondent ever to capture twenty-five Vietcong women and children. I gladly turned them over to the Vietnamese captain.

The troops were remarkably restrained in what was obviously a Vietcong village. At times the quick change in Vietnamese behavior was amazing. At one moment they could be absolutely ruthless; in the next they might be talking to some prisoner as if he were an old friend. It was different with the enemy; I was told by those who had been captured by them during the Indochina war that they were not so tolerant. This was hardly surprising. Much emphasis was placed on teaching them how to hate. They were the have-nots fighting the haves, and even after capture their feelings rarely changed.

We flew back to Baclieu. It had been a good day. There had been few government losses, and there was a chance that from all those prisoners we might learn something important. Everyone was tired and relaxed and happy. If nothing else the day seemed to prove the value of the Huey Eagle helicopter flights. Only Mert Perry, of *Time*, who had also come along to observe the new strategy, seemed a bit depressed. It had been a good day, he agreed, and in one way the government had done very well. But after all, he pointed out, it was a pretty limited business and in the long run it might backfire. There was no follow-up, no one in the villages that night working with the people. These peasants had seen helicopters; they had seen killing, and they had seen their men disappear. The conclusions that the villagers would draw were obvious—particularly if the Vietcong were in those very villages at this moment. Every man taken today, Mert said, must have a brother or a son or a brother-in-law who would take his place after today.

We listened to Perry in silence, for we knew that he was right. The government had scored a quick victory, but in Vietnam victories were not always what they seemed. It was an endless, relentless war to which ordinary military rules did not apply. We went to bed that night a little less confident, knowing that though for a moment the enemy was paying a higher price, he was still out there somewhere in the darkness living close to the peasants.

LARRY BURROWS

"YANKEE PAPA 13"

LIFE, APRIL 16, 1965

Larry Burrows claimed there was only one way to illustrate war: to get out in the field with the men he photographed and take their fears and dangers as his own. Before he arrived in

Southeast Asia, the British-born Burrows had seen sporadic conflict in the Middle East, having covered the Suez crisis, the U.S. landing in Lebanon, and confrontations in Cyprus and the Congo. In 1962 Burrows began snapping pictures in Vietnam and soon became a fixture on the U.S. helicopter patrol circuit for LIFE *magazine.*

*To shoot his pictures, Burrows was out in the field with the men he photographed, their dangers and fears becoming his own. He took risks, but always knowing what he was doing, always planning, always aware of his surroundings and his own vulnerability. His deepest wish—to photograph both South and North Vietnam in a time of peace—was not granted: he died in a helicopter crash in Laos in February 1971. Burrows believed in being prepared and he was easily identifiable by the battery of cameras dangling from his neck and shoulders at all times. The pictures and account of the "Yankee Papa 13" are a testimony to his courage and his influence. (All photos Larry Burrows/*LIFE*, Time, Inc.)*

IT WAS ANOTHER DAY'S WORK for the U.S. Marines' Helicopter Squadron 163 in Vietnam. In the sultry morning the crews huddled at Da Nang for the final briefing on their mission: to airlift a battalion of Vietnamese infantry to an isolated area about 20 miles away. Intelligence reports indicated that the area was a rendezvous point for the Communist Vietcong, who come down the Ho Chi Minh trail from the north.

Among those listening at the briefing were Lance Cpl. James C. Farley, crew chief of the copter Yankee Papa 13, and *LIFE* Photographer Larry Burrows, who had been covering the war in Vietnam since 1962 and had flown on scores of helicopter combat missions. On this day he would be riding in Farley's machine—and both were wondering whether the mission would be a no-contact milk run or whether, as had been increasingly the case in recent weeks, the Vietcong would be ready and waiting with .30-caliber machine guns. In a very few minutes Farley and Burrows had their answer, as shown in his chilling photographic . . . and word report on these pages. And after Yankee Papa 13 had limped back home bullet-riddled and bloodstained, Burrows re-

ceived a special souvenir from Lt. Colonel Norman Ewers, the squadron skipper. Said Ewers as he handed Burrows a set of air crewman's wings, an emblem given to some few Marines and damned few civilians: "You've earned it."

"SEE WHAT YOU CAN DO FOR THAT PILOT!"

"THE VIETCONG, DUG IN ALONG the tree line, were just waiting for us to come into the landing zone," Burrows reported. "We were all like sitting ducks and their raking crossfire was murderous. Over the intercom system one pilot radioed Colonel Ewers, who was in the lead ship: 'Colonel! We're being hit.' Back came the reply: 'We're all being hit. If your plane is flyable, press on.'

"We did, hurrying back to a pickup point for another load of troops. On our next approach to the landing zone, our pilot, Capt. Peter Vogel, spotted Yankee Papa 3 down on the ground. Its engine was still on and the rotors turning, but the ship was obviously in trouble. 'Why don't they lift *off?* Vogel muttered over the intercom. Then he set down our ship nearby to see what the trouble was. One

of the crew of YP3 came lurching across the field toward us, followed immediately by another. They were the copilot and the gunner. Both had been wounded and had to be helped aboard.

"In the cockpit of YP3 we could see the pilot slumped over the controls, 'Farley,' Captain Vogel said, 'see what you can do for that other pilot.' Farley barreled out of the copter and raced over to Yankee Papa 3. I chased after him. From a stone building some 70 yards away a Vietcong machine gun was spraying the area. Farley scrambled up to the pilot and fought to

drag him out but he couldn't be budged. To get into a more upright position so he could exert greater leverage, Farley switched off YP3's engine but the rotor blades kept turning. I was kneeling on the ground alongside the ship for cover against the V.C. fire. Should I try to find another foothold alongside Farley and help him lift the pilot out? Farley hastily examined the pilot. Through the blood around his face and throat, Farley could see a bullet hole in his neck. That, plus the fact the man had not moved at all, led him to believe the pilot was dead.

Machine-gun bullets were tearing holes into the aircraft's skin all around Farley. It would have been certain death to hang around any longer. So, crouching low, we ran back to Yankee Papa 13.

"There Hoilien was pouring machine-gun fire at a second V.C. gun position at the tree line to our left. Bullet holes had ripped both left and right of his seat. The plexiglass had been shot out of the cockpit and one V.C. bullet had nicked our pilot's neck. Our radio and instruments were out of commission. We climbed and climbed fast the hell out of there. Hoilien was still firing gunbursts at the tree line."

TWO MEN RESCUED—THEY'RE IN BAD SHAPE

NOT UNTIL YP13 PULLED AWAY OUT of range of enemy fire were Farley and Hoilien able to leave their guns and give medical attention to the two wounded men from YP3. The copilot, 1st Lt. James Magel, was in bad shape. When Farley and Hoilien eased off his flak vest, they exposed a major wound just below his right armpit.

"Magel's face registered pain," Burrows reported, "and his lips moved slightly. But if he said anything it was drowned out by the noise of the copter. He looked pale

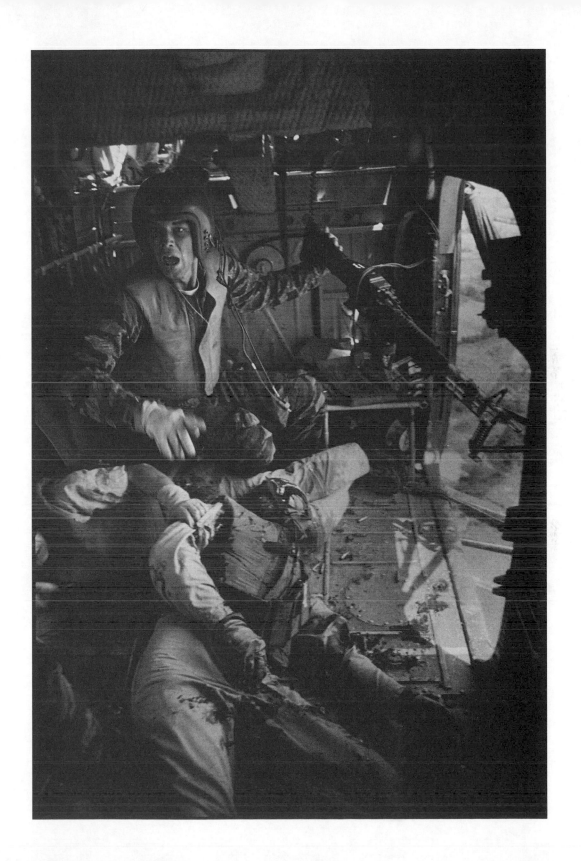

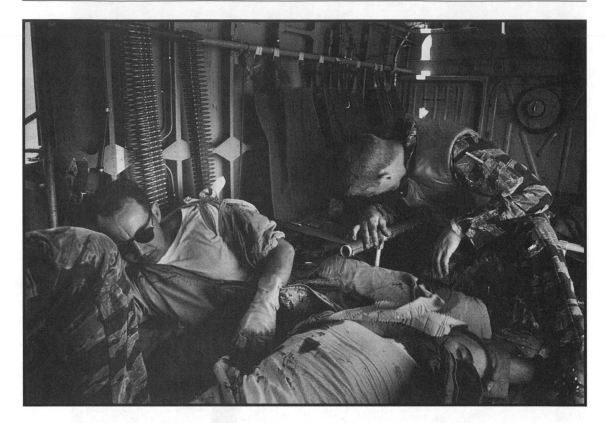

and I wondered how long he could hold on. Farley began bandaging Magel's wound. The wind from the doorway kept whipping the bandage across his face. Then blood started to come from his nose and mouth and a glazed look came into his eyes. Farley tried mouth-to-mouth resuscitation, but Magel was dead. Nobody said a word.

"The other wounded man, Sgt. Billie Owens, his left shoulder smashed by a bullet, lay in shock against the bulkhead. He was watching, but his sunglasses hid any expression his eyes might have shown. Farley poured some water into an empty ammunition can and gave it to Owens. Hoilien took out a cigaret for him but Owens waved it aside. We were all left with our own drained thoughts.

"Suddenly, at the doorway of the chopper, Farley began cursing. Then he broke into tears, first trying to cover his face from the others and then not caring who saw him. I don't know what this young man may have seen of violent death before this day. But compounding his grief and shock, I later found out, were his frustration and feelings of guilt at being unable to extricate the pilot from Yankee Papa 3. What he didn't know then, and what we all were to learn later, was that the pilot was still alive. He was rescued by another helicopter—even as YP 13 was in route to Da Nang."

PETER ARNETT

"THE AGONY AND DEATH OF SUPPLY COLUMN 21"

ASSOCIATED PRESS, AUGUST 19, 1965

Although it came early in the war, the following piece foreshadowed the difficulties the American fighting machine would encounter in the rice paddies and jungle terrain. The symbols of U.S. military muscle, the steel amtraks, the M48 tanks, and the ships anchored offshore, proved useless in the swamps.

Peter Arnett, who joined the Associated Press in 1962, first arrived in Vietnam just as the first U.S. servicemen landed to begin the "police action" in Indochina. By the end of the war, the New Zealand–born journalist was regarded as one of the war's most astute report- ers. Arnett traveled with soldiers to the front lines many times, often carrying a Mauser pistol or a .38; he was a firsthand witness to a war that only got bloodier and bloodier. The dispatch that follows on the ambush of Supply Column 21 was one of the correspondent's initial reports he subsequently won a Pulitzer for other reports.

VAN TUONG, Vietnam

THE MISSION OF U.S. MARINE Supply Column 21 yesterday was simple: Get to the beachhead, resupply a line company and return to the 7th Fleet mother ship anchored a mile out in the bay.

It never found the line company. And it never returned.

Supply Column 21 was a formidable force made up of five steel-shod am- traks—35-ton amphibious vehicles—to carry food and ammunition—and two M48 tanks to escort them once ashore.

The column packed a total of 287 tons of steel. It was made up of 30 men.

The paths that led to its destruction were paved with confusion.

Failing to locate the designated line company immediately, Column 21 set out to look for it.

But the huge amtraks, once out of wa- ter, were unwieldy. They flopped from one rice paddy to another, with their crews calling at one battalion and then the next. No one seemed to pay much attention.

At 11 A.M., Supply Column 21 was about 400 yards ahead of the nearest Ma- rine riflemen. The vehicles were deep in Vietcong territory and, suddenly, were deep in trouble.

Survivors said the Vietcong rose out of hedge rows and swamps.

Lance Corporal Richard Pass of Home- wood, Ill., said his amtrak veered aside as explosions erupted around them. The leading tank was hit with an armor- piercing shell. Two men inside were wounded.

The terraced paddies made maneuver- ing difficult and the supply men were not trained for it. Attempting to get into good firing positions, three of the five amtraks backed into a deep paddy and bogged down.

The other two edged toward the tanks for shelter. One didn't make it. A Vietcong knocked it out by dropping a grenade down its hatch, killing two Americans inside and wounding others.

Mortar fire bounced off the vehicles and cannon put three holes in one tank. The wounded driver squeezed himself through the 18-inch wide escape hatch under this vehicle only to be riddled by bullets.

Corporal Pass saw Vietcong with ammunition bandoliers, black pajama uniforms, and camouflaged steel helmets move right up to an amtrak 30 yards to his left.

He said the doors of the vehicle clanged open as the two drivers tried to make a break to Pass's vehicle. One of the Americans was killed as he leaped out.

The other was plunging through the paddyfield swinging his Marine knife when he went down. When pulled out dead today, he still had the knife clutched in his hand.

Soon after noon, as the hot sun beat down on the scurrying figures and the steel vehicles, the Vietcong knocked out a third amtrak. Survivors massed in the other two.

Corporal Frank Guilford of Philadelphia said machine guns sliced into the guerrillas, but they kept coming.

The men took turns as sharpshooters at peepholes on top of the vehicles. All were wounded in some degree.

"I couldn't maneuver up there," said Pfc. James Reeff of Seattle, who escaped with a slight injury.

A young corporal shouted, "Okay, men, we're Marines. Let's do the job."

He started to climb out of the vehicle but never got his rifle to his shoulder. A bullet hit him between the eyes.

Among those sweltering in the other amtrak was Staff Sgt. Jack Merino of Limita, Calif. He said he almost passed out from heat exhaustion. The men took turns splashing water over each other from resupply cans within the vehicle.

Merino said that in midafternoon he heard a man outside whispering, "Amtrak, amtrak." He proved to be a wounded tank crewman. Merino and others pulled him inside.

"It was a hair-raising moment but we managed it," Merino said.

The Marines continued with the nerve-wracking task of keeping off the attackers. The enemy bodies began piling up.

In late afternoon, air strikes eased the pressure.

By this time, a lieutenant had been killed and another wounded.

Another tank joined the beleaguered group.

At daybreak, a solitary helicopter landed at the scene. It had mistaken the landing zone.

At the drone of the helicopter, the Americans surged from their amtraks like moths to a flame.

Crouched, and with weapons at the ready, the Americans slipped past the bodies of their own and the enemy. They carried the wounded to the helicopter and left the dead.

The helicopter came back once more for wounded.

Ground forces arrived to relieve the others. In the interval they had scoured the nearby paddyfields and brush for Vietcong bodies. They found 18.

Corporal Earle Eberly of Sycamore, Ill., said:

"We don't like being here and killing people and being killed. But this is a job we've been told to do, we have to do it, and we're going to do it."

The fate of Supply Column 21 was sealed at noon.

The men thought the disabled vehicles might be carted off and repaired. But an officer of the relief force told them:

"Take your personal belongings out of the vehicles. We're going to blow them up."

The remains of the amtraks at Van Tuong will be a reminder of Supply Column 21.

LEE LESCAZE

"HUE MARINES: BITTER AS BRAVE"

WASHINGTON *POST*, FEBRUARY 20, 1968

Although normality began to return to Saigon in early February 1968, fighting continued throughout much of the country. In Hue, Lee Lescaze came across marines showing the effects of frustration and confusion. As marines gathered their wounded and dead, Vietnamese civilians and soldiers simply looked on. While South Vietnamese soldiers got patrol duty at headquarters, marines were sent to fight their war. One marine bitterly taunted his commander in chief. The spirit and pride of the marine force was wearing thin in Hue.

Lescaze reported the seeds of what would be the most lasting legacy of the war: the estrangement of its veterans from the society that sent them to fight. Vietnam veterans would segregate themselves—with or without choice—from the larger military and civilian community. Their battles with psychological disorders would become fodder for scores of movies and commentaries. Some returning from the war would be treated as villains, spit on, or derided as "murderers." Reporters, meanwhile, would fare no better. In the years to come, public officials and parts of the citizenry would blame the "disloyalty" of reporters in Vietnam for contributing to the military's defeat.

A S THE AMERICAN MARINES sweep through the southeastern part of Hue's Citadel, Vietnamese are coming back to their homes to recover and evacuate their belongings.

"They've got great intelligence," A Marine said. "Every house we set up in, the gooks are back here the next morning to clean up."

Bravo Company, 1st Battalion, 5th Marines, was set up in a rich man's house this morning. The liquor cabinet was full of Johnny Walker, Seagrams and beer.

A Buddhist altar took up one wall and the other walls had pictures of Vietnamese rural scenes mixed with center-folds from *Playboy* magazine.

"He's the Hugh Hefner of Vietnam," a Marine said, settling into one of the absent host's armchairs.

One Marine was worried. "There's a baby's crib in there. What's a married man doing with all those *Playboy* pictures on his walls?"

The night had been rough for Bravo Company. At dusk firing broke out on three sides of the command post in the house and the Marines waited for an attack that never came.

At 7:00 A.M., as the Marines were opening C Rations and shaking off the cold of the 45-degree night, the rich man's servants came to collect what they could.

They brought a note in English which ended:

"Let us take back my things and come back to the safe region. Thank you very much. We wish you a happy new year and a complete victory."

The note said that rice and salt and "other precious things" were to be salvaged. Bravo Company watched as the servants carried out the television set first, then the refrigerator, then several lamps, plates and small decorations, then the radio phonograph and finally a 100 pound bag of rice. It took four of them three trips before they were finished. They took the Johnny Walker, but the Seagrams bottle had been broken and the Marines had taken care of the beer.

The Marines in Hue are angry. This month, Bravo Company has taken 137 casualties and the other companies of the 1st Battalion have been hit equally hard.

From heavy fighting in Phuloc, a district town south of Hue, they were brought into the former imperial capital on Feb. 12.

At first there were restrictions on the air and artillery support they could have because the Vietnamese government hoped to retake Hue with minimal damage to the city, which houses much of the country's political, religious and cultural tradition. The restrictions have since been lifted but bad weather has held down the number of air strikes.

The street fighting in Hue is terrifying. There is cover everywhere and nowhere. Walk into a street and a sniper may kill you. Stick your head out of a window and you may draw fire. Run into a building and you may find an enemy soldier there, waiting.

"The Vietnamese have better intelligence following our advance than they ever gave us about where the enemy was," one Marine said.

Every Marine casualty who is evacuated, wounded or killed, is driven through the secure blocks of Hue into the headquarters compound of the Vietnamese 1st Infantry to wait for a helicopter. Vietnamese civilians stand along the road watching the dreadful cargo pass by.

In the compound, Vietnamese soldiers look on as the Marines angrily wrap their dead in ponchos and leave them on stretchers by the landing pad until the next helicopter comes in.

Individually, the Marines have shown enormous restraint. Groups of civilians who suddenly appear in front of them looking to recover their possessions from their homes do not draw fire. But the young Vietnamese civilians and the soldiers of the Vietnamese detachment that has been left at headquarters make the Americans angry. Their comrades are dying and being wounded a few blocks away in one of the hardest battles of the war.

For the Marines in the southeast part of the Citadel, it is an American battle against a very good enemy. They don't know anything about what the Vietnamese Marines are doing on the Citadel's west wall.

It has never been clearer that the Marines are fighting for their own pride, from their own fear and for their buddies who have already died. No American in Hue is fighting for Vietnam, for the Vietnamese or against Communism.

They are as bitter as they are brave. "You tell Lyndon Johnson I said 'Hi'," a wounded Marine said to a cameraman as he was carried down the street. The Marine waved his hand at the camera. "Here I am, Mr. Johnson," he said.

One seriously understrength Marine battalion has been given an enormous job here. Their inability to get the job done quickly has angered them and amazed several Vietnamese civilians who don't understand the tactical situation in Hue.

What the civilians see are American troops taking many casualties and making little progress against Vietcong and North Vietnamese soldiers—soldiers who are going to be driven out by air, artillery and U.S. Marines, but soldiers who have put up a frighteningly successful fight.

WILLIAM F. BUCKLEY, JR.

"GO ALL OUT OR GET THE HELL OUT"

NATIONAL REVIEW, MARCH 19, 1968

In 1968 William F. Buckley, Jr., was quickly becoming the conservatives' chief intellect. The defeats of Richard Nixon and Barry Goldwater in 1960 and 1964, respectively, left a void not only in national leadership but in the American Right's brain trust. Just who would articulate and hammer out conservative positions on the key issues of the day? Buckley's series on Vietnam helped him fill part of that vacuum. The report that follows is one of Buckley's numerous editorials on the war effort. It castigated not only the civilian leaders but the military brass who seemingly misunderstood the needs in fighting this war.

GEN. WESTMORELAND HAS ASKED for 200,000 more American troops. They should be denied him.

The easy reasons for doing so are not the best ones. It will be—has been—pointed out, tirelessly, that Gen. Westmoreland's optimism has been oppressively unwarranted. The criticism is just, though not by any means the conclusive reason for ruling against the general, any more than it was conclusively a reason for refusing to go to the aid of England that Churchill had said, Give us the tools and we will do the job. Military estimates are no more reliable than the estimates of economists or political scientists or sociologists. . . .

The call for the resignation of Gen. Westmoreland, in other words, is even less convincing than the call for the abandonment of Lord Keynes as the result of his deficient economic forecasting. The trouble is at the higher level; specifically, the question of the extent to which the United States is willing to use American troops in order to avoid using other weapons which are proscribed by world opinion. This American, for one, resists the convention that the war in Vietnam must be fought by orthodox American military forces so as to avoid the danger of the variant pressures which are open to us but require a heroic act of political will.

It is said so tirelessly that one thinks of it as a platitude, and therefore meaning-less—even though it is never demon-strated as meaningless. Escalation. When, in the Summer of 1967, Secretary McNa-mara testified before a Senate committee and all but drew the rug out from under the rationale of bombing, the senators failed to ask him precisely the relevant question. What McNamara said in effect was that no conceivable amount of bomb-ing by U.S. forces would be sufficient to interdict the supply of material needed by the Viet Cong. His statement was seized by the anti-bombers as conclusive proof of the empirical argument against bomb-ing, an argument which in fact they con-sider redundant, inasmuch as it is easily seen that they would be against bombing even if it did prove effective. But as James Burnham pointed out at the time, the question was not then (and is not now): Can the North Vietnamese succeed in ex-travasating (infiltrating) 100 tons of war material per day into South Vietnam, but is there a point at which they would opt not to do so?

That is the question Lyndon Johnson appears to be impaled upon, because of the schizophrenia that paralyzes him. He is afraid of a world war. He is afraid of offending the Soviet Union. He is afraid

of the world opinion-makers. Curious, considering how dauntless he has shown himself to be on the narrower question of the Vietnam war and its domestic impli-cations. Isn't it curious that he should fear the Kremlin more than he fears Arthur Schlesinger, Kenneth Galbraith, and Rob-ert Kennedy? In a strange kind of a way, the American critics of Mr. Johnson's poli-cies in Vietnam are infinitely more dan-gerous to him and what he seeks to effect than the Soviet Union.

What it comes down to, then, is this: Should the anti-communist community endorse Westmoreland's proposal to in-crease by 50 percent the American mili-tary in Vietnam? Or should the commu-nity insist that President Johnson adopt instead measures calculated to reduce the will of the enemy to prosecute the war? Blockades; economic embargoes; a savag-ing of the overland supply routes, the un-leashing of the Asian anti-Communist ar-mies; the freezing of economic and agricultural credits. It needs to be re-peated that our participation in the Viet-nam war is justified only if Vietnam is the contemporary salient of a world enter-prise, however loosely organized, that aims ultimately at the security of the United States. If that is what it is, we need to hit back with such weapons as we are in a position to use which spare us the most precious commodity we have, the American soldier. If that is not what Viet-nam is all about, then we should get the hell out.

JOHN FETTERMAN

"PFC. GIBSON COMES HOME"

LOUISVILLE *TIMES*, JULY, 1968

In the Pulitzer nomination for the following story, John Fetterman's editor wrote, "'Pfc. Gibson Comes Home' is a simple story. It has meaning, however, for every American." Indeed, the narrative has little noticeable flare in its writing, yet it packs a strong emotional punch because of its painstaking detail and description. Fetterman keeps himself out of the story, allowing neighbors and family to speak for themselves. His descriptions are understated and all the more powerful as a result. The story is a good example of how restraint in writing can be very effective. It won the Pulitzer Prize for local general spot news reporting in 1969.

IT WAS LATE ON A WEDNESDAY night and most of the people were asleep in Hindman, the county seat of Knott County, when the body of Private First Class James Thurman (Little Duck) Gibson came home from Vietnam.

It was hot. But as the gray hearse arrived bearing the gray Army coffin, a summer rain began to fall. The fat raindrops glistened on the polished hearse and steamed on the street. Hindman was dark and silent. In the distance down the town's main street the red sign on the Square Deal Motor Co. flashed on and off.

Private Gibson's body had been flown from Oakland, California, to Cincinnati and was accompanied by Army Staff Sgt. Raymond A. Ritter, assigned to escort it home. The body was picked up in Cincinnati by John Everage, a partner in the local funeral home, and from that point on it was in the care of people who had known the 24-year-old soldier all his life.

At Hindman, the coffin was lifted out while Sgt. Ritter, who wore a black mourning band on his arm, snapped a salute. One funeral home employee whispered to another: "It's Little Duck. They brought him back."

Most of his life he had been called Little Duck—for so long that many people who knew him well had to pause and reflect to recall his full name.

By Thursday morning there were few people who did not know that Little Duck was home—or almost home. During the morning the family came; his older brother, Herschel, whom they call Big Duck; his sister Betty Jo; and his wife Carolyn.

They stood over the glass-shielded body and let their tears fall upon the glass, and people spoke softly in the filling station next door and on the street outside.

The soldier's parents, Mr. and Mrs. Norman Gibson, waited at home, a neat white house up the hollow which shelters Flax Patch Creek, several miles away. Mrs. Gibson had been ill for months, and the family did not let her take the trip to Hindman. Later in the morning, they took Little Duck home.

Sweltering heat choked the hills and valleys as Little Duck was placed back in the hearse and taken home. The cortege had been joined by Maj. Lyle Haldeman, a survival assistance officer, sent, like Sgt. Ritter, to assist the family. It was a long, slow trip—over a high ridge to the south, along Irishman Creek and past the small community of Amburgey.

At Amburgey, the people stood in the sun, women wept and men removed their hats as the hearse went past. Mrs. Nora Amburgey, the postmistress, lowered the flag of the tiny fourth-class post office to half-mast and said, "We all thought a lot of Little Duck."

At the point where Flax Patch Creek empties into Irishman Creek, the hearse turned, crossed a small wooden bridge and drove the final mile up Flax Patch Creek to the Gibson home. The parents and other relatives waited in a darkened, silent home.

As the coffin was lifted upon the front porch and through the door into the front living room, the silence was broken by cries of grief. The sounds of anguish swelled and rolled along the hollow. Little Duck was home.

All afternoon and all night they came, some walking, some driving up the dusty road in cars and trucks. They brought flowers and food until the living room was filled with floral tributes and the kitchen was crammed with food. The people filled the house and yard. They talked in small groups, and members of the family clasped to each other in grief.

They went, time and time again, to look down into the coffin and weep.

The mother, a sweet-faced mountain woman, her gray hair brushed back and fastened behind her head, forced back the pangs of her illness and moved, as in a trance, among the crowd as she said:

"His will will be done no matter what we say or do."

The father, a tall, tanned man, his eyes wide and red from weeping, said:

"He didn't want to go to the Army, but he knew it was the right thing to do; so he did his best. He gave all he had. I'm as proud of him as I can be. Now they bring him home like this."

Around midnight the rain returned and the mourners gathered in the house, on the porch and backed against the side of the house under the eaves.

The father talked softly of his son.

"I suppose you wonder why we called him Little Duck. Well, when the boys were little they would go over and play in the creek every chance they got. Somebody said they were like ducks.

"Ever since then Herschel was 'Big Duck' and James was 'Little Duck.'

"You worked hard all your life to raise your family. I worked in 32-inch seam of coal, on my hands and knees, loading coal to give my family what I could.

"There was never a closer family. Little Duck was born here in this house and never wanted to leave."

Other mourners stepped up to volunteer tributes to Little Duck.

"He never was one to drink and run up and down the road at night."

"He took care of his family. He was a good boy."

Little Duck was a big boy. He was 6 feet 5 1/2 inches tall and weighed 205 pounds. His size led him to the basketball team at Combs High School where he met and courted the girl he married last January.

Little Duck was home recently on furlough. Within a month after he went down Flax Patch Creek to return to the Army, he was back home to be buried. He had been married six months, a soldier for seven.

The Army said he was hit by mortar fragments near Saigon, but there were few details of his death.

THE FATHER, THERE IN THE stillness of the early morning, was remembering the day his son went back to the Army.

"He had walked around the place, looking at everything. He told me, 'Lord, it's good to be home.'

"Then he went down the road. He said, 'Daddy, take care of yourself and don' work too hard.'

"He said, 'I'll be seeing you.' But he can't see me now."

An elderly man, walking with great dignity, approached and said, "Nobody can ever say anything against Little Duck. He was as good a boy as you'll ever see."

Inside the living room, the air heavy with the scent of flowers, Little Duck's mother sat with her son and her grief.

Her hand went out gently, as to comfort a stranger, and she talked as though to herself:

"Why my boy? Why my baby?"

She looked toward the casket, draped in an American flag, and when she turned back she said:

"You'll never know what a flag means until you see one on your own boy."

Then she went back to weep over the casket.

On Friday afternoon Little Duck was taken over to the Providence Regular Baptist Church and placed behind the pulpit. All that night the church lights burned and the people stayed and prayed.

The parents spent the night at the church.

"This is his last night," Little Duck's mother explained.

THE FUNERAL WAS AT 10 O'CLOCK Saturday morning, and the people began to arrive early. They came from the dozens of hollows and small communities in Letcher, Knot, and Perry counties. Some came back from other states. They filled the pews and then filled the aisle with folding chairs. Those who could not crowd inside gathered outside the door or listened beneath the windows.

The sermon was delivered by the Rev. Archie Everage, pastor at Montgomery Baptist Church, which is on Montgomery Creek near Hindman. On the last Sunday that he was home alive, Little Duck attended services there.

The service began with a solo, "Beneath the Sunset," sung by a young girl with a clear bell-like voice; then there were hymns from the church choir.

Mr. Everage, who had been a friend of Little Duck, had difficulty in keeping his voice from breaking as he got into his final tribute. He spoke of the honor Little Duck had brought to his family, his courage and his dedication. He spoke of Little Duck "following the colors of his country." He said Little Duck died "for a cause for which many of our forefathers fought and died."

The phrase touched off a fresh wail of sobs to fill the church. Many mountain people take great pride in their men who "follow the colors." It is a tradition that goes back to October 1780, when a lightly regarded band of mountaineers handed disciplined British troops a historic defeat at Kings Mountain in South Carolina and turned the tide of the Revolutionary war.

Shortly before Little Duck was hit in Vietnam, he had written two letters intended for his wife. Actually the soldier was writing a part of his own funeral. Mr. Everage read from one letter:

"Honey, they put me in a company right down on the Delta. From what everybody says that is a rough place, but I've been praying hard for the Lord to help me and take care of me so really I'm not too scared or worried. I think if He wants it to be my time to go that I'm prepared for it. Honey, you don't know really when you are going to face something like this, but I want you to be a good girl and try to live a good life. For if I had things to do over I would have already been prepared for something like this. I guess you are wondering why I'm telling you this, but you don't know how hard it's been on me in just a short time. But listen here, if anything happens to me, all I want is for you to live right, and then I'll get to see you again."

And from another letter:

"Honey, listen, if anything happens to me I want you to know that I love you very very much and I want you to keep seeing my family the rest of their lives and I want you to know you are a wonderful wife and that I'm very proud of you. If anything happens I want Big Duck and Betty Jo to know I loved them very much. If anything happens also tell them not to worry, that I'm prepared for it."

The service lasted two hours and ended only after scores of people, of all ages, filed past the coffin.

Then they took Little Duck to Resthaven Cemetery up on a hill in Perry County. The Army provided six pallbearers, five of whom had served in Vietnam. There was a seven-man firing squad to fire the traditional three volleys over the grave and bugle to sound taps.

The pallbearers, crisp and polished in summer tans, folded the flag from the coffin and Sgt. Ritter handed it to the young widow, who had wept so much, but spoken so little, during the past three days.

Then the soldier's widow knelt beside the casket and said softly, "Oh, Little Duck."

Then they buried Little Duck beneath a bit of the land he died for.

PETER ARNETT

"IN LIKE HEROES, OUT LIKE FOES"

CHICAGO *TRIBUNE*, APRIL 30, 1975

In April 1975, the stage was set for the last chapter of the war and reporters were on the scene to record the final act of the humiliating defeat. The place was the U.S. Embassy in Saigon. Seven years before, it had been a Tet target. Now it was the departure point for U.S. forces evacuating Saigon. It was fitting that the account that follows of the hurried, chaotic flight from the South Vietnamese capital was filed by Peter Arnett. Having seen the entry of the United States into the conflict, Arnett now watched U.S. servicemen leave with none of the formality and pomp that had greeted them more than a decade before.

Arnett filed the dispatches, one of the few journalists who elected to stay behind and report the evacuation and the takeover of the city by the victorious North. What he recorded was South Vietnamese bitterness at what they perceived as abandonment by Washington.

TEN YEARS AGO I WATCHED THE first United States Marines arrive to help South Viet Nam. They were greeted on the beaches by pretty Vietnamese girls in white silken robes who draped flower leis around their necks.

A decade has passed.

And on Tuesday I watched U.S. Marines, shepherding the last Americans out of South Viet Nam. They were the same, cleancut-looking young men of a decade ago.

But the Vietnamese were different.

Those who didn't have a place on the last helicopters out of Saigon—and there were thousands of them left behind—hooted, booed, and scuffled with the Marines guarding the landing zones.

Some Vietnamese threw themselves over walls and wire fences, only to be thrown back by the Marines.

Bloodshed was avoided seemingly only by good luck and bad aim on the part of some angry Vietnamese soldiers who shot at a few buses and departing helicopters.

But the entire, frantic dash from Saigon by the Americans—and the bitter resentment of the thousands of Vietnamese who couldn't go—seemed a sad but accurate reflection of what relations between Americans and Vietnamese had come to in the 10 years since these flowers were gladly given to the Marines.

Americans and the South Vietnamese used to get along pretty well. That was in the days when the U.S. Marines first arrived in Viet Nam imbued with a determination to see the war thru.

The South Vietnamese army, dispirited then, watched with wonder as first the Marines and then the paratroopers and the American infantry came to steaming hot Viet Nam to trudge the coastal plains and mountain valleys in a punishing, unfamiliar environment.

Vietnamese officers began aping the American way. The Americans seemed always to have better pressed uniforms and more detailed maps and diagrams.

Nearly 20,000 Vietnamese officers flew to the United States for education or advanced training, and they returned with American slang expression and an American taste of firepower and massive military supplies.

But something went wrong along the way. To win a war like Viet Nam, the subject to study was not the American way but the Communist Vietnamese way. They were launching the war in their own country.

The South Vietnamese, instead, learned the American way to use firepower, blasting at the other side with war planes and artillery, effective only so long as there were bombs and shells.

And Saigon also tasted the luxury of the American way, with massive quantities of bombs and equipment. And this was to end, also.

One factor that surely sustained the South Vietnamese for long years after the American ground troops left was hope that the United States would continue to help one way or the other. Or to at least save everyone at the last minute.

That hope died for many on Tuesday.

The days preceding the evacuation were eyeopeners for Americans who had any faith left in the ability of the South Vietnamese high command.

This reporter lunched with a three-star general with critical responsibilities for the defense of Saigon, and he matter of factly explained his own plan of retreat.

He would simply have his helicopter pilot follow the U.S. Marine helicopters ferrying evacuees to 7th Fleet carriers offshore, and set down with them. But what about the defense of the city for which he would be responsible after the Americans left?

"Don't you see," he said, "this will be my last chance to get to the United States. I know I can make money there by writing about my successful military campaigns."

Come Tuesday, and the general followed the Marines to the carriers.

Those officers who left hurriedly on the long journey to the United States were in the minority.

Many thousands of officers in the Saigon army had apparently been promised passage out, or believed that they qualified for it. But the evacuation came so quickly that only a small percentage could be moved.

A Vietnamese infantry colonel complained bitterly that he had been left behind despite a promise "from a friend high in the American CIA."

This sort of bitterness must be felt by thousands of other Vietnamese officers who worked with the American advisers over the years and began believing in "the American way" of doing things.

Two colonels on his staff had less resources. But they simply corralled this reporter outside one of the press buses, changed their uniforms into civilian attire on the curbside, and mingled with the newsmen climbing aboard. Occasionally on Tuesday it became apparent.

A Vietnamese ranger captain surrounded by soldiers and carrying a glass of beer approached a group of newsmen waiting for a bus. Several times he snarled, "American bastards." He caressed the butt of the .45 in his holster, but backed off when the group of Americans insisted they were all French.

The sight of pathetic bands of Vietnamese struggling to board the last helicopters on Tuesday pointed up the failure of the whole war efforts as dramatically as any military defeat.

SYDNEY H. SCHANBERG

"THE FALL OF PHNOM PENH"

NEW YORK TIMES, MAY 9, 1975

Sydney H. Schanberg's story, and that of his Cambodian associate, Dith Pran, is known to many who watched the award-winning movie The Killing Fields. *But while the movie focused attention on the plight of his associate, Dith Pran, not much was learned about the* Times *reporter and his circuitous route to the action in Cambodia. Schanberg joined the* New York Times *in 1959 as a copyboy but soon received a number of promotions. In 1965, just as the Vietnam War was heating up, Schanberg was drafted by the army but was sent to serve his tour in Germany, where he spent his time writing for the military paper in Frankfurt. After his discharge, Schanberg was sent to New Delhi in 1969 as the* Times *reporter on the India-Pakistan War. He later became the newspaper's bureau manager in Singapore, his final stop before Cambodia.*

AFTER LEAVING THE PRISONERS and the military commander at the Information Ministry, we headed for the Hotel Le Phnom, where another surprise was waiting. The day before, the Red Cross had turned the hotel into a protected international zone and draped it with huge Red Cross flags. But the Communists were not interested.

At 4:55 P.M., troops waving guns and rockets had forced their way into the grounds and ordered the hotel emptied within 30 minutes. By the time we arrived, 25 minutes had elapsed. The fastest packing job in history ensued. I even had time to "liberate" a typewriter someone had abandoned since the troops had "liberated" mine earlier.

We were the last ones out, running. The Red Cross had abandoned several vehicles in the yard after removing the keys, so several of us threw our gear on the back of a Red Cross Honda pickup truck and started pushing it up the boulevard toward the French Embassy.

Several days before, word was passed to those foreigners who stayed behind when the Americans pulled out on April 12 that, as a last resort, one could take refuge at the embassy. France had recognized the new government, and it was thought that the new Cambodian leaders would respect the embassy compound as a sanctuary.

As we plodded up the road, big fires were burning on the city's outskirts, sending smoke clouds into the evening sky like a giant funeral wreath encircling the capital.

The embassy was only several hundred yards away, but what was happening on the road made it seem much farther. All around us people were fleeing, for there was no refuge for them. And coming into the city from the other direction was a fresh battalion marching single file. They looked curiously at us; we looked nervously at them.

In the 13 days of confinement that followed, until our evacuation by military truck to the Thai border, we had only a peephole into what was going on outside, but there were still many things that could be seen and many clues to the revolution that was going on.

We could hear shooting, sometimes nearby but mostly in other parts of the city. Often it sounded like shooting in the air, but at other times it seemed like small battles. As on the day of the city's fall, we were never able to piece together a satisfactory explanation of the shooting, which died down after about a week.

We could see smoke from huge fires from time to time, and there were reports from foreigners who trickled into the embassy that certain quarters were badly burned and that the water purification plant was heavily damaged.

The foreigners who for various reasons

came in later carried stories, some of them eyewitness accounts, of such things as civilian bodies along the roads leading out of the city—people who had apparently died of illness or exhaustion on the march. But each witness got only a glimpse and no reliable estimate of the toll was possible.

Reports from roads to the south and southeast of Phnom Penh said the Communists were breaking up families by dividing the refugees by sex and age. Such practices were not reported from other roads on which the refugees flooded out of the capital.

Reports also told of executions, but none were eyewitness accounts. One such report said high military officers were executed at a rubber plantation a couple of miles north of the city.

In the French Embassy compound foreign doctors and relief agency officials were pessimistic about the survival chances of many of the refugees. "There's not food in the countryside at this time of year," an international official said. "What will they eat from now until the rice harvest in November?"

The new Communist officials, in conversations with United Nations and other foreign representatives during our confinement and in statements since, have rejected the idea of foreign aid "whether it is military, political or economic, social, diplomatic, or whether it takes on a so-called humanitarian form." Some foreigners wondered whether this included China, for they speculated that the Communists would at least need seed to plant for the next harvest.

Whether the looting we observed before we entered the French compound continued is difficult to say. In any case,

it is essential to understand who the Communist soldiers are to understand the behavior of some of them in disciplinary matters, particularly looting.

They are peasant boys, pure and simple—darker skinned than their city brethren, with gold in their front teeth. To them the city is a curiosity, an oddity, a carnival, where you visit but do not live. The city means next to nothing in their scheme of things.

When they looted jewelry shops, they kept only one watch for themselves and gave the rest to their colleagues or passersby. Transistor radios, cameras, and cars held the same toylike fascination—something to play with, as children might, but not essential.

From my airline bag on the day I was seized and threatened with execution they took only some cigarettes, a pair of boxer underwear shorts, and a handkerchief. They passed up a blue shirt and $9,000 in cash in a money belt.

The looting did not really contradict the Communist image of rigid discipline, for commanders apparently gave no orders against the sacking of shops, feeling perhaps that this was at least due their men after five years of jungle fighting.

Often they would climb into abandoned cars and find that they would not run, so they would bang on them with their rifles like frustrated children, or they would simply toot the horns for hours on end or keep turning the headlights on and off until the batteries died.

One night at the French Embassy I chose to sleep on the grass outside; I was suddenly awakened by what sounded like a platoon trying to smash down the front gates with a battering ram that had bright lights and a loud claxon. It was only a bunch of soldiers playing with and smashing up the cars that had been left outside the gates.

Though these country soldiers broke into villas all over the city and took the curious things they wanted—one walked past the embassy beaming proudly in a crimson-colored wool overcoat that hung down to his Ho Chi Minh sandals—they never stayed in the villas. With big, soft beds empty, they slept on the courtyards or the streets.

Almost without exception foot soldiers I talked with, when asked what they wanted to do, replied that they only wanted to go home.

IN RETROSPECT

MAX FRANKEL

"A DIVIDED NATION LOST ITS WAY"

NEW YORK TIMES, JANUARY 28, 1973

The ink on the peace treaty between the United States and North Vietnam was not yet dry when the first perspective stories began finding their way into the pages of the country's newspapers. One of the best early pieces was Max Frankel's retrospective story, which appeared in the New York Times in January 1973. Frankel provided the paper with many distinguished reports and eventually became the newspaper's managing editor.

The piece did more than assess the failure of the war: it reflected on the damage the conflict inflicted on American society. "Beside the wreckage of Camelot," he noted, "lies a grounded Great Society, with her cargo of guns and butter both." The disaster in Vietnam was more than a military defeat. It was the routing of a previously indomitable country. That may have been the biggest tragedy of all—the blown opportunity and lost promise of what was once heralded as the "American century."

IT BEGAN AS THAT DIRTY LITTLE war and it expired with those clean massive strikes of eight-engined fury. It was an undeclared war for ill-defined objectives against a foe who never quite fit the concept of "enemy" and became known instead as "the other side" of a four-sided Paris peace table. It was the war of euphemisms: of incursion, escalation, pacification and protective reaction, for which Americans crossed the seas shouting "leave your neighbors alone" until they perceived honor in a vague and ambiguous sheaf of agreements that allowed them simply to leave.

By one measure, the war was the ultimate act of overextension—into a remote civil war mistaken as a global threat to peace and national security. By another, it was the ultimate example of undercommitment—the world's mightiest nation failing to muster the will and the power to defeat a tiny rural country. Either way, it was a searing experience in which Americans felt themselves losing confidence and pride and perspective and patriotism and trust and temper and treasure—however defined.

It was the guerrilla war to end all guerrilla wars until it somehow became simply a war to be ended. It was the proxy war to contain international Communism until it somehow became the central embarrassment to an era of Communist-capitalist detente. It was devised by a generation that wanted no more Munichs, meaning betrayals by appeasement, and it spawned a generation that wants no more salvations by intervention, no more Vietnams.

The toll in lives and limbs is difficult enough to calculate for a conflict whose course came to be measured primarily by some fanciful "body count." But the war's true cost to the United States will never be known, for it was a compound of frustration and guilt, diversion and deception, and a shattering catalogue of might-have-beens.

Here lies domestic tranquility, beside a burning Buddhist and a My Lai infant, roiled by the campus teach-in and shattered by the Chicago chaos.

There lies America the Just, renamed the Bully by some foreign critic—or is it native? A land possessed of a vision of opportunity and optimism suddenly perceived as a nation obsessed by a mission of indiscriminate destruction.

Beside the wreckage of Camelot lies a grounded Great Society, with her cargo of guns and butter both. Programs that promised welfare and equality and jobs and learning have been eroded by inflation and parched by recession in an economy distorted by the war and now cheated of any dividends of peace.

Some think they see the Constitution itself among the victims. Presidents stand accused of imperial arrogance for usurping the war power and for suppressing dissent. They shout back charges of betrayal and stabs in the back and faintheartedness and abetting the enemy. Between the ugly words of impeachment and treason, the center barely held.

The decade now ending had been consecrated to sacrificial strivings for freedom and prosperity everywhere. America's prowess and largesse were to sustain the lonely outposts of Berlin and Vientiane, the reality of her power and wealth to be demonstrated on the moon, and along the Mekong. The volunteers of the Peace Corps and the Green Berets set out simultaneously as the servants of a single ideal. But Vietnam sapped the will and the means for good works and bold deeds. Helping others now no longer appears a worthy enterprise to those who are no longer sure what they want, even for themselves.

Peace, we thought, depended upon the credibility of our military might. Thus a small military venture was deemed necessary to avoid a larger. And thus it became necessary to nurture the venture, to avoid defeat if not to attain victory. Soon the war was its own purpose, and there was no longer any standard by which to measure profit and loss, cost against gain. Peace required war.

Because of the secretive way in which it was begun, the deceptive way in which it was repeatedly proclaimed a success, the brutal way in which it was fought and the unequal way in which it was manned and paid for, the war managed to destroy the confidence of Americans in their purpose, power and institutions.

The draft-age young turned against authority, and before long, so did many of their uncomprehending—or comprehending—parents. An angry minority tormented a confused majority until the enemies among them became more vivid than those of Indochina. It became safer for a President to visit the war zone than to tour among his own people.

To be protected by America in the fashion of Vietnam began to imply the risk of destruction by America, so that those abroad who were meant to take heart from the high resolve of the United States began to doubt its sanity instead.

Once truth and wisdom were counted among the casualties of the war, and victory was clearly beyond reach, it became difficult to defend even the virtue of the enterprise—though many clung to the so lace that at least we meant well. Americans began to perceive other Americans not only as liars or fools or incompetents, but also as criminals and barbarians. Shame and guilt dissolved into hatred, which in turn overwhelmed the politics by which a change of course might have been found.

Now troops and tear gas were needed, or at least summoned, to pacify America. Peacekeepers faced denunciation as pigs and were taunted with stocks and stones and sometimes with crude explosives as well. Protesters risked clubbings and random arrests and sometimes bullets fired in panic. Raised fists and hard hats became the rival symbol of the conflict and the last in a long line of Presidents to preside over the perpetual war, who had begun by pleading for a lowering of voices, wound up proclaiming silence as the highest civic virtue.

It is in the next decade of engagements and competitions that the ultimate costs of Vietnam are likely to be revealed. Exhausted, divided and distracted, America does not yet know how she will recover.

Out damned spot!

THE GULF WAR

OPERATION DESERT STORM

1991

BY **1990 MANY AMERICANS** believed their nation to be an empire in decline. The bright promise of unlimited prosperity had dimmed since the 1960s, as basic industries such as steel, automobiles, textiles, and appliances—the mainstay of the U.S. economy for decades—slumped. The oil shocks of the 1970s alerted vulnerable consumers and corporate and political leaders that the economy would have to become more efficient. Abroad, European and East Asian nations had restored and improved their industrial capacities, and the era of U.S. dominance of the global market had drawn to a close. Matching American economic impotence was a tarnished military reputation. The Iranian hostage crisis of 1979–81 had challenged the United States's once-unquestioned position in world affairs. American voters had punished President Jimmy Carter and elected Ronald Reagan, who promised to make America strong again.

Reagan delivered on his promises. If future detractors would question his methods, his administration and a bipartisan Congress fostered the nation's longest period of economic growth since World War II. Part of Reagan's plan was a massive defense buildup, which he promoted with a healthy dose of anti-Soviet rhetoric. But the second half of the decade saw U.S.-Soviet agreements to reduce both nuclear and conventional forces. By the time George Bush entered the Oval Office in 1989, the Communist bloc was crumbling from within. The Berlin Wall, and the Soviet-style governments of Eastern Europe, tumbled under pressure from citizens eager to found new republics. The cold war was over.

Americans celebrated their victory, but they also faced uncertainty: if the Russians were no longer the enemy, how should the United States measure itself?

From the cradle of civilization came the answer. On August 2, 1990, Saddam Hussein's Iraqi army invaded Kuwait. Within days the Bush administration adroitly organized an international coalition to condemn Iraq's action, deploying troops to the gulf with blinding speed to protect Saudi Arabia and Bahrain. The United Nations condemned Hussein's occupation, but negotiations and economic sanctions proved futile. In mid-October the United States increased its troop strength to 450,000 and issued an ultimatum. The void left by the fall of the Soviet Empire had been filled by a mustachioed thug from Baghdad, whom the politicians and journalists of America gleefully compared with Hitler.

The deadline on the American ultimatum expired on January 15, 1991, and Operation Desert Shield became Operation Desert Storm. Overnight, the air strikes on Iraq became a national fixation. In the past the American soldier—the GI, doughboy, Johnnie Reb, Billy Yank, or buckskin-clad rifleman—had symbolized the nation's resolve. Now technology took center stage in a war televised around the clock. Millions of Americans looked on as Patriot missiles destroyed scores of Soviet-built SCUDs and saw "smart bombs" tear through narrow elevator shafts on the other side of the world. If the American military had bogged down in the rice paddies and jungles of Vietnam, in the sands of Arabia it functioned smoothly. On television back home, the war resembled nothing so much as a giant video game, complete with instant replay. Logically enough, sports metaphors were used to describe the action. One field commander told reporter Larry Copeland, "We're not going to do anything fancy. What we're going to do is an off-tackle play . . . where you apply all the power you can at one point to defeat your opponent."

With Americans at their TV screens scrambling for every detail about Desert Storm, the war may have represented the ultimate triumph of American war correspondence. The Mexican War had seen the first telegraphed dispatches; World War II had bombarded the public by radio wave; Vietnam had burst into their homes in color—but nothing could match the immediacy with which events in the Middle East reached Americans. Networks remained on the air for hours, broadcasting live reports from Iraq, Saudi Arabia, Israel, and Jordan. Fax machines and satellite dishes transmitted written coverage across continents and oceans in seconds.

Yet for all the technology, the scope of the reports and dispatches from the hotel warriors was frustratingly limited. Military censors refused journalists access to the action and herded them together in pools, which restricted their ability to understand the chaos around them. Even when they could break free to roam the desert, sand had a way of interfering with fax machines. There were few Ernie Pyles in the gulf. One *Life* correspondent stayed long enough to write a piece on the soldiers, but his request for another stay with the troops was denied by military brass. Still, dispatches like those of Los Angeles *Times* reporter Janny Scott made it clear that lives, limbs, and futures were at stake in the combat. One lieutenant recalled an attack that pierced his armored vehi-

Preparing for land war in the Iraqi desert. *(U.S. Army)*

cle. "The round, I think, went through the gunner," he said. "As soon as I could see I saw his head limp."

The approach to reporting the war sparked intense debate on the role of the media. Some critics heaped invective on maverick journalists in Iraq who reported the effects of American bombs on civilian life. Cable News Network (CNN) correspondent Peter Arnett found himself inaccurately tagged as an enemy sympathizer. Yet many others bemoaned the press pools and lambasted television networks and wire services for accepting unquestioningly the Pentagon's version of events. Aware of their ambiguous role in Vietnam, it appeared that the press now wished to demonstrate its patriotism. It admonished citizens to trust the administration that had committed their sons and daughters, husbands and wives to the desert four months before Congress even debated the issue.

Just as quickly as the war came—with Iraq's August blitzkrieg in Kuwait—it was over. After a month of bombings established allied air and naval superiority, the final ground offensive began in late February. One hundred hours later President Bush called an end to the assault. U.S. troops had not only liberated Kuwait but pushed to within one hundred miles of Saddam Hussein's bunker. Emaciated Iraqi soldiers, not their elusive dictator, now greeted Americans on their TV screens, asking for food and mercy. Despite grim forecasts that the fighting would last months and cost tens of thousands of casualties, the conflict had lasted a mere six weeks and, incredibly, left only 138 Americans dead.

LANCE MORROW

"A NEW TEST OF RESOLVE"

TIME, SEPTEMBER 3, 1990

A month after Iraqi tanks rolled into Kuwait, Americans were waving to loved ones board-
ing transport ships for the Persian Gulf. Although U.S. troops had been deployed several
times in previous years for "police actions" around the globe, the late summer and fall of
1990 saw a mass deployment unrivaled since Vietnam. Almost before they realized it, civil-
ians began preparing mentally for war.

In this article, Lance Morrow examined the American way of going to war—the "war
psychology" of the American people. By early September, support was building for the war—
but, Morrow wondered, would it remain so? Would this battle for the sands of Arabia be
another "good war," like World War II, recalled nostalgically with flag-waving and stirring
movies, or another Vietnam, in which a weary and frustrated people showered their re-
turning veterans with curses rather than ticker tape?

EVERY NATION INVENTS ITS OWN style of going to war—the myths that it plays in its mind when it marches off to fearsome business. In August 1914 an Englishman placed a personal ad in the London *Times:* "Pauline—alas, it can-not be. But I will dash into the great ven-ture with all that pride and spirit an an-cient race has given me." The man's generation, destined for the trenches at Ypres and the Somme, was almost inno-cent enough to ship off thinking of Hor-ace's lines: *"Dulce et decorum est/Pro pa-tria mori."* Years later, American boys flying to Vietnam sometimes unreeled John Wayne movies in their head. That was the model; that was what a man should look like, act like, when he goes to war.

John Wayne, or possibly John Rambo, was still ghosting around some American imaginations last week. A banner stretched across I-75 in north Georgia—a route the 101st Airborne traveled from Fort Campbell, Ky.—gave the troopers a parting thought: GET THEIR GAS AND KICK THEIR ASS. Adrenaline, jingo and doubt mingled with sheer weirdness and a sort of emergency-issue nostalgia, as if Americans were rummaging through old *LIFE* magazines, dipping back into the lore of World War II to discover the styles of leave taking, of sweethearts' goodbyes. Television-news shows offered small touches of the USO, airing video post-cards from soldiers newly arrived in the gulf, grinning and sweating and reassur-ing Mom. Said a soldier, cheerful and ear-nest: "We're here fighting for America and our way of life. Airborne!" Will Bob Hope be in Riyadh for Christmas? ("Hey, guys, I wanna tell ya, that gal's veil sure didn't leave much to the imagination!")

War, or the possibility of it, is some-thing that a nation has to talk itself into. America has had little time for that. The weeks since the Iraqi invasion of Kuwait have been strange, almost a sort of hallucination. The usual lazy vacuum of high August abruptly filled with urgent, deadly business and martial noises. August 1990 seemed in a way like August 1914. The President's adamancy in sticking to his Maine vacation (the tense, almost angry flailing at golf balls, the powerboat *Fidelity* bucking out of harbor, a war getting organized by cellular phone) contributed to an air of the surreal. So did the alien theater of war: the Saudi peninsula's shimmering heat, its lunar landscapes, its customs and culture out of other centuries altogether.

Amid that air of the unreal, Americans edged themselves toward a war psychology. They supported George Bush's decisions to send the troops and call up the reserves. They signaled that they are ready to endure sacrifices to pursue American objectives, even accepting—for now—the possibility of higher inflation, higher gas prices and fuel shortages.

Americans initially greet almost any military mission by rallying around the President and the flag. It is almost an involuntary reflex. That was even true of Vietnam. "That's usually the way it is at the beginning of these affairs," Dean Rusk, 81, says with a philosophical wariness. As Secretary of State during the Johnson Administration, Rusk watched the radical turning of public opinion against the war in Southeast Asia. "If this conflict in the gulf drags on," Rusk says, and if there are American casualties, "things may change."

The central question is not whether America has the military strength to win against Saddam Hussein. It surely does. The critical question is whether Ameri-cans have the resolve to see the conflict through.

In the high desert of Southern California, 4,000 of the 10,000 Marines at Twenty-nine Palms Marine Corps Air Ground Combat Center were shipping out for the gulf. Two days after the Marines and their families learned of the mobilization, a local wedding chapel performed 30 weddings. Robert Lauffer, editor of the *High Desert Star*, went to dinner at a local restaurant, the Sizzler, and could hardly get past the crowd waiting to be seated. "At practically every table," he recalls, "there was one young guy with short hair, surrounded by family, friends and an equally young wife or girlfriend." The Marines' wives formed support groups, each centered on a wife who has been through this before. The base newspaper is running an ad offering "family services—assistance in deployment stress."

Cavalry and armored divisions were shipping out from Fort Hood, Texas. A lawyer in nearby Killeen executed wills and powers of attorney free of charge. A pawnshop announced it was willing to hold items for a year without charge to soldiers going to the gulf. In Memphis a radio station sponsored an "Iraq-no-phobia" gasoline sale in which a service station, its attendants dressed like Arabs, offered gas for 50 cents per gallon.

On the day when Air Force Sergeant John Campisi was buried in West Covina, Calif., the townspeople turned out in a relatively rare display of community. Campisi, 31, the father of four children, was killed by a truck on a dark Saudi airfield during the first wave of U.S. deployment. He was the conflict's first casualty. The dead man's mother said she received many calls from other mothers whose sons had just left for Saudi Arabia. "All of them seem to support sending our boys there," she said. "They seem to—but with worry." West Covina's grief for Sergeant Campisi had about it a touching purity that typified the first stage of popular sentiment toward the crisis.

In a year of amazing fast-forward history, the later stages of American thinking about the gulf crisis have been swift in arriving. Across the U.S. the element of time began to take on profound importance. The window of popular support for the American mission in the gulf may prove to be narrow. Says Sheldon Kamenicki, a political scientist at the University of Southern California: "As recently as the late '60s, President Bush might have had a couple of years in which to operate. Now he has only a couple or three months."

A formula: the duration of American resolve is inversely proportional to distance, time and size of deployment. It is easier for a vigorous people to summon resolve when they are under direct physical attack (like London during the blitz) than when their luxuries (big cars and air conditioners, for example) are being assaulted in remote places. National resolve fares badly when the fighting is far away and most of the people are mere spectators, watching from the BarcaLounger. Over time, the dominant passion of the war (as with Vietnam) may become a feeling of futility and guilt.

Americans are not sure whether they have mobilized their forces in order to defend principles of international order or merely to maintain their own access to cheap gasoline. National will is difficult to sustain in a self-indulgent, debt-ridden society that is being asked to grow indignant about being deprived of a source of its indulgence. That is the reason time is critical. Americans have traditionally found it hard to proceed in wars without a clear moral rationale for their mission. As time passes in the gulf, more and more Americans may entertain doubts about the validity of the enterprise.

"It's true that there's a moment of tremendous national consensus now," says Robert Karl Manoff, director of the Center for War, Peace and the News Media at New York University. "But it has been only three weeks in the making. If I have one criticism, it is that the really hard questions start getting asked only after the battle is already under way, not before. Questions like, Whom or what are we defending? The Kuwaitis? The Saudis? Cheap oil? Is George Bush doing more to destabilize the Middle East than Saddam Hussein? Are we prepared for popular Arab sentiment to turn against us if we start fighting Iraq?"

"War," wrote Boston *Globe* columnist Mike Barnicle last week, "is popular for the first week or month our soldiers are engaged in combat. Right now, the lust to kill Saddam Hussein and many thousands of his soldiers is thick throughout the land. Toss a few hundred funerals into the mix, add 120 women to each state's roster of Gold Star mothers, and popularity wanes. Our culture is rooted in instant gratification, quick rewards at bargain-basement prices. If the cost is heavy, or the road a bit long, recent history shows we would rather take an early exit. The nation wallows in a tidal pool of huge debt, enormous self-pity and incredible selfishness."

Doubts about the mission in the gulf

are being voiced at both ends of the political spectrum. On the left, former Attorney General Ramsey Clark and others have formed the Coalition to Stop Intervention in the Middle East. The *Nation* condemned the venture as "naked imperial intervention." On the right, some American conservatives, including Pat Buchanan and Jeane Kirkpatrick, are discovering the attractions of neo-isolationism.

During the Iranian hostage crisis in the late '70s, CBS anchorman Walter Cronkite ended his report each night by saying, "And that's the way it is," giving the day's date, and adding, "The 247th day [or whatever] of captivity for the American hostages." The nation came to be festooned in those days with yellow ribbons (after Tony Orlando's "Tie a Yellow Ribbon Round the Old Oak Tree," which sounded like a roller-rink melody).

Yellow ribbons have again made their appearance around the nation, but the American mood regarding hostages seems to have changed considerably. Americans mostly agree that it would be fatal for the nation to become so transfixed by the plight of hostages that it lost the will to act.

Television news has been restrained and responsible on the subject this time. Correspondents and anchors did not use the term hostage until Bush did. What will happen, however, as time passes and the families of hostages appear on the morning television shows, displaying photographs, personalizing the tragedy, breaking everyone's heart? It is almost impossible for television to avoid doing what it does best: to dramatize, to symbolize, to administer the anchor's sympathies and unctions. Wars by definition require a hardness of heart that looks terrible on television. Ulysses Grant would have lost his job in a week if he had had to discuss his methods (industrial warfare: the grinder) with Deborah Norville.

The key to sustaining the American mission in the gulf will be George Bush's leadership and, above all, the way in which he articulates the nation's objectives in the conflict.

Americans may have left remnants of their Wilsonian idealism years ago, somewhere north of the Mekong Delta. They are certainly no longer driven by a desire to "pay any price, bear any burden," as John Kennedy said, to ensure the liberties of others around the world. In a way, the crisis in the gulf brings together a fortuitously crass coincidence of American idealism and materialism; Americans look to punish the aggressor and protect their energy supplies at the same time.

Yet the nation will not long sustain an enterprise whose only object is to keep Americans in the wasteful, oil-guzzling style to which they have become accustomed. As time passes, the President will keep the support of Americans only by giving them a larger and clearer sense of the purpose of the mission. If the stakes are as large as the world's economic order and the danger that Saddam Hussein, armed with nuclear weapons, might eventually set off a Middle East holocaust, Bush should explain that.

RICHARD ZOGLIN

"LIVE FROM THE MIDDLE EAST!"

TIME, JANUARY 28, 1991

Coupled with the technology of war was the technology of journalism that brought it into America's living rooms. Satellites relayed live reports from reporters huddled in hotel rooms, speaking through gas masks worn to protect them from the chemical attack they believed was imminent. Americans had watched the war in Vietnam in bits and pieces on the evening news, but now the drama unfolded live before their eyes, in prime time. Cable News Network even succeeded in keeping reporters behind enemy lines for the first day of the war, dispatching live coverage of the bombs falling on Baghdad.

The jumble of contradictory information that bombarded Americans in the early days of Desert Storm was made possible by space-age technology. Yet it resembled perhaps nothing so much as the reports that reached newspaper editors in the era before trains, steamboats, and telegraphs. Then, more than a century and a half earlier, editors sorted through the information and attempted to present a coherent picture of events to their readers. Now, courtesy of television, everyone could be an armchair editor of sorts.

IT WAS A WAR THAT TELEVISION had spent five months preparing to cover, and the start of hostilities was almost bizarrely well timed: smack in the middle of the networks' evening newscasts. ABC anchorman Peter Jennings had just finished a live phone conversation with correspondent Gary Shepard in Baghdad, who said that all was quiet in the Iraqi capital. A couple of minutes later, however, Shepard was back on the air, reporting that bright flashes and tracer fire were lighting up the sky west of the city. "An attack is under way," he said. So was the TV drama.

For the ensuing hours and days, TV held the nation riveted. Not, for the most part, with pictures; those were meager, slow in coming and tightly restricted by tough Pentagon rules limiting press coverage of the conflict. Not with the sort of gripping combat footage that had

brought the Vietnam War so painfully into America's living rooms. Not (at least, not yet) with heart-wrenching scenes of body bags and grieving families. Mostly, TV conveyed the story in the simple words of reporters: ordinary people caught up in extraordinary events, describing the sights and sounds and feelings of war.

Those words and images had an instant, indelible impact. Across the nation, in homes and offices and bars, people stopped in their tracks, gathered around the TV set and held their collective breath. Like the Kennedy assassination or the space-shuttle disaster, the outbreak of war in the gulf was one of those historic events destined to be remembered forever in the terms by which television defined it.

The undisputed star of the initial coverage was CNN, the 24-hour-news chan-

Gas-masked American soldier.
(U.S. Army)

nel, which affirmed its credibility and world-wide clout with new authority. Though ABC, NBC and CNN managed to air telephone reports with their correspondents in Baghdad during the initial shelling (CBS, unluckily, could not get its phone line working), ABC and NBC lost contact after a few minutes. Only CNN was able to keep its line open and broad-

cast continuously throughout the attack. Three reporters on the ninth floor of the Al Rasheed Hotel—anchorman Bernard Shaw, veteran combat correspondent Peter Arnett and reporter John Holliman—provided an exceptional, and perhaps unprecedented, live account of the start of war from inside an enemy capital.

Their reports were a low-tech throwback to Edward R. Murrow's famous radio broadcasts from London during the blitz. As viewers watched a still screen, disembodied voices described what was happening in graphic, excited, sometimes overwrought language. Holliman: "We just heard—whoa! Holy cow! That was a large airburst that we saw." Arnett: "We're crouched behind a window in here. . . The antiaircraft is erupting again." Shaw: "This feels like we're in the center of hell." The dramatic scene was punctuated by interludes of awkward comedy, as the reporters scurried around the room on hands and knees and exchanged nervous banter. "It occurs to me that I didn't get dinner tonight," said Shaw at one point. "There's tuna fish, Bernie," replied Holliman, "plenty of tuna fish."

CNN finally lost contact with its Baghdad team 16 hours later, when Iraqi military officials shut down its phone line for what they said were security reasons. Shaw, Holliman and most other U.S. TV reporters left Baghdad the next day. (Arnett remained behind, even after Iraqi officials ordered all Western journalists to leave the city "temporarily.") ABC's Shepard, hitching a ride with a CBS producer, reached Amman, Jordan, on Friday afternoon after being stalled for four hours near an air base in western Iraq that was being shelled by U.S. warplanes. "It sure brought back a lot of memories," said Shepard, a former Vietnam correspondent. "But this is the first time I have ever reported from behind enemy lines."

Meanwhile, the TV show back home was in full swing. Once the air raids had begun, all three broadcast networks jettisoned their regular programming and aired continuous coverage for the next 42 hours. Even cable channels like MTV and ESPN, that rarely pay attention to news of the real world, interrupted regular fare to carry President Bush's speech on Wednesday night. The audience was mammoth. According to Nielsen estimates, more than 61 million TV households were tuned to Bush's speech, the biggest audience for a single event in TV history.

With acres of airtime to fill, the networks probed every nook and cranny of the unfolding story. Military experts assessed the capabilities of U.S. and Iraqi weapons; correspondents roamed the halls of the Pentagon looking for scraps of news; foreign diplomats trooped into the network studios to give their perspective on the crisis; reporters looked for fresh angles everywhere, from Wall Street to California protest marches. The networks' star anchors—Jennings on ABC, Dan Rather on CBS and Tom Brokaw on NBC—spent long hours in front of the camera, trying to manage a bombardment of information that was often sketchy, sometimes confusing, ultimately numbing—but somehow indispensable.

In another quirk of timing oddly fitting for the TV age, the drama often heated up just as the prime-time hours approached. On Thursday viewers watched in apprehension as network correspondents in Tel Aviv and Jerusalem relayed tense accounts of Iraqi missiles striking Israel. There were confusing and conflicting reports about whether the missiles were carrying chemical weapons, and scary, surrealistic scenes of correspondents being urged by anchors back home to take precautions—and calmly resuming their reports after donning gas masks. When

NBC's Brokaw told his Tel Aviv correspondent Martin Fletcher to "put on your mask," Fletcher replied, "I think I will. This is no time for heroics."

For any news operation, war is the ultimate stress test, and the networks for the most part performed impressively. ABC's coverage was the most consistently informed and level headed, with anchors Jennings and Ted Koppel doing most of the probing and commentators like military scholar Anthony Cordesman and Admiral William Crowe, a former Chairman of the Joint Chiefs of Staff, providing many of the answers. At NBC, Brokaw was a smooth master of ceremonies, while correspondent Fred Francis proved to be the most enterprising and lucid of the Pentagon reporters. Only CBS, led by the unnerving and overly cautious Rather (with his constant admonitions: "Let me underline for you what we don't know . . ."), seemed creaky and slow on its feet. CBS correspondent Bob Simon, however, got a scoop late in the week, when he drove to the Iraqi border with a camera crew—circumventing Pentagon restrictions—and got footage of a Marine base that had been shelled by Iraqi artillery.

All were overshadowed, though, by CNN's early coup. Both Dick Cheney, Secretary of Defense, and Colin Powell, Chairman of the Joint Chiefs, referred to CNN in their first press conferences following the air strikes. Powell, in response to one question, contended that U.S. bombing had seriously damaged Iraqi communications—"at least according to what Bernie Shaw tells me." Overseas, reporters and world leaders alike were glued to the all-news channel for authoritative word on the crisis. CNN's audience

was by far the highest in its history: 10.8 million households were tuned to the cable channel Wednesday night, in addition to millions more watching it on one of the more than 200 broadcast stations that carried CNN's feed. (Some network affiliates even switched over to CNN in preference to their own network's coverage.) NBC gave its rival perhaps the most gratifying plug on Wednesday night, when anchor Brokaw, with his own Baghdad reporter incommunicado, conducted an on-air interview with CNN's Shaw.

CNN's gutsy performance came as a surprise only to those who still regard the 24-hour-news network as the upstart, shoestring operation started 10 years ago by Atlanta entrepreneur Ted Turner. As the broadcast networks have trimmed their news operations for economic reasons, CNN has developed into TV's most comprehensive and reliable gatherer of news: the wire service of television. CNN has 125 staff members covering the crisis in the gulf region, for example, in contrast to 60 to 80 for each of the three networks. CNN can simply go more places and cover more news without the emphasis on slick packaging and star correspondents that often distracts the Big Three.

Network rivals were quick to point out that CNN's Baghdad scoop was as much the result of Iraqi favor and technical happenstance as journalistic enterprise. Some viewers grew annoyed at CNN's relentless self-promotion of the scoop. And despite its aggressive reporting, the cable network lags behind its broadcast rivals in providing seasoned analysis and thoughtful perspective. Though Shaw will long be remembered for his performance on Wednesday night, few will recall his odd prediction in a phone interview the night before, when war was deemed inevitable even by diehard optimists: "Personally, I do not think there will be a war."

Still, CNN's sheer presence has acted as a spur to its network rivals. Each is spending an estimated $1.5 million a week on its coverage of the gulf war. In addition, pre-empting regular programming cost each as much as $2 million a day in lost ad revenues. By Friday afternoon the three networks had returned to some semblance of regular programming, but they jumped back in frequently for new developments, such as the second wave of Iraqi missile attacks on Israel late Friday night. "It's a balancing act," said ABC News president Roone Arledge. "But as long as we feel there's breaking news, we will stay with it."

The saturation coverage of the gulf war is something entirely new. Vietnam, the last TV war, was reported mostly after the fact on film or videotape. The invasions of Panama and Grenada were over too quickly, and conducted too secretly, for TV to be much of a factor. The gulf conflict—the first full-scale war fought in the age of worldwide satellite communication—is being relayed immediately, moment by moment: every air-raid warning, bombing sortie or peep from the diplomatic community resounds across the globe as it happens. The upside is that the nation and the world are able to monitor a crucial episode in history in unprecedented detail. The downside is that every unconfirmed rumor or twist in the story is exaggerated, with all the attendant swings in emotions and expectations.

There is no telling how long this new TV drama will continue to transfix its audience. TV entertainment, after all, is supposed to have a clean story line, heroes and villains that are easy to tell apart and—most important—a satisfying ending that does not drag on and on. If the gulf war gets more complicated or overstays its welcome, the American audience might eventually grow bored.

Already, as the bombing runs and air-raid warnings have begun to grow chillingly routine, the stretches of live coverage have become somewhat repetitive and less urgent. Yet the war in the gulf has something that TV entertainments can almost never boast: the drama of the truly unexpected. As that drama unfolds, one thing is certain: television will continue to tell the story—and be an irresistible part of it.

RUSSELL WATSON AND GREGG EASTERBROOK

"A NEW KIND OF WARFARE"

NEWSWEEK, JANUARY 28, 1991

Most Americans watching and reading about the war at home found the technology fascinating. During the air war, there was little else to see but the smart bombs, cruise missiles, and aircraft. It seemed as though the entire nature of war had been altered: where once soldiers actually had to go and fight, now they could sit back and let remote-controlled robots do the dirty work, acting out their parts in a giant video game.

It was not so, of course. Left out of most stories about the war's technology was its impact on Iraqi soldiers, to whom the term video game *would hardly have seemed appropriate. And after the war was over, it gradually became apparent to American civilians that smart bombs were not so smart as they had thought—even in the computer age, there was still no such thing as a surgical strike. Still, in the early weeks of the war, the new technology was a hot topic.*

I T SEEMED ALMOST TOO EASY. With eerie precision, "smart" bombs dropped down air shafts and burst through bunker doors. Cruise missiles, lethal robots launched from warships in the Persian Gulf and the Red Sea, slammed into the Defense Ministry and the presidential palace in Baghdad. Hot streams of antiaircraft fire lit up the night, while bomb explosions bloomed above the skyline. Out in the desert, the Iraqi Air Force hid in its hardened shelters; the few pilots who came up to challenge the intruders were quickly shot down or turned tail and fled to the north. To television watchers back home, the bombardment of Baghdad seemed like a kind of video game, at once impersonal and fantastic. It was intensely real to the pilots who had to fly through the Iraqi flak, but even they brimmed with confidence about their high-tech toys. "You pick precisely which target you want . . . the men's room or the ladies' room," said Col. Alton Whitley, who commands a wing of F-117A Stealth fighters.

When Desert Shield turned into Desert Storm last week, aerial warfare seemed to cross a threshold into a new generation. High-tech weapons, maligned in the past for their stratospheric cost and earthbound fallibility, suddenly seemed to work almost flawlessly. The Navy's Tomahawk became the first cruise missile to be used in battle, and of the first 150 that were fired, more than 85 percent hit their targets, Pentagon sources said. The Army's Patriot became the first missile to shoot down another missile under combat conditions, destroying what was thought to be an Iraqi Scud launched toward a base in Saudi Arabia. Electronic countermeasures befuddled Iraq's air defenses. Bombs and air-launched missiles, guided by laser beams, infrared images and television pictures, slammed into target after target, erasing memories of embarrassing misses in earlier attacks on Libya and Panama. It is in the nature of war that some missiles will go awry and some weapons misfire in the campaign ahead. Already the edge has been taken off Desert Storm's triumph by the inability of the air campaign to prevent Iraq from firing Scud missiles at Israel, which raises the specter of a wider regional war. But with most of the technology working well, the strategists' dream of the decisive "surgical strike" may now be one step closer to reality.

The early successes heartened an American public that had dreaded the outbreak of war against Iraq. In a *Newsweek* Poll taken just after the fighting began, George Bush's approval rating soared to 83 percent, the highest of his highflying presidency. Approval of his actions in the gulf surged to 85 percent. The president and his advisers kept pinching themselves: the long-awaited war against Saddam Hussein *had* to be tougher than this. "We must be realistic," Bush cautioned at a news briefing on Friday. "There will be losses. There will be obstacles along the way. And war is never cheap or easy."

'ROPE-A-DOPE'

"WE'RE INTO EUPHORIA CONTROL around here," said one of the president's closest advisers. "It's going to get a lot worse." Even as the air war seemed to be going almost entirely their way, American officials worried that perhaps Saddam was holding back, absorbing the first blow from the allies and saving his strength for a bloody land battle later on. "The guy's doing a rope-a-dope on us," fretted a top U.S. strategist.

Bush tried to keep everyone's eye on the goal: to force Iraq to withdraw unconditionally from occupied Kuwait. But Saddam soon muddied the waters with an old-tech weapon of his own. On Friday and Saturday, his forces fired Scuds into Israel from launchers in western Iraq. Straining at the limit of their range, the obsolescent missiles exploded almost harmlessly and hurt few Israelis. Saddam's intention was to provoke, hoping that Israeli retaliation would transform the fight over Kuwait into an Arab-Israeli conflict, a crusade he would be only too happy to lead. But Israel held its fire. . . . Bush said allied warplanes were conducting "the darndest search-and-destroy effort that's ever been undertaken in that area" to eliminate Saddam's remaining Scuds.

By the end of the week, however, the job still had not been done. Air Force officers believed that Saddam still had about 50 operational Scud launchers. The preliminary air bombardment of Iraq had been planned to go on for nine days before the ground war began, *Newsweek* learned. Now, bad weather in the region and the failure to knock out the Scuds had prolonged the aerial campaign.

That was the only known setback of the campaign's first few days. But in the opening stages of the conflict, the Americans and their partners in the air war— Britain, Saudi Arabia, France, Italy, Canada and exiles from Kuwait—had been lucky. Several factors made the allied forces much more successful than they might have been in another setting. Among them:

THE RIGHT WEATHER

THE NIGHT ON WHICH THE WAR began was clear and dark, with a new moon just arrived. Those are the best conditions for the night-vision equipment used on allied fighter-bombers and for their smart bombs. The climate also was ideal for cruise missiles. The optical scanner that guides a Tomahawk in its final approach to the target can get confused if it has to look through fog, clouds, smoke or dust. After the first 36 hours, however, the weather turned cloudy, and some allied jets were forced to return to base without dropping their bombs, even though some of the warplanes were loaded with "all weather" devices.

Missile attack in the Persian Gulf. *(U.S. Army)*

THE RIGHT TIME

THE EARLY AIR RAIDS WERE EX-
tremely complex, but commanders of the
international coalition had plenty of time
to plan and practice during the five
months they spent waiting for the war to
start. They had time to coordinate different forces so that their planes would not
be jamming or shooting at one another.
They had time to build new airfields in
Saudi Arabia to accommodate ground-
based aircraft and to provide refueling
facilities for carrier-based warplanes
committed to the battle in Kuwait and
Iraq. American commanders also had
time to prepare the elaborate digital maps
that have to be programmed into cruise

missiles in advance of an attack. Such
maps did not exist in early August. Incredulous, the regional commander, Gen.
Norman Schwarzkopf, used his considerable temper to get them made. In a faster-
starting, more fluid war, the cruise missiles might have been much less effective.

THE RIGHT TERRAIN

IRAQ AND KUWAIT ARE OPEN
country, where guidance systems and
night-vision devices can readily pick out
targets. In forests or jungles, the same targets might be harder for pilots and some
of their sensors to locate. And the war is
being fought in a relatively small area,
close to allied air bases and launching

platforms. "You have to wonder if the technology would appear to be working so well against the Soviet Union," says Col. Andrew Duncan, a military-affairs expert at the International Institute for Strategic Studies (IISS) in London. The Soviets have much more sophisticated air defenses than Iraq, deployed over a much larger arena. "Think of a battlefield stretching all the way from northern Norway to Turkey, at least 10 times the current area," says Duncan. "There might simply not be enough technology to cover all of that. In a larger theater, you eventually run out of resources."

THE RIGHT DISPLAY

WHEN THE AMERICANS HIT BAGHdad, television recorded the high-tech blitz. Allied warplanes made their own visual records as well, and when U.S. generals played some tape for the press, they selected highlights from the most successful missions. Reporters were not shown tapes of bombs or missiles that went astray. And no one, except the Iraqi victims, witnessed he old-fashioned onslaught of the giant B-52 bombers dumping loads of bombs on troops cowering in their bunkers. The B-52s attacked targets that were outside the range of television's prying eye.

THE RIGHT ENEMY

IN THE FINAL ANALYSIS, IRAQ IS a dictatorship run by a leader who may be mad in the clinical sense—and whose notions of modern warfare are somewhat quaint. Armies led by tyrants often lack effective officers, because strong opinions

and individual initiative are not encouraged. This was apparent during Iraq's war with Iran. In eight years of fighting against one of the world's most disorganized states, Iraq managed to gain only slivers of territory. Iraqi commanders appeared hesitant and insecure, failing to assert themselves in the most obvious ways, such as pursuing shattered Iranian columns. Last week the Iraqis once again seemed unsure of themselves, except for the diversionary attack on Israel.

Last Tuesday morning, more than 12 hours before the United Nations deadline for Iraqi withdrawal from Kuwait, President Bush signed an order for the war to begin the next day. Wednesday morning, when the deadline had passed without any concessions from Saddam, Bush saw no reason to change the timetable, which called for an air attack to begin shortly before 7 o'clock that night (3 A.M. Thursday in Baghdad). The allies were notified of the pending air war, and doubters climbed on the bandwagon. France, which had failed with a peacemaking effort at the last minute, put its forces in the gulf region under U.S. command—though not for airstrikes deep inside Iraq. Turkey, which had hedged on the question of a second front, eventually decided that bases on its territory could be used for attacks on Iraq by American warplanes.

IN THE CROSS HAIRS

ONE STRATEGIC TARGET ON THE first night of the war was Iraq's command-and-control system, the network of telephone lines and microwave communications that connects Baghdad to outlying Army headquarters and to the country's four air-defense centers. The capital itself was protected by surface-to-air missiles (SAMS), antiaircraft guns and fighter planes, none of which had been knocked out yet. Thus American planners chose to attack the main telecommunications building in Baghdad with an F-117A Stealth fighter-bomber, the angular, slow-flying plane that is nearly invisible to radar. One of the F-117s neatly dropped a 2,000-pound, laser-guided smart bomb onto the building. In a videotape shown to pool reporters later, the cross hairs of the plan's targeting system focus on the telecommunications building and then the bomb hits it, showering debris from all sides. . . .

Other targets on the first day included air defenses, missile launchers and troop concentrations. Some allied planes jammed Iraq radars or knocked them out. . . . Others, including the British Tornadoes, cratered the runways of Iraqi airfields, temporarily closing them down. United States Navy A-6Es and F/A-18s bombed Scud missile platforms in western Iraq, where they threatened Israel. Iraqi troops in or near Kuwait were attacked by tankbusting A-10s and Apache helicopters and by the ponderous B-52s.

Some of the most sophisticated attacks were carried out by single planes delivering single, precisely targeted bombs or missiles, rather than by waves of attack planes, which might have caused enough smoke or dust to confuse one another's guidance systems. To get to the target, however, each attacker was enfolded in what the planners call a "force package," a team of aircraft playing various roles. Standard U.S. tactics against a defended position call for the first players onto the field to be the "defense suppression" air-craft. An EF-111 would jam the Iraqis' long-range radar, forcing the SAM crews to turn on their own battery radar. Then an F4-G Wild Weasel would fire a missile to knock out the radar, grounding the SAMs.

Next would come the fighter planes, such as F-15s or F-16s, to protect the attack aircraft. Finally the bombers would come into play—any of a half-dozen models, depending on the mission. The planes in the force package, which come from different speeds, would not have to fly all the way to the target together. Instead, they would arrive there in a precisely timed pattern, with AWACS command planes acting as traffic cops in the crowded and unfriendly skies.

After 36 hours of almost trouble-free bombing, the weather turned cloudy, and some coalition aircraft with daytime roles were unable to complete their assignments. Their commanders preferred aborted missions over the risk of hurting innocent civilians. So instead of jettisoning their bombs and missiles in the desert or the sea, the pilots returned to their bases and made dangerous landings with the weapons still attached to their planes. Some pilots said cynically that the bombs and missiles were too expensive to dump. While the weather hampered pilots based on the south of Iraq, American warplanes began attack from Turkey, presumably aiming at northern airfields that had provided sanctuary for Iraqi pilots in earlier battles.

PARKED INDOORS

AS THE AIR WAR CONTINUED, THE coalition gradually shifted to new targets. On Saturday, Gen. Colin Powell, the chairman of the Joint Chiefs of Staff, said the attacks would begin to concentrate more heavily on the elite Republican Guards and other Iraqi ground forces stationed in or near Kuwait. But one original objective of the air was still had not been achieved: to knock out the Scuds. Although most of the fixed launches apparently were destroyed, some mobile launchers—no one knew exactly how many—survived the onslaught and were able to hurl rockets at Israel. The threat posed by Scuds tipped with conventional or poison-gas warheads may continue for the rest of the war. "They're parked indoors," said Col. Duncan of IISS. "No matter how many satellites you have overhead or how many search-and-destroy missions you do, nobody can see through a roof."

Even though they held the upper hand technologically, most of the coalition's young pilots found their first experience of combat to be as frightening as it was exhilarating. "It was the most scary thing I have ever done in my life," Flight Lt. Ian Long, the pilot of a British Tornado, told pool reporters. "We were frightened of failure, frightened of dying," he said. Inevitably, a few of them died, despite the weakness of Iraqi air defenses. American, British, Italian and Kuwaiti planes went down in the first two days. The first American plane went down in the first two days. The first American plane to disappear was an F/A-18 from the aircraft carrier USS *Saratoga*, piloted by Lt. Cmdr. Michael Scott Speicher, a 33-year old father of two from Jacksonville, Fla. His plane was hit by a SAM, and by late last week he was still listed as missing.

It may have been some consolation to the pilots of high-tech attack planes that their bombs and missiles produced little "collateral damage"—the military euphemism for death and destruction among civilians. The accuracy of modern munitions permits relatively small war heads. The Maverick air-to-ground missiles, for example, can knock out a tank or a bunker, but its "destruct radius" for that purpose is only about 10 feet, which means that it may cause no widespread destruction if it lands in a suburban street. After the pounding of Baghdad on Wednesday night, some eyewitnesses were surprised by the lack of damage to civilian areas in the city. "You expected to see, the following morning a devastated landscape, but what you saw in fact was a very surgical operation by the Americans," said Nigel Baker, producer for Britain's Independent Television News, who traveled overland from Baghdad to Amman after covering the first night of the war.

'THE STUFF WORKS'

SOME OF THE BEST EXAMPLES of precision bombing were collected in videotape shown to the press last Friday by Lt. Gen. Charles Horner, the Air Force commander in the Persian Gulf region. One clip shows two smart bombs slamming into a Scud missile bunker; in another, a bomb is directed straight down the air shaft in the middle of "my counterpart's headquarters in Baghdad," according to Horner. In other examples shown, there was no smoke or bad weather to disorient the guidance system, and the Iraqi air defenses were not energetic enough to keep the pilots away from the targets. There was no footage of the 20 percent of warheads that missed the target, by official reckoning. Still, the videotape showed emphatically, as Norman Friedman, an American weapons analyst, put it, that "the stuff works. It works unbelievably well."

In the right conditions, unmanned weapons can work even better. The cruise missiles achieved a slightly higher success rate than the bombers, without risk to pilots. Tomahawks are best suited to stationary targets in situations that allow time for elaborate guidance programs to be written. In such circumstances, live air crews are probably a needless risk. The success of the Patriot anti-missile missile was equally impressive. Before dawn last Friday morning, ground crews at the Dhahran air base saw the sky light up with the bright flash of a midair explosion. "They said, 'Oh my, it's a Scud'," transportation Sgt. Robin Milonas, 38, a reservist from Tacoma, Wash., said later. The thunderous boom she heard next was the sound of the Patriot intercepting the Iraqi missile thousands of feet above the runway. "People cheered," said Milonas.

The improved accuracy of high-tech weapons may take warfare into a new era of truly surgical airstrikes. In World War II, the typical accuracy of U.S. bombing put explosives within about a mile of the target. By Vietnam, the circle had shrunk to about a quarter mile, and at the time of the Libyan raid in 1986, it was down to perhaps 500 feet. That sounds impressive, but for many military targets, a 500-foot miss is as bad as a mile. If recent advances have brought the margin of error down to 30 feet or less, as appears to have been achieved during parts of Desert Storm, and if the electronics are now as reliable as they are said to be, then the age of surgical bombing is finally at hand.

To their admirers, smart weapons can seem downright humane. They spare civilian lives, limit destruction and promise quick results. Yet they hold a darker promise, as well. After the gulf war, dozens of other countries will scramble to acquire the technology employed by the United States and its allies. Almost all of it, unfortunately, can be used with nuclear, chemical or biological warheads or with the ballistic missiles that many nations are now adding to their arsenals. In the regional conflicts to come, smart bombs and missiles may be the weapons of choice for any country that can afford them.

TOM MATHEWS AND TONY CLIFTON

"TORTURE AND TORMENT"

NEWSWEEK, FEBRUARY 4, 1991

The apparently easy successes of the first days of high-tech air war might have lulled some Americans into a feeling that victory would be both quick and inevitable. The allied prisoners the Iraqis paraded before television cameras eradicated any such feelings. The captives appeared to have been brutalized, and they made wooden statements condemning President

Bush and the allied war effort. Had the scene been deliberately calculated to galvanize American hatred of Saddam and determination to carry the war through, it could hardly have been more effective.

This article, by Newsweek *correspondents, analyzes the impact on prisoners of war and speculates—with grisly examples from previous American wars—on the fate of these newest POWs.*

THE TOP GUN NEVER BELIEVES it can happen to him. Not when the engines of his F-14 are roaring in his ears, his instruments all check out and the smart bombs and missiles are ready at his fingertips. Not when the enemy won't even come up to fight. Not even when the antiaircraft batteries open up around the target and the night lights up with tracers. Then suddenly he sees a blinding flash and hears the crump of an explosion. Black smoke fills his cockpit. The plane cartwheels out of control. With a sharp bang the ejection seat hurls him into the darkness at 600 miles an hour. Icy wind tears at his face, and his bones shudder with the jolt as his parachute opens. Then down, down he floats, right into the hands of that enemy he was just trying to kill. "One minute you're a hawk in the skies," shudders an old POW who has made the tumble, "the next you are an ant on the ground."

That fall from martial grace, from the warrior ascendant to the captive under the boot, lends the POW his tragic gravity. You could see it at work last week in the swollen faces, glazed eyes and mumbling voices of the American, British, Italian and Kuwaiti airmen that Saddam Hussein dogmarched through Baghdad and grilled on TV. In staging the performance, Saddam added Iraq's name to a tradition of dishonor that snakes from the Third Reich's Stalag 17 and Japan's Bilibid Prison to the POW pens of North Korea

and on to the Hanoi Hilton in Vietnam. President Bush, an old Navy pilot who was shot down and rescued in World War II, swore he would never let Saddam get away with it. What Bush knew and Saddam neglected was a truth as old as combat itself. Nations at war can measure their raw power by success at arms; but the more accurate gauge of their moral fiber is the way they treat their POWs.

Now the war against Saddam will create a new generation of POWs. The dictator chose to introduce his first captives with a television special. Wearing their uniforms, seven allied airmen three Americans, two Brits, an Italian and a Kuwaiti—sat glumly in front of a white wall somewhere in Baghdad. An interrogator questioned and prompted them. He opened with questions about their names, ages, units; then he asked what the fliers thought about "this aggression against Iraq." Like zombies out of "The Manchurian Candidate," Guy Hunter Jr., 46, a Marine warrant officer, said, "I condemn the aggression against peaceful Iraq," and Jeffrey Zaun, 28, a Navy lieutenant, said, "Our leaders and our people have wrongly attacked the peaceful people of Iraq." Hunter also said, "I think this war is crazy," a fresh almost believable opinion; but he quickly reverted to parroting the interrogator's favorite word: aggression.

Images told more than any word about the reality on the screen. Out of consideration for frightened relatives, the Penta-

Refueling over Kuwait. *(U.S. Army)*

gon refused to speculate on whether the prisoners had been beaten. Saddam refused to let the International Red Cross examine them. The trauma of ejecting from a crippled plane could have produced the lumps and bruises on the faces of each man. But, in private, Air Force officers who studied videotapes of the interviews didn't believe that. "It's bulls—t," exploded one angry colonel. "They've been through more than cockpit injuries." The prevailing view was that during the first 48 hours after capture, the men had been beaten into attacking the war. "Forty-eight hours is sufficient time," said Arizona's Sen. John McCain, a Navy pilot who spent nearly six years as a POW during the Vietnam War. "With a skillful interrogator, no food, sleep or water, you can get a statement."

The airmen may not have been entirely helpless. McCain believes they were acting like robots to send a message home. Some new evidence supported the theory. The next day the Iraqis hauled forth Maj. Jeffrey Scott Tice and Capt. Harry Michael Roberts. Speaking in chopped syllables like the Tin Woodsman of Oz, Roberts said, "I-was-shot-down-be-fore-rea-ching-my-tar-get." And mocking the interrogators' accent, Tice said he had been shot down by a surface-to-air "meesile." At the Pentagon, officers scrutinized the tapes and detected a clear signal: the two men were reading a prepared script, not speaking of their own free will.

How to make Saddam change his scabrous behavior was a frustrating problem for the Bush administration. Outraged, Under Secretary of State Robert Kimmitt summoned Iraq's charge d'affaires to the State Department and shoved a copy of the Geneva Conventions into his hand along with a formal diplomatic protest. The conventions, signed by Iraq along with 163 other nations, stipulate that prisoners of war may not be dragged before hostile crowds, beaten or mistreated or used for propaganda. To step up pressure, the department and the White House threatened to put Saddam on trial as a war criminal, but this was a rather moot point until they caught him. The more serious warning came from Defense Secretary Dick Cheney, who said Saddam would not be able to obstruct the air war by using POWs as human shields.

For Saddam the rewards of abusing the POWs clearly outweighed the risks involved in his tactics. Part of his motive was simply to buck up Iraqis, who had seen thousands of American airstrikes. When Vice Adm. James Stockdale, a retired Navy flier who spent more than seven years as a Vietnamese prisoner of war, looked at the videotapes of Hunter and Zaun, he felt a shock of recognition at the behavior of their captors. "They are trying to show that the knights on white horses are reduced to whimpering wimps," he said. "This is supposed to convince Iraqis to 'go get your guns and we can take these people to the cleaners'." By flaunting the captured airmen, Saddam has also elected to wage psychological war against American pilots flying combat sorties. His calculation is that when American pilots see their comrades humiliated on TV, they will lose their nerve on the attack.

For the short term, it is more likely that they will get mad and get even. Pilots flying from airfields in Saudi Arabia and Bahrain watch CNN on local television, and carrier pilots get cassette videotapes a day or two late depending on the weather. When the hostages came on TV last week, Maj. Scott Hill, a Thunderbolt jockey from Chagrin Falls, Ohio, was sitting in a ready room with 10 other pilots. "We will hit 'em harder and make them pay for every violation of decency," Hill told a pool reporter. And that didn't mean going off half-cocked. "When we go to war we go to war smart. We don't go to war with our hair on fire and our fangs out."

While most pilots felt that way, there were a few signs that Saddam's little show had made them edgy. Aboard the USS *Saratoga*, which had lost three planes and had one pilot among the POWs, the crew became so tense the military kept reporters away. The official reason was that "logistical problems" prevented visits to the carrier; but choppers were shuttling back and forth all the time. Pilots who had given their full names and exploits to reporters during the first few days of the air war started using only first names or initials. Some were worried that Iraqi agents would get their home addresses and organize terrorist attacks on their families. Others feared that if they were shot down, the Iraqis would find them boasting of successes on old CNN tapes. Still others decided not to paint silhouettes of destroyed targets on the fuselages of their jets. If the tallies appeared on wreckage, the pilot would be in for double mayhem.

If the way Iraq treated prisoners during its war with Iran is any indicator, wounded American pilots can probably expect only perfunctory medical care. American military doctrine calls for immediately evacuating the wounded from the battlefield. The Iraqis take a different approach. As the ordeal of the first American hostages was playing out on TV, an officer at the Pentagon remembered how an Iraqi had once told him Saddam's doctrine: "When you are fighting you fight. When it's over you worry about the wounded."

SOLID KICKS

SADDAM DIDN'T LET THE RED Crescent inspect his prisoner-of-war camps until his war with Iran was almost over; but a United States study reported many head wounds among POWs, with scars, bruises, broken teeth and other signs of frequent brutality. The Iraqis took reporters only to showplace camps where squatting POWs shouting "Death to Khomeini" were obviously prepped on what else to say. On one such trip to a camp in southern Iraq the guards shouted at their captives in Farsi, who all yelled back in the same language that they were well treated and happy. Suddenly from the back, a young prisoner said in very good English, "They're not treating us well at all; they stole my watch and boots last night." For a moment there was stunned silence. Then the guards dragged the young man off. From around the corner, the reporters soon heard the thump of solid kicks and blows.

The same rules will undoubtedly apply to Saddam's latest prisoners. The Pentagon does not know where he is holding them as human shields and it is too early to say precisely what will happen to them if the war goes on for a long time. But military thinkers have accumulated quite a data bank on POWs from experience in early wars. According to American Ex-Prisoners of War, a national organization of former POWs based in Arlington, Texas, there were 4,120 U.S. POWs in World War I, 130,201 in World War II, 7,140 in Korea and 766 in Vietnam. The shock for all of them was tremendous. Newly captured prisoners are often wounded. Even if they are uninjured they are suddenly under an enemy's total control. A downed pilot's first feeling tends to be one of inadequacy and remorse. "You think 'Hey, I must have screwed up or I wouldn't be in this situation'," says David Hoffman, a retired Navy captain who flew F-4s in Vietnam until he was shot down in 1971. "You have to get at peace with yourself. You have to learn to stay in control."

Pilots can acquire some of this learning through the survival, evasion, rescue and escape training they all undergo before flying into combat. Trainers playing hostile forces "capture" their students. For 24 to 36 hours they isolate them, grill them and manhandle them. The time and details of the program are classified. The aim is to eliminate the fear of the unknown that destroys a downed flier's equilibrium, but there are limits to what drill can do. "You know you are going home on Saturday night," says Hoffman. "The uncertainty of real captivity can't be simulated." Before his captors threw him into isolation for 100 days, they told him his entire life story. "They said, 'We can get to your family any time we want'," he recalls. "I had a lot of time to think what they could really do."

Iraqi interrogators will probably try to pry sensitive military data from Saddam's POWs as fast as they can. On the battlefield, where conditions rapidly change, secrets have a shelf life of a month or so. If the Iraqis follow the model of the Vietnamese, they will try to extract bombing targets and codes first. To encourage Stockdale, a Medal of Honor winner shot down in 1965 after 200 combat missions, Vietnamese interrogators used a torture called "the ropes." They tied him up in ways that caused great pain for long periods of time. When Stockdale saw Zaun on TV, he thought he saw some familiar signs. "He talked to me like a guy who had just come off the ropes," he says. "Your circulation is cut off, you're disoriented. The pain makes you numb."

Saddam and other thugs can use torture in all shapes and sizes. Stockdale spent seven and a half years in the Hanoi Hilton, the Zoo and other North Vietnamese stops. Captors broke his back and shattered his leg trying to make him talk. Finally he signed a letter to the camp commissar purporting to give his captors all the information they were after. He faked everything. Still, the reality is that torture works. The military Code of Conduct used to forbid POWs from giving anything but their name, rank and serial number. Now it requires only that they resist to the best of their ability giving anything but those basics. "The problem is fear—fear and guilt," says Stockdale. Even when anti-American statements are coerced from pilots, they feel ashamed. "It's the worst feeling in the world," says Hoffman. He remembers the pain of returning to an isolation cell or cellblock after saying things he knew he shouldn't have said: "You feel like an absolute piece of crap."

A 'B.A.C.K.' LIST

IT IS DIFFICULT TO FIGHT BACK against an enemy who controls your food, water, clothing, shelter and movement; but it can be done. As senior POW in his camp, Stockdale took command of the other POWs. In prison, where the individual can be isolated and broken, he says, it is vital to maintain a system of orders and communications. This will be impossible for Saddam's prisoners, who are now scattered and deployed as human shields, one of the worst configurations for a POW. Stockdale instructed his own men to refuse in the beginning all objectionable requests from their captors. A POW who cooperated once, then balked, was treated more brutally than a holdout. When the men came to him with a request for a list of other do's and don'ts, he constructed a four-letter formula he called B.A.C.K. The letter B stood for "don't Bow in public"; A was "stay off the Air" (no propaganda broadcasts); C meant "don't admit Crimes." And the letter K was "don't Kiss'em goodbye."

Iraqi cultural values—as well as how much Saddam thinks he can wring from his prisoners—will determine how badly they are treated in the months ahead. Not all countries are as bad as others in this regard. Saddam has always admired Germany, but so far he shows no signs of following German practices for POWs. William Chapin was 25 in 1944 when the B-24 bomber he was flying was shot down over Yugoslavia. A German patrol found him with a badly broken leg. That night he lay in a litter alongside Wehrmacht enlisted men, some wounded by bombs from his own raid. A German surgeon amputated his leg to save his life, treating him before the Germans because he was an officer. He wound up in Stalag 17. "It was rough, but not concentration-camp rough," he remembers. "We were cold as hell and hungry as hell, but we weren't beaten." After seeing the Americans on Iraqi TV he thought, "I got none of the manipulation—where POWs become tools."

The real question is whether Saddam attaches any value to the lives of the POWs or whether he holds them in contempt for being captured. During World War II the Japanese considered surrender a moral disgrace and POWs beyond the human pale. After the fall of Corregidor in the Philippines, Fred Peppers, then a 24-year-old Navy quartermaster, spent three years in camps where POWs were beaten, starved and left to die from diseases. He ate rice crawling with maggots to survive. For a time he was a slave laborer in a coal mine. He stands 6 feet 2 inches tall. When he was released, he weighed 92 pounds. "Next year it will be 50 years," he says. "You don't ever get past it. Every time there's a war, the bad memories come back." What has happened to Saddam's captives, he says, has left him "pretty depressed."

The will to live is the only force a POW can count on to get through the worst of conditions. After North Korean troops overran Lt. Charles Minietta's headquarters base in 1950, he spent 38 months, including a winter death march, as a POW. The North Koreans aimed pistols at the heads of captives to make them do propaganda broadcasts. His comrades suffered from frostbite, dysentery, beriberi, hepatitis, and night blindness. Of 750 men captured with him, 500 died. He would wake up mornings to find the man next to him frozen to death. Others gave up eating their meager rations of two millet balls a day and died of starvation. "They had what we called 'give-up-itis'," he recalled. "A man would tell you, 'I'm not going to be here tomorrow, I'm going to die,' and by God, he would be gone."

LICE AND DOGFIGHTS

NEXT TO THE FEAR OF DYING, A POW's worst torment is the feeling that no one knows where he is or cares. After William Fornes tangled with MiG-15s, he was captured by Chinese troops in North Korea. Neither his outfit nor his family knew whether he was dead or alive. He spent 10 months in solitary counting lice and watching dogfights overhead. Then the dogfights stopped. "That was the worst," he remembers. "I couldn't help thinking, if the war is over, why am I still here?" It was not an idle thought. Unlike German POW camps, Korean and Vietnamese camps were never liberated. The MIA lobby thinks Vietnam is still holding captives, or at least their remains. The Pentagon sees no evidence that any POWs are alive in Southeast Asia.

Fornes didn't know whether he would reach Virginia as a hero or a traitor, and he was surprised when his hometown gave him a parade. After years of nightmares, he found comfort talking to other ex-POWs. Whether they had been held by the Germans, Japanese, Koreans or Vietnamese, they shared a bond that now extends to those held by the Iraqis. Today Fornes is trying to raise $2.5 million for a POW museum in Americus, Ga., near the site of the South's Andersonville POW camp during the Civil War. Andersonville showed what horrors even Americans can work on one another as POWs. When Fornes dies, he wants to be buried alongside the 13,000 Union soldiers who lie there, a Southerner among Yankees. "Andersonville offers me a kinship that transcends everything else," he says. "There I am among my own." A prisoner of war at peace.

EDWARD BARNES

"SURRENDER"

LIFE, FEBRUARY 25, 1991

Edward Barnes is an associate editor for Time *Magazine. Before coming to Time, he was a senior correspondent for LIFE, for which he spent six months in the Middle East covering the Persian Gulf War. During that time, his cutting-edge reporting led him to the Kuwaiti border, where four Iraqi soldiers surrendered to him. He also made news with several Gulf War exclusives, including an interview with a rebel leader in Nasiriyah and a report of mass graves being dug for the allied Arab troops.*

FROM A DISTANCE THEY APpeared to be nothing more than a clutch of soldiers manning another desert checkpoint, four indistinct figures alongside the empty road, waiting to stop cars and ask for the day's password. We had spent the night with an eight-man Kuwaiti patrol unit, at the western end of the front that separates the allied armies from Iraqi troops, but we had left them some time before. It was now 7:35 in the morning, and the sun had only begun to penetrate the smoke and haze of a long night's bombing.

As our car drew closer, someone said hopefully, "Syrians!" But it was clear almost immediately that they were Iraqis—and for a moment we felt the closeness of our own capture or death. And then two of them lifted over their heads the white leaflets allied planes had been raining over Iraqi positions, leaflets that bore instruction in the art of surrender. The other two had draped their AK-47s over their left shoulders, muzzles pointing downward, as the leaflets directed.

Although the men looked healthy, it was clear that they had been through a kind of hell. Their dark-green uniforms were ragged and filthy, their shoes split and torn. Two of the soldiers shrank against the morning chill, wrapped in tattered, thin blankets. But nothing showed their condition more clearly than their blank, accepting faces and supplicant body language. They were putting themselves at our mercy.

As we prepared to drive through the desert to an allied forward reconnaissance post, the four men jammed into the backseat of our gray Land Cruiser didn't say a word. Tony had wedged himself into the luggage compartment, nose to knees with our gear, and Richard and Isabel shared the bucket seat next to mine in front. With our meager Arabic, all we had been able to explain to our captives was that we were *sahafi*—journalists. We passed out cigarettes, bread, orange juice, some slices of Kraft cheese. Throughout the 70-kilometer drive, they barely spoke to one another. But one did say, "Saddam finished, Iraq finished." And one of his comrades added, "George Bush, O.K."

We arrived at our destination within an hour. I had been to this allied commando encampment three times since the war began. It lies three kilometers from the first of two parallel walls of sand that divide the warring armies. Both of these walls run the whole length of the front, relics from prewar days when they were positioned to regulate trade and immigration along the Saudi-Kuwaiti frontier. The sand walls are 15 feet high, with a deep trench dividing them. Now in wartime they separate the allies from the all but unknown men in revetments across the barren plain. In the hours to follow, we would learn quite a bit about them.

The Iraqis were debriefed by an English-speaking Saudi lieutenant based at the commando encampment, a gathering of several large tents behind sand walls pushed hastily into place by bulldozers. Some soldiers gave two large enamel bowls filled with a yellow soup to the Iraqis, and as they ate they answered the lieutenant's questions.

The four men—three privates and a corporal—told us that for three months they had shared a trench three meters long, two meters wide and two meters deep at the very front of the Iraqi lines, in the middle of a mine field. Each of them

had been drafted for what they were told would be three years' national service; all of them, as it turned out, have served at least six years. Mousa, a 35-year-old farmer from Mosul, has been a private in Saddam's army for 11 years. None of the soldiers had had any communication with family members in more than two months.

They told us they had no idea how many other men occupied their position, how many in their company had been killed by allied bombers, or whether reinforcements had been brought in as prelude to the coming ground war. Their commanders had kept each four-man unit separate from the other troops in the 36th Division; the only contact with their comrades was a daily delivery at four P.M. of their single meal: some bread and five spoonfuls of rice. "Usually there is little water to drink," one said, "and none for bathing."

They had subsisted on this meager ration during the endless assaults on their position by allied aircraft. The planes, they explained, "shoot at us with bombs every day. It never stops. Everyone wants to come like us to Saudi Arabia. When the ground attack comes, they will all surrender." But right now, for most of the troops, fight is out of the question: "At night, anyone who gets out of their hole is shot" by Iraqi guards.

This gun-muzzle discipline, it became clear, was only part of a program of terror inflicted on the soldiers by Iraqi commanders. When the surrender leaflets began to drop from the sky, the officers told their troops the paper contained poisonous chemicals. The soldiers were also told that if somehow they evaded the Iraqi sentries who were poised to shoot deserters on sight, then the Americans who captured them would kill them. The land mines ahead of their position threatened any who dared go forward; more mines and the Saddam-loyalist members of the Republican Guard—some of them guarding the supply corridors that led into each trench—lay in wait behind them. "The men fear the Guard," one said, "because they will kill them if they want to stop fighting."

The four, who because of their forward position probably knew the placement of the mines ahead of them, had decided to attempt an escape when they became convinced they could not survive the allied bombing. After sunset on February 5, when darkness had come to the desert and a lull in the bombing raids had calmed the skies, they made their break.

For nearly 12 hours, they said, they avoided barbed wire, mines and their own troops until they were able to cross the no-man's-land between the two sand walls. "We would run and hide, run and hide, all night long," one said.

After 75 minutes, the interrogation was concluded. These men had betrayed neither fear nor relief, neither anger nor vindication. They answered the lieutenant's questions evenly. Now, even as the larger war rages on, their own war is over. "Saddam is stupid," one of them said. "We don't belong here. This has nothing to do with us. It is all Saddam. He is crazy."

It was Mousa, the farmer-soldier who had spent more than a decade in Saddam's service, who summed it up best for all of them. "After the war," he said, "I look only for safety."

EDWARD BARNES

"WHEN FREEDOM CAME"

LIFE, MARCH 11, 1991

Edward Barnes was the first print reporter to arrive in Kuwait City, some thirteen hours ahead of the Pentagon's pool journalists. This is his account of the city's liberation, written for one of LIFE's *special weekly editions on the war.*

THIRTY MILES FROM KUWAIT City, the roads were empty, eerily empty, and the only evidence that the Iraqis had ever been there was the acrid smoke from hundreds of oil well fires, so thick it stung the eyes and cast a pall of perpetual twilight across the sky. Photographer Tony O'Brien and I had been traveling with a Marine scout battalion, part of the lead element of the allied offensive into Kuwait, and we had broken off

to head straight for the capital. We'd be safest driving across the expanse of sand using a string of power lines for bearings, a Marine captain had told us; it was the best way, he'd said, to avoid the minefields spread throughout the desert.

There was nothing to guide us but a compass, the six months of experience we'd had in the desert and the simple urge to avoid danger. We were afraid of the mines. We were afraid of the ambushes. Most of all, we feared we might be coming into the city on the same roads that the Iraqis were using to leave it. We scrambled across the barren sand until we connected with an advance column of Kuwaiti tanks rumbling toward town. If they were safe, so were we.

As the Kuwaiti unit got closer to the city, we passed a row of squat houses set back from the road, and their residents emerged—tentatively at first, then with growing boldness—to wave Kuwaiti flags. And that's when I realized exactly what was happening: This was the liberation of Kuwait City.

We sped ahead of the Kuwaitis and arrived in a deserted downtown. The sidewalks were empty, as were the roads; there weren't even any cars parked on the streets, since most Kuwaitis had long since hidden them from their occupiers. But as soon as we pulled into the city center, a great flood of Kuwaitis began to appear—by car and foot, laughing, crying, waving flags, hugging one another, hugging us, shooting into the air and honking their horns in manic jubilation.

Some of those early moments seemed like replays of the liberation of Paris. Others had a logic all their own. At the outskirts of town, a white Chevy with two Kuwaitis had pulled alongside us. The driver rolled down his window. "Thank you for coming," he said politely. "Is there anything I can do for you?" Then he handed me a gin and tonic.

Everywhere, the first question we were asked was the same: "American?" Then the Kuwaitis would touch us, to make sure we weren't some surreal apparition brought on by despair. An old man, blinded by cataracts, ran his hands across my face; a woman thrust her baby into my arms. One man—an obvious CNN watcher—grabbed me by the neck and kissed me. "God bless George Bush!" he cried. "God bless James Baker, God bless Dick Cheney, God bless Margaret Tutwiler!"

The displays of affection were almost overwhelming, and at times I felt close to tears. Remaining an observer seemed an impossible task just then, but I did notice one thing in the crush of a thousand people pressing against me as if I were the embodiment of their liberation. Through the thick black clouds, a thin sun began to emerge, and amid the devastation of this nearly ruined country, that in itself seemed a miracle.

JANNY SCOTT

"HOSPITALIZED U.S. SOLDIERS FACE SCARS DEEPER THAN THEIR WOUNDS"

LOS ANGELES *TIMES*, JUNE 9, 1991

As the first extensive military commitment since Vietnam, the Gulf War reflected the changes in American society that had occurred in the 1970s and 1980s. One of those was

Oil fields burn in the aftermath of the war. *(U.S. Army)*

the increasing number of women fighting and writing on the front lines. Janny Scott of the Los Angeles Times *was one of these women. Her report from a Frankfurt hospital shed light on a part of the war that Americans rarely glimpsed, the recovery of the wounded. Despite the sterile feel of the "video war," Scott's report made clear that the Gulf War nevertheless produced wounded and maimed soldiers, just as past conflicts had. In the age of CNN, her work also showed that writing was not yet a lost craft.*

FRANKFURT, GERMANY

IT WAS VALENTINE'S DAY. THE SUN was shining in the desert. A round of ammunition ripped into Spec. Scott Gill's left leg. Blood started spraying everywhere. A hard-rock song came into his head. Appropriately, it was Guns N' Roses.

"Take me down to Paradise City," Spec. Gill recalls murmuring, "where the grass is green and the girls are pretty."

Then someone was slicing off his clothes. An intravenous tube got snagged on a cot, yanking the needle from his elbow. He came out of surgery delirious, mumbling infantry cadences.

Spec. Gill met an Egyptian nurse in a hospital in Riyadh, Saudi Arabia. She said she had been in Kuwait when Iraq invaded. She told a tale so horrible that even now Spec. Gill can't bring himself to repeat it. For the first time, he decided the

Persian Gulf was about more than oil. The nurse's story justified it.

"I feel I've paid my dues," said Spec. Gill, 21, an infantryman from The Dalles, Ore., a small town on the Columbia River. Sitting in a hospital in Frankfurt, confronting the possibility that he might never regain full use of his left foot, he said with certainty, "I want to go home."

They sat in U.S. military hospital wards across Germany and England this week, some of the first combat casualties evacuated to Europe—men in blue-striped bathrobes with shrapnel wounds in their heads and legs, watching the war wind down on television and pondering what they had been through.

One had lost sight in one eye. Another had a shattered kneecap. There were burns, bullet wounds, a lot of shrapnel. Even so, some said they regretted having been evacuated and would have gone back. Only one, Pfc. Robert Gebhard, admitted anger.

"I think about it every day," said Pfc. Gebhard, who survived an attack of "friendly fire" that killed two of his friends and injured five others. "Why did they confuse us with the enemy?. . . . It really does make me mad. . . . I don't think there's any excuse for shooting your own."

Like many others, Spec. Gill enlisted in the Army for lack of choices—not enough money for college, too much for a grant. But he found that he liked the military, particularly being a "grunt"—an infantryman.

Then he learned in October that he was going to Saudi Arabia. He was skeptical about the conflict.

"A white-collar war," he called it, about nothing more noble than money and oil.

It also interfered with his wedding plans. But he never hesitated to go. He says he rarely thought about dying. He was sure he'd be fine.

Spec. Gill won't say exactly what he was up to when he was injured Feb. 14. But he and his platoon were doing something called "military operations in urban terrain"—going from house to house, checking out rooms, either by tossing in a grenade or rushing the door.

Rushing through the door, Spec. Gill led with his left leg. As it crossed the threshold, the enemy bullet split his calf open "like you stepped on a grapefruit." Fragments ricocheted off the door frame into his thigh and forearm. Falling backward, he grabbed his leg "to hold it together."

Spec. Gill's recovery will determine his future in the Army. Because of nerve damage, he has lost some control of his foot. But leaving the Army wouldn't bother him now, he said. He'd like to go home, have that wedding and start a business.

Unlike Spec. Gill, Army Lt. Christopher Robinson, 25, of Atlanta wasn't confident that he'd be fine. Just the opposite. On Christmas Day, he made his wife a tape:

"I'm going to get hurt, but I'm not going to die," he said in the tape.

It happened Feb. 20, about 11 miles into Iraq.

Lt. Robinson was in one of several Bradley Fighting Vehicles that had just taken seven prisoners. He was in the turret, on the radio, when Iraqi artillery hit. The turret exploded. A fire broke out, then fire extinguishers went off. Lt. Robinson came to, unable to breathe, seeing only in black and white.

"The round, I think, went right through

the gunner," he recalled Friday at the Landstuhl Army Regional Medical Center. "As soon as I could see, I saw his head in his lap. I'm not sure where his arm was. His right arm was missing."

Someone dragged the lieutenant out of the turret by his collar and over to another vehicle. Then that vehicle was hit. But it was able to move, at least in reverse. Carrying six wounded men, it backed all the way to the aid station. Lt. Robinson learned that three men had died on the way.

Shrapnel had riddled his left leg and his hands. His hands, face and eyes were burned, and his lungs and ribs were bruised. He feels like he was hit in the chest with a baseball bat. Every day, he can make out a few more lines on the eye charts.

But in sleep, two nightmares recur.

In the first, he's in the Bradley on the radio. He asks the gunner to change frequencies, but nothing happens. So he ducks down into the turret to find out why. And he sees the gunner, headless, as he saw him in reality that day.

In the second, Lt. Robinson has a new crew. But he's sent back out to the battlefield with all his injuries. They get hit again, but he is unable to help because he can't see.

"I don't worry about the future," he said. "But I wonder what it is. I'm sure that after this, my wife doesn't want me in the Army. I wonder if I'm going to stay in. If I don't, what will I do? If I do, what effect will it have on me and her?"

"I thought about changing branches. But if I'm in the Army, I want to be a grunt. . . . If you're in the Army, you want to be in combat arms. And I'm not sure I can do that any more."

Pfc. Gebhard, too, was in a Bradley when he was hit. He and his crew were out on reconnaissance about 1 A.M. Feb. 17. There was a radio report of Iraqi tanks. The battalion commander dispatched helicopters to take them out. He told Pfc. Gebhard's vehicle and one near it to sit tight.

'A BIG FLASHBULB'

THEN THE VEHICLE JUST EXPLODED, "like a big flashbulb," Pfc. Gebhard recalled. He could hear the crew screaming. He leaped out of the driver's hatch to help. Suddenly, there was a second missile hurtling toward him, like a white ball of flame. It hit the adjacent vehicle dead center.

The impact sent two crew members flying into the dirt. Then Pfc. Gebhard saw one of them, his poncho on fire, running between the burning vehicles "like a wall of flame." He grabbed the other soldier and they fled into the night, lit up by the exploding vehicles as though by a giant spotlight.

"I didn't think anybody else made it," said Pfc. Gebhard, who is recovering from burns and shrapnel wounds to his thigh. "I thought it was just me and him. Because I had heard people screaming, and I didn't hear them any more."

On the evacuation helicopter, he recognized the voice of one of the scouts from his Bradley.

"I said, 'Hey! Is that you?' I wanted to jump down and hug him," Pfc. Gebhard recalled. There, he learned that two of the crew had died. He and the other two had lived.

A former high school boxer and triathlete, he plans to head home to Brainerd, Minn. to see his family. Then he plans to return to Germany to complete his tour of duty, which ends in July 1993. After that, he's not sure what he will do.

Maybe race motorcycles, he said.

IN RETROSPECT

DAVID H. HACKWORTH

"LEARNING HOW TO COVER A WAR"

NEWSWEEK, DECEMBER 21, 1992

David H. Hackworth was a retired U.S. Army colonel and the most decorated veteran of the Vietnam War.

To get around the difficulties of covering the Gulf War in press pools, Newsweek *hired Hackworth and dispatched him to Saudi Arabia. "While the rest of us slaved compliantly in specific pools out in the field during the windup to the air war," wrote reporter John J. Fialka afterward, "Mr. Hackworth moved from division to division like a wraith, relying on a network of officer cronies to float through the controls." Hackworth's military experience also made him an adroit analyst of war, as this essay demonstrates.*

THE PENTAGON JUST DOESN'T get it. During Desert Storm, press officers treated reporters as the enemy and kept them pinned down. This time the brass gave away every detail of Operation Restore Hope: mission, assault beach, objectives, troop strengths, even commanders' names. To lurch from thought control to no control is plain stupid. When the press corps beats the Marine Corps to the beaches, everybody loses.

Part of the problem is that war correspondents aren't what they used to be. Gone are the Walter Cronkites, Ernie Pyles and Ward Justs, "upfront" reporters who landed with the first wave at Anzio, flew in bombing raids over Berlin and tagged along with patrols in Vietnam. Today's war story comes from another breed. His or her base is more often a five-star hotel than a foxhole. Few have served as soldiers. Most of the almost 1,500-member U.S. press corps I saw during Desert Storm couldn't tell a tank from a turtle. Only a score were qualified to report on military matters. Many arrogantly refused to learn even the basics like: *this* is a squad, *that* is a squadron.

It didn't used to be that way. When I was a boy soldier in Italy right after World War II, Robert Ruark, one of the old shoe-leather war correspondents, turned up at my platoon. He wore a uniform that was the same as ours except for a "war correspondent" insignia. Our skipper didn't tell us what to say or not say to him. Ruark respected our mission. He got his story by being one of us. During the Korean War, all dispatches and photos were censored to ensure that the security of the troops was never put at risk. But the story still got told to the American people, who had every right to know how the war was going. A good war correspondent doesn't have to be a man. My Wolfhound Regiment became the darling of the public because Marguerite Higgins of the New York *Herald Tribune* stayed with us for months. She made us famous and we loved her for doing it.

The right kind of war correspondent has plenty of experience, nerve and sense of proportion. In Vietnam, reporters could go where they wanted to go. They sent their stories directly to their editors, bypassing the military. The best got the truth out. The worst didn't. Once during a fire fight a reporter came in wearing a yellow shirt and a baseball cap. "Where's all the action?" he said. I pointed. A few minutes later I noticed that he was poking his head up too high, taking photographs. "Hey," I said. "Stick your camera up, not your head." He ignored the advice. Not five minutes later he'd taken a slug between the eyes. We shipped his body out on the next chopper.

Of the many myths fathered by the Vietnam War, probably the biggest was that we lost because of uncensored, free-ranging press coverage. But most professional officers believed that myth and still do. Young Turk generals coming into power, like Colin Powell and Norman Schwarzkopf, said never again would reporters roam free to criticize our wars.

Until Somalia, the Pentagon has been working to muzzle the media. During the initial stages of the 1983 invasion of Grenada, the Pentagon shut the press out of the operation. The brass told the American people that Grenada was a splendid little victory. It took more than seven years before the full story came out: the planning and execution had been Keystone Cop, the wrong objectives were taken, 18 paratroopers were hit by our own airstrike, SEALs drowned because of stupid mistakes. Bluster and blunder cost many other lives.

'FRIENDLY' WEAPONS

AFTER SADDAM HUSSEIN INVADED Kuwait, reporters became prisoners of war in their own hotels. Those few pool members who were out with the troops became part of a military machine that imposed total control over what the public would see, hear and read. I tried to short-circuit the system by talking to grunts the way Walter Cronkite, Ernie Pyle and Ward Just had done. On sprints through the desert, I had more weapons pointed at me by "friendlies" trying to block my story than by anyone from Saddam Hussein's side.

If trying to hamstring reporters is wrong, it also makes no sense to jettison all control. The idea in Somalia, apparently well meant, was to show the world that the good guys had arrived while signaling the warlords of Mogadishu to get out of town. But the result was the beach party at Half Moon Bay. The solution is for the Pentagon to go back to a revised version of the system used in World War II: the military fights the war, the press covers it and the public is told what's happening. But everyone agrees to play by suitable rules.

Reporters should be free to visit units without minders. Editors and the Pentagon need to work out a compromise on what constitutes reasonable military censorship. Mutual paranoia now distorts the issue along with the coverage. The two sides need to devise a way to reduce the size of reportorial contingents without returning to the pools that gave the Pentagon its one-sided advantage in Desert Storm. To cover the complicated world of modern soldiering, editors should assign people who understand the profession of arms, not people in little caps with the logo of their news organization on top. The most important thing is for everyone to quit treating military operations like celebrity weddings or bowl games. Nobody at home is going to trust reporters or press officers who run into battle yelling, "Ready, fire, aim."

(*Larry Burrows*/LIFE, *Time, Inc.*)

BIBLIOGRAPHY

GENERAL/MISCELLANEOUS

Armstrong, David. *A Trumpet to Arms*. Los Angeles. J. P. Tarcher, 1981. Dist. by Houghton Mifflin, Boston.

Beach, Edward L. *The United States Navy: A 200-Year History*. Boston: Houghton Mifflin, 1987.

Belford, Barbara. *Brilliant Bylines: A Biographical Anthology of Notable Newspaperwomen in America*. New York: Columbia University Press, 1986.

Berger, Meyer. *The Story of the New York Times, 1851–1951*. New York: Simon and Schuster, 1951.

Bigart, Homer. *Foward Positions: The War Correspondence of Homer Bigart*. Edited by Betsy Wade. Fayetteville: University of Arkansas Press, 1992.

Bleyer, William. *Main Currents in the History of American Journalism*. Boston: Houghton Mifflin, 1927.

Blythe, Samuel G. *The Making of a Newspaper Man*. Philadelphia: Henry Altemus, 1912.

Born, Donna. "The Image of the Woman Journalist in American Popular Fiction, 1890 to the Present." Paper presented to the Committee on the Status of Women at the annual convention of the Association for Education in Journalism, Michigan State University, East Lansing, August 1981.

Brady, James. *The Press Lord*. New York: Delacorte, 1982.

Broder, David S. *Behind the Front Page*. New York: Simon and Schuster, 1987.

Bullard, F. Lauriston. *Famous War Correspondents*. Boston: Little, Brown, 1914.

Butler, P. R. "Unwelcome War Correspondents." *Army Quarterly* 48 (April 1944): 96–100.

Cannon, Lou. *Reporting: An Inside View*. Sacramento: California Journal Press, 1977.

Cray, Ed, Jonathan Kotler, and Miles Beller. *American Datelines*. New York: Facts On File, 1990.

Davenport, Diana. *The Power Eaters*. New York: William Morrow, 1979.

Dewey, George. *Autobiography of George Dewey*. Annapolis, Md.: Naval Institute Press, 1987.

"Dialogue on Military/Media Relations." *Military Review* 67 (February 1987): 70–84.

Emery, Edwin. *The Press and America: An Interpretative History of the Mass Media.* Englewood Cliffs, N.J.: Prentice Hall, 1972.

Garraty, John A. *Henry Cabot Lodge: A Biography.* New York: Alfred A. Knopf, 1953.

Goulden, Joseph C. *Fit to Print.* Secaucus, N.J.: Lyle Stuart, 1988.

Greene, Graham. *The Quiet American.* New York: Viking, 1955.

Hagen, Kenneth J. *This People's Navy: The Making of American Sea Power.* Free Press, 1991.

Halloran, Richard. "Soldiers and Scribblers: A Common Mission." *Parameters* 17 (Spring 1987): 10–28.

Hammond, William M. "The Light of Controversy: Five Essays on the Rise of the War Correspondent, 1848–1916." Ph.D. diss., Catholic University, 1973. Microfilm.

Harbaugh, William H. *The Life and Times of Theodore Roosevelt.* New York: Oxford University Press, 1975.

Harrison, James G. "American Newspaper Journalism as Described in American Novels of the Nineteeth Century." Ph.D. diss., University of North Carolina, Chapel Hill, 1945.

Herr, Michael. *Dispatches.* New York: Alfred A. Knopf, 1977.

Hogarth, Paul. *The Artist As Reporter.* London: Gordon Fraser, 1986.

Hohenberg, John. *Foreign Correspondence: The Great Reporters and Their Times.* New York: Columbia University Press, 1978.

Howarth, Stephen. *To Shining Sea: A History of the United States Navy, 1775–1991.* New York: Random House, 1991.

Hutchens, John K., and George Oppenheimer, eds. *The Best in the World.* New York: Viking, 1973.

Irwin, Will. *The American Newspaper.* Reprint. Ames: Iowa State University Press, 1969.

Johnstone, John W. C., Edward J. Slawski, and William W. Bowman. *The News People.* Urbana: University of Illinois Press, 1976.

Juergens, George. *Joseph Pulitzer and the New York World.* Princeton: Princeton University Press, 1966.

Just, Ward. *Stringer.* Boston: Little, Brown, 1974.

Knightley, Philip. *The First Casualty: From The Crimea to Vietnam: The War Correspondent as Hero, Propagandist, and Myth Maker.* New York: Harcourt Brace Jovanovich, 1975.

Kobre, Sidney. *The Yellow Press and Gilded Age Journalism.* Tallahassee: Florida State University Press, 1964.

Langford, Gerald. *The Richard Harding Davis Years: A Biography of a Mother and Son.* New York: Holt, Rinehart and Winston, 1961.

Lee, James Melvin. *History of American Journalism.* Garden City, N.Y.: Garden City Publishing, 1917.

Leekley, Sheryle, and John Leekley. *Moments: The Pulitzer Prize Photographs.* New York: Crown, 1978.

Lewinski, Jorge. *The Camera at War.* New York: Simon and Schuster, 1978.

Mander, Mary Sue. "Pen and Sword: A Cultural History of the American War Correspondent, 1895–1945." Ph.D. diss., University of Illinois, 1976.

Mathews, Joseph J. *Reporting the Wars.* Minneapolis: Univesity of Minnesota Press, 1957.

Mathews, Lloyd J., ed. *Newsmen and National Defense: Is Conflict Inevitable?* New York: Brassey's, 1991.

May, Antoinette. *Witness to War: A Biography of Marguerite Higgins.* New York: Beaufort Books, 1983.

McAuliffe, Kevin Michael. *The Great American Newspaper.* New York: Scribner's, 1978.

McLuhan, Marshall. *Understanding Media: The Extensions of Man.* 1964. Reprint. New York: New American Library, 1966.

Mott, Frank Luther. *American Journalism. A History: 1690–1960.* New York: Macmillan, 1962.

———, ed. *Journalism in Wartime.* Washington, D.C.: American Council of Public Affairs, 1943.

Mullenix, J. C. "Freedom of the Press in Time of War." Student paper, School of Foreign Service, Georgetown University, 1942.

Musicant, Ivan. *The Banana Wars: A History of the United States Military Intervention in Latin America from the Spanish-American War to the Invasion of Panama.* New York: Macmillan, 1990.

Neider, Charles, ed. *The Autobiography of Mark Twain.* Harper and Bros., 1959.

Pauly, John J. "The Ideological Origins of an Independent Press." Paper presented at the convention of the American Journalism Historians Association, Las Vegas, October 1985.

Regier, C. C. *The Era of the Muckrakers.* 1932. Reprint. Gloucester, Mass.: Peter Smith, 1957.

Ross, Walter. *Coast-to-Coast.* New York: Simon and Schuster, 1962.

Sarkesian, Sam C. "Soldiers, Scholars, and the Media." *Parameters* 17 (September 1987): 77–87.

Schneir, Walter, ed. *Westmoreland vs CBS: Guide to the Microfiche Collection.* New York: Clearwater, 1987.

Sigal, Leon V. *Reporters and Officials: The Organization and Politics of News-making.* Lexington, Mass.: D. C. Heath, 1973.

Smith, Jeffrey G. "The Literature of Disillusionment: Public War Correspondence from Waterloo to Khe Sanh." Ph.D. diss., Princeton University, 1992.

Smith, Page. *America Enters the World.* Vol. 7. New York: McGraw-Hill, 1985.

"Soldier Journalists." *Soldiers,* August 1974, 50–51.

Stein, M. L. *Under Fire: The Story of American War Correspondents.* New York: Messner, 1968.

Stephens, Lowndes, F. "Political Socialization of the American Soldier: The Mass Media as Agent." *Armed Forces and Soc.* 9 (Summer 1983): 595–632.

Tebbel, John. *The Media in America.* New York: New American Library, 1974.

Thomas, Hugh. *Cuba: The Pursuit of Freedom.* New York: Harper and Row, 1971.

Weber, Ronald. "Journalism, Writing and American Literature." Occasional Paper No. 5, Gannett Center for Media Studies, April 1987.

Wendt, Lloyd. *Chicago Tribune: The Rise of a Great American Newspaper.* Chicago: Rand McNally, 1979.

PRE-1860

Botein, Stephen. Introduction to '*Mr. Zenger's Malice and Falsehood': Six Issues of the New-York Weekly Journal, 1733–34.* Worcester Mass.: American Antiquarian Society, 1985.

Carter, Samuel III. *Blaze of Glory: The Fight for New Orleans, 1814–1815.* New York: St. Martin's Press.

Copeland, Fayette. *Kendall of* The Picayune: *Being His Adventures in New Orleans, on the Texan Santa Fe Expedition, in the Mexican War, and in the Colonization of the Texas Frontier.* Norman: University of Oklahoma Press, 1943.

Morazan, Ronald R. *Biographical Sketches of the Veterans of the Battle of New Orleans, 1814–1815.* Berkeley, Calif.: Legacy, 1979.

Russell, William Howard. *Russell's Despatches from the Crimea, 1854–1856*. Edited by Nicholas Bentley. New York: Hill and Wang, 1966.

Spell, Lota M. "The Anglo-Saxon Press in Mexico, 1846–1848." *American Historical Review* 38 (October 1932): 20–31.

CIVIL WAR

Andrews, J. Cutler. *The North Reports the Civil War*. Pittsburgh: University of Pittsburgh Press, 1955.

———. *The South Reports the Civil War*. Princeton, N.J.: Princeton University Press, 1970.

Chester, Thomas M. *Thomas Morris Chester, Black Civil War Correspondent: His Dispatches from the Virginia Front*. Edited by R. J. M. Blackett. Baton Rouge: Louisiana State University Press, 1989.

Crozier, Emmet. *Yankee Reporters, 1861–65*. 1959. Reprint. Westport, Conn.: Greenwood, 1973.

Endres, Fredric F. "The Northern Press and the Civil War: A Study in Editorial Opinion and Government, Military and Public Reaction." Thesis, University of Massachusetts, 1975.

Hazen, William B. *A Narrative of Military Service*. Boston: Ticknor, 1885.

Marszalek, John F. *Sherman's Other War: The General and the Civil War Press*. Memphis, Tenn. Memphis State University Press, 1981.

Sherman, William T. *Memoirs. . . .* Vol. 2. New York: D. Appleton, 1875.

U.S. War Department. *General Order No. 67*, August 26, 1861. Invokes the 57th Article of War against journalists, subjecting those convicted to death penalty.

LATE NINETEENTH CENTURY (TO 1898)

Barth, Gunther. *City People: The Rise of Modern City Culture in Nineteenth-Century America*. New York: Oxford University Press, 1980.

Hankinson, Alan. *Man of Wars: William Howard Russell of The Times*. London: Heineman, 1983.

Knight, Oliver. *Following the Indian Wars: The Story of the Newspaper Correspondents Among the Indian Campaigns*. Norman: University of Oklahoma Press, 1960.

Mahan, Alfred Thayer. *The Influence of Sea Power Upon History*. Boston: Little, Brown, 1890.

Morison, Elting E., ed. *The Letters of Theodore Roosevelt: The Years of Preparation, 1868–1900*. Vols. 1 and 2. Harvard University Press, 1951.

Stearn, R. T. "War and the Media in the 19th Century: Victorian Military Artists and the Image of War, 1870–1914." *Royal United Service* 131 (September 1986): 55–62.

Walker, Dale L. *Januarius MacGahan: The Life and Campaigns of an American War Correspondent*. Athens: Ohio University Press, 1988.

SPANISH-AMERICAN WAR ERA

Allen, Douglas. *Frederic Remington and the Spanish-American War*. New York: Crown, 1971.

Barron, Carlos G. "Spanish Press Reaction During the 1898 War." *Mid-America* 61 (January 1979): 25–33.

Blow, Michael. *A Ship to Remember: The Maine and the Spanish-American War.* New York: William Morrow, 1992.

Brown, Charles H. *The Correspondent's War: Journalists in the Spanish-American War.* New York: Scribner's, 1967.

Chadwick, French Ensor. *The Relations of the United States and Spain: Diplomacy.* New York: Scribner's, 1909.

Chidsey, Donald. *The Spanish-American War.* New York: Crown, 1971.

Crane, Stephen. *Active Service.* New York: Frederick A. Stokes, 1899.

———. *The Correspondence of Stephen Crane.* Vol. 2. Edited by Stanley Wertheim and Paul Sorrentino. New York: Columbia University Press, 1988.

Creelman, James. *On the Great Highway.* New York: Lothrup, 1901.

Davis, Richard Harding. *The Cuban and Porto Rican Campaigns.* New York: Scribner's, 1898.

———. *Notes of a War Correspondent,* New York: Scribner's, 1911.

Friedel, Frank. *The Splendid Little War.* Boston: Little, Brown, 1958.

Jackson, Bennett L. "General Shafter Meets the Press." *Military Review* 42 (September 1962): 58–68.

Mason, Gregory. *Remember the Maine.* New York: Henry Holt, 1939.

Musgrave, George Clark. *Under Three Flags in Cuba: A Personal Account of the Cuban Insurrection and Spanish-American War.* Boston: Little, Brown, 1899.

O'Toole, G. J. A. *The Spanish War: An American Epic, 1898.* New York: W. W. Norton, 1984.

Rickover, Hyman G. *How the Battleship Maine Was Destroyed.* Washington, D.C.: U.S. Government Printing Office, 1976.

Stallman, R. W. *Stephen Crane. A Biography.* New York: George Braziller, 1968.

Wilheim, Marcus M. *Public Opinion and the Spanish-American War.* Baton Rouge: Louisiana State University Press, 1932.

Wilson, Herbert W. *The Downfall of Spain: Naval History of the Spanish-American War.* London: Sampson, Low, Marston, 1900.

SINCE 1900: GENERAL/MISCELLANEOUS

Barton, William E. *The Life of Clara Barton.* Boston: Houghton Mifflin, 1922.

Beale, Howard K. *Theodore Roosevelt and the Rise of America to World Power.* Baltimore: Johns Hopkins University Press, 1956.

Churchill, Winston S. *My Early Life: A Roving Commission.* London: Oldham Press Ltd., 1930.

Coblentz, Edmond D. *William Randolph Hearst: A Portrait in His Own Words.* New York: Simon and Schuster, 1952.

Michelson, Miriam. *A Yellow Journalist.* New York: D. Appleton, 1905.

Roosevelt, Theodore. *An Autobiography.* New York: Macmillan, 1914.

Schuman, Edwin L. *Practical Journalism: A Complete Manual of the Best Newspaper Methods.* New York: D. Appleton, 1903.

Tuchman, Barbara. *The Proud Tower: A Portrait of the World Before the War: 1890–1914.* New York: Macmillan, 1966.

Wilheim, Marcus, and Joseph Wisan. *The Cuban Crisis in the New York Press, 1930.* New York: Columbia University Press, 1934.

Wilkinson, Glenn. "'There is No More Stirring Story': The Press Depiction and Images of War During the Tibet Expedition 1903–4." *War and Society* (October 1991): 1–16.

WORLD WAR I ERA

Ashley, Perry J., ed. *American Newspaper Journalists 1901–1925.* Vol. 25, *Dictionary of Literary Biography.* Detroit: Gale Reserach, 1984.

Conway, William P., Jr. "They Danced in the Streets—Four Days Too Soon: False Armistice Day, 1918." *Army* 24 (September 1974): 25–27.

Crozier, Emmet. *American Reporters on the Western Front, 1914–18.* New York: Oxford University Press, 1959.

Gero, Anthony, and Dale Biever. "Observations on the Uniforms of Accredited War Correspondents, American Expeditionary Force, 1917–1919." *Military Colleges and History* 39 (Winter 1987): 158–60.

Hudson, Robert V. *The Writing Game: A Biography of Will Irwin.* Ames: Iowa State University Press, 1982.

Lytton, Neville. *The Press and General Staff.* London: Collins, 1921.

Palmer, Frederick. *With My Own Eyes: A Personal Story of Battle Years.* Indianapolis: Bobbs-Merrill, 1933.

U.S. War Department. *Regulations Governing Correspondents and Photographers with the United States Army.* Spec. reg. no. 102, September 1918.

SINCE 1919: GENERAL/MISCELLANEOUS

Carlson, Oliver, and Ernest Sutherland Bates. *Hearst: Lord of San Simeon.* Westport, Conn.: Greenwood, 1936.

Culbert, David Holbrook. *News for Everyman: Radio and Foreign Affairs in Thirties America.* Westport, Conn.: Greenwood, 1976.

Lundberg, Ferdinand. *Imperial Hearst: A Social Biography.* New York: Equinox Cooperative Press, 1936.

Older, Mrs. Fremont. *William Randolph Hearst.* New York: Appleton-Century, 1936.

Reynolds, Michael. *Hemingway's First War.* 1976. Reprint. New York: Basil Blackwell, 1987.

Swanberg, W. A. *Citizen Hearst.* New York: Scribner's, 1961.

Tebbel, John. *The Life and Good Times of William Randolph Hearst.* New York: E. P. Dutton, 1952.

This Fabulous Century: 1930–1940. Vol. 4. New York: Time-Life Books, 1983.

Winkler, John K. *William Randolph Hearst: A New Appraisal.* New York: Hastings House, 1965.

WORLD WAR II ERA

Allen, Ann. "The News Media and the Women's Army Auxiliary Corps: Protagonists for a Cause." *Military Affairs* 50 (April 1986): 77–83.

Allied Expeditionary Force. Supreme Headquarters. *Regulations for War Correspondents Accompanying AEF in the Field, 1944.* Pocket booklet. England, 1944.

"Army News Policy." *Army Navy Register* (April 8, 1944): 9. Letter from Army PR director explaining delays in release of information on three incidents: Patton soldier slapping, Bari Harbor air attack, and friendly fire on U.S. troops over Sicily.

Army Navy Journal (April 21, 1945): 1055. Article on Ernie Pyle's death notes that twenty-three war correspondents died in service.

Army Navy Register (April 21, 1945): 7. Lists correspondents who died in service.

Collier, Richard. *Fighting Words: The War Correspondents of World War II.* New York: St. Martin's, 1989.

Dunn, William J. *Pacific Microphone.* College Station: Texas A and M University Press, 1988.

Forde, H. M. "Strategic Censorship in World War II." *Military Review* 28 (September 1948): 33–36.

Irwin, Will. *The Making of a Reporter.* New York: G. P. Putnam, 1942.

Lewis, Boyd. "Sortie to Reims: The Inside Story of a Controversial 'Scoop.'" *Army* 25 (June 1975): 28–31 and 34–37.

Murrow, Edward R. *This Is London.* Edited by Elmer Davis. New York: Simon & Schuster, 1941.

Oldfield, Barney. *Never a Shot in Anger.* 2d ed. Santa Barbara, Calif.: Capra, 1989.

Pogue, Forrest C. *The Supreme Command.* Washington, D.C: Office of the Chief of Military History, 1954.

Quetchenbach, Raymond. "The Leyte Landing and the Japanese Controlled Press." *Leyte-Samar Studies* 11, no. 2 (1977): 42–51.

Sawyer, Bickford E., Jr. "The Normandy Campaign from Military and Press Sources." Master's thesis, University of Missouri, 1957.

Steele, Richard W. "The Great Debate: Roosevelt, the Media and the Coming of the War, 1940–1941." *Journal of American History* 71 (June 1984): 69–92.

U.S. War Department. *Military Intelligence, Counterintelligence.* Field Manual 30-25, February 1940.

———. *Regulations for War Correspondents Accompanying U.S. Army Forces in the Field.* Field Manual 30-26, January 1942. With 3 changes.

Wagner, Lilya. *Women War Correspondents of World War II.* New York: Greenwood, 1989.

Weithas, Art. *Close to Glory: The Untold Stories of World War II by Yank Magazine Correspondents.* Austin, Texas: Eakin, 1991.

SINCE 1945: GENERAL/MISCELLANEOUS

Agee, James, and Walker Evans. *Let Us Now Praise Famous Men.* Boston: Houghton Mifflin, 1960.

Baker, Carlos. *Ernest Hemingway: A Life Story.* New York: Scribner's, 1969.

Barris, Alex. *Stop the Presses! The Newspaperman in American Films.* South Brunswick, N.J.: A. S. Barnes, 1976.

Bent, Silas. *Buchanan of the Press.* New York: Vanguard, 1952.

Bliss, Edward, Jr., ed. *In Search of Light: The Broadcasts of Edward R. Murrow.* New York: Avon, 1967.

Braestrup, Peter. *Battle Lines: Report of the Twentieth Century Fund Task Force on the Military and the Media.* New York: Priority, 1985.

Capa, Cornell, and Richard Whelan, eds. *Robert Capa: Photographs.* New York: Alfred A. Knopf, 1985.

Capa, Robert. *Slightly Out of Focus.* New York: Henry Holt, 1947.

Chiaven, Frederick J. "Ethics and Responsibilities in Broadcasting." *Military Review* (August 1991): 64–76.

Cumings, Bruce. *War and Television.* New York: Verso, 1992.

Fuentes, Norberto. *Ernest Hemingway Rediscovered.* New York: Scribner's, 1988.

Goldberg, Vicki. *Margaret Bourke-White.* Reading, Mass.: Addison-Wesley, 1987.

Hooper, Alan. *The Military and the Media.* Aldershot, England: Gower, 1984.

Koropey, O. B. *The Media and the Political Milieu: How the Sergeant York Became the System that Everyone Loved to Hate.* Booklet. History Office, Army Material Command, 1992.

Lowenstein, Ralph L. "Military Press Censorship in Israel." *Military Review* 50 (February 1970): 3–9.

Miles, Donna. "Beetle Bailey Turns 40." *Soldiers,* June 1990, 21–24.

Persico, Joseph E. *Edward R. Murrow: An American Original.* New York: McGraw-Hill, 1988.

Trotta, Liz. *Fighting for Air: In the Trenches with Television News.* New York: Simon and Schuster, 1991.

White, William, ed. *By-Line: Ernest Hemingway.* New York: Scribner's, 1967.

KOREAN WAR ERA

Clearly, Thomas J., Jr. "Aid and Comfort to the Enemy." *Military Review* 48 (August 1968): 51–55.

Gibbons, Edward. *Floyd Gibbons: Your Headline Hunter.* New York: Exposition Press, 1953.

Hymoff, Edward. "The Fallen Reporters in the Forgotten War." *Media History Digest* (Fall/Winter 1990): 12–40.

Osmer, Harold H. *U.S. Religious Journalism and the Korean War.* Washington, D.C.: University Press of America, 1980.

U.S. Department of the Army. *Armed Forces Newspaper Editor's Guide.* Pamphlet 20-23, October 1952.

———. *Public Information: Correspondents Accompanying Armed Forces of the United States.* Army Reg. 360-60, December 1951.

———. Office of the Chief of Information. *Handbook for Public Information Officers.* Pamphlet 21-64, 1951.

VIETNAM WAR

Carpini, Michael D. "U.S. Media Coverage of the Vietnam Conflict in 1968." In *The Vietnam Era: Media and Popular Culture in the U.S. and Vietnam,* edited by Michael Klein. Winchester, Mass.: Pluto, 1989.

———. "Vietnam and the Press." In *The Legacy.* Boston: Beacon, 1990.

Davis, Franklin M., Jr. "The Military and the Media: A Proposal for a Cease-Fire." *Army* 24 (September 1974): 16–20.

Deakman, Elizabeth. "Dickey Chapelle's Lifelong Quest . . ." *Vietnam* (Spring 1989): 8 and 61–64.

Dougan, Clark, and Stephen Weiss. *The American Experience in Vietnam.* New York: W. W. Norton and Boston Publishing, 1988.

Elwood-Akers, Virginia. *Women War Correspondents in the Vietnam War, 1961–1975.* Metuchen, N.J.: Scarecrow, 1988.

Faulkner, Francis D. "Bao Chi: The American News Media in Vietnam, 1960–1975." 2 vols. Ph.D. diss., University of Massachusetts, 1981.

Goodnow, Chandler, et al. "News Coverage of the Tet Offensive." Student paper, USAWC, 1969.

Havach, Emil L. "The Watchdog Barks at Snooping: Army Political Spying from 1967 to 1970 and the Media that Opposed It." Master's thesis, University of Arizona, 1974.

Kiernan, David R. "The Case for Censorship." *Army* 33 (March 1983): 22–24.

Kinnard, Douglas. *The War Managers*. Hanover, N.H.: UP of New England, 1977.

Knightley, Phillip. *The First Casualty*. New York: Harcourt, 1974.

Lucas, Jim G. *Dateline: Viet Nam*. New York: Award House, 1966.

Mandelbaum, Michael. "Vietnam: The Television War." *Daedalus* (Fall 1982). Reprinted in *Parameters* 13 (March 1983): 89–97.

Minor, Dale. *The Information War*. New York: Hawthorn, 1970.

Osborn, George K., et al., eds. *Democracy, Strategy, and Vietnam: Implications for American Policymaking*. Lexington, Mass.: Heath, 1987.

Peake, Louis A. *The United States in the Vietnam War, 1954–1975: A Selected, Annotated Bibliography*. New York: Garland, 1986.

Pratt, John Clark, ed. *Vietnam Voices*. New York: Viking, 1984.

Rigg, Robert B. "How Not to Report a War." *Military Review* 49 (June 1969): 14–24.

Salisbury, Harrison E., ed. *Vietnam Reconsidered: Lessons from a War*. New York: Harper and Row, 1984.

Sheehan, Neil. *A Bright Shining Lie: John Paul Vann and America in Vietnam*. New York: Random House, 1988.

Turner, Kathleen J. *Lyndon Johnson's Dual War: Vietnam and the Press*. Chicago: University of Chicago Press, 1985.

U.S. Army War College. "Press Coverage of the Vietnam War." Study, 1979.

U.S. Department of the Army. *Public Information, Establishment and Conduct of Field Press Censorship in Combat Areas*. Army Reg. 360-65, August 1952.

U.S. Military Assistance Command, Vietnam. *Public Information, Policies and Procedures*. Directive 360-1, May 15, 1972.

———. Office of Information. "Guidance on Public Release of Information," April 1, 1967. File no. 2012, VNDocs.

———. "Accreditation of News Media Personnel," n.d. File no. 2012, VNDocs.

———. "Accreditation Procedures for Unconfirmed News Agency," July 17, 1970. File no. 2012, VNDocs.

———. "Appeal of the Suspension of Accreditation of Mr. Alan Dawson, UPI Correspondent." Memo, December 3, 1972. File no. 2012, VNDocs.

———. "Denial of Intelligence Information to the Enemy." Memo for the press, February 26, 1968. File no. 2012, VNDocs.

———. "Disaccreditation Action—Mr. Richard A. Pyle." Disposition form, August 1, 1972. File no. 2012, VNDocs.

Westling, Frank S. "*TIME* and the Vietnam War, 1965–1969." Master's thesis, University of North Carolina, Chapel Hill, 1971.

Wyatt, Clarence R. *Paper Soldiers: The American Press and the Vietnam War*. New York: W. W. Norton, 1993.

SINCE 1975: GENERAL/MISCELLANEOUS

Banks, Louis. "Memo to the Press: They Hate You Out There." *Atlantic Monthly,* April 1978, 35–38.

Behrens, John C. *The Typewriter Guerrillas*. Chicago: Nelson Hall, 1977.

Dorfman, Ron. "Journalists Under Fire." *The Quill,* October 1985.

Drury, Allen. *Anna Hastings: The Story of a Washington Newspaperperson!* New York: Warner Books, 1977.

Dygert, James H. *The Investigative Journalist: Folk Heroes of a New Era.* Englewood Cliffs, N.J.: Prentice Hall, 1976.

Fisher, Mark. "Whatever Happened to the Tough-fisted, Hard-drinking ME?" *Associate Press Managing Editors News,* April 1985.

Forester, Tom, ed. *The Information Technology Revolution.* Cambridge, Mass.: MIT Press, 1985.

Grant, Lee. "Images of the Journalist." *Bulletin of the American Society of Newspaper Editors.* (April 1982): 5–12.

Halberstam, David. *The Powers that Be.* New York: Alfred A. Knopf, 1979.

Henry, William A. III. "Journalism Under Fire." *Time,* December 12, 1983, 77.

Huisking, P. V. "Afghanistan and the Soviet Press." *Military Intelligence* 11 (January/February 1985): 40–45.

Rich, Frank. "Stage: Echo of Vietnam. How I Got That Story." *New York Times,* December 9, 1980, C9.

SINCE 1985

Anderson, Mary A. "Thomson Merger Plan Set for June Vote: Knight-Ridder to Seek Protection from Acquisitors." *Presstime,* April 1989.

Associated Press. Biographical sheet on Terry Anderson. May 1989.

Bagdikian, Ben H. "The Lords of the Global Village." *The Nation,* June 12, 1989, 805–20.

Bonafede, Dom. "Taking on the Press." *National Journal,* April 8, 1989, .

Brady, Patrick H. "General Brady Replies to Criticism of his Article on Army and Media." *Army* (January 1991): 10–11.

Braestrup, Peter. *Battle Lines: Report of the Twentieth Century Fund Task Force on the Military and the Media.* New York: Priority, 1985.

Cook, Philip S., Douglas Gomery, and Lawrence W. Lichty, eds. *American Media: The Wilson Quarterly Reader.* Washington, D.C.: Wilson Center Press, 1989.

Diebold, John. "Newspapers and Information Technology: Some Strategic Options." A paper presented at a meeting of the American Society of Newspaper Editors, Washington, D.C., April 15, 1988.

Edwards, Julia. *Women of the World: The Great Foreign Correspondents.* Boston: Houghton Mifflin, 1988.

Glickman, Norman J., and Douglas P. Woodward. *The New Competitors.* New York: Basic Books, 1989.

Kellner, Douglas. *The Persian Gulf TV War.* Boulder, Colo.: Westview, 1992.

Logan, Joe. "2014: A Newspaper Odyssey." *Washington Journalism Review,* May 1989, .

Normann, Roderick de. "To War with the Press: Some Recollections of the Media in the Gulf." *Army Quarterly* (October 1991): 430–36.

Noyes, Harry F. III. "Like It or Not, the Armed Forces Need the Media." *Army* (June 1992): 30–34 and 35.

Parenti, Michael. *Inventing Reality: The Politics of the Mass Media.* New York: St. Martin's, 1986.

Patten, Dave. *Newspapers and New Media.* White Plains, N.Y.: Knowledge Industries Publications, 1986.

Schwartz, Thomas A., and David Fletcher. "The Newsperson as TV Character." *Media History Digest* (Spring/Summer 1988): 48–57 and 64.

Sidle, Winant. "A Battle Behind the Scenes: The Gulf War Reheats Military-Media Controversy." *Military Review* (September 1991): 52–63.

Summers, Harry G., Jr. "Western Media and Recent Wars." *Parameters* 66 (May 1986): 4–17.

Taylor, Philip M. *War and the Media: Propaganda and Persuasion in the Gulf War.* New York: Manchester University Press, 1992.

U.S. Department of Defense. *Conduct of the Persian Gulf War.* Final report to Congress, April 1992.

U.S. Marine Corps. Public Affairs Office, New York. *From the Battlefield to the Newsroom: A Limited Review of How the Marine Corps Story Was Told in Operations Desert Shield and Desert Storm.* August 1991.

Williams, Pete. "The Press and the Persian Gulf War." *Parameters* 21 (Fall 1991): 2–9.

Zoll, Donald A. "The Press and the Military: Some Thoughts After Grenada." *Parameters* 14 (Spring 1984): 26–34.

ACKNOWLEDGMENTS

Arnett, Peter. "In Like Heroes, Out Like Foes," Chicago *Tribune*, April 30, 1975 (© 1975, Associated Press). Reprinted by permission of the Associated Press. All rights reserved.

———. "The Agony and Death of Supply Column 21," August 19, 1965 (© 1965, Associated Press) Reprinted by permission of the Associated Press. All rights reserved.

Barnes, Edward. "Surrender," *Weekly LIFE In the Time of War series*, February 25, 1991 (© 1991, *LIFE* Magazine). Reprinted with permission of the author and *Time*, Inc. All rights reserved.

———. "When Freedom Came," *Weekly LIFE In the Time of War series*, March 11, 1991 (© 1991, *LIFE* Magazine). Reprinted with permission of the author and *Time*, Inc. All rights reserved.

Beech, Kayes. "This Was No Retreat," Chicago *Daily News*, December 11, 1950 (© 1950, Chicago *Daily News*). Reprinted with permission of the Chicago *Daily News*. All rights reserved.

Buckley, William F. Jr., "Go All Out or Get The Hell Out," *National Review*, March 19, 1968. (© 1968, William F. Buckley). Reprinted by permission of the author. All rights reserved.

Burrows, Larry. "Yankee Papa 13," *LIFE*, April 16, 1965 (© 1965, *LIFE* Magazine). Reprinted by permission of Russell Burrows and courtesy of *Time*, Inc. All rights reserved.

Clifton, Tony. "Move Forward & Shoot the Things," *Newsweek*, March 11, 1991 (© 1991, Newsweek, Inc.). Reprinted by permission of Newsweek, Inc. All rights reserved.

Corwin, Norman. Selections from *A Note of Triumph*, broadcast May 8, 1945 CBS (© 1945, CBS Inc.). Reprinted with permission of CBS Inc. All rights reserved.

Fetterman, John. "Pfc. Gibson Comes Home," Louisville *Times*, July 1968. (© 1968, Louisville Times). Reprinted courtesy of the *Louisville Times*. All rights reserved.

Frankel, Max. "A Divided Nation Lost Its Way," from the *New York Times*, January 28, 1973 (© 1973, The New York Times Inc.). Reprinted by permission of the New York Times, Inc. All rights reserved.

Grover, Preston. "Russian Downers of Plane Receive Medal Rewards," May 8, 1959 (© 1959, Associated Press). Reprinted by permission of the Associated Press. All rights reserved.

Gunther, John. *Inside Europe* (© 1940, Harper & Brothers). Reprinted by permission of HarperCollins, Inc. All rights reserved.

Hackworth, Col. David. "Learning How to Cover a War," *Newsweek,* December 21, 1992 (© 1992, Col. David Hackworth). Reprinted by permission of the author and Newsweek, Inc. All rights reserved.

Halberstam, David. "The Face of the Enemy in Vietnam," *Harper's Magazine,* February, 1965 (© 1965, *Harper's Magazine* Inc.). Reprinted courtesy of Harper's Magazine, Inc. All rights reserved.

Hersey, John. "Major Rings a Bell in Licata," *LIFE,* August 23, 1943 (© 1943, *LIFE* Magazine). Courtesy of Time, Inc. All rights reserved.

Higgins, Marguerite. "My God! There Are Still Some Left," New York *Herald Tribune,* September 18, 1950 (© 1950, New York Herald Tribune Inc.). Reprinted by permission of the New York Herald Tribune, Inc. All rights reserved.

Hightower, John M. "MacArthur Tries to Take Over U.S. Policy in Warzone," March 26, 1951 (© 1951, Associated Press). Reprinted by permission of the Associated Press. All rights reserved.

"How Goes the War?" from *Newsweek,* January, 1, 1968 (© 1968, Newsweek, Inc.) reprinted by permission of Newsweek, Inc. All rights reserved.

Jones, Russell. "For the First Time Since I Was a Boy I Wept," *United Press International,* October 29–December 3, 1961 (© 1961, United Press International). Reprinted with permission of United Press International. All rights reserved.

Lescaze, Lee. "Hue Marines: Bitter as Brave," Washington *Post,* February 20, 1968. (© 1968, Washington *Post*). Reprinted by permission of the Washington *Post.* All rights reserved.

Lippman, Walter. "Kruschev to Lippman—Face to Face No. 1." from New York *Herald Tribune,* April 17, 1961 (© 1961, New York Herald Tribune Inc.). Reprinted by permission of the New York Herald Tribune, Inc. All rights reserved.

Lucas, Jim. "Our Town's Business is War," *Scripps Howard,* January 3, 1953 (© 1953, Scripps Howard). Reprinted courtesy of the Scripps Howard Foundation. All rights reserved.

Manegold, C. S. "Avoiding the Next Crisis," *Newsweek,* March 11, 1991 (© 1991, Newsweek, Inc.). Reprinted with permission of Newsweek, Inc. All rights reserved.

Martin, Douglas D. and others, "Millions Watch Legion Veterans March for Hours," from Detroit *Free Press,* September 23, 1931 (© 1931, Free Press Plus). Reprinted by permission of Free Press Plus. All rights reserved.

Martin, Robert P. "Jungle War From the Inside: An Eyewitness Report," *U.S. News & World Report,* October 30, 1961 (© 1961, *U.S. News & World Report).* Reprinted by permission of *U.S. News & World Report.* All rights reserved.

Mathews, Tom and Tony Clifton. "Torture and Torment," *Newsweek,* February 4, 1991 (© 1991, Newsweek, Inc.) Reprinted by permission of Newsweek, Inc. All rights reserved.

Morin, Relman. "Hatred to Stay," September 25, 1950 (© 1950, Associated Press). Reprinted by permission of the Associated Press. All rights reserved.

Morrow, Lance. "A New Test of Resolve," *Time,* September 3, 1990 (© 1990, Time Inc.) Reprinted by permission of the author and Time, Inc. All rights reserved.

Murrow, Edward R. *A Report During the Blitz,* broadcast September 13, 1940. (© 1940, CBS Inc.). Reprinted courtesy of CBS Inc. and Mrs. Edward R. Murrow. All rights reserved.

"News Beat or Unethical Double Cross?" from the *New York Times,* May 8, 1945 (© 1945, The New York Times Inc.). Reprinted by permission of the New York Times, Inc. All rights reserved.

Pyle, Ernie. "This Is The Way It Was. . . ," June 16, 1944, Washington *Daily News* (© 1944, Scripps

Howard Foundation). Reprinted by permission of the Scripps Howard Foundation. All rights reserved.

————. "The Death of Captain Waskow," January 1, 1944, Washington *Daily News* (© 1944, Scripps Howard Foundation). Reprinted by permission of the Scripps Howard Foundation. All rights reserved.

Salisbury, Harrison E. "Beria's Troops Held Moscow, But He Hesitated and Lost," from the *New York Times*, September 21, 1954 (© 1954, The New York Times Inc.). Reprinted by permission of The New York Times, Inc. All rights reserved.

Schanberg, Sydney H. "The Fall of Phnom Penh," from the *New York Times*, May 9, 1975 (© 1975, The New York Times Inc.). Reprinted by permission of The New York Times, Inc. All rights reserved.

Scott, Janny. "Hospitalized U.S. Soldiers Face Scars Deeper Than Their Wounds," from Los Angeles *Times*, June 9, 1991 (© 1991, Los Angeles Times Syndicate, Inc.). Reprinted by permission of the Los Angeles *Times*. All rights reserved.

Sheehan, Neil. "The Secret War in Vietnam," from the *New York Times*, June 13, 1971 (© 1971, The New York Times Inc.). Reprinted by permission of The New York Times, Inc. All rights reserved.

Shirer, William T. "A Broadcaster Reports the Start of the War," in *Berlin Diary*, (© 1939, Alfred A. Knopf, Inc.). Reprinted courtesy of Alfred A. Knopf, Inc. All rights reserved.

Simpson, Kirk L. "Bugles Sound Taps for Warrior's Requiem," November 11, 1921 (© 1921, Associated Press). Reprinted by permission of the Associated Press. All rights reserved.

Thompson, Dorothy. "Radio Broadcast of a Jewish Youth in Paris," from *Let the Record Speak* by Dorothy Thompson (© 1939 by Dorothy Thompson Lewis, © renewed 1967 by Michael Lewis). Reprinted by permission of the Houghton Mifflin Co. All rights reserved.

Warren, Robert Penn. "Looking Back," *LIFE*, March 17, 1961 (© 1961, LIFE Magazine). Reprinted courtesy of Time, Inc. All rights reserved.

Watson, Russell and Gregg Easterbrook. "A New Kind of Warfare," *Newsweek*, January 28, 1991 (© 1991, Newsweek, Inc.). Reprinted by permission of Newsweek, Inc. All rights reserved.

Zoglin, Richard. "Live from the Middle East!" *Time*, January 28, 1991 (© 1991, Time Inc.). Reprinted by permission of the author and Time, Inc. All rights reserved.

Bourke-White, Margaret. Photograph © Time Inc., courtesy Time Inc. All rights reserved.

Burrows, Larry. Cover photograph © Larry Burrows Collection. Reprinted with the kind permission of Russell Burrows.

Capa, Robert. photograph © Magnum Photos Inc. Courtesy of Magnum Photos.

INDEX